PRINCIPLES
OF POLITICS
AN INTRODUCTION

W9-DGS-358

John J. Schrems

Villanova University

PRENTICE-HALL, INC., Englewood Cliffs, New Jersey 07632

Library of Congress Cataloging-in-Publication Data

Schrems, John J. (date)
   Principles of politics.

   Bibliography:
   Includes index.
   1. Political science. I. Title.
JA66.S36 1986   320   85–12108
ISBN 0–13–701806–1

Editorial/production supervision: F. Hubert

Interior design: *raoul*

Cover design: Ben Santora

Manufacturing buyer: Barbara Kelly Kittle

*To Mellie Tirador Schrems, Juanita,
Josephine, Maria, John, George*

Printed in the United States of America

10 9 8 7 6 5 4 3 2 1

ISBN   0-13-701806-1   01

PRENTICE-HALL INTERNATIONAL (UK) LIMITED, *London*
PRENTICE-HALL OF AUSTRALIA PTY. LIMITED, *Sydney*
PRENTICE-HALL CANADA INC., *Toronto*
PRENTICE-HALL HISPANOAMERICANA, S.A., *Mexico*
PRENTICE-HALL OF INDIA PRIVATE LIMITED, *New Delhi*
PRENTICE-HALL OF JAPAN, INC., *Tokyo*
PRENTICE-HALL OF SOUTHEAST ASIA PTE. LTD., *Singapore*
EDITORA PRENTICE-HALL DO BRASIL, LTDA., *Rio de Janeiro*
WHITEHALL BOOKS LIMITED, *Wellington, New Zealand*

CONTENTS

CHAPTER TWO
THE POLITICAL SYSTEM   *43*

CHAPTER THREE
POLITICAL SCIENCE: SCOPE AND METHODS   *59*

PART II   THE STATE

CHAPTER FOUR
THE NATURE OF THE STATE   *86*

CHAPTER FIVE
POLITICAL AUTHORITY/SOVEREIGNTY   *101*

CHAPTER TEN
THE INDIVIDUAL AND THE STATE:
A FOCUS ON RIGHTS *166*

CHAPTER ELEVEN
THE STATE AND GROUPS *191*

CHAPTER TWELVE
CONSTITUTIONALISM *225*

PREFACE

In the last two decades most "introduction to political science" studies have come to emphasize behavioral oriented information such as socialization, public opinion, voting behavior, communications, the governmental process, competing systems, functionalism, and developmental patterns. Missing has been a consideration of principles and fundamentals, which underlie and give meaning to the familiar events observed in the everyday political world. This book combines a consideration of the political science of recent decades with a traditional and now reemerging attention to underlying principles.

The main features of this work are:

- provocative yet open discussion of three contrasting views of democracy;
- up-to-date and balanced presentation of the scope and methods in political science;
- emphasis on principles which explain government from three dominant points of view;
- full development of the analytical principles of the nature and purpose of the state and the justification for governmental actions;
- extended use of the principle of subsidiarity applied to rights, private property, groups, church-state, and international relations (following E.F. Schumacher's suggestion that

this principle, which informed his *Small Is Beautiful,* was intended for society as a whole;

* traditional explication of constitutionalism innovatively combined with discussion of political culture and political structure;
* unusual but compelling discussions of federalism and separation of powers.

What will be clear is that there are alternative views of the political world and that these views make a difference. Disagreements based on principles should convey to the reader that politics is important and the importance flows not from facts alone but from choices.

ACKNOWLEDGMENTS

Many have helped in the preparation of the work. Professor Ernest Giglio, of Lycoming College, read and commented on an earlier draft. Dr. Morris Nossov provided detailed comments on a more recent draft. Former students Dennis Ricci and Nancy Patrick assisted at different stages in the preparation of the manuscript. My daughter, Maria, and Anne Cassidy Bowden, secretary to the Political Science department at Villanova, typed the earlier draft. Professor Howard Lurie of the Villanova Law School provided advice and encouragement. Material support was provided at just the right time by John Driscoll, President, and Lawrence Gallen, Vice-President, of Villanova University. Stan Wakefield, Audrey Marshall, Frank Hubert, and the editorial and production staff at Prentice-Hall provided a quality of professional assistance which made this an astonishingly smooth endeavor.

Many other individuals over the years have contributed to this text although this notice will be the first that they are aware of it. Bob Horwitz, Harry Clor, and Pat Coby of the Kenyon College Summer Institute on "Teaching Introductory Political Science" are three such individuals. So also are the many colleagues from that Kenyon Institute of 1982 where agreement was not required but the friendship, intellectual stimulation, and professionalism reinforced the importance of continuing this work. An even more unaware contributor is Henry J. Schmandt, Professor of Political Science, St. Louis University. I quote Professor Schmandt's book (co-authored with the late Paul G. Steinbicker), *Fundamentals of Government,* several times. I used the first edition of that work when I was an undergraduate, and as a professor I assigned the second edition until it went out of print.

The encouragement and assistance of colleagues, friends, and my wife Mellie contributed to this final product. Needless to say, however, the responsibility for what appears here is mine. The reviewers for Prentice-Hall—Dr. Douglas A. Brown, Arizona Western College; Dr. Stephen Francis Coleman, Northeastern University; Dr. Philip Abbott, Wayne State University—made sound and constructive suggestions which have been incorporated in this book. I hope that what I have done reflects adequately the seriousness of their suggestions. The reader, student, and professor alike is invited to continue this most serious of academic dialogues by sending me his or her brief comments or extended remarks so that constructive examination of this material may continue.

Jack Schrems

INTRODUCTION

The usual activity of political science is to describe the relations between nations, how the bureaucracy or the courts operate, how a budget is prepared, how and why citizens vote and in what numbers, how groups influence the political process, and the role of institutions and culture in individual political behavior. Much has been written about each of these and many more topics. Volumes of information, however, can be of little value unless principles are available to help organize and give meaning to that information.

In its effort to be scientific, political science runs into difficulty at the very beginning of the science routine. Scientific knowledge requires several steps. These steps, called the *scientific paradigm*, require observations organized into or reflected in concepts, generalizations that relate those concepts, and theories which collect those generalizations. Explanation and prediction follow the theories. Political science and other social sciences, by virtue of the word ''science'' in their titles, imply that they follow these scientific requirements. In reality, however, they have few validated generalizations since the scientific paradigm breaks down at the concept level. Ironically, however, political scientists do not lack theories which attempt to explain and predict political events. These theories come from diverse sources: some are speculations following approximations of the scientific paradigm; some are the byproducts of generalizations derived from other social sciences. Some theories are the residue from tens of centuries of Western thought.

Later in this work the procedures and approaches of political scientists will be examined. For now it should be pointed out that whatever the scientific requirements, there is a precondition which makes political science different from sciences like physics or chemistry: the political world cannot be taken into a lab. The discipline of political science must accommodate the world of real political life, which can change with no discernible pattern and with no forewarning. In other words, political science must adjust to the nonstatic political reality instead of the other way around. It is upside down to expect the political world to fit neat scientific requirements of academic categories and conceptual patterns. One of the many challenges with which studies of the political world must contend is the conventional explanations of political life held by the public. Those conventional explanations may or may not be correct but they are formidable nonetheless in that they can constrain the most perfect of scientifically discovered truths about the political world. The political scientist must consider the goals, purposes, and values of ordinary political life as well as the other forces of political life and the scientific constructs of the academic world.

The Political World
and the World of Nature

It is remarkable that many of the common assumptions and theories about the political world are valid but unexamined, some are inconsistent but seemingly plausible, and some are illusions. Most people have what might be called "poetic understandings" of some parts of nature and of social and political reality. Poetic understandings are a temporary way of explaining situations until a more logical and scientific explanation is available. In the context of physical nature, it is common to speak in a poetic way of the sun rising and setting even though it is scientific fact that the earth rotates and the sun is stationary. The ancient description has given way to scientific explanation, but the language of everyday discourse has not changed. Similarly, it is common to speak of astronauts being "up" in a satellite even though they may be on the other side of the earth and logically "out" in the satellite instead of up. Strictly speaking, an airplane goes in and out from an airport even though generally it is referred to as going up and down. Likewise, the wind is commonly referred to as blowing, as if a force were pushing on the air, although the scientific explanation is of a low pressure zone drawing or pulling.

All these poetic expressions, about sunsets, blowing winds, etc., are inaccurate from a strictly scientific and logical perspective. The scientific language is employed only in scientific situations as, for example, in planning and carrying out the launch of a space station. Even in that situation the astronauts will speak of the many beautiful "sunsets" they witness. The poetic language of everyday usage does not interfere with brilliant scientific activities, or vice versa.

In the context of the social and political world, there are many poetic expressions. Here too they are used to describe concrete phenomena, but in this instance the poetic version can have a pernicious effect on political life. If democracy is understood in common discourse to be "popular control over political leaders," and that view is explained through scientific methods to be a myth, the contrast between the common view and the scientific has the potential for being greatly disruptive. If the state, or any organization, is said to serve the individual or, contrariwise, to be served by the individual, the consequences of believing one and being subject to the other can be personally and politically disrupting. If federalism or the usual description of the separation-of-powers doctrine are revealed to be more fiction than fact, there is a personal effect well beyond the world of academic discourse.

General assumptions, traditional theories, scientific explanations, and poetic understandings need to be sorted out. To have a clear understanding of political reality and to avoid disruptiveness and confusion, valid and inaccurate explanations must be distinguished. In the world of physical science, once it is discovered that the earth is spherical instead of flat or that the planet is not the center of the universe, it does not matter that an overwhelming number of people still hold to the old beliefs. Navigators will thereafter explore the oceans or the stars using the new discoveries, no matter what the rest of humanity may think. That equanimity in the physical sciences is not true of the social and political world. If a majority of people hold to an erroneous belief on childrearing or political organization or democracy, harm can result or, at least, a potentially harmful distance can be created between a knowing elite and an unknowing public. It is especially important in the political world therefore to sort out the facts, theories, popular beliefs, myths, generalizations, and principles.

What will be done in this work is to show that there are at least three different ways to understand each of the political topics considered. Each separate way is a sharply distinct understanding of the same basic phenomenon. The views reflected in these three approaches come from ancient and modern theory, philosophical and scientific attempts at generalizations, and the summary conventions of centuries. Each view has consequences that affect ordinary political life. What will be emphasized in this work are principles that underlie and explain political life. There are many principles of this nature; principles of organization, democracy, morality, and action. They will be sorted out in the succeeding chapters.

Balanced Presentation
and the Author's Views

It is commonplace to expect descriptions of political phenomena, but the most encyclopedic collection of facts is useless without some meaningful way to handle them. Since the scientific paradigm has technical difficulties in application in political science, the different views and principles are the best means available to approach an understanding of the political world. The use of principles, especially competing principles, does not force a point of view on the reader. It instead opens horizons and provides a guide for discovering new dimensions to reality. That is not to say that the author does not have a point of view or a preference in the theories and principles which will be discussed. The author does have his own views. The other views discussed, however, will all be presented in a balanced and objective manner. Where a personal preference enters in, it will be in such a manner that it will not affect the fair presentation of the other views. With the premises and assumptions of all the positions examined openly, the reader will be free to weigh and balance the arguments and ultimately come to a personal choice, or to no choice. What will be clear is that there are different views of the political world and that those views make a difference. In this way it is hoped that the reader will grasp that politics is important and that the importance flows not from the facts but from the choices.

The Plan of What Follows

This text is divided into three parts. The first part, Chapters 1–3, gets immediately involved with the political world, the activity of political scientists, and then gives a description of the discipline of political science itself. The second part, Chapters 4–8, examines the state under a number of aspects, from the abstract to the practical. The third part, Chapters 9–15, deals with multiple aspects of governing, from principles of operation to forms of government.

The first chapter begins by plunging into a discussion of democracy. That immersion technique continues in the following chapter on the political system. Democracy will be looked at in terms of three different views. One view will be favored, but the others will have sufficient merit that the only result from the preference indicated will be insight instead of a prescribed answer. The discussion of the political system is designed to introduce the student to the predominant organization schema used by political scientists in describing the vastness of political reality. Having acquired information and some understanding of both democracy and the political system in the first two chapters, a discussion of the scope and methods of political science follows.

It may be argued that the sequence of the first three chapters ought to be reversed. I prefer the designated sequence because of the immersion technique. Even though not universally agreed upon, the immersion technique is a legitimate introductory approach. Some desire and others expect a type of systematic development in political science texts. According to this expectation the text should begin with formal introductions followed by formal definitions. But such a plan is not universally agreed upon. As one political scientist points out, there is as much a tradition for a formal procedure in political science as there is a tradition to "simply plunge in and study whatever the student of politics finds interesting and significant."[1]

Those who urge the formal approach fear that without definitions as a starting point the discipline will amount to "a mountain of data surrounding a vacuum." That fear is the same as one that argues the importance of principles in understanding facts. The problem with starting with definitions, however, is that such an approach gives greater prominence to the discipline than to the political world. Only after experiencing some exposure to the political world, if merely to democracy and the political system, is it possible to appreciate the variety of approaches within the discipline. Part One therefore both employs the immersion technique and the systematic technique by fully developing the dimensions of the discipline after experiencing some part of the real world and real political science. In Chapter 3 the scope and methods of political science will be explained as important for the light cast on the understanding of real political issues. Important principles of politics are found in the discussion of methodology as well as in the more substantive political topics dealt with elsewhere in the text.

Some of the more critically important principles for the organization and justification of government are found in the discussion of the nature of the state, the nature of political authority or sovereignty, the origin of the state, and the purpose of the state. Principles and theories establish parameters and bases for a considera-tion of the range and limit of governmental activity. Whether government can or should engage in certain activities is no less relevant today than 200 or 2000 years ago. The first four chapters in Part Two deal with four different aspects of the state: its nature, authority, origin, and purpose. Each aspect, which constitutes a principle for later practical action, is presented from three different points of view. The dif-ferent views have historical and logical roots. Furthermore, they are totally at odds with one another.

One may be tempted to take each of the views in the four chapters and tie them together to form organic wholes. That indeed can be done, but it is best not to do so at this stage. The four aspects of the state will be viewed as discrete topics to be understood in themselves. As progress is made through the four chapters, the possible linkage of the different views can be kept in mind, but no great effort should be made in this regard. Within the chapter on the purpose of the state, a preliminary drawing together of the different views will be done. The different pur-poses of collectivism, individualism, and the common good are more fully appreci-ated by seeing their roots in the origin and nature of the state and authority. In the eighth chapter, ''Ideologies,'' the linking of the four topics and the different points of view will be carried out more formally.

Linking the different aspects of the state together with varying emphases pres-ents the core of many contemporary ideologies. In other words, all the elements of ideologies are contained within the four aspects of the state. The ideological impli-cations depend on the combination and emphasis given to the earlier elements. These four aspects (nature, authority, origin, and purpose) should in themselves give an overall appreciation of the state. In addition they should give an apprecia-tion that the state can be looked at in three basic theoretical ways. There is not al-ways a necessary linkage of one aspect of the state to another. Rational or logical linkages about aspects of the state are always tentative. Discussion of ideologies is presented to show some of the linkages. Also seen are some of the limits of ideolog-ical linkages since ideologies give the appearance of certainty to topics that are only tentative. Such appearances are both the appeal and the weakness of ideology.

The aspects of the state constitute the principles upon which different political attitudes, policies, and practices are based. These applications need not always take an ideological form. One must be cautious in handling these topics. Ideologies, or applications, are not to be overemphasized because they are frequently too far re-moved from the principles or aspects to hold up logically. What can be gained from these theoretical and ideological dimensions of politics is an appreciation of some of the principal foundations for the divergent political views in daily political discourse. An appreciation of these underlying views will serve as the basis for one's insight into the dynamics and contradictions of the political world. If knowledge of principles leads to understanding, even if that understanding is not complete or perfect, then that knowledge has been successful. All approaches and methods in political science mentioned in the chapter on scope and methods and all the principles mentioned in the rest of the text have at least that common goal: a contribution to understanding. Success in this goal can be measured by the logic of what is said and by the appreciation that is gained in the process.

Mention was made a little earlier of the importance of the range and limit of governmental activity. The different views of the purpose of the state and the different ideologies are theoretical expressions of range and limit. More practical expression is found in concrete treatment of individuals, groups, and intragovernmental relationships. In Part Three these more practical concerns of government are described. Though these practical concerns might be explained as flowing from the earlier discussion of purposes and ideologies, they will instead be presented quite independently. The theoretical principles will not be totally discarded, but it is important at some point to investigate more concrete events as a separate development.

The different views of the purpose of the state affect how governments will regard their relationship to the public and to other states. All governments claim to be concerned in a general sense with the common good. What each government specifically means by that general sense of the common good, how it is defined, who defines it, and what price must be paid to achieve it are critical in determining good government. These latter concrete concerns can be arrived at by understanding the principles of justice, rights, constitutionalism, the treatment of groups within society, and intragovernmental relationships.

Although every country desires stability and tranquility, both developed and underdeveloped countries can be beset with chaotic or repressive regimes. Authoritarian regimes often define the common good in a collectivist manner. They broach no disagreement with their constructs, they are repressive to those who would challenge them, and they sacrifice any individual to a promised better day which seems never to arrive. However, an authoritarian regime need not be collectivist in a final sense. Some may truly pursue the common good in both a formal and practical sense. The actions they undertake may be necessary to overcome corruption, chaos, internal subversion aided by outside forces, or to respond to overt external aggression. The actions of the regime test the principles of government in both a theoretical and a practical sense.

The critical difference between acceptable and unacceptable authoritarian rule is the extent to which they truly approach the common good. That difference is marked in a variety of ways: the extent to which efforts are made to respect the integrity of the individual in opposition (assuming that the opposition acts with integrity too), the extent to which arbitrariness or fairness prevails, the extent to which the rule is consistently harsh or merciful. Matched pairs of contemporary regimes can be imagined in terms of these criteria, for example, United States / Soviet Union; Philippines / Argentina; India / China; South Africa / Libya; Israel / Iran; El Salvador and Nicaragua. In some instances it may seem easy to decide which is repressive and which operates for the common good. In other instances it would not be easy to judge. Some governments may be perceived to be the enemy of the individual while they in fact seek an order within which the individual may be free. Other governments proclaiming individual freedom may serve only a few wealthy individuals at the expense of many. In other situations the neglect of the few may cause irreparable harm to the entire community.

The difficulty in making these distinctions between regimes does not render the distinctions irrelevant. A fuller appreciation of the practical aspects of the state and the distinction of regimes requires an examination of particular relationships within the state. This is what is done in Part Three. The relationship between the state and the individual in terms of citizenship and personal rights will be examined. Also to be examined are the relationships between the state and various groupings within the state. The freedom and limit of groups, individuals, and the state itself must be scrutinized to make theoretical differences meaningful. Primary attention for these relationships is directed to examples within the North American experience. This American focus occurs because of familiarity and the need to clearly establish the principles involved in order to facilitate wider application on one's own.

The principle of subsidiarity provides an organizing schema throughout the initial chapters of Part Three. The principle is at the same time empirical and normative. It is empirical in the sense that it describes the actual practice of the relationship of the individual and of groups to the state. It also describes major aspects of justice, constitutionalism, and federalism. Subsidiarity is normative in the sense that it may be used as a norm and as a guide for future understanding. It will be seen that this role as norm and guide applies to undeveloped rights, such as privacy, and to other relationships between the individual and the state. Although subsidiarity may be unfamiliar as a term, the concept is not new. As will be shown, it is little more than a way to summarize and describe how the political world of our immediate experience really works. Its presence or absence will serve as a guide for understanding relationships in the political community and as a test for regimes.

Subsidiarity has been used by E. F. Schumacher, the author of *Small Is Beautiful*[2], as the first principle in his theory of large-scale organization. Schumacher, a British economist, states the formulation of the principle as: "It is an injustice and at the same time a grave evil and disturbance of right order to assign to a greater and higher association what lesser and subordinate organizations can do. For every social activity ought of its very nature to furnish help to the members of the body social and never destroy and absorb them." Although he applied this formulation to large organizations, Schumacher indicates that the principle was meant for society as a whole.

The application of subsidiarity to society as a whole provides special insights to a range of topics which ultimately measure the difference between repressive and just regimes. Justice, rights, world government, church-state relations, constitutionalism, and federalism viewed in the light of subsidiarity constitute an attitude toward government which gets at the heart of the governing principle itself. A grasp of this governing principle will give any student of political science a firm foundation from which to proceed into the many dimensions of the political world.

Justice, rights, constitutionalism, the relationship between a political regime and its cultural setting, the forms of governments and the structural permutations of forms will each be described to gain an appreciation of who does what in the political world. They will also serve as principles or bases by which one can judge acceptable and unacceptable regimes. The concern with these practical aspects of government does not mean that all theoretical dimensions are to be forgotten. The thread of earlier theoretical principles will be found recurring from time to time. For the most part, however, Part Three will describe practical aspects and relationships of government so that politics may be approached in terms of both theoretical and practical principles.

NOTES

1. Alan C. Isaak, *Scope and Methods of Political Science* (Homewood, Ill.: The Dorsey Press, 1981), pp. 14–15. Isaak is also the source of the steps in scientific activity mentioned at the opening of this Introduction.

2. E. F. Schumacher, *Small Is Beautiful: Economics as if People Mattered* (New York: Perennial Library of Harper and Row, 1973).

CHAPTER ONE
DEMOCRACY:
THREE VIEWS

Democracy has been discussed since the earliest times. Before Socrates, Plato, and Aristotle, questions of the relationship of rule and ruled occupied thinkers about the state. The ancient discussion, like that today, was two-sided. On the one hand democracy was viewed as the entitlement of each citizen to participate in ruling and being ruled. On the other side democracy was regarded as a device for exploiting the rich by the incompetent masses. Of all the enormous volumes that have been written on the topic of democracy, the discussion still resolves itself into a question of "elite guidance versus democratic participation." The question is seen as "among the oldest problems in political science."[1]

One task of the political scientist is to clarify concepts of common usage. The goal is to give these concepts accuracy and precision so that agreed-upon universal understandings can be achieved. Clearly democracy is one political concept which can stand such clarification. Most of the ancient or contemporary discussion about democracy dichotomizes it between rich and poor, elite and mass, informed and uninformed, "anti" and "pro." Today in Nicaragua, El Salvador, the Philippines, South Korea, South Africa, and Pakistan local partisans are readily evaluated in these terms. However, as most would quickly realize, the matter is not that simple. Few people admit to being anti-democratic. The appeal of democracy is so strong that its most severe critics claim that they represent the true sense of the doctrine. Even totalitarian regimes that are portrayed as the antithesis of democracy make that claim.

Since democracy is one of the most common and at the same time most fund amental political concepts, our introduction to political science begins by examining three views of democracy. The first to be examined is the most familiar. It is designated or referred to as the "traditional," "conventional," or "consensus" view. The second view will be a rational criticism, called "challenge," of that traditional view. The challenge view agrees with the definition and terms of the traditional view but disagrees with what they lead to. The third view takes the first two and reexamines them to produce a distinct, if not startling, alternative. It does show that there are three clearly separate perspectives on democracy. By examining these alternatives we begin the study of the principles of politics.

TRADITIONAL VIEW:
POPULAR CONTROL

The basic terms of the traditional, conventional, or consensus view of democracy are fairly well known to all. These terms are repeated here so that there can be recognized agreement on them. What is intended, and will occur with most readers, is that everyone recognizes his or her own view of democracy in the description. In one respect that personal view is simple and uncomplicated. It is the democracy of everyday conversation, of election arguments, of editorials and sermons. Nonetheless, despite that simple and uncomplicated understanding there is some sophistication to it. Thus an initially satisfying definition of democracy as "government or rule by the people" is unacceptable. One must know what is meant by "rule" or "government." One must know who the people are and to what effect they govern. From such questions sophistication develops.

To the initial description of democracy as government by the people must be added the understanding that government involves the making and enforcement of decisions of public consequence. Two tasks are involved. One is the making of decisions affecting the public, the establishment of policy which directly or indirectly affects everyone. The other task is the enforcement of those policies. All governments have these two tasks whether the form is democratic, representative, totalitarian, authoritarian, monarchical, or any other. Every government must make decisions and all governments must enforce them.

Democracy's uniqueness is generally understood to be in the role that the people have in the ruling process. The character of that role must be explained more fully. Accordingly, it is safe to say that the business of enforcing and administering public policy cannot rest in any immediate sense with the public in general. There must be some fixed collection of government personnel to carry out law enforcement responsibilities, foreign policy objectives, economic or health and welfare programs. Those who carry out the policies in particular areas are, respectively, the police, the diplomatic corp and military services, or, more generally, "the bureaucracy." The enforcement and administrative function is not carried on by a random selection of "the people" rotating on some fixed cycle in those positions. These tasks are either professional or clerical and as such require a permanence in staffing for purposes of both efficiency and effectiveness.

Small town meeting democracies are said to be different because of their size. They are said to be able to run themselves directly without the need of elected officials. But even they must have a town clerk-manager who supervises the day-to-day running of local affairs. Communities with large populations, complex domestic and foreign problems, technical procedures, and intricate safeguards designed by previous generations make it impossible for the daily activities of government to be conducted by anyone other than specialists and professionals. These specialists and professionals, the bureaucracy, are merely the differentiated versions of the small town clerks.

Jacksonian Democracy

The concept of "Jacksonian democracy" once current in the United States maintained that any ordinary person, the so-called "common man," could hold any ordinary governmental office. This common-man rule, in the Jacksonian conception, combined with frequent turnover of officeholders, would bring government closer to the people. In this way government was supposed to be more directly democratic. The Jacksonian direct democracy language is still attractive as campaign material one hundred and fifty years later. Historical evidence would suggest, however, that beginning with Jackson himself and lasting for many years it was a camouflage for the spoils system. The spoils system was the practice of replacing government workers in the previous administration with the supporters of the challenger. These supporters were labeled in Jackson's instance as the "common man."

History reveals no evidence of an attempt to institutionalize "Jacksonian democracy" during the Jackson years (1829–1837) by legislating strict limits on the terms of all offices. Such a limit would have mandated a system of rotation of office, thereby legally expanding the number of people who directly participate in government. It is safe to say, therefore, that even the Jacksonian practice, as opposed to the "theory" of Jacksonian democracy, does not contradict the contention that the business of administering and enforcing government obligations cannot rest with the public in general. Jackson only chose *some* of the many job applicants who flooded Washington after his victory.

The recognition of the reality of practical job effectiveness over the theory of rotation was later expressed in the professionalization of government employment in merit selection civil service practices. It took years, until 1883, but eventually it replaced the spoils system. Professionalism and civil service are what we call, in the more common terminology, the "bureaucracy." It is through them that the administrative and enforcement functions of government are accomplished today. The bureaucracy may be either the small town clerk or the nearly three million national civil servants. In neither case does the government run itself.

Since the public cannot claim enforcement responsibilities democracy's distinguishing characteristic must therefore be found elsewhere. For some authors democracy's distinguishing characteristic was localized in the legislative and policy framing function and the argument is presented in this fashion:

> What is more important than the method and details of administering a national health insurance law is the question as to whether such a program should be undertaken by the government. This is a matter of public policy; and here the people should have their say. The administrators or experts may point out to the electorate the advisability and the need for such a law, but the final decision as to whether government should assume the task must rest directly or indirectly with the electorate. If it does not—if popular participation in the formulation of policy is excluded—the resulting government will be authoritarian or dictatorial but not democratic.[2]

The point being made is that broad policy issues should be determined by the public if the system is to be considered democratic. To this democratic imperative of popular policy determination the logical next point is how this popular decision making is to be accomplished. In practical terms the traditional view of democracy maintains that "if the citizen body is to share meaningfully in the business of framing public policy there must be procedures and machinery through which this participation can take place."[3] The procedures and machinery are provided in the system of democratically elected representatives. Democracy is thus more specifically called representative democracy.

Town Meeting Democracy

In the history of local government in the United States, town meetings were gradually replaced by what was called "representative town meetings." What most American towns have today in their city council, town board, or whatever, is still often technically and legally a "representative town meeting." In this way the procedures and machinery through which democratic citizen involvement takes place is generally called *representative government*. In this system of representative government individual representatives are periodically elected for some limited and fixed term. Many variations of length of terms, number and responsibilities of offices, and various qualifications occur but the representative feature of the many electing the few is essential. It is this characteristic of elected representatives making the legally binding decisions for the community that distinguishes democracy from all other forms of government. This characteristic applies at local, state, and national levels.

Some additional comments must be made about the so-called direct democracy of the small town. Many contend that the democracy of the small town is an idyllic exception to the hard practicality of the more general form of representative democracy required by the more remote, larger, more complex governmental experiences. The ancient Greek city-state, Swiss cantons, and New England towns are said to be examples of the more personal display of the sovereignty of the people. There the people are said to rule "directly" by popular assemblies. Aside from the point previously mentioned that each such community must have a clerk who carries on the daily functions and who, not incidentally, is largely responsible for preparing the agenda of the annual or semi-annual meeting, the very meetings of the town are themselves representative rather than truly direct.

It may sound like philosophical nit-picking or semantics but actually it is a simple political reality that any town meeting is a representative form. No matter what the composition of the membership in terms of age, sex, property, or no such terms, the meeting represents the members of the community who are *not* present. If the authority upon which the direct democracy operates comes from "the people," then the annual assembly of those over eighteen, or whatever, years of age *represents* those of the community below that age or those otherwise not present.

This debate is somewhat trivial because there are, have been, and will be few claimed direct democracies in practice. Furthermore there is never an accompanied part of the theory of direct democracy that no administrative or executive role exists in these communities. All governments relegate these implementing functions to some officers. Ancient Athens had its popular assembly but it also had a policy-making council. In addition it had a special institution of independent but influential generals. Little is heard of these institutions when praise is given to the Athenian direct democracy. The New England town had its clerk and its town fathers. The reality of these town fathers, clerks, generals, and councils contradicts the imagined self-management of direct democracy. So direct democracies are no exception to either the representative or administrative roles which all governments have.

The Role of the Representative

Representativeness is the common feature of all democratic governments, large or small. How then should the representative conduct herself or himself? What is the representative's relationship to the constituents? Once elected, must the representative continually seek contact with the district, not just to be reelected, but to get the views of the constituents on the topics of the day? Is the representative bound in theory to vote according to the preference of the district if that preference is known? What is the obligation of the representative if he or she holds a view which is opposed to the preference of the district?

This question of the role of the representative is not a factual matter. It is not a matter of the actual vote of elected representatives. Various studies have been made which show the correlation or lack of correlation between the voting records of elected officials and the attitudes of their constituents.[4] One scholar concludes that, in general, representatives know little of their constituency's issue preferences and that the constituents in turn know little of the representatives' policy stands.[5] This political scientist does not find the situation alarming since it is offset by the close correlation between the voting record of the representative and the characteristics of constituencies. For example, representatives in Congress from "liberal" districts vote "liberal" and those from "conservative" districts vote "conservative." This latter correlation is explained by a sociological identity between the representative and the district. The representative is so much "of" the district, belonging to similar social, economic, and organizational groups, that conflicts seldom occur.

Lack of knowledge of the constituents' preferences or the representatives' voting record does not diminish the representativeness.

The crucial question about the role of the representative is how the representative should vote when there is a known discrepancy between the district and the representative and all sides are fully aware of the discrepancy? The answer to the question is usually put in terms of two theories: virtual representation, and actual representation. Virtual representation is also known as the "trustee" theory or the "independent judgment" theory. Actual representation is likewise known by the alternate titles of "delegate" theory or as the "mouthpiece" theory.

Virtual Representation

"Virtual" means that physical characteristics are present but substance or essence is missing. The intention of the word "virtual" is usually the opposite of that just explained: that something exists in essence or effect though not formally recognized or admitted, hence we say, for example, that one is a "virtual slave." Translated into the elected representative situation, virtual representation in the strict sense is supposed to mean that the representative votes on policy issues as a virtual slave to the interests and wishes of the constituents. But that etymological sense of "virtual" reflects neither the current nor the classical political sense of the phrase virtual representative. How the "representative" decides on policy reveals the true sense of the term.

According to virtual representation, policy decisions are made in terms of the representative's own judgment of what is in the best interest of the constituents, not in terms of the constituents' actually stated preference. The argument for virtual representation was classically expressed by Edmund Burke, a member of Parliament from 1765 to 1795, in his "Speech to the Electors of Bristol." Burke states that the member of Parliament owes to the constituents one's best judgment, whether it agrees with theirs or not.

> Certainly, gentlemen, it ought to be the happiness and glory of a representative to live in the strictest union, the closest correspondence, and the most unreserved communication with his constituents. Their wishes ought to have great weight with him; their opinion, high respect; their business, unremitted attention. It is his duty . . . to prefer their interest to his own. But his unbiased opinion, his mature judgment, his enlightened conscience, he ought not to sacrifice to you, to any man, or to any set of men living. These he does not derive from your pleasure; no, nor from the law and the Constitution. They are a trust from Providence, for the abuse of which he is deeply answerable. Your representative owes you, not his industry only, but his judgment; and he betrays instead of serving you, if he sacrifices it to your opinion.[6]

Such a dispute about the role of the representative is not abstract political theory or history. It is part of contemporary political life as revealed in the 1978 debates in the U.S. Senate over ratification of the Panama Canal Treaties. Senate Majority Leader (at the time) Robert C. Byrd (D., W. Va.), in supporting the treaties, invoked Burke saying, as quoted in *The New York Times* on February 10 of that year, "I'm not going to betray my responsibility to my constituents. I owe them not only my industry but my judgment. That's why they sent me here." Byrd added, "If I were to make a judgment based on the names on a petition or on the mail, what we'd need is a computer or a set of scales to represent the people of West Virginia."

Actual Representation

The counterpoint, actual representation, was not absent from the Canal debates either. Senator Bill Scott (R., Va.) argued that senators must vote as their constituents would vote. Expressing himself in opposition to Senator Byrd he said, "We also have a responsibility to listen to the voice of the people, and when the overwhelming majority of the people of the United States are opposed to this treaty, it should be persuasive." The theoretical position of Scott was that of actual representation—the representative must vote as the constituents would *actually* vote. Hilaire Belloc and Cecil Chesterton articulated the argument in a classical way:

> Either the representative must vote as his constituents would vote if consulted, or he must vote in the opposite sense. In the latter case, he is not a representative at all, but merely an oligarch; for it is surely ridiculous to say that a man represents Bethnal Green if he is in the habit of saying "Aye" when the people of Bethnal Green would vote "No." If on the other hand, he does vote as his constituents would vote, then he is merely the mouthpiece of his constituents and derives his authority from them. And this is the only democratic theory of representation.[7]

The language of the classical debate between the theories of virtual and actual representation come to the surface only rarely, as in the Panama Canal debate. The essential question is present, however, in all major political issues. Votes on MX missile systems, covert aid to "contras" in Nicaragua, nuclear freezes, and budget deficits can all be translated into the question of virtual versus actual representation. To understand democracy adequately the question of the proper role of the representative must be answered. Which theory of representation best registers the traditional consensus view of democracy must be resolved.

The attempt to unravel the question of the role of the representative should not be distracted by such speciously practical concerns as the need or the desire of incumbents to be reelected. Nor should attention be diverted by the knowledge or, more likely, lack of knowledge on the part of the public of what the representative is doing on many other issues. Despite these distractions the question of virtual representation versus actual representation is one that should be answered when the vote is cast. The question is important when the issues are clear to the public. Later, at the time of an election, the issues will be blurred.

Of special interest are the situations when the public is informed on the policy issues and the representative disagrees with them. The question is critical in those voting situations where the action taken is irrevocable, for example, to start a war or to end one, to dispose of a canal, to end a life, or to change constitutional or institutional arrangements. In more relaxed situations the question is somewhat academic, for the role of the representative may not be critical. But even in these situations the question can influence whether the representative or the public will be passive or active in their conduct. Such an influence can have a long-term effect on the political system.

The question of the role of the representative is important in another dimension. It is important in light of the challenges to democracy found in academic literature. This challenge to democracy will be more fully explained in the next section but for now we should say a few words about it. Democracy is described by some noted scholars as a "myth" or an "illusion." Gabriel Almond, for example, declares that "popular control over political leaders is the sustaining myth of democracy."[8]

Almond is no frantic revolutionary. He is instead, as past president of the American Political Science Association, the quintessence of the academic establishment. Robert A. Dahl, another past president of the association with credentials similar to Almond, also speaks of the myth of democracy. In a careful study of the politics of a contemporary American city Dahl has concluded that the "ancient myth about the concern of citizens with the life of the democratic polis is false in the case of New Haven. Whether or not the myth was reality in Athens will probably never be known."[9] Dahl's research concluded that concern for the ongoing issues of the city has not been found and so the perpetuation of such discussion was more mythical than real. In a similar vein the French political theorist and analyst of bureaucracy Jacques Ellul refers to democracy as an illusion. He has written, "it is precisely here that the political illusion resides—to believe that the citizen, through political channels, can master or control or change th[e] state."[10]

For the present discussion about representation it is important to see that the challenge to democracy is significant only if the role of the representative is understood to be or held to be actual instead of virtual. The challenge therefore can be seen as well focused for, as Almond says, the conflict is between elite guidance and democratic participation. Common democratic theory, in the view of Belloc and Chesterton, holds that actual representation is "the only democratic theory of representation." For the conventional view of democracy when there is a conflict between the representative and the constituents "the verdict of the majority ought to prevail."[11] Clearly popular control is under challenge.

Popular Control

It should be made clear that the theory of popular control is not naive. On the one hand it does not ignore the possibility that the public may be wrong at times and the system may thereby be weakened. Yet on the other hand conventional-traditional democratic theory has an optimism to it based upon a profound faith in mankind. As expressed and developed through Locke, Rousseau, Jefferson,

Madison, Jackson, and Lincoln, modern democratic theory has maintained that the people are a better judge of their interests than some rulers who claim to make judgments for them. From this position the claim of public jurisdiction over policy has followed.

The contention of popular democracy is that the individual and the community ought to make judgments on matters affecting their own lives. Traditional democracy maintains that those judgments should not be imposed by others who claim to know better. Furthermore, the experience of making such judgments now will improve the exercise of such judgments in the future. Letting others make the decisions "until the individual or the community is mature enough," as is so often the rationale of authoritarian decision makers, will constantly delay the realization of that maturity.

There was a clamor for "participatory democracy" in the United States and elsewhere during the 1960s. Our public memory of the period is often limited to the protests about the Vietnam war. In reality the political movement which surrounded those protests was broad both in content and time. A representative but by no means exclusive expression of the goals and principles of this participatory democracy was found in the organization called Students for a Democratic Society (hereafter referred to as SDS).

The goals and principles of the SDS were set forth in a document called the "Port Huron Statement," written by Tom Hayden in 1962. The SDS was an amalgam of students and others of "the New Left" who gained notoriety in anti-war protests of the 60s and riots at the Democratic National Party convention in Chicago in 1968. As the date of their opening statement indicates, however, the SDS's founding preceded the Vietnam war as an immediate issue.

A reading of the Port Huron Statement indicates concern with many particular issues of that time. Among the issues raised were: the seniority system of selecting congressional committee chairpersons, which led to Southern conservative domination in Congress; the localized nature of the political party system; racial discrimination and gerrymandering in voter registration and districting procedures; an enormous lobby force selfishly distorting national interests for business interests; and political campaigns of personality and image instead of campaigns of issues and options. All these concerns were expressed in that original statement. And all of them were legitimate democratic issues irrespective of immediate partisan consequences.

Although there have been noticeable changes in most of these areas of original concern, the fundamental point of the SDS about participatory democracy had an enduring quality that linked it to traditional democratic values.[12] The SDS spoke of a basic "faith" in the worth of the individual. This is similar to the faith expressed by Rousseau, the eighteenth-century French theorist, the authors of the Declaration of Independence, or Lincoln in his belief that not all of the people can be fooled all of the time. The SDS's call for participatory democracy starts with a regard for men "as infinitely precious and possessed of unfulfilled capacities for reason, freedom, and love." They see men as having:

. . . unrealized potential for self-cultivation, self-direction, self-understanding, and creativity. It is this potential that we regard as crucial and to which we appeal, not to the human potentiality for violence, unreason, and submission to authority.[13]

This statement of man's worth is followed by the disclaimer that in so appraising man they do not "deify" him. They claim instead to "merely have faith in his potential." Because of this faith in man the SDS calls for "the establishment of a democracy of individual participation, governed by two central aims: that the individual share in those social decisions determining the quality and direction of his life; that society be organized to encourage independence in men and provide the media for this common participation." The SDS was not widely applauded at the time because they had an accompanying rhetoric and disruptiveness which stirred, and often rightly so, negative reactions. As a result the common inclination was to classify the group as radical. Since many years have passed and the passions of the sixties have waned, the statement of the SDS can be looked at less passionately. It can be seen as another version of the dichotomy between elite guidance and popular control.

The sentiments of faith in the individual, human potential, and collective good sense are constants in the literature on democracy. Two authors cited earlier explain the underlying assumption of democracy as

an act of faith in the abiding good sense of the average human, and . . . the belief that the consensus of common opinion in matters which vitally concern the community is a wiser and safer guide to decision than the dominating leadership of one man or select class of men.[14]

These same authors go on to say that

the proponents of the democratic form of government feel that in a society of rational beings, the judgment and experience of the many will, in most instances, be superior to the judgment and experience of the few; and hence, that the verdict of the majority ought to prevail in case of conflict.[15]

An intriguing comment immediately following acknowledges that the device of the majority, which ought to prevail, is a "practicable rule of law" but it is said to be like other human instrumentalities, "subject to weaknesses and imperfections." This acknowledgement of limit is in contrast to the Port Huron Statement, which mentions no weaknesses and imperfections (save for the "potential" of violence).

That earlier work, again in contrast to the SDS statement, indicates that "the people" are subject to error "through ignorance, shortsightedness, prejudice, passion, and hysteria."[16] This unenviable litany does not dissuade from the democratic faith. Despite these limitations it is held that in the long run self-interest and happiness keep humans on the right course. By contrast the judgments of the few are made faulty by the temptations of power, position, and wealth. It may or may not be significant that the New Left proponents of participatory democracy do not mention this fallibility in their advocacy. That omission will not be explored in the present discourse. Our attention instead will be focused on the joint interest in positive democratic values by conventional and contemporary advocates.

The democratic values of individual worth and collective wisdom are ancient in origin. They can be found in the discussions of democracy in Athens from the sixth to the fourth centuries before Christ. Aristotle, one of those fourth century Greek philosophers, discussed these themes in his *Politics,* one of the earliest full treatises on democratic government. Aristotle's philosophic comments on democracy were preceded only by his teacher, Plato, who wrote the anti-democratic *Republic*. Aristotle, drawing an analogy with other activities, observed that "the many are better judges than a single man of music and poetry; for some understand one part, and some another, and among them they understand the whole."

What Aristotle had in mind was that "the many, of whom each individual is an ordinary person, when they meet together may very likely be better than the few good."[17] It is helpful to call attention to the qualifiers, "may" and "very likely," in Aristotle's observations. This hesitancy is a function of the human error and imperfect judgment he finds common to mankind. It is even more useful to point out the practicality of Aristotle's avowal of democracy. He admits that there is danger in allowing the mass of people to share the offices of state since "their folly will lead them into error, and their dishonesty into crime." He maintains, however, that there is danger also in excluding large numbers of people from these duties. The reason for this danger is that "a state in which many poor men are excluded from office will necessarily be full of enemies."

Concern for potential enemies is a backdoor way to support democracy. It nonetheless is an interesting point to reflect on in the light of the many contemporary authoritarian and totalitarian regimes. Poland, El Salvador, and Nicaragua may be useful immediate examples. A little more thought may include Chile, Pakistan, and the Philippines as regimes that may be skirting further unrest as they remain authoritarian. How one might consider the situation of the sharing of the offices of state in Russia, China, the Middle East, and Africa would take a bit longer to figure out.

Aristotle's support for democracy may not be as indirect as it first appears. He comments a little later that "if the people are not utterly degraded, although individually they may be worse judges than those who have special knowledge, as a body they are as good or better." He extends his point by another analogy to various arts in observing that not all arts are judged solely or best by the artists themselves:

> For example, the knowledge of the house is not limited to the builder only; the user, in other words, the master, of the house will be even a better judge than the builder, just as the pilot will judge better of a rudder than the carpenter, and the guest will judge better of a feast than the cook.[18]

The point of this analogy is that politics can be judged by the recipients of policy and not just the policy planners.

Clearly there is a role for the people in ancient and contemporary commentary on government. Much of the modern writings have developed the specific public role to the degree where, as quoted above, the majority "ought to prevail in case of conflict." There are many contemporary mechanisms for the majority preference to be asserted. Regular and periodic elections are an obvious and primary example. There are numerous other expressions of majority rule, for example, "initiatives" where the public can in some jurisdictions through petition get policy issues placed on the ballot. Through this process the legislature is bypassed and "the people's" will is expressed directly in law. Proposition 13 in California is a famous recent example. The referendum, where the legislative body in some jurisdictions may choose to, or be forced to, present some issues for the public ballot approval, is another illustration of direct majority preference. Its most obvious exercise is in state constitution and local charter amendments. It also comes into play in some states limiting local property tax increases and in local option provisions for limiting liquor sales.

Other examples of majority assertion are petitions, polls, and constituent surveys by elected officials. Similar surveys claiming to reflect majority preference are conducted by citizenry interest groups like Common Cause, Ralph Nader's Congress Watch organization, or local and state citizen environmental and public utility vigilance groups. The exact effectiveness and accuracy of these various mechanisms may be challenged on several grounds but they are uncontestably expressions of popular feelings about policy. The extent to which members of Congress or other legislators are influenced by questionnaires which they sponsor or by other manifestations of public opinion is debatable. There are few elected officials, however, who fail to see the public relations merit in soliciting the views of the constituents and then publicizing the results of their findings.

Much fanfare is given to democratic citizenry control. Common Cause, a so-called public citizen's lobby, was founded (according to their literature) "out of a desperate need for a citizen's lobby—to work as a movement of the people, by the people and for the people on issues before our legislature." This group laments that full democratic control is not entirely realized. They strive for the accomplishment of democratic control and they practice it within their own organization by annual referenda of their members about preferences. What the members are asked, however, is their preference for emphasis among a list of preselected issues. The preselecting is done by the central staff of the national group. Such a process may remind the reader of what was said earlier about the town clerk preparing the agenda for the annual meeting in the allegedly directly democratic New England town.

Without doubt the stated intention of Common Cause is democratic. So also is the revival of efforts of SDS founder Tom Hayden for democratic control of the economy in his new organization, Campaign for Economic Democracy (CED). As mentioned earlier the SDS was perceived as extremely negative in their rhetoric during the 1960s but their message, surprisingly, was conventional democracy. Although the earlier organization faded with the decade, the essential democratic theme, "that decision-making of basic social consequence be carried on by public groupings" and that "the economy . . . should be open to democratic participation and subject to democratic social regulation," had no time limit to it.

Those quotes from the Port Huron Statement are the essential ingredient of the new organization's appeal for "economic democracy with workers' and community control."[19] This economic democracy theme is similar to workers' management or the workplace democracy phenomenon discussed and written about in Europe, particularly Eastern Europe. It alleges, as stated in Hayden's recent "Introduction," the "constant tension between the forces of order, authority, privilege, and elite rule, and the rebellious, iconoclastic forces of change, progress, pluralism, and self-determination" with the latter, democratic side "prevailing." The general notion is that people should control things that affect their lives, whether social, economic, or political.

It is more than fascinating that the same themes of political and economic democracy are the tenets of the Sandinists in Nicaragua and the insurgents in El Salvador. It should give us pause to note, however, that they were also the tenets of Castro in the 1950s before he succeeded in overthrowing the dictator Batista. For the time being we will not analyze this Cuban or others' hiatus in democratic theory and practice. Our purpose at this point has been to indicate (1) the common and universal dimension to the democratic formula of popular control, (2) that "popular" is used in the sense of widespread, and (3) that "control" is used in the sense of the verdict of the majority prevailing.

THE SECOND VIEW:
DEMOCRACY IS A MYTH

There are many challenges to democracy today. The essential point of the present discussion is the internal logic of democracy. That logic will be critically examined in this section. First, however, it should be acknowledged that there are external challenges to democracy, which is different from the internal logic of it. The external challenges come as ideologies like Nazism, Fascism, Marxism, Communism, etc.

Ideology is an elaborate system of ideas possessing a distinctive core used to · explain political events. There are numerous and disputed definitions of the term ideology as well as many and disputed definitions of the particular forms of ideology. A more developed discussion of these matters will be presented in a later chapter. Additional ingredients must be developed before a fuller explanation is possible. For the present it should be mentioned that though ideology is referred to as an external challenge to democracy it sometimes uses or incorporates democracy. Fascism is the example of a system which directly challenges democracy and the competence of the people. Marxism, on the other hand, claims to be the epitome of democracy. It claims that the Western forms of government are really antidemocratic and that only with the demise of these pretenders will true democracy prevail.

It will not be possible to settle the questions raised by the external challenges until the later discussion. Many things must be discussed beforehand, including various views of the state, the treatment of citizens, constitutions, and even forms of government. It is possible that a final answer to satisfy all questions will never be found. Judgments and opinion cannot be suspended, however. For that reason it is important to explore the logic of democracy because the external challenge is linked to the inner one. With an understanding of the inner logic of democracy the challenges to it can be viewed and analyzed from a more secure perspective.

Reflective proponents of the conventional view of democracy[20] simply hold that in the long run the judgment of the people is a sounder basis for decisions than the judgment of the few. The judgment of the few is said to be deficient because it is subject to temptations of office, power, position, and wealth. The preference for the majority rests on a basic faith in the average person and a basic distrust in position or office holding. It is precisely to the point of the competence for decision making and judgment of the average person that the challenge to democracy is raised. The very faith in the people and the capability of the democratic system are challenged as *myth*. The reader should be forewarned that in coldly logical terms the analysis by critics of democracy, Almond and others, is largely irrefutable. This is a difficult but honest admission. A sound case, it is hoped, was made for popular control in the previous section. That case, however, will be unable to withstand the challenge to it.

Almond's Analysis

Almond argues in effect that for the people to control it is necessary for them to have sufficient information and that they lack this requisite knowledge. Put simply, it is argued that to exercise reasonable control it is necessary for the people to be informed, but the people are not informed, therefore it is not reasonable for the people to control. Instead, and this also is reasonable, those who are informed should control.

The reason the people are not informed has three aspects as explained by Almond: (1) the difficulty of assessing responsibility because of the inability of establishing definite cause-and-effect relationships in the world of politics, (2) the technological complexity of most matters of importance, and (3) the remoteness of the public from most political issues except those that affect them personally.[21]

It is necessary to reflect only briefly in the light of these factors on such issues as current foreign policy, international and domestic economics, energy policy, environment problems, urban bankruptcy, health care concerns, social security, crime, and atomic energy to get a quick grasp of Almond's point. Experts have difficulty enough assessing responsibility, or understanding technical problems, or keeping abreast of issues in other experts' fields. To claim that ''technical'' matters are ''the people's'' responsibility reveals its impossibility by definition. Such complexity of government prevails that one can state syllogistically, with us:

In a democracy the people should decide everything but what is technically complex, but everything is technically complex, therefore the people should decide nothing.

If everything is technically complex and the people should be adequately informed before they exercise control, then it is unreasonable that they should attempt to exercise control. This is the dilemma of democracy.

The complexity of politics makes it impossible for the average citizen to sort out the various parties involved in any particular policy area and ascertain who is primarily responsible for things going wrong or right. Whom can the public hold responsible for inflation? The President with his fiscal recommendations? The Congress with its budgetary procedures? The Federal Reserve Board with its independent monetary policies? The Democratic Party with its spending proposals? The Republican Party with its tax attitudes? The international economy? The capitalist system? Before some "rascal" currently holding office can be kicked out for what he or she has done or has failed to do to the economy, one ought to be able to establish some semblance of a cause-and-effect relationship between that rascal and the condition of concern.

In reality politics has a quality to it where, although everyone claims responsibility when things are going well, everyone can disclaim responsibility, and correctly so, when things are going poorly. Wars are a primary example. Presidents, generals, and congressional leaders are all given, and take, credit when things go well. When things go poorly each leader has many fingers of blame pointed in directions *away* from himself or herself. The recent Grenada and Lebanon experiences confirm this point.

The Vietnam experience is an especially curious example of this phenomenon of fixing responsibility. There one could push the arrow of responsibility back from the "military industrial complex," to Congress's original hawkish reception of the administration's initiatives, to a "cold warrior" Secretary of State, to a "macho" President, Lyndon Johnson, who did not want to be the first in American history to suffer defeat. One might continue to push that arrow of responsibility to that president's mother who, according to the exponents of psycho-history, planted those inclinations in the future president in her childrearing practices. That string of responsibility seems a little far-fetched but some travel its full length to come up with explanations of historical events. Others for no more obvious reasons stop at earlier points to fix responsibility.

The string of whom to hold responsible for the Vietnam policy is more than curious because until just recently most of the blame was centered within the boundaries of the United States. This parochial focus was encouraged ironically by the practice, in administration testimony before congressional hearings throughout the period of the conflict, of a constant reference to "the other side" without specifically identifying who the other side was. The public knew that there was an "other side" but they were never helped by their government in identifying exactly who that was. If the opponent is not identified an abstraction is held responsible.

Only years later was any information forthcoming about the amount of assistance provided by the Soviet Union or China to the North Vietnamese and the

Vietcong. There also was no public awareness of the rivalry between the two suppliers. Having this additional information gives some more precise definition to the composition of the other side. Only in 1979 did the American public learn that Peking sent 300,000 soldiers to Vietnam, including antiaircraft crews, from 1964 to 1971. It was the Chinese government itself and not the United States which supplied this information at the later date. It was supplying the information in 1979 not as a service to the American public but as a diplomatic tactic in its own ongoing border conflict with Vietnam. And, it should be made clear, even these numbers are no basis for establishing that China was the principal supplier since the Soviet figures have never been given. Until all the figures are known it will still not be possible to clearly identify "the other side."

A credible explanation about why the United States did not attempt to fix blame by specifying who the other side was during the days of the conflict is that to do so could easily have resulted in an undesirable escalation of the conflict. Even at this late date one still has to ask if any useful, or (more likely) harmful, result would follow a full disclosure of the respective degree of involvement of the superpowers in that war. Such a disclosure could easily kindle resentments and adversely affect current foreign policy efforts. One has to ask oneself if revelation of the identity of our principal enemy in the 1960s would improve or damage current foreign policy needs. To "set the record straight" has an abstract appeal but it may be practically foolish.

The problem of information as seen in the Vietnam example constitutes a double dilemma for the open democracy. Maintaining limits on information given to the public and being taken advantage of by the enemy, or supplying the information and escalating the conflict is the first dilemma. The second dilemma is the democratic propensity of inevitably finding someone to blame at home if a clearly recognizable foreign adversary cannot be found versus the possibility of irresponsibly blaming someone abroad to distract attention at home. The Vietnam example points out dramatically the complexity of the issues which the public is supposed to assess and the dependence of the public on information supplied by the government.

The public cannot make accurate assessments of politics unless information is available. If information on foreign policy is available the public is incapable of deciphering it since it involves so much complex material. Strategic multinational choices of the superpowers, aligned and nonaligned powers, Third World conflicts, traditional rivalries, and economic competition are involved in almost all foreign policy issues. On such choices even the experts disagree. To this consideration must be added that most of the adversaries of the United States, an open democracy, do not have to pay attention to public displeasure since the media and public opinion are largely controlled or stifled. For the United States to have its policies freely debated can handicap it in comparison with its foes.

Openness can therefore be an inherent liability in the strategic conflict, which enemies are able to exploit. As alluded to earlier, in the Vietnam conflict the other side could easily have had a strategy of dragging on the war and delaying the negotiations to end the war on the expectation that the American public would become impatient and clamor for a quick, though imperfect solution. Some then extend this line of suspicion to interpret the current Central American and Middle East conflicts, and other conflicts throughout the world, in this same way.

Issues of war and peace affect the public by way of arousing more immediate concerns even though intellectually the cause-and-effect relationships, the complex issues, and the facts may remain remote. The emotional closeness of war and peace issues makes them no less remote in analytical terms. One may feel close and directly affected by an issue especially as one reacts to the possibility of being drafted, having loved ones drafted, or as one begins to hear of casualties. Nonetheless, these complex issues, though they appear direct, are remote by way of the public's ability to know and effect action.

There are many other issues from which the public is similarly remote. For example, the general public is usually uninformed about issues of farm policy unless they live on a farm or unless the price of bread rises inordinately. The public is uninterested in dam and water projects unless they live in an unpredictable flood area or until they suffer from drought. In time of either flood or drought the general public's concern is too late and even that concern will abate when the immediate situation passes. Such short-term concern has been demonstrated any number of times with the energy issues.

The factor of remoteness therefore reinforces the other factors of technical complexity and the assessment of responsibility. Together these factors argue the inability of the public to control leaders or policy. Either the democratic public must handle all issues or it must handle none. Since it is remote from most if not all issues the public should handle none. If the public cannot know and understand the issues it is not possible or reasonable for them to control the political leaders who decide the policy.

The claim of popular control is further exacerbated by the inability to know exactly what decisions the political leaders have made. Legislators and executives make thousands of decisions and the public might be aware of ten of them. The ten decisions about which the public is aware are those that the individual politician or that politician's opponent chooses to tell the public. Little real control can be exercised under these circumstances.

A further consideration is that the public does not know when it is going to receive information or whether the information it receives is correct. Usually a barrage of information comes at election time from candidate and opponent. These are unreliable circumstances for careful assessment of facts and responsibilities. While election periods are the main source of information for the public on what their representative is doing, the circumstances are less than desirable for objective or dispassionate evaluation.

Elections as Carnivals

A major reason the election period is not reliable for objective information about public officials is because of the carnival atmosphere of elections. What takes place in an election is not the dissemination of information but the reversing of roles as in the Caribbean carnival or medieval festival. As one author expressed it, a "central function of elections like carnival, is to symbolically turn the world upside down for a day so people will acquiesce in its being substantively right side up the rest of the time."[22]

In a carnival the common folks wear masks and dress like kings and queens and princes and the real royalty wear masks and dress like clowns. This one-day pretended reversal of roles is for fun. In an election, office holders become like all the other simple folk, who in their turn become decision makers, rulers, for a day. Even while we are told that the election is serious business, it can otherwise be looked at as great fun. Much hoopla is found on television and in the press and radio in the time surrounding Election Day. Political party workers come to the "party" part of their activity after spending many weekends and working days knocking on doors, stuffing envelopes, telephoning prospective voters, and scheduling Election Day efforts. The "party" takes place whether the workers' candidate wins or loses.

In this pandemonium the winning candidate regards the voters as wise, attentive to issues, responsible, and selective. The losing candidates regard their supporters in that same way but they have an opposite view, despite some complimentary words they might utter, of the general public who voted against them. The view that the public is not wise, selective, attentive, responsible, etc., finds support in the contradictory votes cast by any particular community for President, governor, senator, congressperson, and state and local offices.

A prominent display of carnival is found at political conventions where the celebration of democracy is marked by rhetoric and "planned spontaneous demonstrations." In his acceptance speech at the Democratic Convention in 1972 George McGovern made a statement which is particularly revealing of the democratic theory we have been discussing. Quoting Woodrow Wilson, McGovern proclaimed, "Let me inside the government, and I will tell you what goes on there." In the atmosphere of distrust and suspicion that existed then the promise of openness brought a thunderous response from the partisan crowd. The statement by McGovern and the response can be taken as a revealing admission for candidate and audience. Both are claiming that although they do not know what goes on inside the government they ought to know. What is ironic is that the audience responded approvingly to the promise sixty years after Wilson made the same promise. And Wilson won his election.

It might seem that the audience, instead of being enthusiastic, would be cynical. In sixty years the openness had not been achieved. But even the Wilson and McGovern statements are minor in importance. What should be noticed is that almost all candidates running for office make the same offer. All claim that they will let their constituents know what is going on. This promise is common stock in elections. The election is the symbol of popular control and the candidate wants to establish himself as subservient to the general will. The promise, however, merely confirms the basic point of the *lack* of adequate information. In sum, the inability of the public to assess responsibility, the technical complexity of particular issues, and the remoteness from all but the most immediate issues are found in not only the substantive policy areas but in the voting process itself. Even an occasional professor of political science admits imperfect knowledge on policy issues and the best candidate.

Groups of many different types espouse popular control. Common Cause, mentioned earlier, presents itself as a broad based citizen's lobby seeking "government of the people" and opposing government by special interests. There are a couple of assumptions built into that proposition. Common Cause's statement assumes that government is not currently "of the people" and that it is instead "by special interests." Much of politics proceeds in the same way that proposition does. It operates by way of unexamined or unproven assumptions. The intention of this introductory text is to examine or open for discussion some of the principal ingredients of such assumptions.

Various groups that advocated war resistance in the 1960s and early 1970s, public anti-nuclear energy demonstrators, pro-nuclear freeze marchers, demonstrators for jobs and justice, as well as the established interest organizations, all implicitly, if not explicitly, endorse the popular control view of democracy. The phenomenon of interest group activities is a concomitant of democracy. It assumes the wisdom of the give-and-take process for reaching public policy decisions.

Within this view of democracy there is a debate between "pluralists" on the one side, who advocate the interest group competition process for making public policy decisions, and "anti-elitists" on the other side, who distrust the interest groups. The anti-elitists, frequently just called "elitists" with the prefix assumed, view the interest groups as infringing on the primacy of the individual as democratic decision maker. This anti-elitist position is part of the SDS-CED thesis which sees government and the economy in the control of special interest elites rather than the masses.[23] What is most informative for our current examination is that the debate nonetheless has both sides assuming the same view of democracy. Both assume the fundamentals of public decision making and popular control as opposed to governmental decision making and the impossibility of popular control.

The pluralists prefer interest group rivalry as the major determinant of policy. The pluralists join the anti-elitists in opposing "authoritative" policy making by "government experts." On the other side the anti-elitists want popular determination of policy. They join the pluralists in opposing authoritarian governmental decisions. Common Cause and the National Rifle Association, for example, are particularly prominent groups that alert their respective members to lobby for or against specific measures in the name of the public. In proceeding in this way both organizations are pluralists, anti-elitists, anti-authoritarian, and they oppose one another.

The members of these groups, or any such group, are urged to speak as "the public." They are not directed to say, "As one of 250,000 members nationally of group X . . . ," or "As one of 1.8 million members nationally of group Y . . . ." Each group writes on behalf of the public even though they constitute an extremely small percentage of the more than 230 million members of the public. They make their claim to being heard on the grounds that democracy is popular control and they are the public. In this way group activity is a manifestation of the traditional view of democracy. It is also a manifestation of democracy's mythicalness because the members of a group have no more technical knowledge of a particular policy area than what is contained in a eight page newsletter discussing seven issues. For an individual to be one newsletter closer to policy issues than the general public is not very expert.

This discussion, which rests on the lack of information and expertise of the public, does not claim that the people do not in any way influence events. Democracy, it should be noted, is indeed said to be a "sustaining" myth, albeit still a myth. Ellul acknowledges that the people influence the course of political events but their influence, he says, is all for the worse: "If the public is not aroused nothing can be done and if it is aroused, moderate, equitable, and provident solutions are no longer possible."[24]

Ellul's point is borne out by the excitement concerning the gasoline shortage in the winter of 1973 and the wide public clamor over the home fuel shortage in the severe winter of 1976–1977. Despite the clamor the government was unable to pass an energy bill. During a crisis if a bill were ready it could be passed quickly. When the crisis has abated proposed legislation drags on for years even though all recognize theoretically that delay may cause even greater harm in the future. The conclusion which one might draw is that instead of popular control *or* elite guidance it is a matter of *neither*.

Neither popular control nor elite guidance prevail since, as Ellul appears to suggest, nothing gets done. This view is too cynical to be true, but Ellul's comments do have some appealing aspects to them. They point out the real questioning of public influence and political leadership. Ellul ultimately will find the leadership function neither in the public nor in elected officials. He finds leadership in a hidden elite of the bureaucracy. That particular proposition should not concern us here except as it is continuing evidence of the basic question under consideration.

The basic consideration is that the question of elite guidance versus democratic control is real.Elite guidance is the corollary to the logical criticism of popular control. Since the public can control neither the specific policy decisions nor the decision makers by electing them on any semblance of full knowledge, the correlative of elite guidance is the only alternative normally available for consideration. The elites merely operate by way of elections in democratic systems instead of by way of private appointments or blood relationships in nondemocratic systems. In hereditary monarchies the elite is the royal family and their chosen associates. In the Soviet Union according to their own doctrine of democratic centrism the elite is the Communist Party hierarchy. The criticism of popular control claims that traditional democracy has its own elite even though it may be well hidden even from itself.

Elite leaders need not know or at least need not acknowledge their elite character since the democratic myth is so ingrained. It is, to remind ourselves once again, a *sustaining* myth. Only the type of academic analysis which has been going on in this portion of the discussion can point out the clear alternatives. Put simply, the alternatives are the inabilities of the traditional view and the conclusion, if merely by default, of elite guidance. Elite guidance may come disguised as virtual representation but in any case the public does not control, the verdict of the majority does not prevail.

THE THIRD VIEW:
POPULAR SELECTION

The alternatives already discussed are self-defining and self-defeating. If popular control is the defining difference of democracy then any lack of it puts one automatically in the elite guidance category. Likewise, if elite guidance is the starting point the only generally acceptable alternative is popular control. These two alternatives are logically and practically interconnected. Almond speaks in exactly these terms. Dahl speaks of the myth of the citizen's concern for public affairs. Participatory democracy's advocates see themselves at odds with power rooted in possession, privilege, or circumstance. All the analyses in effect see democracy as the verdict of the majority, actual representation. The dichotomy cited in the beginning prevails. It prevails up to this point.

There are problems with the given alternatives, however. A central problem is that the whole discussion is put in the context of the proverbial two equally unacceptable alternatives: "Yes or no, have you stopped breaking the law?" "Yes or no, have you stopped cheating on exams?" Given the alternatives there really is no acceptable answer. One is indicted, self-indicted, no matter which alternative is chosen. As a personal strategy one might decline to answer such questions, or one might provide a third alternative of one's own choosing. Politicians, who are almost universally accused of never answering any direct questions, have actually developed the skill of regarding *all* questions as "Yes/No" alternatives. For this reason the politician responds to questions by talking around the subject instead of accepting the questioner's alternatives. The politician's strategy is to avoid problems that might be created by someone else's alternatives.

The problem with the two democracy alternatives under discussion is the prominence, indeed primacy, given to the notion of *control*. The "verdict of the majority prevailing," "actual representation," "popular control" all impute public policy making, immediate and direct impact on policy. One might ask, whoever said that democracy requires public control? To that question the answer is clear. The traditional view requires it, as was pointed out in the first section. Almond, Dahl, and the other critics reviewed in the second section do the same. The focus is on control, the verdict of the majority, determination of policy. The focus is too narrow.

Aristotle classified democracy simply. Democracy was "the good form of government by the many." Some modern authors look at this ancient scholar with only historical interest; others have formed a prejudice and do not give him even that much attention. Our interest is in what he said and not who said it. The classification of democracy as good government by the many does not mention control. It merely differentiates democracy from other good forms of government in terms of numbers. This is an important point. It is addressed to the number of persons eligible to participate in the ruling process. Democracy speaks of the many. Monarchy and aristocracy, the other good forms of government, were rule by one or few respectively. This is an elementary but, as will be seen, important point.

The other distinguishing quality in this ancient classification scheme was that the three forms were "good" governments as opposed to "bad." The bad forms were tyranny, oligarchy, and mob rule, respectively following the numerical order of one, few and many. The feature of bad versus good was a separate quality. It held that good rule was for the sake of the common good and bad rule was for the benefit of the ruling person or group. The monarch ruled for the good of the people and the tyrant ruled for his own sake, aristocracy was for the common good and oligarchy for the benefit of the few, and so also for democracy and mob rule. There is a modern prejudice against anything that does not proclaim itself democratic but this category implies that it is possible to have a good government by one or few. The "monarch" need not be a king or queen. It could be any one person who rules for the good of the community. Many contemporary governments could be looked at as versions of this form. Whether they are monarchies or tyrannies would depend on the quality of the rule. (The classical schema is sketched below.)

	Good	Bad
One	Monarchy	Tyranny
Few	Aristocracy	Oligarchy
Many	Democracy	Mob Rule

The traditional classification of monarchy and aristocracy as "elite" was because of the qualifications that limit the number of persons eligible for holding office. If ruling is limited to the oldest male heir of the current ruler or to those who have an exceptionally large amount of property, then most citizens are ineligible to take part. Democracy was "nonelite" in making it possible for most to participate. Disputes arise over the ancient classification as to how many were really able to participate. Such disputes merely divert attention from the basic fact that there is a clear distinction between the many and the one or few.

Even in the modern context the question of how many are among the many may raise problems. Nonetheless, the essential feature is unchanged. Democracy is defined in terms of numbers of people *eligible* for office. Given this classification scheme it would not matter if the office holders were selected by rolling dice as long as the scheduled turnover of office occurred. In the other forms fewer participated and the turnover was much more infrequent. The essential character of democracy was that the many were eligible to rule and in fact ruled by reason of the frequent turnover. It is precisely this democracy, people rule, as prescribed by the constitution of Athens which was so much discussed by Socrates, Plato, and Aristotle.

With these two criteria of rotation and numbers, democracy can be stated simply as the form where all are eligible to rule and the rulers are selected by all. The term all is used merely as a substitute form of the term many. It is not meant to mean that children or noncitizens must share in the eligibility. In this way it is possible to understand that earlier forms of democracy which, for example, excluded women from an active political role were nonetheless democratic. They were democratic in the sense that all of the adult males were eligible to rule and to select the rulers. Today women are included in our community of eligible participants for active political life but we do not include children and adult noncitizens. In this way we retain the basic distinction between the many and the whole community. This is the basis of the earlier point that all democracies were representative since even the popular assembly of all adult men and women would represent the other members of the community, children and others, not present.

The specific provisions which affect who can be included and to what extent they may participate can vary widely from place to place. The fullness of participation in Athens, Tokyo, Dallas, or Boston is affected by different rules about the number of offices to have in the government, the length of the terms, whether successive terms are possible, qualifications for specific offices, the mode of elections, and the condition of the franchise. The original point of these specific provisions was to ensure democratic rule. All these provisions were designed to see that all had their turn at office.

Continued modifications in these rules have occurred over the years and centuries. The changes which have occurred have, however, not always been done with full awareness of how they will affect the general democratic experience. Even unchanged rules need periodic scrutiny to ensure that they remain true to their democratic intent. For example, normally in a democracy there are no property or wealth qualifications for holding office since such provisions would render the supposed democracy an aristocracy by limiting qualification to a few. It is this precise danger which explains the recent concern about the costs of political campaigns. If, as seems increasingly the case, only wealthy individuals can afford to campaign and hold office then an aristocratic element has been unwittingly injected into the democratic process. Attention to such matters helps maintain the true democratic character. Such vigilance alone, however, does not guarantee correct solutions.

Now to bring these points together, if the classical aspects of democracy are applied to the contemporary scene, a solution is available to the impasse between elite guidance and popular control. The problems with those two alternatives is that elite guidance generally excludes the public and popular control has a difficult time including efficient and wise rule. It is true that in the classical formulation the many were at times acknowledged as wiser than the few even though it admits that their folly may lead them into error. Democracy was about *the people ruling in turn*. It is not that the people should rule all at the same time all the time. This role in ruling and at the same time not ruling presents a solution to the impasse. The public's role is not so much controlling rulers as "selecting" them.

Understanding democracy as *popular selection* of political leaders overcomes at the same time both the limitations of popular control and the impudence of elite guidance. It should be noted that this view does not alter the reality described or the activities associated with it. One explanation that describes democracy better than other explanations does not change the reality but only the perception of it. Popular control describes the reality one way, elite guidance describes the same reality another way, and popular selection is a third way of describing the same set of circumstances and events. This third alternative should not be viewed as a threatening situation. It is simply a substitute way of looking at the same facts to see if there is a better explanation.

Popular *selection* is not just a matter of substituting the word selection for the word control. Control was used in the first place to reflect a particular perspective of the political world. Control meant that the verdict of the majority ought to prevail, that actual representation should be the practice, that immediate and direct impact by the public on policy should be realized. Control meant that if the public wanted a certain war turned off it should be turned off, if they wanted taxes lowered they should be lowered, if the people want international justice they should have it. Because the democracy of popular control was so unvarnished it was easy prey for its critics.

The third alternative, popular selection, says that the public selects the rulers. It does not imply immediate and direct impact of the public on policy. It does imply mediate and indirect effect. The public selects an officeholder from among the available candidates. The officeholder determines the policy. But the particular individual is only one member of an elaborate system of various officeholders. No one official decides policy entirely.

The public, the individual voters, may know something about the position of many of the candidates on some of the issues. The public does not know the position of all the candidates on all the issues. There are many possibilities: the voters may act on erroneous information about the candidates, they may vote in a contradictory fashion on specific issues and particular candidates, or the public may be almost completely uninformed on the candidates. You and I may vote for a particular candidate for opposite reasons, or we may vote for opposing candidates for identical reasons even though one of us is wrong in our perception. We may be equally informed, or we may be equally uninformed. Even in the best case we are only partially informed.

About ten percent of the public at the most are careful followers of public affairs. Being a regular follower of current events does not make one capable in policy making. However, for the case of popular selection, though intelligence is not unimportant, what the voters do, and all that they need do, is *select* the candidate. The popular selection position does not deny the importance of adequate information in the selection process, but it does recognize the limitations of information usage. This third view argues that the public selects the candidate in whom they have greatest confidence, with whom they are most comfortable, who sounds most credible, and to whom there is most personal compatibility.

How the Public Selects

The suggestion that candidate selection can be based on personality may come as a shock to some. It is especially shocking to those who operate from the traditional perspective of the "rational man–intelligent voter" syndrome. This perspective is part of the thesis that the public controls policy and therefore the voter must be intelligent and the citizen rational. Such a thesis may be less a description of how the citizen and voter acts than it is prescriptive. It assumes what it would like to see instead of describing what really occurs. In addition it places a heavy burden on the citizen as voter which may, if we were to engage in speculative theorizing, explain nonvoting more than the usual socio-economic hypotheses.

There is much to suggest that voters decide between candidates based on personality. In voting on personality the individual works from a familiar foundation. In everyday activity individuals make frequent personality decisions. They decide to associate, to continue to associate, or to break off contact with other individuals. Usually some common background characteristic such as neighborhood, school, church, club, ethnic origin, sports activity, etc., is the occasion for first contact. Acquaintance follows, building on the original contact and common interest. If compatibility is not found or reinforced, individuals drift apart or completely break off contact. The common background characteristic serves as a screen for the first contacts and judgments. The meetings and discussions that follow serve as a more refined screen by which more personality judgments are made. In persons of the opposite sex this is the personality dimension of the dating process.

Voters go through the same steps. There is the first contact with a candidate, followed by getting acquainted, usually through the communications media, and lastly there is judgment or a preliminary judgment about the candidate. Political parties, organizations, and affiliations serve as the common background characteristics. The campaign serves as the more refined screen which reinforces or diverts the first inclination. Letting party affiliation or similar factors serve as the initial screen for meeting candidates is no different than having social characteristics screen friends. Neither screening process is normally so rigid that other, so-called "outside" factors cannot at times supersede. We do on occasion meet new friends "by accident." Even there, though, personality judgments still prevail in the end.

Where a lifelong Republican votes for Kennedy or a lifelong Democrat votes for Reagan, that individual voter will not deviate from his or her normal voting pattern for other offices or in the next election. The normal pattern will prevail unless continuing factors reinforce or strengthen the deviating choice. If the first deviation is an indication of a change in general pattern, that voter can still be seen as acting according to a personality judgment. Personal comfort directs the individual instead of a rigidly rational and scientific analysis of candidate and issue options. Few if any voters can operate according to these rigid standards.

Winter and Bellows[25] approvingly cite Campbell et al. in this regard. They explain that "presidential elections in the United States do not decide policy but at most determine '*who shall decide* what government shall do.'" Two pages earlier those same two authors, in summarizing the significance of elections for Western democracies, had stated that "free elections . . . do not mathematically reveal popular sentiment about a long list of controversial public issues. At best, competitive elections are only a rough approximation of popular feeling." And reiterating the point on the next page they state that "a vote for a candidate or a party cannot be interpreted as support or even awareness of each item in the electoral program."

There is only one reasonable conclusion to draw from these observations. Either democracy is indeed a myth *or* the popular control definition of democracy is incorrect and popular selection is all that democracy intends. Now to the selection view of democracy should be added the reminder that though the public selects candidates on personality judgment, that judgment is not mere whim or impulse. The personality judgment has a quality based on the individual's experiences of everyday living. Decisions about friends and associates are not regularly whimsical. They are instead the products of our inner and habitual self. Such judgments involve many things and are seldom capricious. We generally succeed with our lives and with our friendships.

The argument should be augmented with the reminder that Asher gives that "much more enters into citizens' assessments of candidates than simply the candidate's personality, speaking style, and the like."[26] The candidate's personality is not the point. The personality of the voter is the locus of the selection judgment. The voter may, but need not always, begin with the candidate's personality. The starting point may instead be some particular issue, party, or friend's recommendation but eventually some decision will be made to vote based on what the voter is comfortable with, on the candidate's or the party's credibility, or some other default mechanism. In this way the personality dimension is a starting point for many factors to follow. The central point however is that the voter's first competence is never rejected; it is always assumed. It may be that it is never surpassed.

The rational man–intelligent voter thesis inflates and thereby distorts the quality of the voting act. The suggestion that the voter should carefully study all the candidates and issues requires such a high standard that *few if any* voters would qualify as intelligent in these terms. Thomas Dye writes that, "Voters who make up their minds on the basis of the specific stand of the candidates probably compose less than 10 percent of the electorate."[27] Even the seemingly simpler choice between the two major parties is one on which very few could confidently qualify as intelligent. The Republican party cannot be definitely classified as conservative nor can the Democratic party be classified as liberal. The public is deprived of an easy and accurate categorization on which to judge parties and then candidates. The terms liberal and conservative cannot be readily defined and so the beginning ingredients for sorting out candidates and parties is unavailable.

The average voter rejects the burdens of the rational man–intelligent voter thesis but usually has no ready substitute to explain their voting behavior. It is as if the burdens talk increasing numbers of citizens into either not voting or voting out of habit but at a reduced rate. The popular control thesis and its accompanying voting behavior syndrome creates an inferiority complex in the voter. This complex diminishes voting and lends support to an elite guidance reality. The suggestion that voting is a personality judgment begins more positively by its premise of individual competence. The reflective voter does not want to be burdened with the responsibility of *deciding* policy. The individual may express an opinion but does not want to decide whether the United States should introduce troops into Lebanon, whether the United Nations should be funded, whether the Olympic Games should be boycotted, or how the Russians should or should not be dealt with. These are matters on which the voter may have strong feelings but the voter recognizes a personal lack of adequate information for deciding the policy itself.

Critics of governmental policy, particularly foreign policy, defend their second-guessing the government by saying that everything one needs to know to make a valid judgment on such matters could be gained in a daily and careful reading of *The New York Times*. There are several things wrong with this answer. For one thing that newspaper may be the single best public information source but only a very few people read it. In numbers alone it is an elitist proposition. Furthermore the reply, although traditional, patronizes the public with something patently false. If it were true that all one needs to know can be found in the leading newspaper, the United States or any government could be well advised to scale down intelligence gathering and policy research activities and simply subscribe to their best newspapers.

Jacques Ellul has observed that "undigested up-to-the-minute information is not enough. We have to know what to do with it and how to utilize it."[28] Any reasonable person would acknowledge that the public has neither the latest information nor the immediate capacity to know what to do with such information. The public does not have the information on foreign policy. The voter wants to make the decision that taxes should be lowered, that public services should be increased, that the local elementary school should not be closed. All instances of such direct public decision making have only served to prove the occasional and temporary folly, to use Aristotle's word, into which democracies can get themselves.

A prominent recent example of folly is the public tax cutting or tax-limiting referendum, Proposition 13, in California. That proposition, which the public approved as redounding to their benefit, really was of most immediate benefit to large landlords. It was of little or no corresponding benefit to renters. All property owners realized some decrease in property tax but the ultimate results were not entirely salutary. The author's small plot of undeveloped land in California saw a property tax decrease from $52 per year to $27 per year. Shortly thereafter, however, there was a noticeable increase in weed-abatement fees and cost for water services even for undeveloped land.

It is a common phenomenon that as a cap is put on taxes the fee for services, like water, sewer, and trash collection, go up. In similar fashion when students succeed in arguing against a tuition increase, arbitrary fees increase. On a long term scale the result of Proposition 13 in California was to deprive the cities and local units of government of flexible revenue decisions and to make them more, rather than less, dependent on Sacramento, the state capital. Public referenda are blunt instruments whose decision-making effects are more apparent than real. Most referenda are devices utilized by politicians to shift the burden of hard decisions to the public. Instead of the triumph of popular democracy, referenda might well be looked at as symptomatic of its weaknesses.

Contrary to the popular control view, the third alternative sees the voters' role as more indirect and mediate. Voters make the choice of placing confidence in one candidate instead of another by a judgment of personality registering personal credibility. The elected candidate then decides the policy in combination with many other officials. Personality, as all know from individual experience, is not a one-dimensional quality. Some candidates can have a high personality quotient and maintain it. They can lose it by a low credibility rating. An individual or candidate may be outwardly pleasing but lose the initial credibility by later actions or statements. Similarly, an initially displeasing individual may gain credibility by later actions or statements.

In the period of a political campaign the public may be convinced of one candidate's superiority over another. Later the public may find out that they were mistaken in that judgment. There may develop a "credibility gap," as it was called in the later Lyndon Johnson years, between the elected official and the public. When such a breakdown occurs between the initial expectation of the public and the perceived performance, the public may express and record its changed view at the next election. The public gets to take out its frustration on that candidate, if again running, or on that candidate's party, even if neither is truly responsible for the policy which incurs the public wrath. In that new election the public may make another "mistake" on the individual selected. The most critical point is however that if the public makes "mistakes" on candidates, the situation would be far worse if matters of policy, war, peace, the economy, racial justice, were being decided in such a manner.

The central democratic thesis therefore becomes evident. Faith in the good sense of the average human comes about not in the assumption that the public is infallible in all of its choices of particular candidates. Faith in the average human choice is a result of the large number of well-chosen officials responsible for any one decision. This good-sense human will prevails unless the collectivity of decision makers are wholly corrupt and the public is wholly corrupted in choosing them. In instances where particular officeholders lose public credibility the official either resigns, chooses not to seek reelection, is defeated, is opposed by an even worse opponent, or some corruption occurs.

Democracy is not a Delphic wonder where an otherwise fallible public become miraculously the profound arbiters of the public good. Democracy in the sense of popular selection merely requires a process whereby the ordinary competences of members of the public are utilized to produce extraordinary results. The public does not have extraordinary competence, the system has that competence. It takes normal capacities and the using of them to produce extraordinary results. For this reason we will later take a careful look at the forms of government through which democracy works.

RETROSPECTION AND PERSPECTIVE

Three views of democracy have been presented in this chapter: (1) that it means popular control, (2) that popular control is a sustaining myth, and (3) that democracy means popular selection. The view that democracy is a myth has particularly strong analytical appeal. The information requirements for real popular control of leaders and policy has been shown to be lacking for the public. The solution often offered for this lack of information is that the public should be better educated, that more information should be supplied to the public, that more news programs should be available. This solution is not satisfactory. On the one hand the assumed task of providing more information and education is truly massive. Beyond that the problem is not essentially a matter of the amount of information available.

The percentage of people in the United States with some college education has doubled in the last twenty-five years from less than 15 percent to more than 30 percent. This does not make popular policy making more tenable. Popular control and its informational and educational implications give an excessively rational interpretation to democracy. Such an interpretation is appealing but misleading and dangerous because it gives encouragement to, if not gives way to, popular demagoguery.

Popular selection changes the perspective upon which democracy is conceptualized. It does not change democracy; it changes the perception of democracy. Candidates and voters are still seen doing what they have always done. Popular selection merely gives greater credit to the system of selecting candidates than to the determination of policy issues by the public. And, it should be made clear, this third interpretation does not revive elite guidance disguised as virtual representation. Popular selection insists that virtual representation is the logical and natural result of the reality of popular participation and selection. In that reality the essence of democracy is, in the classical phrase, "the public ruling in turns." Any manipulation of the selection process, by wealth or any form of corruption, is not elite guidance but tyranny.

Surprisingly, popular control itself manifests the character of tyranny. It does this by distorting and imposing an unrealistic interpretation on the selection process. Popular control expects the public to both select candidates and determine policy. For the public or anyone to determine that which they are incapable of is a tyranny. The popular selection view does not see the public determining policy. Its position is a more modest one. It sees the process of selecting candidates as affecting the long-term character of the community.

The discussion up to this point has been predominantly American from the American perspective of Western democracies. In the United States, Canada, England, France, Sweden, Germany, and even Japan and occasionally India, the alternatives make sense. Popular control, elite guidance, and popular selection are realistic ways in which the experiences of these different countries can be interpreted. In some of the less stable Western democracies like Italy, Spain, Portugal, etc., the alternatives become less tenable since it is difficult to interpret their more fluid situations. In developing settings like Latin America, the Philippines, South Korea, and others that make some attempt at democracy, the alternatives are hardly extant. This is so because of the infrequency of regular election in these countries and because of the generally acknowledged low relative information quotients of the political process.

In unstable and developing countries the pretense of popular control is particularly transparent except, so it seems, when it is offered as a revolutionary alternative to the living reality of elite dominance. In this setting the less dramatic alternative of popular selection would have more credibility if given a chance by the other two theories. Unfortunately, moderation is seldom a quality found in turbulent circumstances. The ruling elites, even those who have come to office by use of the democratic process or who advocate eventual restoration of democracy, are blunt and apodictic about the capabilities of the masses. They tell of a reality which the popular conception of democracy just does not acknowledge. The president of Brazil defended his country's indirect system of presidential election by saying that such a choice could not be entrusted to people who did not know how to brush their teeth or bathe.[29] President Zia of Pakistan pleaded that his country not be looked at with American eyes saying, "Seventy-five percent of the people of Pakistan are illiterate. How do you expect illiterates to decide for themselves what is good and what is bad for them?"[30]

The assumptions of the political literacy of Americans themselves may be a flawed criterion by which to judge the democratic process. Polls show that three out of four Americans do not know what the First Amendment deals with, and six out of ten people with college backgrounds were likewise unaware.[31] Other surveys show that roughly half the public do not know how many U.S. Senators there are from each state, that U.S. Representatives are elected every two years, who their representatives or senators are, what the Bill of Rights is, and almost never watch the evening news on television. Further, about one in fifty watch the network news every evening, and one in a hundred give full attention to that news. These figures may change but they will not change drastically.

We look back at the famous, or notorious, Smathers-Pepper senatorial primary of 1950 in Florida with embarrassment and with a smug feeling that it could never happen today. Smathers is supposed to have impressed rural voters by charging his opponent "a shameless extrovert," "a man reported to practice nepotism with his sister-in-law," a person who "before his marriage habitually practiced celibacy," and that he had a sister "who was once a thespian in wicked New York." Smathers, who won the primary, denies that he ever said anything like that. Pepper, the incumbent at the time and (subsequently) reelected to Congress, claims that the quotes at least represent the tone of the election. On tone Smathers might agree with Pepper if it applied to both sides.

Elections today may not be as obvious in casting aspersions but the subtle coded rhetoric of racism, loyalty, integrity, sexism, and other innuendo does not make modern campaigns greatly different from earlier ones. The knowledge and alertness of voters has not shifted in any major way in thirty-five years. And, it should be emphasized, American election campaigns are not alone in presenting unclear but simplified rhetoric to the voters. About a recent (March 1983) West German election it was reported, for example, that "mudslinging, slander, innuendo and the manipulation of information have reached new lows."[32]

West German elections involve a complicated electoral procedure of direct election of some members and proportional representation of other members. In a previous election a poll showed that "a majority of West Germans will not know how their ballots work or understand the decisive element in their choice of a Chancellor.''[33] Studies in Britain show political awareness levels there to be comparable to those in the United States. British teenagers were unaware of the most important function of Parliament, the requirement that general elections there must be called at least every five years, and that the Irish Republican Army was a Catholic and not a Protestant organization.[34]

Such ignorance appalls the well-informed and makes them despair for democracy. Such insights make us concede that if democracy is difficult, to say the least, under favorable circumstances in developed countries, it has a much more difficult task in the developing or unstable setting. There especially the proposition that the people determine policy would test credulity.

It is rude to criticize and at the same time it is unjust to distort reality. In the developing situation there is a dilemma that popular control is unrealistic and yet without it there is no guarantee that the elite can be checked. Democracy has a powerful hold on the imagination in such countries at least insofar as it suggests a restraint on arbitrary power. So powerful is the appeal that revolutionaries use it to substitute the established elites with themselves. And the elites use it to maintain themselves in power. Recent elections in the Philippines, El Salvador, and other Latin nations confirm these points.

Where revolutionaries are successful they inevitably become a new elite that once again do not allow freely contested elections. Cuba and Nicaragua are prominent examples but possibly so only because other examples are so glaring that they are usually overlooked as not even in the democratic category. The Soviet Union and the Eastern European countries view government and democracy in a special way such that they insist that they are truly democratic and the West is not. This view will be discussed in a later chapter on constitutionalism where the principles can be brought out most effectively. Until then it will be necessary to sidestep the democratic dimension of their situation. It most definitely should be tabbed for future reflection though, since it forms such a large dimension of contemporary political reality.

Mexico is another special case of democracy. It has the appearance of holding free elections. Since there is for all practical purposes only one political party in those elections no real choice is available. Mexico is in this respect only slightly more democratic than Cuba or other revolutionary regimes where even the appearance of elections is not saved. Again, that is not to comment on the larger issue of democracy in communist countries mentioned above. It is just to take elections as they are generally presented to us and compare how they are conducted in one-party and, what appear to be, ''no-choice'' states. The similarity and contrast between Mexico and Cuba shows, however, that we have been dealing with democracy in little more than a voting and elections sense. That sense is a valid but incomplete way to consider democracy. Mexico, for example, may be somewhat more democratic concerning freedom of movement, speech, religious practice, union activity, etc. These freedoms are generally lacking in authoritarian regimes. Where they are maintained, future elections may become more competitive.

Developing countries are really the battleground of competing traditional elites amongst themselves and between them and revolutionary elites. In a pessimistic global perspective one could look at the whole world as offering the alternative between unrealistic popular control and inevitable elite guidance. Even American elections, where candidate images are manufactured and presented, it is said, like toothpaste commercials, could fit into this pessimistic picture. The only saving alternative is to view elections in the United States in the more modest perspective of popular selection.

The view of democracy as popular selection seems not to have as much to offer as popular control. Yet if the view is indeed realistic and achievable it offers more than the traditional view. The merit of an election in the popular selection view is chiefly the ability to freely reject unconvincing incumbents. There may be limitations to this ability in many situations but clearly in that case there is no democracy. It is for that reason that Mexico with its one-term presidency and one-party choices is hard to classify as democratic. There it is not even possible to vote against the incumbent. But with these comments we must bear in mind that most of the Middle Eastern countries, except Israel and Egypt, and many other countries around the world do not even make a pretense at democratic processes.

A somewhat overly vehement case has been made in the preceding pages for popular selection as the correct understanding of democracy instead of popular control or elite guidance. The zealousness of the presentation may turn some readers against what has been said. Such a reaction cannot be denounced as entirely unreasonable. Moderation, not zealousness, is a normal sign of a rational argument. However, the reader's indulgence is requested on the grounds that the vehemence was necessary to offset the longstanding dominance of the other two positions.

In the remaining sections of this text, much material will be presented which can be read as completely independent of this first discussion of democracy. The future sections, however, can also be found to provide material to support one or the other of the three interpretations just discussed. At times those connections will be brought out directly. At other times the reader can make the relationship between the versions of democracy and the later material on their own. The point of this opening chapter has been more than just to discuss democracy. The point of the chapter has also been to plunge directly into a substantive question in political science. As Almond states "the basic question of the proper relationship between individual and society is among the most significant, as well as among the oldest, problems in political science."[35] It was the intention of this first chapter to plunge in, to splash around, to be immersed in, to almost drown in a real-life political question. The discussion of democracy satisfies that intention.

To this plunge into democracy it is necessary to now add that the water has not been especially deep, though deep enough to drown in to be sure. It has not been that deep because the discussion of democracy has been limited to a consideration of the relationship of the public to leaders and policy. There are other aspects to democracy: as a way of life, as an economic phenomenon, as a part of the legal process through a jury system. In Athenian democracy, for example, the court was the heart of the system more so than the assembly. It would be necessary to go into these other dimensions and to show their parallel to the alternative views of democracy to cover the topic thoroughly. Enough has been done, however, to have adequately established the principles of democracy for an introduction.

The next chapter will also use the plunge-in approach. There the subject is the political system. That topic, however, is unlike the current chapter in that the discussion is not of a real-life political question. The next chapter is instead about a real political science phenomenon. We will also become fully immersed in this new topic before we are finished. Lastly, however, we will pull ourselves out, crawl to the side, dry off, and examine where we are at. That examination will occur in the third chapter where, after having experienced the political system, what political scientists do will be discussed.

NOTES

1. Gabriel Almond and G. Bingham Powell, Jr., *Comparative Politics* (Boston: Little, Brown, 1966), p. 189.

2. Henry J. Schmandt and Paul G. Steinbicker, *Fundamentals of Government* (Milwaukee: Bruce Publishing Co., 1963), p. 203. The example of national health insurance cited in this 1963 text was at least fifteen years old at that time and is more than twice that old now. The United States still does not have a national health insurance program.

3. ibid.

4. cf. Warren E. Miller and Donald E. Stokes, "Constituency Influence in Congress," *American Political Science Review*, 57, March 1963, pp. 55–65; Charles F. Cnudde and Donald J. McCrone, "The Linkage Between Constituency Attitude and Congressional Voting Behavior," *American Political Science Review*, 60, March 1966, pp. 66–72. See also Edward T. Jennings, Jr., "Competition, Constituencies, and Welfare Policies in American States," *American Political Science Review*, 73, June 1979, pp. 414–429.

5. Thomas R. Dye, *Understanding Public Policy*, 4th ed. (Englewood Cliffs, N.J.: Prentice-Hall, 1982), pp. 343–344.

6. Edmund Burke, "Speech to the Electors of Bristol," November 3, 1774, *The Works of Edmund Burke* (London: Bell and Daldy, 1872), Vol I, pp. 446–447.

7. Hilaire Belloc and Cecil Chesterton, *The Party System* (London: S. Swift Co., 1911), p. 17.

8. Almond and Powell, *Comparative*, p. 186.

9. Robert A. Dahl, *Who Governs?* (New Haven: Yale University Press, 1961), p. 281.

10. Jacques Ellul, *The Political Illusion* (New York: Knopf, 1967), Chapter 4.

11. Schmandt and Steinbicker, *Fundamentals*, p. 222.

12. For a copy of the "Port Huron Statement" see Kenneth M. Dolbeare, *Directions in American Political Thought* (New York: John Wiley, 1969), pp. 468–476; or see Ernest D. Giglio and John J. Schrems, *Future Politics* (Berkeley: McCutchin Publishing, 1971), Part 1.

13. Found in Giglio and Schrems, *Future Politics*, p. 11.

14. Schmandt and Steinbicker, *Fundamentals*, p. 218.

15. ibid., p. 222.

16. ibid., p. 218.

17. Aristotle, *Politics,* III, 1281b.

18. Aristotle, *Politics,* Bk. III, 1282a, 20–25.

19. cf. Tom Hayden, *The American Future: New Visions Beyond Old Frontiers* (Boston: South End Press, 1980).

20. Schmandt and Steinbicker, *Fundamentals.*

21. Almond and Powell, *Comparative,* pp. 186–189.

22. Terrence E. Cook, ''Community Assemblies Democracy: A Latent Theme in Democratic Theory,'' paper presented at the 1978 American Political Science Association convention, p. 18.

23. For a clear theoretical presentation of that debate, tilted in favor of the radical or mass view, see: Shin'ya Ono, ''The Limits of Bourgeois Pluralism,'' found in Charles A. McCoy and John Playford, *Apolitical Politics* (New York: Thomas Y. Crowell, 1967), pp. 99–123.

24. Ellul, *Political Illusion,* from the ''Introduction'' by Konrad Kellen.

25. Herbert R. Winter and Thomas J. Bellows, *People and Politics* (New York: John Wiley, 1981), p. 230.

26. Herbert Asher, *Presidential Elections and American Politics* (Homewood, Ill.: The Dorsey Press, 1980), p. 138.

27. Thomas R. Dye, Lee S. Greene, and George S. Parthemos, *Governing the American Democracy* (New York: St. Martin's Press, 1980), p. 247.

28. *The New York Times,* July 1, 1973, op-ed page.

29. *The New York Times,* March 16, 1979.

30. *The New York Times,* January 18, 1980, p. 8.

31. *The New York Times,* January 18, 1980.

32. *The New York Times,* March 3, 1983, p. 8.

33. *The New York Times,* October 1, 1980, p. 3.

34. *The New York Times,* August 14, 1977.

35. Almond and Powell, *Comparative,* p. 189.

CHAPTER TWO
THE POLITICAL SYSTEM

Many political scientists organize the political world into what is called the "political system." This is a way of presenting complex realities in an initially simplified manner. For some political scientists the political system has scientific value, while others dispute this. Methodology will be discussed in the next chapter where the place of the political system and many other ways of looking at the political world will be described. For the present, the political system framework will be described simply as a model. A model is a metaphor, something in the mind of the person who made it up. It is a simple, organized portrayal of the things of the political world. Models are "good or bad" depending on their accuracy and whether they aid understanding. They are like maps in that they can help us find our way or make us more confused than ever. We will describe a system in its most elementary respects and then adapt it to the political world. The discussion will be illustrated with concrete examples, with a final application to the previous discussion of democracy.

THE SYSTEMS MODEL

A "system" is understood to be an identifiable whole composed of identifiable and interrelated parts. There are initially three parts or functional operations within every system: input, core-conversion, and output. The three activities or parts are interrelated. Together they define the inner boundary of the system. As a simple example we might use a toothpick-making system. The input in such a system would be some pieces of wood. A machine, perhaps even a jackknife, which splinters and smooths the raw material into fine, thin pieces is the core of the system. Of course the output, what the conversion process did to the input, is toothpicks.

The toothpick example could be extended by adding some sulphur material to the input and by finding some means of combining the sulphur compound and the splinters in the conversion process. The output would then be sulphur matches. (These are the old type of wooden matches, now outlawed for safety reasons, which could be lit by scratching the match head against or with any abrasive surface, even a fingernail or the seat of one's pants.) Additional input and conversion processes can lead to more sophisticated output. An automobile or a space-craft are the products of enormous numbers of input items and an elaborately designed conversion process.

The political system is an attempt to look at the political world in the organized fashion of the simple systems model just described. In a political system the input are public interests and demands of various sorts. The core is the process whereby decisions about demands are made. The output is public policy. These three activities define the boundary of the political system. The boundary itself can expand and contract according to the amount of input, conversion, and output activity. The larger the domain of public policy the larger the system. The fewer number of policies the smaller the system, or at least so we imagine.

The political system operates, as do all systems, within an environment of outside forces. Toothpick making operates within the environment of primitive and medical dentistry. Automobile making operates within an industrial environment. The political system operates within the environment of many other systems. The outside environment of the political system includes the economy, the geographical setting, and the demographic factors of size, density, and distribution of the population. The full extent of the influence of environment on the system will be considered in a moment. The other parts of the political system should be explained first.

Input: Political Interests

Input is of two kinds, substantive and functional. The substantive input of the political system are demands, supports, and apathy. Apathy is an interesting item since it is usually assumed from its definition that it is not an input at all. The accompanying diagrams (Figure 2-1) depict the various parts and activities of the po-

---

FIGURE 2-1   There are many different depictions for the political system. All are some adaptation of David Easton's seminal effort, *The Political System* (New York: Alfred A. Knopf, 1953). The basic design for this depiction of the political system is from M. D. Irish and J. W. Prothro, *The Politics of American Democracy* (4th ed.) © 1968 pp. 9, 15. Adapted by permission of Prentice-Hall, Inc., Englewood Cliffs, N. J.

Simple System:

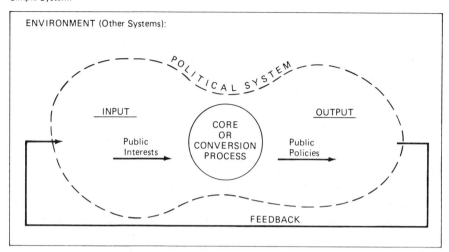

More Detailed System:

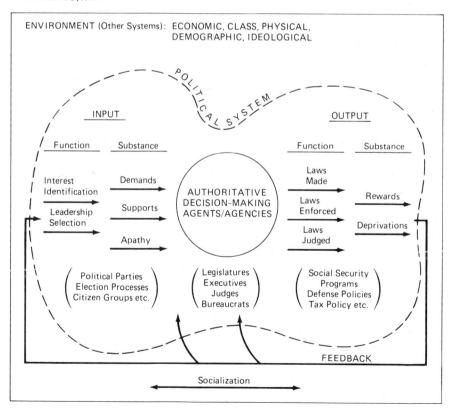

litical system. The simple systems diagram applies to the political world showing the input, core, and output. The second diagram shows more detail of the political system. On the input side, demands and supports sound like the more important factors in comparison to apathy. But apathy may provide a cushion of leeway for decision makers which frees them from immediate demands of particular groups. In this way the system is not responding just to the tabulated demands and support at one point in time. This enables the schema to suggest that the political community has a variety of substantive ways to express its interests.

Demands and supports are designated as input to the decision-making core of the system because they feed definite information into the core of the system. But apathy is also a definite bit of information, a reflection of public attitudes. In fact, in many elections, constitutional amendment referenda, and other public votes, apathy is as much a determinant of results as the actual ballots. A curious anomaly in American politics bears this point out. No winning Presidential candidate has ever received support from as high a percentage of the total eligible public as the percentage of nonvoters in that particular election. Assuming that the nonvoters preferred "none of the above," that designation would always have won. This is a strong affirmation of the role of apathy in American politics and the political system schema.

Functionally the input constitutes two things: (1) the expression or articulation of various interests and (2) the selection of political leaders. Demands, supports, and apathy are the substantive expression of the interests of the community and its choice of leaders. The two functions are interrelated, as are all parts of the system. The interests are articulated by individuals, groups, political parties, or governmental units themselves. Some leaders are selected because of the interests they represent, and some interests are advanced because of the leaders who have been selected. The selection process can be appointive, rotational, or by voting. The diagram suggests that the information processed by the system is in one direction. Considering the interrelatedness within the system this cannot be correct. Nonetheless, for a first impression the one-directional character creates no problem. Therefore we envision the input as fed into the core where a sorting-out process decides the policy output.

Core: Authoritative Decision-Making Agents

The core of the political system is understood to be the authoritative decision-making agents or agencies. The core "converts" input into output. In the United States this core would be the Congress, the President, and the courts. In England the core would be the Parliament and the prime minister. In every system a decision-making operation would exist but the exact agency performing the function may differ from system to system. In the Soviet Union, for example, the decisions may be made by the legally designated Supreme Soviet or they may be made by what is ostensibly an input mechanism, namely, the Communist Party. What is important in a simple systems' description is locating and designating the agency by the function performed instead of by the title of the agent. If in the Soviet Union or in a small town in Michigan the political party boss rather than the legal official makes the important decisions, it is important to be able to recognize that functional distinction. Sometimes the actual designation may be politely overlooked for political purposes. What is important is to appreciate the difference between what is polite and what is actual.

Output: Public Policy

The product or "output" of the decision-making process is public policy. Public policy in this respect is understood to be laws which are made, enforced, or adjudicated. In the United States there is a tendency to link in a commensurate way substantive parts of the core of the system to the output. It is said that, "Congress makes the law, the President enforces the law, and the courts judge the law." Such a linkage is not necessary. It is sufficient to visualize the core as preceding and responsible for the output. The linkage can be left for a more detailed treatment at a later point. Some of that treatment will occur in the later chapters on constitutionalism and on the forms of government.

Feedback

The output, whatever its form, will substantively constitute a reward or a deprivation to those affected by it. A new social security law will reward those who receive increased benefits and, temporarily at least, be a deprivation for those who must pay increased tax withholdings. A popular court ruling may appear to be beneficial to all lovers of justice but years later harmful consequences may become evident. In this way rewards and deprivations set up a "feedback." The feedback may take the form of new interests, more support, or less apathy. More benefits and less taxation may be sought as one is respectively rewarded or deprived. A reexamination of the justice system may be insisted upon as the effects of the earlier ruling become more evident.

The political system with the three internal steps plus feedback takes on the appearance of an ongoing process of input, conversion, output, feedback, new inputs, new conversions, new outputs, etc. The passage of the Eighteenth Amendment and its subsequent repeal by the Twenty-first Amendment shows this process. The Eighteenth Amendment which established Prohibition, was the result of the demands of a few, the support by some, and the apathy of many. Prohibition, the public policy result of the amendment, produced a reward for some and a sensed deprivation for a great many more. The secondary result of Prohibition was the creation of new demands in greater number for its repeal. This feedback saw more insistent demands accompanied by much more active support and much less apathy in general on the issue.

Environment

The interaction of the basic operations of the system takes place within the environment. The environment influences not only the input but also the conversion process and the output. The environment consists of all those other systems that affect the political system. Among these would be the economic system, the system of basic ideas of the community, the class system, the culture and specifically the political culture, the demographic or people dispersal system, and the geographic environment. All these systems interact and influence one another and the political system. The full extent and precise manner in which the other systems affect the political system is beyond the scope of our immediate concern. It is enough to elaborate on just two of the other systems, people and geography. Citing these two factors can suggest the way the environment affects the political system and contributes to making one system different from another.

Think of Japan! (It's marvelous what the mind can do in response to one word isn't it?) Japan has an area roughly equivalent to that of California, yet it has a population of more than half that of the entire United States. Because of this combination of population and area, the political system in Japan would be different from the United States as a whole or, for that matter, the response mechanisms of California. California has in recent years indicated concern over its large (from its perspective) population and made efforts to curb it. California would be much more concerned about expansion if it had to contend with a population almost five times as large, which would make it comparable to Japan. For example, a political demonstration of hundreds of thousands of participants would take months to organize for Washington, D.C., weeks for Sacramento, and twenty-four hours for Tokyo. Accordingly the system, the response mechanisms, the traffic control arrangements, the public and portable comfort facilities, would have to be different in one place over the other.

To push the illustration one step further, Canada can be brought into the picture. Canada has an area roughly equivalent to that of the United States and a population roughly equivalent to that of California. Once again, the two factors of people and geography alone would induce a different response in Canada than in California, the United States, or Japan. As indicated previously there are many more than two factors for any complete analysis. People and geography merely suggest the environment's effect on the system. To bring the point home, family and residence may be substituted for people and geography, and then one might reflect on one's attitude and actions as a function of one's own environment.

It may be contended that other factors such as the economic system or the class system are more important than people and geography or others. The economic environment is obviously important and one does not have to fear being called a Marxist to say so. However, no priority of environment systems need be established at this point. It is sufficient to acknowledge the impact of environment as a whole on the political system. This does not mean that the environment determines the behavior of the affected system. Some may hold that position but we are not in a position to discuss it yet. All we are suggesting at this point is that the environment influences the system and that it is important to acknowledge this influence.

It is now possible to summarize what has been described so far. In any consideration of the political system five factors and their interaction must be taken into account. The five are the three parts of input, conversion, and output, plus feedback and the environment. It may be quite impossible to study all five parts definitively in every undertaking or, indeed, in any one endeavor. What is important is to acknowledge, as the political system model does, the immense context of the integrated social and political universe that is the subject of political studies.

Assumptions of Application

The system-schema or model approach to political studies holds that the basic parts of the system can be found in any country and at any level of government. The system schema is, as the name implies, a universally applicable framework. It is assumed that all countries and levels of government have a system, that all the functions are in each system, that differentiation within and between each system is by degree, and that all systems have mixed environments. According to these assumptions, as has been suggested, the United States, Japan, Canada, or any other country will each have the basic functions, activities, or parts, differing only by degree.

As the system is applied to successively lower levels of government within a particular country, the surrounding higher levels of government assume a position as part of that lower level's environment. The United States has the international arena as part of its environment, Tennessee has the United States as part of its environment, Chattanooga has Tennessee as part of its, and so on. This shows that the system schema can be applied horizontally and vertically. The value of the system is that it gives a framework by which the political world can be grasped in an orderly fashion at any level and to any country.

It is an altogether separate question whether the orderly framework of the system schema is a deductive imposition deceptively suggesting an order not warranted by reality. That question should be mentioned but is not decided now. What is important at this point is to see the organizing utility of the framework and then to use that framework without prejudice or commitment. Later in the discussion of methods the merits of the framework as such will be given more attention. Even if in the end one decides against the system approach no substantive harm can be done in learning about it. The political system is used by many political scientists. Some try to use it in a rigid way. Others merely employ it as a broad organizing framework. Others make use of the language borrowed from more scientific disciplines for the convenience of the terminology. Whatever usage may finally prove best, it is wise to be familiar with the political system.

APPLICATION TO A SCHOOL DISTRICT

It was mentioned earlier that the political system model applies horizontally and vertically. In other words the model can be used at the local, state, and national and international levels. It can be applied to and within all countries. To bear out the horizontal and vertical application and the general adaptability of the system approach a brief consideration of the school district level of government can be helpful. An appreciation of the general adaptability of the model can be gained by seeing its application to this lowest of levels of the governmental ladder. At the same time the consideration of the school district can serve to tie this discussion to the earlier chapter on democracy.

It is convenient to start with the core of the system, the authoritative decision-making activities or agents. In a school district policy is set by either the board of school directors or the superintendent. Do you know which one is *really* in charge? Legally the responsibility is that of the elected officials! Practically, even though appearance supports the elected officials, the policy is set by the superintendent.[1] The relationship between the board and the superintendent can be visualized as like that between a married couple, George and Martha, in an old story. As the story goes, upon first being married the couple agreed that Martha would make all the little day-to-day decisions and that George would make all the big decisions. After many years of happily married bliss George found that there had been no big decisions.

An evaluation of the way problems are analyzed, options are developed, and solutions are presented to school boards by superintendents would strongly suggest that there are no big decisions, only a series of little decisions or agenda alternatives decided or scheduled by administrators. This should not be taken as an attempt to say that school boards do nothing. That clearly is not the case. They spend an unbelievable, some would say an inordinate, amount of time on school board matters. (There is another old story about a school district in which candidates had to be recruited, begged, to serve on the school board. The recruit was told, "Look, it's only one evening a month!" Being convinced of his civic duty the individual got on the board and found that the one evening a month was with his family. What the story does not convey is the number of districts in which this is common practice.)

The story of George and Martha illustrates the problem of identifying functional roles within a school district. The resulting contention is that school boards do not so much formulate policy as ratify it. It is generally assumed that the board makes the decisions. That is only formally accurate. The same principle applies at other levels in the governmental ladder. It is said by some critics that Henry Kissinger as National Security Advisor and as Secretary of State wanted the same relationship with Congress. They would make all the big decisions and he would make all the little day-to-day decisions. Whether the story is true or not is not our current concern. It does point out the similarity of questions at a variety of levels provoked by the framework.

The debate about roles seeks to determine just who the decision-making agent is. Is the superintendent or the board the real decision maker? Is the President or Congress the real maker of foreign policy? Maybe a political microscope would aid in answering the questions; maybe not. At least the schema helps us to look in the right direction and to ask some meaningful questions about the core of the local school system.

Specifying input aspects of the school district is a matter of discovering the agents of interest articulation and leadership selection. Here the quest is for how demands, supports, and apathy are fed through the system to be brought to bear on the decision-making process. The agents of interest would be individuals or groups such as parents, voters, taxpayers, teachers, unions or teacher's associations, local political parties, and even students. Which input vehicle is important is hard to say. As with students, the extent and weight of each of the groups would have to be determined according to the peculiarities of the particular district before any accurate impression could be established. At one time one group may have more influence—parents who support the band program for example—only to be replaced later by a taxpayers group who could care less about a drum line or new uniforms. Thus input activities are no more static that any other part of the system.

Students might more likely be found on the output side of the system. In that respect they are products which reflect the qualities of the system rather than simply the raw input processed by the core. The output of a school system is difficult to measure because the time for optimal measurement cannot be easily determined. Should student output be measured simply by the percentage that graduate from high school after a four year enrollment? Should it be measured in terms of the average SAT scores for the graduating class? The number who go on to college and promising careers? The number who finish college? The number that learn "worthwhile" values? The number that lead a "good" life?

Even before such questions could be answered it would be recognized that they are addressed to only a few of the functions of a school system. Although the educational function of learning certain courses and their content may still be thought of as primary, school systems today do many things other than simply instruct in reading, writing, and arithmetic. In fact schools have had many additional functions for a long time, even though it may be only recently that these other activities have been separately recognized. Schools have social, health, welfare, and entertainment roles. They provide athletic training grounds, music and band programs, and they provide for general physical development. They teach job skills, combat drug abuse, provide sex education, inspire loyalty to the country, train good drivers, feed many of the poor with breakfast and hot lunches, run adult centers, and tend to many children who otherwise would have little adult care both during school hours and after.

It is not our concern in this chapter to discuss whether schools should have all these roles. Questions about the extent of the general role of government will be taken up later in our discussion about the purpose of the state. As the role of the state is large or small the role of the schools would correspond. The immediate concern is different. Here the concern is that if we can identify some of the roles of the schools, what criteria can be used for measurement of successful accomplishment of those roles? Furthermore, what reasonable and proper time period should be used in measuring success? The answers to these questions are not obvious. This set of unanswered questions establishes a useful backdrop for continued reflection on the democracy issue. The functions of the schools and the competing legitimate standards of success reveal the limitations of accurately grasping and subsequently judging the performance of this familiar governmental activity.

The output of a school district, like the input and the decision process, can be seen to be multifaceted. To specify each would be a large task. To show their interrelationship and full bearing on the overall system would be an effort of monumental proportions. The environment of a school system is no exception to the magnitude of such efforts. In this instance the environment consists of all the political systems that are physically proximate. Even though education is said to be nonpartisan it is in reality never completely independent of the political community. The local subculture, the local economic system, particularly the tax base, and the State Educational Code are all part of the larger environment of a school district. The State Code is surprisingly broad and detailed in what it requires of a local school system. It specifies the legal liabilities and responsibilities of each district, the minimum number of days the district should operate each year, the certification requirements for teachers and administrators, building requirements for air circulation, whether corporeal punishment (spanking) should be allowed and under what circumstances, the minimum content of the curriculum, minimum and maximum age of attendance, the size of athletic fields and classrooms, and much more.

Beyond the provisions of the Code the tax base probably more than anything else determines the extent of the program of one particular district as opposed to another district. Affluent suburban school districts have a high tax base and a low tax rate while urban districts have just the opposite. The revenue from taxes makes it possible for one district to afford programs that another district cannot. Tax revenue means that the benefits to children are affected by a factor over which the school directors have no control. That tax factor is not likely to improve soon. The revenue situation is likely to get worse because state-mandated tax systems rely primarily on local property tax revenues. Property tax systems encourage the movement of tax rateables from city to suburb as businesses and individuals seek more favorable tax opportunities. If a business now located in the city can build a new complex in the suburbs where the tax rate is lower instead of in the central city, the city loses and the suburb gains. The suburbs are not likely to discourage that move.

Only the political environment of the state legislature or, at an extreme, the judicial environment of the state or United States Supreme Court can bring about a change in this taxing system with its drastic effect on schools. Such a large environmental change might occur once or twice a century. The school district is clearly circumscribed in its latitude for independent actions. It is affected by factors over which it has little or no control. Neither the central city nor suburban school boards in themselves can control the larger political question of the appropriate and fair tax system.

RELATIONSHIP TO DEMOCRACY

The discussion of the local school district shows the general applicability of the system schema. The first assumption is that the basic system framework can readily apply to the school district to indicate the local examples of input, core, etc. At first mention the framework and district seem to fit together nicely. Further examinations, however, show complexities which complicate the original clear picture. Input, core, output, environment, and feedback become more difficult to specify. Who should decide on appropriate school books, the number and kind of required courses in the program, or the range of high school elective courses? Should the decisions be made by parents or teachers or principals or school boards or the state legislature? Should legislatures, local districts, or professional experts decide on statewide testing programs? Should local elementary schools be consolidated so that the district can continue to afford interscholastic sports and a low student/teacher ratio?

These are but a few of the recurring questions in local education. But one need not go to any depth to discover difficulty. Even on a superficial level few citizens know name and number of officials, their term of office, the pay of the school board members, or simple budget figures. The intriguing thing about the school district is that it is the level of government with which citizens have the closest direct contact for the longest continual period of time. The only place they could have longer direct contact with a governmental unit is if they spent a fairly lengthy term in jail. Yet the school district is the level of government about which the citizen appears to know the least.

The local school district spends more tax dollars on an average, on a ratio of two to one, than the local government. The local unit of government responsible for ordinances, police, trash, fire, traffic lights, and stop signs, etc. is known better but does less. The citizens know less about the school district officials than about the town officials—which is not much even in the latter case. Most citizens do not know how many school board members there are, what their term of office is, what they get paid (usually nothing), how the superintendent is selected, and what he or she is paid (usually a great deal), or even whether they have a right to know these things.

The myth of popular control comes back with a vengeance when democracy and the system schema are combined in application to the local school district. With the considerations of local offices and responsibilities it becomes evident that although democracy may still be a sustaining myth it is manifestly a myth. Indeed, it may be speculated that as the complexities of the local level are revealed the myth may be more appropriately applied at the local level than at higher and more remote levels of government. It is a commonly held view in politics that citizens know most about the level of government to which they are closest. That assumption is not

challenged here. What is challenged is the degree of citizen knowledge of local government and correspondingly the even greater lack of knowledge of higher levels.
The degree is sufficiently low at the local level to support the contention of elite
guidance, whether in the person of superintendent or, as Zeigler and Jennings point
out, the self-perpetuating members of the school board.

The principal reason for the suggestion that popular control is a myth on the
local level as well as at other levels of government is that the complexity of government is beyond the grasp of the ordinary citizen. The political system schema, instead of simplifying understanding, codifies the complexity of political life. It is not
new to say that government is complex. Edmund Burke wrote on that theme, "Why
Government Is Complex?" in his *Reflections on the Revolution in France,* and most
other political writers reflect his views, although they may not admit it. As seen in
the last chapter, some want to believe that government can be grasped and
controlled by ordinary citizens. Those holding this view emphasize the simplicity of
governmental issues. The discussion of the system model suggests complexity. It is
not clear if this was the intention of the originators of the model. In any case complexity is confirmed.

Albert Einstein, in explaining why his writings on politics were not as clear
and easy to understand as his writings on physics and relativity, said, "Politics is
infinitely more complex than physics." Einstein grasped what some political scientists and many advocates of popular control have not. The problem of elite guidance
versus popular control can only be resolved not by dissolving complexity but by
recognizing it. This recognition of complexity is especially needed when the system
schema is combined with the democracy issue in the developing setting. In the development setting it first appears that the model is especially helpful in identifying
performers of functions and roles. To identify the decision-making agents and the
leadership selection process in various settings may be rewarding in the beginning.
When the subtleties of the process are discovered the simplicity assumption
evaporates.

It should be evident that as Western social and political scientists dispute the
nuances and intricacies of government of a particular country, the citizens of that
country could hardly be expected to understand their government in similarly complicated or scientific terms. It is important to remember from the first chapter that
because government is complex and because the system schema helps reveal that
complexity, it does not follow that elite guidance is the only alternative to the impossibility of popular control. A third alternative of popular selection was explained
earlier and that alternative is particularly applicable, analytically at least, to the developing setting. The popular selection view is handicapped practically by the lack
of appeal of moderate proposals in the developing context. That handicap is
nonetheless the ultimate advantage of popular selection over popular control and
elite guidance. Later considerations of the nature and end of the state will bring out
enough dimensions of political life that a better grasp of the profound nature of the
three alternatives can be gained. Strong and moderate positions are frequent in political disagreements. Discussion of democracy and the political system are only a

beginning introduction to such disagreements and their contribution to the richness of political reality.

CONCLUSION AND PERSPECTIVE

Long ago Cicero spoke of the state as a *res populi*, a *res publica*, a thing of the people, a public affair. This view did not necessarily imply democracy but it did stress the intimate relationship between the people and the state. A balance in that relationship has been the eternal puzzle of government. The relationship is no less puzzling under the guise of the political system schema with its appearance of "a place for everything and everything in its place." That appearance may be sustained after an introductory description but only by way of a great increase in "things" and "places." Some imagine the systems model to be a means of bringing state and people into closer proximity by increasing awareness of the vast network of interrelated forces and interests. If that awareness is achieved it can only be to the point of realizing more fully the earlier insight of Cicero.

Criticism

The political system diagram has been called throughout this discussion a schema, a framework, a model. The more common usage is model but all the words can be used interchangeably. Model suggests a more formal and scientific character, which is why some prefer it. However, that formal and scientific appearance may be misleading. It gives the impression of an order where it may not exist, by giving the impression of a causal relationship where there is merely a co-existence or at best a correlation. In other words, model suggests a formality and significance which reality may not warrant. Consequently, although the political system as an adaptation of the general system model may accomplish the task of bringing an orderly description to the understanding of the political world, it by no means is the agreed upon, one and only, accurate and verified approach to the understanding of that world.

There are in political science many competing models of how best to organize and describe the political world. The political system is only one of many models. Others are the group model, the game model, the rational model, the power model, the psychological model, the institutional model, and the communications model. There are more. Some of these models are accepted by some political scientists, some are not. All models, according to Dye, must meet certain criteria. The criteria should try to:

1. simplify and clarify our thinking about politics and public policy;
2. identify important aspects of policy problems;
3. help us to communicate with each other by focusing on essential features of political life;

4. direct our efforts to better understand public policy by suggesting what is important and what is unimportant; and

5. suggest explanations for public policy and predict its consequences.[2]

Dye's comments are particularly intended to apply to the use of models in public policy studies, a special subfield in political science. The criteria can be easily applied, however, to models in general. It is fascinating that the criteria used for models in political science are, with a few modifications, similar to the classical tests put forth for good literature. Those tests are that the work should be congruent with reality, that the work direct our attention to important aspects of life, that it suggest insights, communicate its points well, and have a message of some worth. With literature it is known from the beginning that each author has his or her own perspective with which the final literature product is shaped. With models there is the aura of scientific authority. It is this scientific authority and the precision implied which is the point of debate among political scientists. Some political scientists do not use and do not accept models in attempting to understand the political world. This attitude may appear Neanderthal but a judgment either way should be reserved at least until the topic is more fully discussed in the next chapter.

As in the previous chapter some final words should be said about what was not covered in this chapter. The political system framework was discussed in broad outline, some aspects of the outline were developed, and then the system was applied to a local level of government. Many social scientists in general and many political scientists in particular have written about the political system. Many use slightly different and some use considerably different terminology. The basic aspects of the system described in this chapter show through all the different accounts.

Political Socialization

Some authors go beyond the outline of the system and its workings to a consideration of the internal workings of the political culture and how it affects the system. Political culture may be viewed as part of the environment, the attitude environment, which affects the operation of the entire system. An integral part of political culture is political socialization, which is the process whereby political attitudes are acquired. In one respect it is a subphenomenon of the political system. In another respect the political system is viewed as a subphenomenon of socialization. A way of understanding the difference between political culture and political socialization is to understand culture as something given, a noun, and socialization as something done, a verb. Culture is relatively fixed but it has to be acquired by children and by individuals who change their physical residence. Culture can be understood simply as the way people go about doing things, habits. Socialization is the way habits are learned.

Many political scientists pay a great deal of attention to political socialization. It is, indeed, another competing model. It is for some the principal way of studying the political world—describing the process whereby attitudes, orientations, and practices are acquired and transmitted. Other models were mentioned above. Some of these will be discussed in later chapters. Political socialization will be discussed again in the context of constitutionalism and of political change. At this point it may be helpful to list briefly a series of topics considered in connection with political socialization. This may give an idea of the variety and breadth of the interest.

Specifically, political socialization is distinguished from nonpolitical socialization in order to differentiate between direct learning about politics and indirect learning. Formal socialization is the deliberate effort to instruct in certain attitudes or values by parents, school, or society. Informal socialization is incidental, coming about as the result of other events. There is cognitive socialization, which is what hopefully takes place in government courses. Affective socialization, like affective learning in general, is the development of feelings about personal and group characteristics. In addition to these general topics there is specific attention given to the political socialization of children, political socialization of adults, and role socialization. Furthermore, it is important to discuss the specific agents of socialization like the family, schools, peer groups, mass media, and traumatic events. All these agents shape attitudes and practices. One important realization, however, is that the agents and events which influence attitudes and practices do not have identical effects on everyone. So another important topic is the nonuniformity of socialization.

The topic of political socialization seems large and important. It has not been discussed fully here. As mentioned earlier it will be considered in a number of places later in this text. It is important to understand its place as a means by which we appreciate the process of acquiring political attitudes and habits. At times that process may seem very definite. At other times it is less clear. We may appreciate that our inclinations to be Republican or Democrat, liberal or conservative, active or apathetic, were acquired around the dinner table of our parents. That appreciation works until we think about our sister or brother being almost completely opposite in political orientation with no apparent difference in their socialization. That reflection should convince us of the inexactness of socialization.

"We simply do not know the mechanism by which child socialization affects development of later policy orientations,"[3] is one way of summing up the results of socialization studies. Much information about the percentage of inclinations in one direction or the other may establish probable predictions of behavior or attitudes. Percentages, however, do not establish certitude and so socialization ends up in the same situation as the political system where the scientific appearance does not ensure scientific application. Given that result, information about socialization may be extremely fascinating and generally enlightening but not particularly practical. A further consideration is that, though we have additional knowledge, it is not clear whether or how that knowledge should be used. That latter concern is true of all knowledge whether it is called scientific or general.

How Knowledge Is Used

The question of whether and how knowledge is to be used is a moral consideration. It is a good point on which to end the discussion of the political system because it reminds us of one of the central concerns of politics and of disagreements within political science. It brings to the surface an often neglected dimension of political learning. Political scientists and others in the social sciences and the humanities are widely agreed that scientists whose studies make the building of bombs possible should be concerned with whether and how their scientific knowledge is put to effect. That conclusion about scientists may or may not be correct but the point does seem to apply at least to the social scientists and others who make that case. It therefore seems appropriate to now examine political science as a discipline and to see what views and procedures exist within it.

NOTES

1. A good discussion of this is found in L. Harmon Zeigler, M. Kent Jennings, with G. Wayne Park, *Governing American Schools* (North Scituate, Mass.: Duxbury Press, 1974).

2. Thomas R. Dye, *Understanding Public Policy,* 4th ed. (Englewood Cliffs, N.J.: Prentice-Hall, 1982), p. 19.

3. Herbert R. Winter and Thomas J. Bellows, *People and Politics* (New York: John Wiley, 1981), p. 112.

CHAPTER THREE
POLITICAL SCIENCE: SCOPE AND METHODS

Political science is what political scientists do. Scope and methods in political science are considerations of how they go about it. Some of what political scientists do has already been experienced in the first two chapters. They talk about democracy and they delineate the political system. Political scientists also debate how they should approach the discussions of democracy and they debate the employment of the system model. In this chapter we will describe various ways in which political scientists in the past and today organize their descriptions of the political world. There is no unanimity. There may be a dominant method, yet even that is no guarantee to success or to truth.

Some political scientists really enjoy this scope and methods topic. Some, like many students, could easily do without it and prefer talking about "real" things like Congress or court cases or voting. Those who enjoy the topic regard it as a real thing. They see their colleagues involved in its full implications whether those colleagues are aware of it or not. The insights from a full appreciation of scope and methods add an otherwise unavailable dimension of understanding to the so-called real world. This chapter is written from that point of view.

The chapter will be divided into four parts. There will be a brief discussion of broad approaches, a discussion of the relation of political science and the other social sciences, a larger discussion of methodology, and lastly a conclusion and perspective.

APPROACHES

One broad way to begin looking at political science, before looking at particular methods with their history and rationale, is to consider what might be called "approaches." By approach is meant a broad way of looking at or investigating the political world. One way of visualizing this is to look back to the political system diagram in the previous chapter and ask: What does it portray? What goes on there? What permeates it? What does it tell us?

Policy Approach

From one perspective the political system is no more than an ongoing five part process of input through feedback and then new input. From this perspective the system, and the world it portrays, is merely a closed loop system, an elaborate process which can be known in large relief or in minute detail. The object of political science then is to know and describe the observed process. From this start the next step is to point out possible insights. This approach is called a "policy approach." From this approach political science is viewed principally as a "policy science." In this perspective political science looks at the refinement of the input, conversion, output, feedback process and points out where it might be improved with a view in particular of improving the output.

In this respect policy study is akin to management studies with their interest in improving the way a system runs. In this connection then political science would point out the important public problems, the important output or policy issues (e.g., crime, welfare, taxes, defense), show how other social sciences can be coordinated in bringing about solutions to these problems, and provide the principles and know-how for making decisions about these solutions. The focus in this approach is on the process, its continued functioning, and the avoidance of dysfunction. This approach has some traces of what used to be called public administration. Its intention and perspective is broader than just administration, though it does look on the political world as a process which can be managed.

Power Approach

Another way of looking at the political world and the political system that attempts to portray it is to say that the system and the process are a facade. This point of view says that what dominates the political world is power and struggle. Power and struggle are of the essence in politics. Any attempt to portray the world other than in power terms is an exercise of missing the forests for the twigs. Peel back the veneer of the political system and one will see the "real" politics. That real politics is a world of power brokers, bosses, power elite, Fortune 500, Forbes 400, and the powerful few. Thus this approach is far different from the first. It sees politics not as an orderly process subject to systemic models. Politics is a hidden world of arbitrary will, competitive struggle, fiat, and actions which must be read between the lines or below the surface.

The power perspective suggests that some individual or group dominates the system in such a fashion that the operation of the system is explained more in terms of their nonobservable activities than in terms of the observable process. Politics, according to this approach, is a study of power, how it is acquired, used, and maintained. Professor Hans Morgenthau, whose *Politics Among Nations* was a major text for more than two decades in international relations courses, wrote from a power perspective. This point of view, however, is not new in political studies.

A disputant in Plato's *Republic* argued that justice, or politics, is merely the interest or preference of the strongest element of the community. Machiavelli and Hobbes saw politics as primarily a matter of power possessed by the strongest and most skillful person. Marx saw power in the economic system, which determined all other behavior. Many today, focusing on international competition or domestic events, see conspiracies of social and economic elites maneuvering to maintain and increase their power. Some see revolutionaries as alternate elites in the power struggle.

The point of the power model is not the intricate and elaborate functioning of the process of the political system. Politics in this view is not so much a function of reason as it is of will. Certain unidentifiable parts dominate and direct the many other parts. Approaching politics from this power perspective is said to be the most practical and realistic way to understand and explain winning and losing in the political world.

Like the policy-process approach, the power approach both leads and follows reality. In other words, both approaches find support in reality and they in turn shape a view of reality. Power can be found in the real political world— *A* influences *B* to do *C*— and then that finding can be used to explain. In the policy approach *A* (input) precedes *B* (conversion) which precedes *C* (output) which leads to a systemic explanation. It is left unexamined in both cases whether *C* as an impersonal goal had more of an influence on *B* than the person or impersonal *A*. For both approaches the possible independent quality of *C* as a "goal" is unexamined. Both approaches are well established in the discipline of political science and both have many adherents. Neither approach concedes much to the other or to the suggestion that both might be deficient.

Moral or Goals Approach

What should be made clear here is that we are talking about broad approaches, starting perspectives, and not methodology. Methodology, which will be described later, is the particular way one operates within an approach or perspective. Each of the methods described later can be used by any of the approaches. What approach and methodology have in common is that both can ultimately be put to the test of how they adequately explain reality. That test is at the center of disputes within academic disciplines. It will not preoccupy our attention but it is a reminder that however esoteric the disputes may sound they must ultimately "answer to" reality.

The third broad approach is distinct from the other two. This approach does not pay attention to the ongoing process of the political system or political world. It does not point to the power aspects of politics. The third approach is concerned with the direction and goals of politics. Simple power or process is not its concern. Its concern is the purpose of power and the goal of the process. This approach is called a moral approach. It can also be called a goals approach as long as the moral quality of goals is fully recognized.

Moral is used not in the sense of an assumption about rightness. It is used in the sense of saying that consideration ought to be given to what is right, correct, appropriate. These qualities are to be determined not in terms of "what most do," "what most favor," or "what the most powerful prefer." They are to be considered in terms of the nature, the character, the appropriateness of politics and its parts. Something more is involved than merely an attempt to determine how the policy approach decides what is important or what variety of purposes are related to power. What is involved in the third approach is a concern for the purpose of politics, government, and the state. This is a concern for the range and limits of politics.

A moral approach must know the facts. It must understand the process. It must be aware of power. It must also consider, however, whether there are any external limits to the political domain and whether there are any internal objective factors which can affect its shape. Answers to these concerns are not as readily available as in the other two approaches. There is wide disagreement about a moral approach. Even within the approach one finds disagreement. Because of the disagreements many tend to disregard the approach. Many find it easier to attend to processes and power. The tendency, although understandable, may be myopic. It may attend to what is near at the expense of what is important.

Like the power and the policy approaches, which have traces of ancient thought in them, the third approach is an ancient way to comprehend the political world. Aristotle, if not Plato before him, was principally concerned with the end of the state. Plato's concern was the good and just state, though he did tend toward overly rational processslike answers. Aristotle saw politics as the architectonic or master science. That does not mean that he had a philosopher-king approach like Plato. For him politics meant concern with not only the internal workings of the state but also its purpose, its justification, its relationship to all other sciences and to the ends of life. In Aristotle's view politics is concerned with a great deal more than the other two approaches, separately or combined. This larger concern does not necessarily make it better. It does explain its moral or teleological dimension. That greater dimension means a study of design or purpose, especially of the purpose of nature or of life.

Support for the third approach is small if one considers the percentage of political scientists using it, but numbers do not determine the worth of points of view. There will be many points discussed in the ensuing chapters which have a small number of adherents but which can have a massive effect on the political world and life. These many points are taken up, as are these various approaches, because they have a serious basis and because upon reflection they have proven over time to be significant. They will not go away and it is best that they be understood.

Many of the discussions in later chapters will have three parts, and occasionally there will be a fourth, which may parallel the three approaches just discussed. No extended attempt is going to be made to draw out that parallel. On a casual basis those relationships may be more than fascinating. The final answer as to what view is best may come, as we will see about competing political methodologies, in terms of what is best for one's own particular purpose. Such an answer may appear unprincipled. It may also appear unsatisfactory to individuals who want ready-made answers. As the discussion unfolds it is hoped that a fuller appreciation of the variety in political science and in political life will make that undogmatic answer more acceptable and complete. It is based on the assumption that there may indeed be a one right answer to any question but its formulation is not agreed upon. There is room for much debate and dialogue. Debate and dialogue are the heart of politics and political science.

POLITICAL SCIENCE
AND THE OTHER SOCIAL SCIENCES

In discussing the scope and methods in political science, we have discussed so far the three broad approaches to viewing the political world and to appreciating the political system. Another way to come to an understanding of political science is to compare it to the other social sciences, to see its focus and theirs. By this comparison an appreciation of political science and the other sciences as distinct disciplines can be gained.

The other social sciences to be considered are sociology, psychology, economics, and history. There are many other social sciences and divisions and combinations of each which could be mentioned but which will not. It is sufficient to consider the focus of these few as compared and contrasted with political science. It should be pointed out that only a brief description will be given of each of the disciplines. Much more could be said and for that the reader is encouraged to go to appropriate sources like the *International Encyclopedia of the Social Sciences,* a reference source available in most libraries. Some of what will be said in describing the other social sciences may initially sound facetious. Upon full consideration the points will become clear and any offense will be mitigated.

One way of visualizing the relationship of political science with the other social sciences is depicted in the accompanying diagram (Figure 3-1). This diagram depicts each of the social sciences as having a specialized and limited focus on society. Each has open communications with political science. Political science is depicted as having both a direct and specialized focus on society and as having the benefit of the knowledge gained from the other social sciences. In this design no attempt is made to imply the order or importance of the other disciplines. Furthermore, the diagram fits political science no matter which of the three previously discussed approaches is preferred.

Political science is portrayed in an architectonic or master science relationship to the other fields. This relationship reflects both the nature of the discipline and the

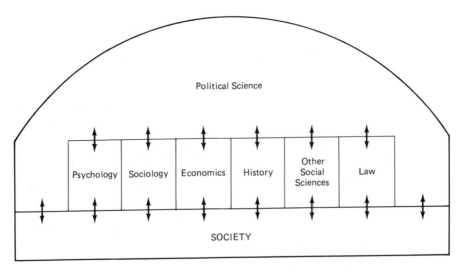

FIGURE 3-1   The relationship of political science to the other social sciences.

nature of politics itself. Politics is authoritative in the sense that it is concerned with all aspects of life. It can command that actions be taken or courses be studied that affect life itself. Defense and military sciences are examples. The well-being of the community and the promotion of science are more general examples.

Political science is architectonic in the sense that it is concerned with the things of politics. The master character also applies to its concern with the extent to which the other sciences are helpful to politics. In this respect, however, political science is not authoritative. It does not interfere in the other disciplines or tell them what their conclusions should be. It is authoritative only in pointing out the extent to which they might be used in matters of state. Political science or politics does not interfere in the "truths" of psychology, economics, or other social sciences. If the other disciplines affect political decisions, political science wants to know that. This is one reason why it is important to describe the focus of the other social sciences.

Psychology

Psychology's concern is with human behavior. Some might say from casual observation that psychology ought not be classified with the social sciences since some in the discipline are known to give a great deal more attention to rats and pigeons than to humans. Electrodes attached to the head of a rat and pigeons poking a dot in a cage are common fare in the discipline. The psychologist would explain that from these other organisms one can learn about behavior in general and then attempt to make applications to human behavior. It is better to do this than to attach electrodes to humans or put them in cages. Those who object to the human applications from animal experiments should be reminded of the simple analogy, "They acted *like* animals." In psychology that common analogy is undertaken with greater scientific exactness and logical care than in casual conversations.

Political science is also interested in human behavior. It is interested in human social behavior. Psychology is interested in the more general ways in which all behavior is influenced. Political science has a much more specific concern, which may not come under psychology's general propositions. The psychologists may give the political scientist much useful information on how people acquire attitudes, what shapes opinions, what might influence a voter or a decision maker, or how crowds may behave. The psychologist stops at this point and the political scientist only begins there.

Psychologists describe general patterns of human behavior, authoritarian personalities, and obsessive-compulsive characteristics. It is up to the political scientist to show whether and how this information is applicable to the specifics of the political world. Political science must be skeptical of the pronouncements of psychologists because psychology, like all the social sciences, is rife with internal competing approaches and methods. This means that the solidly held views of one expert may be easily disputed by another expert. Psychology has its psychodynamic or Freudian approach, its behavioral or Skinnerian approach, and its humanistic-existential approach. Specific methodological rivalries abound.

One should not be dismayed at this division since, as was said, it is common to *all* the social sciences. It should also be remembered that each social science and division within it is substantially better and more systematic than street corner insights of common discourse. The point then is that psychology is a legitimate social science. Its efforts are related to political science but political science has a definite focus which is different from that of psychology.

Economics

Some know economics as "the dismal science." Some maintain that it does not exist, or that if it does exist it ought to be abolished. The "dismal science" title was attached to economics in the nineteenth century when the predictions of Malthus foretold a gloomy future. Whether economics still deserves this title is for its friends and foes to debate. The confidence with which many proclaim the saving power of economics is sharply undercut by a quote attributed to Dr. Kenneth E. Boulding, a former president of the American Economic Association. Boulding once wrote, "I have been gradually coming under the conviction, disturbing for a professional theorist, that there is no such thing as economics."[1]

Many would be aghast at such an utterance. The situation is not helped much when it is heard that Nobel Laureate in Economics, Professor Gunnar Myrdal, has called for the abolition of the Nobel Prize in economics because it is a "soft" science.[2] Soft means an inexact science as opposed to the "hard" sciences of physics and chemistry. Myrdal's proposal was occasioned by, but not aimed directly at, the awarding of the prize to Professor Milton Friedman, who held widely divergent views from Myrdal. The retaining of the prize is defended by others since peace, for which a significant Nobel Prize is also given, is likewise not a hard science.

The dispute over the Nobel Prize merely shows some of the heat that can be generated over an insubstantial matter. No one really questions whether economics really exists. Boulding is not saying that the discipline in which he and others have spent so much time is all smoke and no fire. What Boulding is doing is acknowledging that there is no one economics. He is saying that there is no one way to approach economics. This point seems confirmed by the general disagreements over the strategies of the Federal Reserve Board. The Board's activities are more genuinely economic than any other governmental agency and still the disputes rage among economists. Fluctuations of the money supply, for example, occur because there is not even an agreed upon definition of the simple term "money." That disagreement is of a technical nature but it does reflect the fundamentals which keep economics from being one unified discipline.

It was previously mentioned that this characteristic of disagreement on approaches and methods is shared by all the social sciences. That diversity may be a product of many factors. It stands in contrast to the image of the physical sciences, the so-called "hard" sciences, which are regarded as operating from a unified base. The contrast bothers many in the social sciences. It motivates some to seek greater unity in their respective disciplines or in the social sciences generally.

For others the diversity in the social sciences is more a strength than a defect. For them it is a manifestation of the internal natural liberty of human endeavors. The challenge of natural liberty is not to homogenize human activities but to accept and work with diversity. Acceptance can bring either cooperative accomplishments or respected divergence. The imagined abasement of the soft/hard contrast evaporates in the good-humored observation that the hard sciences always have answers in the back of the textbook and use different colored chalk in the classroom. For their part the soft sciences lack ready-made answers and they generally use only white chalk. The comparison proves nothing. It does raise questions about what kind of fundamental differences should be looked for, however.

Some of the social sciences, particularly psychology and even more so economics, take on the appearance and character of the physical sciences with experimentation, formulas, equations, and statistical and mathematical analyses. In this regard it is said that economics, "though it is not reckoned among what are sometimes called the exact sciences, is undoubtedly in some ways more rigorous and precise than what goes by the name of political science."[3] Experience attests to Plamenatz's point. Still, rigor and precision will neither establish economics nor subordinate politics.

Insistence on pure economic handling of societal problems is attractive to many thoughtful individuals. It remains attractive until one considers personal options like a new pair of shoes for one's self versus piano lessons for one's child. A pair of shoes can be the equivalent of ten to twenty piano lessons. Despite the attractiveness of the economist's imagined "economic man," that explanation of the choice only works as a generalization. The vision of humans making decisions based purely on costs is contrasted with too many piano lessons. The choice is not made with the expectation that the child will earn a large amount in the future as a musician. Choices are made on noneconomic principles all the time. Government makes many of them, as its support for the arts attest.

Because of the diversity of both economic and political views no government can operate on pure economic principles. No reasonable person or party is so certain that a particular plan will be successful that they will stake everything on a single approach. The effect of a single approach would be so massive that society could not handle it. Governments and presidents often announce a single new economic plan. Proponents and opponents talk about the plan for years. The actual operations of successful governments and administrations, however, are always mixed plans. Single plans are great in textbooks but vulnerable to all sorts of predators in practice.

Some—notably Marx, but he is not alone—have appeared to argue that politics and economics are identical. This is a theoretical as well as a practical proposition. Whatever the theoretical side, for practical academic purposes they are separated. The theoretical issue will have to be debated elsewhere. For our purposes the separate academic discipline is viewed as considering among other things the production, distribution, and consumption of goods and services. Divisions among economists occur over the weight and value of all the factors which produce wealth. Those factors and the conclusions about them are of interest to politics and political scientists as well.

Although economists stick to their charts and figures, politicians, and hence political scientists, must pay attention to those who press for action instead of analysis. The student of political science would be well advised to study economics, along with many other diverse subjects. The need for a knowledge of diverse subjects explains why political science programs are usually found in a liberal arts curriculum.

History

The focus of history is the past. Such an attribution may offend some historians who like to point to the contemporary importance of their works. It is clear, though, that the first effort of the historian is to accurately describe and portray some past event or events. History may or may not have secondary, contemporary purposes. The tools and training of the historian, however, are designed to make them skillful at accurately discerning the past. Whimsically it may be said that the historian is an antiquarian, a collector of antique events.

The historian collects and authenticates antique events and puts them in a certain order on shelves or, in their instance, in books. This description of the historian's work is not meant to be invidious. Events and antiques need to be authenticated if they are to assume proper importance. From time to time they have to be rearranged and displayed differently to appreciate the material in a new or better light. Through such rearrangements historical events stand out more clearly. In this way collectors and historians are seen to be similar. A thoughtful reader might respond that not much credit or significance is given to the historian's work in this description. That observation, however, overlooks the value inherent in knowing the past. It ironically only imputes value to some external utility of that knowledge.

David Herbert Donald, an historian, got to the true value of historical study in a little article surprisingly entitled, "Our Irrelevant Past." Donald is Charles Warren Professor of American History at Harvard and is the author of a Pulitzer Prize winning biography of the abolitionist Charles Sumner. Professor Donald wrote that since the past was an age of abundance and the present one of paucity, the lessons learned were "not merely irrelevant but dangerous."[4] The role that he saw for a historian in our "new and unprecedented age" was to "disenthrall" undergraduates from the spell of history, "to help them see the irrelevance of the past, to assist them in understanding what Lincoln meant in saying, 'The dogmas of the quiet past are inadequate to the stormy present.'" An even more important role, he suggested, was "to make it easier for some to face a troubled future by reminding them to what a limited extent humans control their own destiny."

Professor Donald takes a profound lesson from history. His lesson is not deterministic, cynical, or presumptuous. One finds these qualities in many so-called relevant historians. Donald's lesson is the limited extent to which humans control events. He does not deny some control but he does not exaggerate it either. He seems to be saying that a proper appreciation of the past should make us humble but not fatalistic. In that balance there is extraordinary room for both courage and determination in our, or any, unprecedented age.

Clearly the role of the historian is of a proper appreciation of the past. Lessons can indeed be learned for the future. The lessons are not exaggerated ones, however. The role of the historian can relate to current politics and correspondingly to political science. Nonetheless, the primary efforts of the political scientist and the historian remain different by reason of their particular focus.

Sociology

Taking off from the previous discussion, it can be said that sociology is the history of the present. The focus of the sociologist is on *present* artifacts. Some sociologists may not like this depiction any more than some historians do theirs. Once again, the purpose is not to demean. The intention is to bring out the primary focus of the discipline. Sociology's forte is in attempting to accurately describe the many different aspects and dimensions of society. To collect vast amounts of data and to describe it in a meaningful way is an enormous task. Only with such information accurately gathered and presented can society begin to know itself.

Knowledge gained through sociology helps in the attempt at understanding society. It is false, however, to claim that sociology leads to politics, just as it is false to claim that history leads to politics. That "history repeats itself," or that "those who are ignorant of the past are condemned to repeat it" cannot be proven scientifically or logically. A similar claim that some particular future is contained in a sociologically demonstrated present is also unjustified. In an abstract or metaphysical sense those statements may contain elements of truth. That truth, however, cannot be tapped in any practical way.

Sociologically or historically determined outcomes are unverified and unverifiable. Claims about the meaning of past events or predictions about the future are poetic generalizations at best. They assume a determinism which careful historians, like Professor Donald, and sociologists[5] cannot accept. Sociology attempts and succeeds in giving society a better knowledge of itself. It, like history, does not pretend to know all that must be known to verify any determinism. Political science will make use of sociological information. It will not be led solely or exclusively by that information. Political science will have a focus different from sociology or history or the other social sciences.

Political Science

Political science's focus is on the future. Now the reader can see the design of the earlier discussion relating history to the past and sociology to the present. The descriptions were accurate and not contrived even though they do contribute to the unusual focus stated for political science. The focus of political science needs justification much more than do the other disciplines.

To speak of a focus on the future is not to say that political scientists gaze into crystal balls or predict future events by tarot cards. The discipline of political science is concerned with the same thing with which the political world is concerned. In the political world any action, any decision, any policy, can affect nothing except the future. The past or the present cannot be changed. They are already settled. This is, of course, a truism. It is one which, however, instead of being banal, clarifies.

All governmental acts, even the slightest local ordinance altering the flow of traffic at an intersection, have future implications. Acknowledging this simple truth is what gives pause to the policy maker or traffic coordinator to consider the consequences of their actions. By insisting on attention to the future, decision makers are drawn away from dependence upon the historical record or contemporary demands alone. The actions of Congress, the President, a governor, a king, or a dictator are similar in their futurological implications.

The futurity of political actions is unavoidable. No political figure, however powerful, will ever change the past or the present. Someone, perhaps close to a President, may change eighteen minutes of a tape-recorded conversation. That erasure does not change the past. It changes only the record of the past. Such an erasure, however, drastically affected the future of a former President.

Too much should not be made of this one word, "future." Not many political scientists or political science textbooks currently describe political science in this manner. But the description in terms of the future is not entirely new. Definitions in political science today are usually in terms of government or power or in terms of derivations of "political" from the Greek word *polis*, meaning city-state, and the Latin word *scire*, to know. These usual definitions, however, add little to our knowledge. We might as well be told that orchestras are about music. The future adds a new dimension of concern and involvement to our understanding of political science and politics. Aristotle seems to have perceived this element. In his *Ethics*, which is normally understood to be the first book of his *Politics*, he observed that,

"No one deliberates about the past but about what is future and capable of being otherwise."[6] Dante observed many centuries later that legislative acts deal with "general issues of the future."[7] Professor Samuelson, the Nobel laureate and textbook author, has a grasp of this too. He observes that "economic activity is future-oriented."[8] While he appears to be talking about economics he is really speaking of the consequential character of its concern. It is here that it forms a common bridge with political science.

Investors in stocks and all business activities have a future-oriented concern. Theirs, however, is not so much a responsibility for the future in general as a matter of making limited domain predictions which will shape the future. Politics, and hence political science, is responsible, like it or not, for decisions which set the framework in which those individual investments and choices are made. Decisions about economic policy, nuclear power plants, MX weapons systems, or the local traffic light all have a delayed, general orienting effect. That is the essential nature of a political decision; it affects the community on a long-term basis.

That long-term effect makes politics different from all other activities. Political science follows politics in this way. Later it will be seen that this point about the character of politics is the subject of disagreements. Discussion of the nature and purpose of the state brings out that disagreement. One's view of political science is influenced by one's view of the political world and vice versa. There is an extraordinarily rich relatedness to the political world. What we are doing in an introductory political science text is sorting out some of the elements and putting them back together gradually. What we should end with is a clear awareness of the rich but varied views of the political world.

METHODOLOGY

Methodology or method is the way one goes about one's work. No matter the definition or approach, some particular method is followed. It may be random or it may be systematic, regular, and replicative. Several methods in political science will be described. Each has been used by the various approaches. Each has strong proponents and opponents. The point of contention in the disputes is how scientific the method makes the discipline. The answer to that question is not readily available because it is ultimately tested by how accurately the political world is understood. Rivalries about approach and procedures, common to all social sciences, are related to the "Einsteinian" complexity of the political world.

There is the inherent problem in applying the so-called scientific method, as modeled from the physical sciences, to the social world. No one pretends that the laboratory experimental studies of the physical sciences can be copied in political science or sociology or economics. It is maintained nonetheless that the general procedures or outline of scientific method can be employed in the social sciences. That claim has to be examined further.

According to Professor Isaak, the building blocks of science are

- *observations* and attempts to classify and analyze them
- the formulation of empirical *concepts* that organize the observed phenomena
- the discovery of laws or *generalizations* that state relationships between the concepts
- the construction of *theories* that are collections of logically related generalizations
- *explanations* and *predictions* based upon the theories and generalizations.[9]

Political science makes some claim to working within the framework of these building blocks. An honest examination of the discipline in terms of these criteria, however, would reveal serious shortcomings from the concept level on down. Isaak admits that "political scientists can be empirical and scientific only on a very general level."[10] He allows that "political science is relatively immature" as a science[11], and he explains that universal generalizations are "the most powerful kind in the scientist's arsenal" but political science has "few, if any" of these.[12]

Isaak, like many in the social sciences, gets carried into the specious logic—it might be called wishful thinking—that because objective science is important it is possible and must be pursued. This imperative quickly forgets the weakness in political science's use of concepts, generalization, and theories. For example, if in using the power model or approach an intuitive grasp of power is all that can be effectively formulated[13], then the scientific prospects of the study are highly circumscribed. Isaak brings out fully the problem of concept formulation as it is associated with power. A careful reading of his remarks shows the systematic and even empirical limits of their use in political science in general. Isaak cites another political scientist, Arnold Brecht, who in his *Political Theory: The Foundations of Twentieth-Century Political Thought* speaks of the importance of "intersubjective transmissible knowledge." Put simply, that intriguing phrase means "an agreement on terms." It is desired because it does not now exist. That admission speaks directly to the missing concept level building block in political science.

Some would look on the admission that rigid scientific study is not possible in political science as unwise and as likely to drive prospective students from the discipline. The frank admission that political science is no more than it realistically can be ought, however, to be more of an inducement to intelligent students than making false promises would be. For a period of time the statistical, mathematical, and other quantitative efforts in the areas of voting studies, decision making, coalition building, and the like gave the impression of a rapidly advancing scientific discipline. More recent evaluations seem to mitigate this conclusion. Almond[14] recently expressed the character of political science as being "more cloud-like than clock-like." There is a precision and exactness to clocks and an imprecision and inexactness to clouds. To string out the analogy one may point to meteorology and its scientific knowledge of clouds but remind ourselves that we still tell time by watches rather than sundials.

In Isaak's terms, political science lacks "nomological" or "covering-law" explanations[15]; we lack theories which organize and explain existing knowledge.[16] All our particular efforts, all the detailed research, even as it is specifically informative, fall short of genuinely scientific explanations. Many political scientists, and Isaak is one, are determined to pursue rigid scientific goals and feel that it is achievable and near. Almond, however, after decades of scientific efforts himself, demurs. Professor Lindblom, both a political scientist and an economist and also a past president of the American Political Science Association, seems to concur with the demurral. Lindblom[17] advises less emphasis on the promise of social science. He wonders aloud, in the very title of his book, just how "usable" the social sciences are. The answer to that question is that they are not very usable. These more reflective views do not abandon the social sciences altogether, however. They do not advocate tearing down political science departments and replacing them with squash courts. Some systematic knowledge is better than none. The knowledge gained through political science efforts may not be perfect but to proceed on it is better than to proceed on whim or caprice.

The psychologist B. F. Skinner is known for a lifelong insistence on subjecting *all* human behavior to scientific study. This study has come to be known as "behavioralism." Skinner sought[18] "a technology of behavior," "a science of human behavior." In his novel, *Walden Two,* published in 1948, he has the principal character, who he acknowledges in a later edition[19] speaks for him, proclaim euphorically the "fact" of "an effective science of behavior." In a later reflection, however[20], Skinner acknowledges that behaviorism "is not the science of human behavior" but is "the philosophy of that science." Here is the commonly acclaimed father of the scientific study of human behavior admitting that it is not a science but a philosophy, an approach. Such an acknowledgement should enhance rather than lessen the academic standing of the social sciences. Proceeding from such an honest base makes the disciplines more creditable. Disagreements will still be present. The honest discussion of them, instead of one position claiming "scientific" preeminence, will ultimately benefit all sides.

Because of the variety of methodologies in political science it is important to describe each, to relate some of the history of the various approaches, and to attempt to show some order to the methods. Many different lists and possible categories are available. The particular methods presented here and the order of the presentation is used because of its historical-developmental and logical aspects. Its basic validity is tested by the reality it seeks to explain and by the insight it gives. The reader and colleagues in the profession can be the judge of its passing the test.

The list of methods which will be described is as follows: philosophical, historical, comparative, juridical, behavioral, and postbehavioral. The behavioral method is the most widely used within the discipline today. Some would maintain that it is the only method worth giving much attention to and that the others are only of historical interest. Due credit will be given to the behavioral method. However, to fully appreciate the behavioral method and the more recent criticisms of it, a wider spectrum of methods must be reviewed. Furthermore, some of the other methods, although not in wide usage, have their own intrinsic merit. The other methods should not be neglected simply because of the number of practitioners.

Philosophical Method

In the philosophical method the investigator asks "why" questions: why the state exists, why some men rule over others, why we cannot be left alone, the "nature" of the state, the "purpose" of government, the limits on rule, why states differ so much. The philosophical method is deductive in nature. Deductive means it proceeds from certain general propositions about man, for example, that he is a "social and political animal," and arrives at particular conclusions or applications. Plato in talking about the ideal republic used this method as did Aristotle in his disagreement with Plato's design.

The "American fathers," Jefferson and Madison for example, can likewise be said to have proceeded in this manner. They started with "self-evident" truths or deductive propositions and applied them to particular circumstances. Contrary to the impressions given by some, this approach is not *a priori* in the sense of operating without examination or analysis. It is not exclusively speculative since a grounding in the empirical setting is a prerequisite to any attempt at political explanation. Aristotle's *Politics* may properly be regarded as a philosophical work but it is a mistake to forget the sound empirical base he had in the study of 158 Greek constitutions before his reflective efforts.

The philosophical "why" is not something which was settled in ancient writings or in nineteenth-century revisions. Contemporary political scientists, even those of a decidedly empirical orientation like Almond, are known for their Aristotelian or philosophical generalizations. As will be seen a little later, the philosophical method still has an important, although historically smaller, place in political inquiry.

Historical Method

The historical method inquires into the conditions that gave rise to the particular institutions and practices about which the philosophical method speculates. The historical method is distinct from history as a discipline. As indicated earlier, historians are intent on accurately portraying the past. Some historians may attempt through extrapolation or through ideological predisposition to apply the past to the present or to the future. It should not be forgotten, however, that the historian's primary training is knowing the past.

Political scientists use the historical method by borrowing some of the historian's tools. They do not adopt the historian's primary focus. Political science, for example, may inquire into the origin of American political parties or the origin of the electoral college. The inquiry is interested not so much in the details of the historical period as in the structuring principles which were present and may continue to be present or which have changed over time. The political scientist is interested in the implications of structuring principles and their continued relevance to changed circumstances.

The political scientist may show that the electoral college's indirect system of selecting the President continues to apply. This is so not because of an unyielding past but because the electoral principles remain constant even when the conditions which gave rise to that particular device no longer obtain. At an earlier time most political scientists used the historical method. Some still do. It is as legitimate— more so from the view of the political scientist—a method as history is a discipline.

Comparative Method

The comparative method is in many ways a continuation of the historical method. As the latter inquires into the conditions that gave rise to the particular state or governmental practice, the comparative method inquires about whether others had similar experiences. No one culture is totally the product of one historical condition and so the comparative method begins to look into other conditions that may influence particular or divergent outcomes. The comparative method expands on the area of investigation. ''Comparative European Governments'' is a course in nearly every political science curriculum reflecting this approach. In addition one can usually find comparative or area study courses on Africa, the Middle East, Asia, or practically any part of the globe.

Each of the other methods can be used in a comparative way. There could be a comparative philosophical investigation, a comparative juridical investigation, etc. The comparative method is singled out for description at this point in the list because it has a logical and chronological closeness to the historical method and because it is best to make its characteristics clear before discussing the other methods.

The comparative approach at times assumes a very large role within political science. At one time almost all political scientists engaged in comparative analyses. The particular techniques are derived from the parent method (philosophical, historical, juridical, etc.) and from the ordinary rules of fairness and scientific exactness. Comparative voting studies, for example, would take studies of American voting behavior and compare it to French voting behavior with due care about isomorphic settings and similar statistical procedures. Comparative institutions would start from legal structures or historical settings.

Juridical Method

The juridical method emphasizes laws, institutions, structures, and roles founded upon law. This method is most likely the one which was in use in the student's first contact with the study of government. That contact was probably in a junior high school or high school course. There the Constitution, Congress, President, and courts were described. There were probably a few preliminaries about voting, elections, and political parties. This general orientation or method is juridical.

The emphasis on law, institutions, and the Constitution and the progression of topics probably followed the outline of the Constitution. Much detail can be developed in using this method. The jurisdiction of the courts, qualifications for voting, the committee system in Congress, civil rights, and how a bill becomes a law are all expressions of a juridical approach. In these studies the juridical base is dominant. Legal definitions are controlling. This emphasis is justified because law plays such a large role in modern society. The extent of that role will be seen in later chapters discussing rights, constitutions, and forms of government. This method is a model for many political scientists. In employing this approach the political scientist has the appearance of a lawyer. Lawyers, however, get into even more detail. It is the juridical orientations in political science that encourage many students to enter legal studies.

Behavioral Method

The behavioral method is interested in the actual behavior of political actors. It does not matter whether those actors are individuals, institutions, or groups. The behavioral method is not concerned with theories about the state's existence, historical conditions, or legal expectations. It is interested in what actually happens. The law may say that all citizens are eligible to vote but many do not. The Constitution may say that "Congress shall declare war" but the President may be the principal initiator of war in ninety-five out of one hundred cases. The courts may rule in favor of constitutionally guaranteed equal protection of the laws but actual behavior may deny it to many minorities.

The behavioral method inquires into the facts without juridical or other presuppositions. In this way the behavioral method presents itself as objective, empirical, scientific, and value-free. Statistical, mathematical, and other quantitative analyses of vast amounts of data are part of the behavioral approach which work to guarantee the scientific objectivity. Value judgments are eschewed, while data collection and analysis are prized.

A chasm is set up between the behavioral method and all previous methods on the grounds that the behavioral is "scientific" and all the others are "normative." The philosophical, historical, and juridical methods are said to be normative in the sense that they reflect some norm, some predisposition or starting point, some "value." These methods are said to assume some preexisting values in the settings, conditions, theories, or institution from which they begin. Assumptions about the conduct of war from the Constitution or assumptions about voting from the eligibility rules are examples. The behavioral method claims freedom from these presuppositions by reason of its scientific procedures.

METHODS:
THEIR CHRONOLOGY AND LOGIC

The five foregoing methods are listed in the order of their chronological development within the discipline as dominant methodologies. They are also listed in the order of a certain logical development. The chronological development is on two scales, the one classical, the other American.

Classical Chronology

The classical chronology starts with the consideration that the original dominant method within political science was philosophical. Starting with Plato and Aristotle the philosophical method remained dominant for many centuries. The next dominant approach to political studies was the historical method, which was employed much later by Machiavelli. The social contract writers of the seventeenth and eighteenth centuries were legalists or juridical in their approach to discussing the state. The dominant concern of the nineteenth and twentieth centuries has been behavioral.

Such a "classical" chronology is painted with a broad brush. Nonetheless, it gives a fairly accurate picture of the long development of political science. This chronology follows the outline of the development of the discipline presented in Isaak and in most "scope and methods" books. The particular American chronology is suggested in the fine history of the discipline by Albert Somit and Joseph Tanenhaus.[21]

American Chronology

On the American scale, Madison, sometimes called the first American political scientist because of his writings in the *Federalists Papers* and because of his *Journal* about the Constitutional Convention, was philosophical in his approach to the discussion of government. The formal American beginning of the discipline of political science at Columbia College (now University) in the late nineteenth century was historical in its methodology. In this connection, for many years political science was taught from within the history department at most colleges. Political science courses also had a largely historical content. The content changed with the dominant method. The early twentieth century was juridical in its dominant approach. Professor (later President of the United States) Woodrow Wilson's *Congressional Government* was an early sample of its institutional dimensions. Since the 1950s the concern has been behavioral, and in the 1960s and after, this has been the dominant methodology.

Logical Development

The chronological listing is not a point of major importance. It does give some slight sense of the history of political science. The developmental order assumes a greater importance when it is seen in its "logical" dimension. By logical order is meant that the list of methodologies moves from the most deductive to the most inductive. The philosophical method is said to be deductive in the sense of arriving at conclusions about particulars by inference following necessarily from general or universal premises. The historical method is then understood to be more inductive than the philosophical but less so than the comparative, and so on.

This ordering is being used in an ordinal and not an interval sense. No suggestion is being made that there are increments of deduction or induction as one moves from the philosophical to the behavioral method. Almond[22], in describing the emergence of the behavioral method in the period after World War II, spoke of the previous approach and methods as being too limited in scope and the desire for a new approach which was more comprehensive. The fascinating thing about Almond's comment is that it could have been made about each new methodological development as it succeeded earlier study. The historical method could claim that it was more comprehensive than philosophical speculation. The historical approach would base this claim on its investigation of the actual conditions which gave rise to particular institutions and practices as opposed to the limited scope of linking general propositions about the nature of man and the origin of state to particular circumstances.

The same comment about greater comprehensiveness could be made by the comparative approach and in turn by the juridical approach. The juridical claim to comprehensiveness is that historical and other background information is summarized in the basic law or constitution of a country. By concentrating on the constitution belabored historical and comparative studies could be circumvented. Work could begin on "true," juridical, political matters without the necessity of plowing through superfluous material.

The behavioral method, which is Almond's interest, is said to have found that all the previous approaches were "parochial," "configurative," and "formalistic." What he is saying is that the previous approach concentrated on what was familiar, illuminated peculiar characteristics of systems, and tended to focus on institutions, legal norms, rules, and regulations. What was desired was an approach which was broader and focused on performance, interaction, and behavior. Along these lines new effort and experimentation in the post-World War II period sought a more comprehensive scope, greater precision, greater realism, and a new, more comprehensive theory.

The new effort is reflected in the political system model described earlier. The political system is an outgrowth and expression of behavioralism. Its comprehensiveness is seen in the inclusion of "everything" in its range of investigation. As explained earlier the core or authoritative decision-making agencies are included as well as political parties, elections, interest groups, policy output, feedback, communications, political culture, the economic environment, socialization, and all their linkages.

The behavioral approach can be called the "Dragnet school of political science." By this is meant that the behavioral approach is known to consider "just the facts." The facts which it considers are *all* the facts. No presuppositions are made about voting, war powers, judges, or constitutions. No values intervene. Through careful observation and analysis objective, empirical, scientific, and value-free investigations are made into the moving forces behind political events. No philosophical, historical, juridical, or moral preconceptions get in the way of the scientific study of the facts. This is the behavioral credo.

POSTBEHAVIORALISM:
A NEW METHOD?

In the words of a song from the musical *Oklahoma,* political science methods appear to have "gone about as far as they can go." If the philosophical approach is on the deductive end of the scale, the behavioral is at the opposite end. One cannot be more inductive than gathering all the facts. It is with some surprise then that another method is announced. This new approach is "postbehavioralism." Its legitimacy is denied or at least disputed by many behavioralists. Similar contentions about the succeeding method occurred all along the chain of methodological development. The test of a new approach is what it does.

It is intriguing to see again the pattern of claiming that the previous approach was too limited in scope and that there is a need to be more comprehensive. It may be difficult to first imagine how behavioralism, which includes "everything" in its domain, can be too limited. How is it possible for postbehavioralism to be more comprehensive when the previous method includes all the facts? The answer relates to that which by definition behavioralism leaves out—"values."

Values Postbehavioralism

The behavioral method declares itself to be "value-free." Values are that which the postbehavioralists would go beyond the behavioralists to include. It must be carefully noted that the point of including values is not one of taking values into consideration as an object of study. Behavioralists do study values. The point is a matter of "having" values. Postbehavioralists want to proclaim their value preferences. They want to make value judgments about the politics they study.

In their effort to be objective and to leave out all presuppositions, the behavioralists studied only the facts. For that approach postbehavioralists have them criticized[23] as being conservative, antidemocratic, and antipolitical. That criticism is another way of saying that the previous approach is too limited and that the discipline must be more comprehensive. Apparently the postbehavioralists would prefer that political science be liberal, democratic, and political. According to McCoy and Playford the behavioralists are conservative in a double way. On the one hand there is the question of "whether an empirical science, which can only study what is and not what will be, much less what ought to be, must not be inherently conservative." On the other hand there is the matter of the inherent values of equilibrium, stability, balance, and internal self-direction of the system which is their base. The concepts of "functional" and "dysfunctional" contain hidden status quo norms which work against entertaining the possibilities of dramatic change. These inherent conservative characteristics may not show up in the nonprofessional conduct of behavioralists. Some may proclaim themselves to be political liberals. They usually talk about wearing two or more hats, suggesting by that comment that there is a separation between their private conduct and their professional conduct. It was anomalies like this that led Aristotle to observe, "what a man says, he does not necessarily believe."[24]

The antidemocratic allegation refers to reports and studies done in the name of behavioralism. Behavioralists' studies, for example, have reported on the low level of democratic participation in voting and on other low levels of citizenry involvement. The professional response of the behavioralists is that their responsibility is to explain the phenomenon, not to change it. An explanation for the low levels of citizenry involvement goes along the lines of contributing stability to the system by providing a cushion of those undisturbed by passing events. This assigned functional evaluation of apathy is criticized by postbehavioralists. They see the evaluation as antidemocratic since it fails to promote democratic values. On these same grounds many behavioral social scientists fail to take a stand on issues, from pornography to guerrilla movements.

Behavioralists justify their detachment on the grounds of scientific and professional requirements. They cannot be true to "white coat" professionalism if they were to be influenced by particular sets of values. This leads their critics to the charge that the behavioralists are also antipolitical. They contend that the imputed objectivity, value-freeness, and scientific pretension predetermine and limit the content of political studies and leave out the very political dimension of the political world. As the authors of *Apolitical Politics* also argue:

> In their attempt to turn political studies into a value-free "science," they have shown a marked tendency to throw out politics altogether. They seem to select their topic not by any criteria of political significance but rather by criteria determined by their methodology, e.g., "Is the matter to be examined subject to empirical verification, can it be quantified?" Thus they become prisoners of their own methodology. Since they fail to address themselves to questions of great concern to their students and to the public at large, such as Vietnam and the civil rights movement . . . their work often seems trivial, narrow and apolitical.[25]

The conflict between these two approaches escalated to the point where the behavioralists were being called "pseudo-scientists" by the postbehavioralists. This escalated language appeared in a report[26] about the discussions at a meeting of the American Political Science Association in September of 1970. A year before, *The New York Times*[27] had reported on the "fiery week" of Association meetings where the behavioral approach was "under attack from many younger scholars who feel that the profession has been too concerned with gathering facts and too little interested in finding out how it might influence immediate policies."

The younger scholars' concern was that "it is no longer practical or morally tolerable to stand on the political sidelines when our expertise alerts us to disaster." For these critics the profession was guided by "an elitist oligarchy" seeking "to insure the status quo rather than to promote change." In the Association meetings of 1970 the postbehavioral position on values was expressed forcefully: "We feel there should be more of a role for people who have more value-oriented interest." They are further reported to have said, "We are concerned about how to create a society that is free of racial oppression or how to control the military-industrial complex, but these are antithetical to the group which dominates the profession today." The critics' explanation for this lack of concern for pressing problems was that, "People who claim they are being objective presuppose the existing value structure. We feel that political science has to relate more directly to the pressing concerns of American and world society."

In these remarks the value preferences of the postbehavioralists are not hidden. They have clearly expressed attitudes toward American foreign policy, civil rights, domestic political orientations, and toward the behavioralists. Theirs is a salient point about the hidden value perspective from which the behavioralists operate. Now a subtle point must be noted. The behavioralists are not being charged with having no values. The behavioralists, according to their credo, would like that. They are being charged with having unacknowledged norms or values. They are not so much value-free as value blind or dishonest. The place of values in political science from the postbehavioral point of view is clear and definite. That is their postbehavioral characteristic. This normative quality is explicit with the postbehavioralists and implicit with the behavioralists. The thing not discussed in either method is the content of those norms.

Formalistic Postbehavioralism

There are other expressions of a postbehavioral outlook than the one just described. These other forms are not as explicit in their discussion of values. For example, some political scientists use an approach that is more formally mathematical. Noting the emphasis on a wide variety of statistical techniques in the behavioral approach, these other scholars, who like to be called formalists, emphasize more formal mathematics. They regard statistics as marginally useful and would like the beginning political science student to have a couple of semesters of statistics plus two semesters of calculus and then differential equations. They claim that with this formal math more interesting political science can be done.

The formal mathematical preparation would lead to analysis of competition, coalition formation, voter preferences, and war games. Discussions of ''a calculus of voting,'' ''game theory,'' and ''decision-theoretic models'' are part of their efforts. Political scientists such as William Riker, Peter Ordeshock, and Steven Brams are a few of those who approach the political world from this formal mathematical perspective. The efforts of these formalists parallel what the postbehavioralists have done. The parallel is in method-predetermining answers. Approaching the world of events from a statistical perspective gives a set of answers dictated by that method. Mathematical analysis is open to a wider range of answers. Statistical analysis, it can be said, lets the data speak to the researcher. Mathematical analysis brings competing formal models to speak to the data. Political coalitions, for example, can be explained in terms of survey research or in terms of mathematical models of minimal winning coalitions. The challenge of the formalists therefore merely brings out the hidden, perhaps unwitting, value orientation of the behavioralists and the more overt values of their critics.

Biopolitical Postbehavioralism

A third group of postbehavioralists has emerged in recent years. Their concern is with *biopolitics*. They too are critical of the behavioralists but their criticism is more sweeping even than the others. Biopolitics claims[28] that the social sciences have ''attempted to build a superstructure without a base.'' These scholars explain that social scientists have attempted to comprehend the hierarchy of interacting and constraining systems of society by "referring only to the two or three top-most layers (and only in terms of the past two or three thousand years)." They add a most revealing comment from the viewpoint of the methodological survey in this chapter: "we feel that this perspective is too limited." They want, apparently, to be more comprehensive than the narrow range of "everything" encompassed by the behavioralists.

Biopolitics wants to inquire, for example, about the extent to which crowding, birth ordering, body rhythm, nutrition levels, and biological instincts influence behavior. Crowding, for example, produces biochemical changes and stress in animals and it would be important to know whether it has similar results on humans. Another example of biopolitical inquiry are the questions raised about how the medication taken for physical ailments affected Anthony Eden or John Kennedy in their appraisal of political events.[26] What the biopolitical approach is looking for is a deeper and more satisfying explanation for political behavior than can be gained through the more sociological techniques of the behavioralists.

Evaluation of Postbehavioralism

All three groups of postbehavioralists have pertinent criticism of behavioralism. It must be made clear however that they are precisely *post*-behavioralists and not *anti*behavioralists. They come after and they would go beyond the contributions of the behavioralists. There are some political scientists who for their own reasons still have an antibehavioralist perspective. The "anti" viewpoint sees greater merit, for example, in classical theory, in the historical method, or in juridical investigation. It sees little merit in behavioralism. The postbehavioralists do not consider behavioralism in that way. Although they claim that more must be included, they accept what has been done.

Each of the postbehavioral groups would add a dimension to political studies which the behavioralists do not include. They would add, respectively, values, formal mathematics, or a biological base. The first group of postbehavioralists do not seek to reopen a discussion of values such as characterizes classical political theory; they simply want to have their values assumed as right. They want the war in Vietnam condemned, the military-industrial complex controlled, colonialism rejected. Their values and insights are present as unquestioned values and insights. From their perspective implementation should begin! The formalists are not as pushy, but they nonetheless would add a dimension which, from all appearances, is arrived at deductively. Why one mathematical model is preferred over many other possibilities is a deductive choice of the investigator. Like the other postbehavioral views, the biopolitical approach arbitrarily adds a new dimension, justified though it may be, to the spectrum of methodology.

A logical response to these additions may be, why these particular values, why these particular models, why this biological rather than astrological base? What these questions do is add a seventh step to the chain of methodology. The seventh step asks once again "why" type questions. The chain of methodology looks like this:

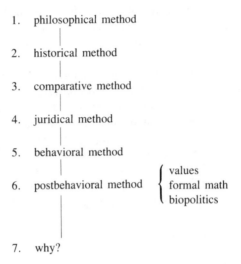

1.   philosophical method

2.   historical method

3.   comparative method

4.   juridical method

5.   behavioral method

6.   postbehavioral method { values / formal math / biopolitics

7.   why?

It should be almost immediately apparent that the seventh step is a return to the philosophical method of the first step. In other words, the development from one through six, from the philosophical method through the postbehavioral method, was in a respect linear. The seventh step reveals the development as curvilinear. Now the methodologies are seen to be different vantage points in a circle around the political world, each seeing it differently but all seeing the same thing. It is as if the methodologies occupy different sections of a baseball stadium. Some occupy more of the stadium than others, some are out in left field, some claim to have an umpire's view or a manager's view behind home plate or in the dugout. The point is, they all see the same events but from different perspectives.

This equanimical view of political science methodology has always been possible. All critics of behavioralism prior to the postbehavioralists were not necessarily antibehavioral but they were, and often still are, looked at that way. The contribution of the postbehavioral development is that all can come to see the whole dispute in larger perspective. All can begin to see the differences as merely alternative ways of attempting to understand the same phenomenon. The only thing that can be said about which method is "best" is that it is whatever is most appropriate to a particular task. No one method is definitively best. Each has something to offer but each is limited in certain respects, as the other methods point out. One should therefore feel free to undertake whatever study in whatever way best satisfies the important items under investigation.

CONCLUSION AND PERSPECTIVE

There is a story of six or seven Indian blindmen, each feeling different parts of an elephant and none being able to discern either individually or collectively exactly what it was. Political scientists with their different methodologies are like the Indian blindmen. It may appear that many have been working too long on the rear quarters of the elephant. (That's not intended to be a partisan political joke, but take it that way if you can.) The analogy with political science is that each separate method is blind *if* it proclaims itself to be the definitive method for understanding the political world. One method is blind if it proclaims that only it has the exclusive way to correctly know politics. "20/20" vision is possessed in knowing one's own approach and its limits and in knowing the same about the other methods. With such respect for all approaches and methods political science shows a wisdom and maturity which will contribute to the advancement of understanding.

Near the end of the nineteenth century, in a general infatuation with the accomplishments of science, Seurat and some other neoimpressionist painters proposed techniques for making painting an exact science. They proposed that lines, color, proportion, space, etc., could be subjected to mathematical analysis and formulation. Their immediate technique was pointillism, a process whereby the picture on the canvass was constructed out of dots of color. Many of their paintings are very beautiful and most fascinating. They created a brief stir in the art world and have long since given way to the ongoing creative efforts of other artists.

Some people in the world of music and other performing arts attempted to adapt their artistic field and science. Such endeavors are not without justification. Music, for example, has an exact mathematical basis. Still, scientific formulation can never capture the creative, emotional dimension of art. Shakespeare, Beethoven, or Monet cannot be expressed in a mathematical formula. Some of their work may be better appreciated with the insights contributed by scientific studies, but their creative spirit cannot be captured except through the imagination.

The shades of interpretation and appreciation of a work of art are as varied as its audience. The political world has also had a fascination with scientific analysis. Much of the political world can be captured to a greater degree by science than the world of art. However, it can be captured only to a degree. The part captured may be, as the postbehavioralists suggest, the least interesting and the least important. The contributions of such endeavors have to be proven on a large scale and not assumed from a methodological technique.

It would be unusual indeed to expect that political science had come to a definitive way of understanding the political world. If a "correct" approach had been found the path to the door of the discipline would be well trod with individuals and world leaders seeking solutions to political problems. From time to time some scholar is thought to have uncovered a remarkable new way to understand and bring order to political reality. No one is opposed to such a true discovery. In the lifetime of any of the readers of this work such new discoveries will come and go and the world will not change for them. The world is not obstinate. The discoveries are just not as definitive as first believed.

Many centuries ago Plato proposed an ideal republic with an elaborate educational system that would remedy the defects of the political world. Aristotle also saw the defects of the political world but he opposed Plato's solutions because they "disregard the experience of ages." He commented further that "in the multitude of years these things, if they were good, would certainly not have been unknown.''[30]

The world does not perversely avoid things that will work. The same is true of methodological and other innovations in the world of political studies and politics. Aristotle's comments conform with those of Einstein about the greater complexity of the political world and the difficulty of understanding it through purely rational constructs. Rational efforts are not to be disregarded. They should, however, be in accord with ''the experience of ages.'' If it is not always or usually possible to test political science methods by their results because of problems with time frame, at least they should be tempered by the experience of ages.

NOTES

1. *The New York Times Book Review,* September 19, 1976, p. 2.

2. *The New York Times,* March 31, 1977.

3. John Plamenatz, *Democracy and Illusion* (London: Longman Group Limited, 1977), p. 5.

4. *The New York Times,* September 8, 1977.

5. Robert A. Scott and Arnold R. Shore, *Why Sociology Does Not Apply: A Study of the Use of Sociology in Public Policy* (New York: Elsevier, 1979).

6. Aristotle, *Ethics,* 1139b, 6.

7. Cited in William Ebenstein, *Great Political Thinkers* (Hinsdale, Ill.: Dryden Press, 1969), p. 245.

8. Paul A. Samuelson, *Economics,* 5th ed. (New York: McGraw-Hill, 1961), p. 49.

9. Alan C. Isaak, *Scope and Methods of Political Science: An Introduction to the Methodology or Political Inquiry* (Homewood, Ill.: Dorsey Press, 1981), pp. 29-30.

10. ibid., p. 26.

11. ibid., p. 87.

12. ibid., p. 115.

13. ibid., p. 79 and p. 97ff.

14. Gabriel Almond and Stephen J. Genco, ''Clouds, Clocks, and the Study of Politics,'' *World Politics,* July 1977, p. 505.

15. Isaak, *Scope,* p. 136.

16. ibid., p. 173.

17. Charles E. Lindblom and David K. Cohen, *Usable Knowledge: Social Science and Social Problem Solving* (New Haven: Yale University Press, 1979).

18. B.F. Skinner, *Beyond Freedom and Dignity* (New York: Bantam, 1971), chapter 1.

19. B.F. Skinner, *Walden Two* (New York: Macmillan, 1976), p. viii.

20. B.F. Skinner, *About Behaviorism* (New York: Vintage Books, 1976), p. 3.

21. Albert Somit and Joseph Tanenhaus, *The Development of American Political Science: From Burgess to Behavioralism* (New York: Irvington Publishers, 1982).

22. Gabriel Almond and G. Bingham Powell, *Comparative Politics* (Boston: Little, Brown, 1966), chapter 1.

23. Charles A. McCoy and John Playford, *Apolitical Politics: A Critique of Behavioralism* (New York: Thomas Y. Crowell, 1967), introduction.

24. Aristotle, *Metaphysics,* 1005b, 24.

25. McCoy and Playford, *Apolitical Politics,* introduction.

26. *The New York Times,* September 11, 1970, p. 24.

27. ibid., Sept. 9, 1969.

28. Peter Corning, Joseph Losco, and Thomas C. Wiegele, "Political Science and the Life Sciences," *P S:* Published quarterly by the American Political Science Association, Volume XIV, Number 3, Summer 1981, pp. 590–594.

29. Thomas C. Wiegele, *Biopolitics: Search for a More Human Political Science* (Boulder, Co.: Westview Press, 1979). And cf. the new journal *Politics and the Life Sciences* published by an association of the same name.

30. Aristotle, *Politics,* II, 1264a.

CHAPTER FOUR
THE NATURE
OF THE STATE

Some political scientists, particularly those of a behavioralist outlook, have disowned the state. They regard the concept of the state as an inappropriate orienting idea in analysis and research about the political world. David Easton[1] sees the concept of the state as laying "siege" to the preferred concept of "the political system" and threatening a "conceptual morass from which we thought we had but recently escaped." Easton's concerns are what he regards as the methodological impurity and grossness of the concept of the state. He also objects to the theoretical or ideological disputes evoked over the state in modern political literature.

As will be seen, there is indeed an inexactness to the term and there are profound disagreements about its meaning and application. However, as the previous discussion about behavioralism and postbehavioralism revealed, to simply substitute the term political system for the term state does not magically purify political science. It merely replaces one set of assumptions with another. The new set often has hidden implications which only later become evident.

The clarity and measurability of the "scientific" language of the political system is set off against the ambiguity and divisiveness of the traditional language about the state. There may indeed be a richness to the political system approach. Some was displayed in Chapter 2. However, to simply replace the state with the political system is to neglect the experience of ages. There are valid concerns about the direction, origin, purpose, and justification of the system that are just not discussed in the political system approach. According to Easton the reason the political system was consciously designed was precisely to avoid such questions. But it is just those questions that must be addressed if the system is to attend to the real world beyond its idealized constructs. These are indeed value questions but if they are avoided on methodological grounds then the purported science is truncated.

A consideration of the various theories of the state will do no harm to the political system model if both the theories and the system are presented fairly and objectively. If seen as alternative points of view with some base in reality, the theories of the state will constitute a backdrop against which the system can be viewed, proving its resourcefulness or revealing its limits. The conclusion in the last chapter was that the best method was that one most appropriate to a particular task, and that each method made a positive contribution. From this perspective, in distinction from Easton, the state has a contribution to make even to the political system approach.

Easton is far from alone in desiring the "interment" of the state. Almond[2] also sees the term "state" along with the terms "government" and "nation" as "older terms . . . limited by legal and institutional meanings. They direct attention to a particular set of institutions usually found in modern Western societies."

Another author explains the viewpoint in this way:

> The traditional study of "state" and "sovereignty" is an unnecessary, and misleading, restriction of the scope of political science. There are several reasons for this position. For one thing, the terms "state" and "sovereignty" are badly culture-bound. It can be shown that the origins of these concepts is intimately tied up with the rise of a centralized monarchy and a territorial national state in the West. In their recent discovery of the non-Western world, the social sciences generally, and political science particularly, have learned that there are numerous societies which have nothing remotely resembling a "sovereign." Hence a dilemma arises. Either one is forced to say these societies have no politics, or the definition of politics employed is inadequate.[3]

That author, as well as Almond and Easton and others, chose the latter alternative. It may be that they responded too quickly to two equally unacceptable alternatives.

The discussion in Chapter 2 of the political system revealed the broad usefulness of it. It is systematic, universally applicable. It integrates a diversity of parts, shows their relationship, and fits them into a larger whole. However, there are assumptions built into the phrase "political system," just as there are said to be assumptions within the older terms of state, government, sovereignty, and nation.

It is said that the "recent" discovery of the non-Western world has uncovered societies without sovereigns in the Western sense. This cannot be all that recent because seventeenth century Englishmen made the same discovery when they met the American Indian. In each newly discovered society, there was some organized entity, some authority structure, with which the newcomers had to deal, whether in stealing land or fighting wars. It is the nature and origin of that entity or authority with which those who deal with the nature of the state or sovereignty concern themselves.

Proponents of the power approach view the political system assumptions as presupposing in the same manner as the system proponents view the state and sovereignty. Each approach views the others as starting from undemonstrated assumptions. The perspectives reflected in the three broad approaches to the political world are repeated in a surprisingly parallel fashion in the traditional debates about the purpose of the state. Some initial time may be saved by formulating new language to avoid old problems. The reemergence of the methodological debates over behavioralism and postbehavioralism plus the debate about such fundamental terms as democracy shows, however, that the problems of authority and power and theory will not go away. The parameters of the traditional theories must be dealt with, or one's political science lacks depth.

It might be easier in some respects if all political scientists used the same terms in exactly the same way. Some, such as Brecht with his notion of intersubjective transmissible language, see uniformity as the goal and major contribution of political science and the humanities in general. That uniformity may be debated by some as a goal. It certainly does not exist at the present. Whether it should is a point that requires an understanding of the alternatives. The superiority of one approach cannot be foisted on would-be students of political science without doing a disservice to the students and to the discipline. For this reason, the historical worth of the topic and the merit of the topic itself, there should be a discussion of the nature of the state.

ELEMENTS OF THE STATE

It can be reasonably assumed that the state is familiar to all and that it is necessary only to identify certain elements of it. Those elements are people, territory, government, and some unifying element or principle which ties the first three together. From the beginning the unifying element needs elaboration and clarification. It comes in three forms: organismic, mechanistic, and what will be called here synergistic.

Each version or theory of the unifying element of the state argues something different and each claims to be the only correct theory explaining the binding force of a political community. The terms themselves may not be familiar to all. As will be explained later, synergistic is here substituted for the more common term, "organic." Even with that change the terms may not be familiar. Sometimes the terms used are monistic, pluralistic, and holistic, respectively. Confusions abound. It is often semantic or the result of overlapping use of the terms. Although there may be some benefit in reconciling all the usages, that will not be done here. We will do here two things: (1) clarify that there are three different theories and (2) explain each, whatever it might be called.

The immediate need to explain the unifying element stands in contrast to the apparent simplicity and clarity of the first three elements. Little clarification appears necessary about people, territory, and government. The elements are material, tangible, familiar. They are easy to recognize and—at least the first two if not the third—are measurable. People can be numbered. Territory can be calibrated. Government can be accounted for at least in a nominal sense if not in the degree of effectiveness.

A caveat can be entered however. As to the point of measurability, most students, when asked to list the top ten nations in the world according to population, will include West Germany, Italy, England, and France along with China, India, the Soviet Union, and the United States. Japan is usually included at some point and the tenth country mentioned is often Israel, Korea, Spain, Egypt, Canada, Poland, or some other country currently in the headlines.

That West Germany, Italy, England, and France are not among the top ten in population is never considered. (They rank twelfth, fourteenth, fifteenth, and sixteenth respectively.) The ten in correct order are China, India, the Soviet Union, the United States, Indonesia, Brazil, Japan, Bangladesh, Pakistan, and Nigeria. Mexico is in eleventh position and Vietnam is thirteenth. Many of these states, such as Indonesia, Bangladesh, Pakistan, and Nigeria, are unknown to the beginning student.

The assumed familiarity of the concept of state is slightly diminished. Importance is not *determined* by numbers, but reflecting on a list of states ranked according to population and geographical area gives some surprises. It should open one's thoughts to just how familiar the term state is.

MiniStates

A second point which can be made in questioning the assumed familiarity of the state is to inquire into the full extent of measuring the state. There are currently 159 members of the United Nations. Some of the members are exceptionally small in terms of population and geographic area. Seychelles, for example, has a population of 65,000; Sao Tome & Principe has a population of 88,000; Grenada, 119,000; St. Lucia, 119,000; Maldives, 168,000. By contrast, and to get some perspective, there are four hundred and thirty-five congressional districts in the United States, with each district having an average population of 530,000.

There are many other small members of the UN like Western Samoa, Qatar, Solomon Islands, Bahamas, and Bahrain. A few years ago the UN addressed the problem of size. Its concern was not the size of existing members but of potential members. New countries applying for membership or considered as potential members provoked the full problem of measurability. According to its charter the United Nations is open to all "peace-loving states." According to that charter provision, two things qualify a country for membership, being peace loving and being a state.

The Secretary General at the time of this earlier question described these potential members as "entities which are exceptionally small in area, population and human and economic resources, and which are now emerging as independent states."[4] That these entities were defined by the Secretary General as "states" shows the problem. "Peace loving" is the only means test for membership. At the time of this discussion the usually understood to be conservative *Wall Street Journal* proposed an arbitrary quantitative means test of "a population of at least 10,000; a territory of at least 360 square miles; a budget of at least $15 million a year; and a foreign trade worth at least $15 million a year."[5] Except for the last item many universities and small towns could consider seceding in order to petition the UN for membership. They might even apply for United States foreign aid.

The problem of size at the UN is not entirely playful speculation. Nauru, a small South Pacific island, was cited as an example during this discussion of size. One year their population was reported to be 3000 [6] and the next year it was reported at 4914.[7] That increase would certainly seem to qualify them as peace-loving. Fourteen years later it has jumped to 9000. It is not just the matter of population increase that interests us in Nauru and its theoretical problem for the UN. More importantly, Nauru controls about 98 percent of the world supply of phosphate. Its peace-loving status is therefore of interest to the general UN membership.

The matter of UN membership, however, is not the principal concern here. The chief concern is whether or not Nauru is a state. Whether it is called a state or a political system does not make any difference. In neither case are there any minimum specifications for population, area, etc. It possesses the criteria whether these be people, territory, government, and a unifying principle or input, output, feedback, and authoritative decision-making agents. The issue gets a little stickier on the consideration that if Nauru qualifies then one can ask about other non-UN entities. Attention must be given to Vatican City (population 1000), San Marino (22,000), Liechtenstein (26,000), Andorra (42,000), Monaco (28,000), and Tonga (104,000). Even more interesting would be the answer to the consideration of Pitcairn Island; area 1.75 square miles, population 61.

Our imagination could get carried away in thinking about these figures. The point is that there are no minimum specifications for the size of the "measurable" elements of the state. There are no maximum specifications either. China is accepted as a state because it has "always" been called a state, as has India. Given the elements one could easily visualize an even larger entity, a world state consisting of the human race as the people, spaceship earth as the territory, and the UN as the government.

The very thought of a world government would cause some to cringe, others to revel. The point is that there are no self-evident minimum or maximum specifications which would ordain or preclude *mini-* or *maxi*-states. Analogously, we might ask, when in the world of fashions is a miniskirt no longer a miniskirt or a necktie no longer a tie? in either direction? Answers for skirts, ties, or states are arbitrary. The answers are not necessarily right but they set the current parameters with which one has to work. The assumed familiar and measurable aspects of the state become less familiar and more immeasurable after first contact.

THE UNIFYING ELEMENT

The discussion of state size shows that the unifying element of the state is not alone in being unfamiliar. Coming to understand the unifying element of the state will not unravel the mysteries of the minimum or maximum size of the state. The answer to those questions will continue to be arbitrary and political as occurs at the UN and in the relation between states. The examination of the unifying principle looks into what it is that holds a state, any state, together. It can be understood to be a "glue" that holds a certain people in a certain territory under a certain government. Sociologically or behaviorally this glue is referred to as "patterns of allegiance."

Political theory traditionally speaks of three theories of the state. They will be examined. It should be understood from the beginning that the theories discussed here and in the following chapters are intended to be exclusive. By exclusive is meant that each theory presents itself as the only correct view of the nature or unifying element of the state. Each will be presented fairly so that the reader can fully appreciate what is seriously intended. No one theory should be dismissed out of hand. Some preference will be in evidence for one particular line of thought but eventually all the theories (three parallel theories in each of four chapters) will be balanced out. In the end a choice should be possible depending on the premises established.

A unifying element or principle may at first appear unimportant to the practically oriented reader. The practical mind notices that there are enough states with enough problems to be settled that one does not need to create investigations into the theory of the state. That practical reader would want to get on to "real" things.

Most likely to such a reader Lebanon is a real political problem in need of solution, so also with Northern Ireland or the problem of the two Chinas. With Lebanon, it should be pointed out, there is a serious question about whether it is a state. If it is a state there is the further question of what holds or can hold it together. In Northern Ireland there is not only domestic turmoil, as in Lebanon, there is also the long standing historical question of rightful jurisdiction, arbitrary force, and popular will. The same questions exist about the China of Taiwan and the China of the mainland. These are but three of the contemporary political question areas relating to state identity.

There are similar problems or potential problems in almost every state in the world today. There is the potentially explosive problem of an entity called Baluchistan, which is a territory somewhat equally overlapping Iran, Pakistan, and Afghanistan. If someone were to stir up the Baluchis to seek "national unity and statehood" the repercussions could be earth shattering. Similar problems exist within Spain, France, South Africa. Within the Soviet Union there is a problem, as some see it, of the captive nations which should be independent but are not. Some claim that the problem is the same with the French in Canada and with Puerto Rico within the United States. The communities along the Mexico-United States border and the Canada-United States border are often reported to have much more in common with themselves than with their respective political centers.

What makes each and every claimant to separate identity truly a state or not may be settled arbitrarily, as with the question of size. Many existing states may be said to be arbitrary constructs. Individuals, groups, and other states do not accept the claimed statehood of many prominent states today. The problems of colonialism, imperialism, and nationalism are all expressions of, or at least can be expressed in terms of, the unifying bond of the state.

A discussion of the nature of the state and the nature of its unifying principle will not settle any of the existing disputes. The discussion will lead, however, to an appreciation of the depth of the issues involved and the intensity with which the positions are held by the contending parties. If one has to be practical about this appreciation, there is a humanizing and potential problem solving utility to understanding fully the position of opposing parties in any political dispute.

Organismic Unity

The organismic theory maintains that the state is like an organism where the parts are intimately tied to the whole. No part acts except as the whole acts. There are two variations on the organismic theme. One speaks of a spiritual force, the other of a biological force. The force controls human actions in organizing, moving, and directing the state. In either form the power is not subject to human control.

Hegel's theory is a classical representation of the spiritual force. He views the state as the embodiment of the "Divine Idea as it exists on Earth." For Hegel the individual receives his worth only through the state and the state receives its worth only by the Divine Idea which controls it. All parts are uniquely fitted into the whole that controls. Hegel writes:

> Since the state is mind objectified, it is only as one of its members that the individual himself has objectivity, genuine individuality, and an ethical life. . . . The state in and by itself is the ethical whole, the actualization of freedom . . . . The state is mind on earth and consciously realizing itself there . . . . In considering freedom, the starting-point must not be individuality, the single self consciousness, but only the essence of self-consciousness; for whether man knows it or not, this essence is externally realized as a self-subsistent power in which single individuals are only moments. The march of God in the world, that is what the state is. The basis of the state is the power of reason actualizing itself as will. . . . Man must therefore venerate the state as a secular deity, and observe that if it is difficult to comprehend nature, it is infinitely harder to understand the state.[8]

For Hegel neither man nor the state itself controls the dynamic by which the state comes about. The dynamic is all a product of the larger unfolding process. It is this force, this power over which men have no control, that holds the state together, not men's separate wills.

The biological version of the organismic theory does not grant the spiritual character to the state which Hegel grants. The factor of control is nonetheless the same. The biological form regards the state like any other organism where, for example, the hand cannot live separate from the body, the eye cannot see independent from the person, the petal cannot live separately from the flower. The state and the individual are seen as having the same dependent relationship. Some versions of this theory ascribe birth, maturation, reproduction, and death to the state. A state is said to be founded, grows in strength, becomes imperial, has colonies, withers under the stress of time, and eventually dies from internal or external causes.

More recent versions, coming in popularized forms of biopolitics or sociobiology, suggest that human behavior can best be explained in general terms of animal behavior. Some of the popularized expressions of this view are found in the writings of Robert Ardrey: *The Social Contract, Territorial Imperative, African Genesis;* and Desmond Morris: *The Naked Ape, The Human Zoo.* These writings contain fascinating accounts about human and animal behavior. It should be understood, though, that these books present a theoretical position as well as interesting stories.

B. F. Skinner presents the same theory, where humans are directed by a force over which they have no control. With Skinner, however, it is much more evident that his is a definite theoretical position despite his interesting stories and arguments. For Skinner the environment controls. The human being's behavior is conditioned and reinforced by all the factors of the environment. There is a uniqueness to the individual for Skinner but there is no individual control or free will. Humankind can only design, as Skinner suggests in his *Walden II,* more or less efficient responses to the environment. This is not the place to argue the merits or demerits of Skinner's theory. Here the only point is to acknowledge that for him, as for Hegel, people are controlled by some external power.

The organismic theory is not flattering because we like to think of ourselves as in control. Its affront to our pride is not reason in itself for dismissing the theory, however. Hegel, Skinner, and others who take the so-called organismic position are not naive dreamers leading the gullible without good basis. Their explanations satisfy many if not most of the observed facts. Their conclusions are based on reasoned observations of reality. Put simply, the organismic position might be expressed in this way: (1) men exist and so does the state, (2) men's existence is ephemeral compared to the state, therefore, (3) the state (or the environment in Skinner's case) is of paramount importance and men ought to be seen as serving it.

There is a cogency to this argument. If we think in terms of just our own existence and then extend that to our parents and grandparents and then to our children, we can acknowledge that the state existed before us and will in all probability exist after we are gone. We are ephemeral; the state is not. Like the animal herd, humans live in the political community not by individual choice but by reason of some force over which they have no control.

Individual examples of apparent independent action do not refute the theory because the examples are small relative to total numbers. These independent acts can be dismissed as mere aberrations. The organismic theory has to be faced in its own terms. The total picture has to be grasped and it has to be dealt with in terms of the weight and merit of the premises and conclusion. Independent actions can give one pause for not accepting the theory outright. The theory has to be evaluated in comparison with alternative views.

In reference to the earlier cited practical question of the unity and identity of the state, the organismic theory would say that manifestations of the underlying unity are seen in common language, culture, beliefs, ethnic qualities, and habits. One state is clearly distinct from another. Political arrangements, like boundaries and autonomy, are but reflections of the more basic unity. When political events appear to contradict this unity, as in the federation of disparate groups or the fission of an established state, they are explained as manifestations of a yet unrecognized greater unity or as isolated deviations.

The basic underlying unity explains the individual's place within the state. One speaks that language and therefore one is *of* that state, etc. The roots of nationalism are seen here. So also can one see in skeletal form the theory of socialization which says that one is conditioned and reinforced to certain relatively constant behavior. In whatever expression, the organismic theory says that individuals act primarily as parts of a whole and the whole controls.

An interesting but clearly unintended expression of the organismic view is reflected in the quote attributed to Robert Strauss, a former government official and chairman of the Democratic party: "Everybody in government is like a bunch of ants on a log floating down a river. Each one thinks he is guiding the log, but it is really just going with the flow." Strauss was making a rhetorical political remark, not a philosophical one. Taken philosophically, the remark can be viewed as consistent with the organismic theory. The theory holds that the human role is merely to know and describe the state and its parts, not to change it.

Mechanistic Theory

The mechanistic theory is at a minimum flattering. In it the unity of the state is controlled by people. A machine, a watch, and an automobile have mechanistic unity. The parts are put together at the direction of the person who designed the machine. In the mechanistic theory of the state, the state is viewed in exactly the same sense. The state is viewed as completely subject to human control.

As there was a cogency to the organismic theory so there is a cogency to the mechanistic theory. The mechanistic view argues that: (1) as long as states have existed they have been directed in some fashion by people, whether one person, a few, or many; (2) we may not like the direction in which the state is going but that complaint indicates that it could be "directed" better; (3) therefore, human control is the constant in political life.

The organismic theory regards this supposed "direction" as no different from the behavior of the "alpha" or lead animal in a herd. The lead animal does not control its actions any more than all the other members of the herd. Hegel made a similar observation about the contribution of a Caesar or a Napoleon to their armies or empires. The mechanistic theory just draws a different conclusion from the same observed situation. The mechanistic theory concludes that there is human control; the organismic concludes the opposite.

The mechanistic understanding of the state is that it is artificial in its origin and mechanical in its nature. It views the state as held together by human design. It may not be subject to the design of the individual who is at the moment in disagreement with the government and its policies. To that individual the state assumes an organismic character. However, that individual is assuaged by the promise that with a gain in support the direction of the government may change. The possibility of changing the government with popular appeal argues human control. Traces of traditional democracy (see Chapter 1) are present here. No such consolation is available in the organismic theory.

Practical examples of the mechanistic view of the state are found in the fixing of territorial boundaries by treaties, the establishment of states by compacts, and the specification of the role of the government by contracts or constitutions. All such arrangements are humanly determined; they are arbitrary and artificial. There may be "natural" borders, but they may not be respected. Where the boundary is located is ultimately determined by human agreement. People draw the line or agree to it. It is that human act which defines one as members of country X or country Y.

Occasionally an individual may not be happy in a particular location and will move. The person might also begin a movement to redefine the boundaries or the terms of a constitution. All this manifests human control. In the making of a watch one may choose, if skillful enough, to make an analog watch or a digital watch or a sundial. Whatever the choice, the product is subject to the watchmaker. The maker gives the unity, the springs and wheels and dials, the computer chips, or angled uprights. The mechanistic theory applies the same argument to the state and its parts.

Compared to the organismic theory, the mechanistic unity is flattering. The organismic would say that the mechanistic can only point to the "appearance" of control. The pragmatist would comment that instead of debating theories we should find solutions to real political problems. A concern for solving problems is probably the foremost of all political interests. Theories affect conduct, however. Solutions will not be lasting unless the theoretical positions that people bring to problems are understood. One must also realize that there are limits to solutions. This is a significant challenge to the mechanistic theory. There are many goals upon which there is universal agreement but complete human control of even these is frequently lacking. No one opposes the elimination of poverty, inflation, or pollution, yet these goals have not been achieved. Disagreements rage about the means. The disagreements reflect different views about the level, and desired level, of control needed to accomplish the goals.

The mechanistic theory speaks in terms of "complete human control." Whether it can or cannot exist according to the mechanistic and organismic theories one must consider its nature and consequences. To maintain, as the mechanistic theory does, that the state is completely subject to human control concedes to human control the ability to impose in some way a temporal human will on everybody. Whether it can be done or not, it has certain frightening aspects. Its theoretical dimensions ought to be understood clearly. It is one thing to disagree with the lack of human control; it is quite different to accept complete human control as the only alternative.

We come to the point where, for various reasons, neither the organismic nor the mechanistic theory is completely acceptable. Both have strong arguments in their favor, both are subject to reasonable doubt. To concede complete human control is as unacceptable as no human control. In such a situation of equally unacceptable alternatives, compromise is usually in order.

Synergistic Theory

Synergy means combined action or operation. It means the behavior of a whole which is unexplained by the behavior of the parts or any subassembly of the parts. In a casual reading synergy may imply compromise, but strictly understood it does not. An example of synergy is the tensile strength of an alloy steel. The alloy is greater in strength than the separate strength or the conjoined strength of its components. Buckminster Fuller gives as an example of synergy the formula that one plus two equals four:

> Take three equi-edged triangles. Stack them together edge to edge as a three-sided tent. Inadvertently you have produced a fourth equi-edged triangle at their base. All together they form a tetrahedron. This is synergy. One plus two equals four. Take one away from the four and only two remain. The one that was lost was annihilated.[9]

The synergistic theory maintains that events are to some extent subject to human control but also to some extent uncontrollable. The components are combined together by human effort but the exact results are unexpected. Synergy may be said to be "organic" in the sense of forming an integral part of a whole. Organic is the term that has most often been associated with the third theory of the unifying principle of the state. One problem with the word organic is its too easy confusion with organismic. Another problem is that the term has far too many different definitions and usages in the history of political thought. Aristotle's theory is said to be organic, as are Hobbes', Rousseau's, Burke's, and others. The term synergy makes it possible to explain an ancient concept in a new and more effective way.

On the unifying principle of the state, the synergistic theory views unity as a product of both human control and the lack of such control. Synergistic unity is opposed to the organismic view of no human control and the mechanistic view of complete human control. The Sperry Rand Corporation, in a interesting series of ads, once claimed itself to be "synergistic." That corporation had several different divisions producing quite unrelated—or so it would normally appear—items. One division made hay balers, another made typewriters, others made electronic amplifiers, computers, and electrostatic copiers. Sperry Rand claimed, "We're synergistic." And it said: "We do a lot of things at Sperry Rand. And we do each one better because we do all the rest." The claim is that Sperry Rand makes a better hay baler because they make electronic amplifiers no larger than a pinhead. These two divisions and their products are completely unrelated, as are all the other divisions and their separate products. The divisions and products are unrelated in an ordinary, mechanistic or organismic sense. They are related, according to the ad, synergistically.

Sperry Rand is claiming that there is a synergy to their corporate structure.

This synergy is lacking, or so it is implied, in their competitors, who may be organized merely mechanistically. No effort should be made to ascertain whether Sperry Rand's claim is true or not. What is important is the concept of synergy versus mechanistic versus organismic.

Synergy implies that what holds a social entity together and what makes it work is some unity subject to human control and lacking human control. The other two theories speak of either complete human control or no human control. Synergy appears to be a compromise of the other two theories, but that compromise is in appearance only. Synergy is the synergistic conjoining of organismic and mechanistic. It is, like the alloy and the tetrahedron, a separate entity.

As to the unifying principle of the state, the synergistic theory says that the political community has a unique existence. Individual human efforts contribute to the existence of the state. This contribution is similar to combining divisions in a corporation or stacking equi-edged triangles into a tent to form a tetrahedron. Individual efforts also could destroy the state. In the nonpolitical examples individual efforts could break up the corporation or pull away one triangle and cause the tetrahedron tent to collapse.

A concrete example of political building and destroying would be Lebanon. Lebanon was built using some natural foundations in the 1920s. It was destroyed in the 1970s and 1980s. It would be best if this destruction did not take place, especially because of the many innocent victims of such a tragedy. The problem may be that there was no real, synergistic unity in the beginning. The building of a corporation and the stacking of three triangles are human efforts. The results are unexpected. The state is the product of human efforts and it can be destroyed by human effort. The state is different, however, in that it cannot be completely controlled, even synergistically. It will not completely collapse like the tent or the corporation. It arises in some new form, either broken in many new states or dominated by some external power.

This last point, which assumes a continued existence of the state in some form, is an important dimension of the synergistic theory. This aspect picks up from the organismic and mechanistic theories the observed, long-standing existence of the state. More will be discussed about that dimension in the later consideration of the origin of the sate. As in the first two theories, there is a cogency to the synergistic view. As with the other theories, there is a realistic base: (1) individuals do act independently, (2) there are things about the state which individuals do not control, and (3) most human endeavors, including the state, are conducted in this same way.

CONCLUSION AND PERSPECTIVE

At this juncture there may be an inclination to conclude in favor of the third theory, synergistic unity. The discussion may seem convincing and the appearance of compromise may be persuasive. Although that inclination is understandable, the conclusion is not warranted at this point. All that has been done is to juxtapose three different views of the unifying element of the state. We may be inclined to settle the question and to get on to other matters. Patience, however, should be practiced.

Judgment should be suspended until the other characteristics of the state have been considered. In each of the remaining topics—sovereignty, origin, and purpose—three views will be presented which parallel the three just considered. Although these topics will not be systematically woven together, when they are finished there will be three distinct and coherent views of the state. At that point one may want to draw a conclusion. At that later point a decision may also be avoided. Knowledge of the three views and the principles involved may lead to recognition of the distinctness of the theories with no judgment between them.

There may appear at times a preference for the third option. Such a perception of bias may be justified. The implications, however, will be balanced out when, upon examining the purpose of the state, the full dimensions of the third theory will be evident. At that point the three theories will stand in balance as three equal alternatives whose distinctness is based on their fundamental assumptions. Then the alternative views of the nature of the state will be fully appreciated and the reader can freely choose between them.

A final word should be said about immediate practical applications of this topic. In developing countries there is an especially evident struggle with problems of identity and allegiance. Most emerging nations, although claiming historical roots frustrated by colonial domination, are themselves the amalgam of diverse groups welded or bandaged together by the will of a dominant or temporarily dominant force. An examination of these countries in the light of the three theories, although never considered in this way by those involved, reveals the character of the contending forces within such a nation. Some groups or individuals, in an organismic way, seek to dominate by right and will. These forces are oblivious to any separate point of view. Others, in a mechanistic form, contend that they act for the majority. It is a separate and usually unexamined question how the majority is discovered or whether it is competent. Some speak synergistically and act on behalf of the common good. There is no full indication how that good is determined. Conflicting factions with these different points of view is the common tribulation of developing nations.

A recent article about India[10] explored once again the question of unity and identity in a large and diverse country. The article examined the question, "Is India a Nation?" As mentioned earlier, the same type of question could be raised about China and many other countries. Pakistan, Lebanon, Ethiopia and many African countries, the Middle East in general, Northern Ireland, Yugoslavia, and many others are beset with problems of internal composition and national unity.

A resolution to the problems of particular countries will not result from solving the question of the correct theoretical unifying principle. A consideration of the theoretical unifying principle can give insight into the depth of the conflict. The study can make clear the patience needed to avoid exacerbating existing divisions. This theoretical knowledge will complement the historical, economic, cultural, and sociological dimensions of the problem. All these factors must be known and utilized in any attempt to improve the situation.

Humankind meets in many different ways and at many different levels. Face-to-face contact in itself involves many different things. In any meeting there is the contact of behavior, opinion, attitudes, beliefs, values, and theory. From a theoretical perspective the dimensions of human contact may be diagrammed in this manner:

PERSON
|
THEORY
|
VALUES
|
BELIEFS
|
ATTITUDES
|
OPINION
|
BEHAVIOR
|
PERSON

It is easiest to meet and interact with the person. Sometimes we meet the person from the theory perspective, sometimes from the behavior. Each step further into the person is complex and difficult. Theory constitutes a summary attempt to describe and understand human activities. Because theory is complex and difficult and because each of the preceding steps has not been traversed does not mean that theory should be avoided. Where it is avoided, behavior is the dominant way in which individuals are known. There is nothing wrong with this in itself. It should be noticed, however, that we are constantly pushing beyond that point to "understand." Theory accepts, indeed embraces, the effort to understand.

The discussion in this chapter of the unifying principle of the state is a plunge into the theory dimension of the person. If theory is good it will explain behavior. As a bonus, it will be more parsimonious. If one were to explain the state starting from behavior, one would (as was discussed in the chapter on methodology) never reach beyond the level of statistical generalizations and partially sufficient conditions for causal situations. It is the old situation of missing the forest for the trees, or, more likely once again, the twigs!

NOTES

1. David Easton, "The Political System Besieged by the State," *Political Theory*, Vol. 9, No. 3, August 1981, pp. 303-325.

2. Gabriel Almond and G. Bingham Powell, Jr., *Comparative Politics* (Boston: Little, Brown, 1966), p. 16.

3. Don Bowen, *Political Behavior of the American Public* (Columbus, Oh.: Ch. E. Merrill, 1968), p. 10.

4. *The New York Times,* September 20, 1967.

5. *Wall Street Journal,* August 25, 1969.

6. *The New York Times,* September 20, 1967.

7. *The New York Times,* September 15, 1968.

8. Hegel, *Philosophy of Law*, found in William Ebenstein, *Great Political Thinkers* (Hinsdale, Ill.: Dryden Press, 1969), pp. 618-619.

9. As reported in *The New York Times,* November 16, 1969. Similar formulations of a definition of synergy are found in most of Fuller's many writings.

10. Krupsdanam J. B. Bella, "Is India a Nation?" *Journal of South Asian and Middle Eastern Studies,* Winter 1980, pp. 49-70.

CHAPTER FIVE
POLITICAL
AUTHORITY/SOVEREIGNTY

It may come as somewhat of a disappointment to learn that the previous discussion has not been necessarily about the state. The discussion could just as easily have been about corporations. Political sounding terms such as state, government, citizens, and territory have been used. Nonpolitical terms could just as easily have been used. Corporation, management, personnel, and property would fit nicely. The various theories of unifying principles can then be applied to corporations as they were applied to states. One corporation, Sperry Rand (to mention them for a final time), could be synergistic in its corporate makeup. Another's corporate unity could be mechanistic. In this case the corporate whole would merely be the sum of its component divisions. General Motors might fit that mechanistic category.

A third corporate form could be organismic. Here a spiritual force is said to inspire and guide the corporate existence. Claimants to this structure are rare in American experience, with the possible exception of some entities like the Amana Corporation. It is not as rare in non-Western settings, where the corporate structure is often perceived in a more godlike fashion.

What Makes the State Different?

The use of political or nonpolitical terms does not determine the political quality of an entity. The political quality is determined by some unique feature which describes or explains why one entity defers to another, why the corporation defers to the state. The unique feature of the state explains why when the government says to a corporation, "Jump!" the corporation ends up saying, "How far?" What the state possesses that makes it unique is said to be "political authority" or "sovereignty." Sovereignty is a term like state which, as explained earlier, some authors say is badly culture-bound and which therefore should not be used in political science.

Origin of the Term "Sovereignty"

It is true that the origin of the term sovereignty is tied to the rise of the centralized monarchy and a territorial national state in western Europe. Jean Bodin, a French theorist, coined the term in the late sixteenth century under circumstances of great religious feuding which threatened the breakdown of the state. Bodin felt that the disagreements about the responsible implementation of authority could be avoided by recognizing the king's "supreme power over citizen and subjects." This supreme power was called sovereignty. Bodin's definition or explanation of sovereignty can only be understood in terms of Bodin's purpose. Bodin sought to focus attention on the king and the state in order to get away from scandalous religious disputes which were destroying France.

The focus of political discussion did change and France survived; whether Bodin was responsible need not be examined. The term sovereignty did become widely used. The concept or reality which the term represented, however, was not new with Bodin. Supreme power over citizen and subject is not fundamentally different from the "supreme authority" to which Cicero had referred seventeen centuries earlier, nor is it different from the "supreme power" of the state referred to even earlier by Aristotle. However culture-bound the modern term, the concept is ancient. It continues to accommodate the diversity of Greece, Rome, and Europe, as well as America, Africa, and Asia.

THREE VIEWS OF SOVEREIGNTY

Whatever the history of the term sovereignty, there is an important debate about the meaning of the concept. Often there is a desire to avoid the debate because it is unpleasant and because it has not been settled. This desire is understandable enough. As the desire succeeds there is an unfortunate consequence of missing one of the crucial considerations in politics. By avoiding the debate on the meaning of sovereignty a basic consideration of the range and limit of political decisions is overlooked.

Absolute

On the one side of the debate on authority—the terms sovereignty and authority will be used here interchangeably—are those who maintain that it means the absolute, complete, and unlimited power of the state over the life, rights, and duties of every one of its members. In a word this position views the state as "absolute." The reason individuals, businesses, groups, or whatever, obey the government is because there is no other choice. There may be deviations from this expectation but according to the absolute view they are precisely deviations. Order should be restored and the law enforced according to the absolute position.

Relative

To this absolutist view there is opposed what may be called a relativist view. This second position maintains that the state is on the same level as other institutions and denies that the authority of the state is essentially different from that of corporate associations. In this last view authority is "relative" to time and place. In this view prior to the sixteenth century, in the feudal milieu, the state was not absolute, but during modern times the state may have become absolute. For a variety of reasons, according to this position, the situation has changed. The absolute state is in the process of being replaced by other social arrangements.

John Kenneth Galbraith talks about the emergence of the "corporate state"[1] and Charles E. Lindblom speaks of public policy made by corporations.[2] These views are within the relativistic framework. The authors do not address the theoretical topic formally, nor do they advocate a relativist view as such. They simply describe what they observe in the behavior of corporations. The corporation may become or may already be dominant. Many corporate apologists severely critical of the large role of government are oblivious to the large role of corporations. The decision on the location of a headquarters building or plant has a dramatic effect on a local government or school district's tax base. The decision will affect teachers' salaries, educational programs, swimming pools, day-care centers. The decision makers are neither elected by nor answerable to the affected community. Theirs is an exercise of corporate sovereignty touching the political realm, corporate sovereignty replacing local political sovereignty.

Another example of the replacement is the recent display of power by the banking community. International banking agencies acting for large private banks who supply the funds have forced countries such as Poland, Brazil, Argentina, and the Philippines into policy and structural changes to avoid sanctions from the financiers. These may not be Galbraith's or Lindblom's versions of the new industrial state. They do give some credence, however, to the general proposition of the relative view of sovereignty. The role of multinational corporations in developing countries gives further substance to the view. What is a more difficult proposition, and this is what Galbraith, Lindblom, and others attempt, is to show the extent to which corporations have replaced political sovereignty in developed countries.

Responsible

Opposed to both the absolutist view and the relative view of sovereignty is one that can be called "responsible" or "proper" sovereignty. This third view, for which there is not much literature, merely strikes the logical alternative to the other two. It holds that the state's authority should be neither absolute nor relative. It maintains that there should be a certain "proper" activity for government and all units in society. The authority of the state should be neither too great nor too little. Government, in this view, should not interfere unduly with corporations and it should not shrink from intervening where appropriate.

What is proper, where the line of responsibility can be drawn, and what is appropriate, is not immediately specified. This unspecified character makes this third position appear weak in comparison to the other two views, whose contents are more self-specifying. Once again we should be reminded of our logical duties. Because something is not immediately apparent does not mean that it should be abandoned. Such impatience is neither intellectually nor practically wise. The way to specify the content of responsible authority requires inquiry into more concrete experience of authority before the theoretical positions can be debated.

POPULAR SOVEREIGNTY
AND LEGAL SOVEREIGNTY

Most students have come across the term sovereignty before in two different contexts, one as popular sovereignty, and the other as legal sovereignty. Popular sovereignty, sometimes called political sovereignty, is associated in American and English tradition with authority coming from the people. It is a notion that the authority of the state resides in and flows from the people. In exactly what character it resides or exactly how it flows from the people is usually not specified.

The government deriving its "just power from the consent of the governed," as stated in the Declaration of Independence, is an expression of popular sovereignty. History texts and some introductory American government texts frequently explain sovereignty in this way. Sometimes popular sovereignty is associated with direct democracy. It suggests that since the people possess authority they can rule themselves directly without any specific ruling personnel. As discussed in Chapter 1 on democracy there are theoretical and practical arguments against the assumption of direct democracy. That caveat, however, need not weaken the character of popular sovereignty. It is perfectly possible for the authority to come "from" the people, as Cicero's *res populi* and the Declaration of Independence suggest, without it being exercised by them all the time. This will be discussed more in the next chapter.

The other context from which students may know the term sovereignty is that of legal sovereignty. Upon first mention this may appear unfounded. Few of us can remember any contact with legal sovereignty. However, everyone has an awareness that courts and other legal bodies make binding decisions. Whether dealing with a simple traffic ticket, a zoning law, or a major constitutional issue some final rule-making authority is accepted. That decision, or the framework within which it is made, is the legal sovereign. The character of legal sovereignty is more definite and specific than popular sovereignty. It is found in some agency or person. One knows that there is a final disposition of one's case. One knows who decides the case.

There is no vague reference to a decision by the people in matters of legal sovereignty. Occasionally there may be some allusion to a constitutional amendment or a decision by the ballot box in some legal controversies. For the most part such allusions are more rhetoric than substance. The rhetoric occupies the attention of large numbers of people. The rhetoric of appeal beyond the legal authorities does not, except in exceedingly rare instances, change the legal decision. Proof of this can be found in the small number of popular referendum amendments to the United States Constitution. The specific amendments will be discussed in a later chapter on constitutionalism; in the present context the only amendments which might be said to have been brought about by popular acclaim are those on women's suffrage and prohibition. Most of the other amendments are really extensions of the legal environment instead of the other way around. This relationship between popular referendum and legal decision making brings to the fore again the question of how authority, which is said to reside in the people, exactly flows from them. That question of the relation of popular and legal sovereignty must be postponed until the full character of legal sovereignty has been explained.

ATTRIBUTES OF LEGAL SOVEREIGNTY

The specific or inherent characteristics of an item are its attributes. By knowing the attributes of legal sovereignty it will be possible to appreciate better what the unique authority of the state is supposed to be. Understanding the ascribed attributes may make it possible to finally decide between the absolute, relative, and so-called proper views of political authority.

The plan in this discussion is to describe how authority behaves and how it is regarded in order to determine whether it is absolute, relative, or proper. This should make it possible to decide whether sovereignty is indeed unique or merely an historical convention. Such a plan might entail a multivolume effort. Here we will only review the attributes ascribed to legal sovereignty and attempt to understand their implications. That should give enough information to appreciate fully what the state is all about, which will lead into the more general questions of its range and limit.

Determinate

The attributes of legal sovereignty are determinate, indivisible, and omnicompetent. *Determinate* means that legal authority is found in some definite agency, body, person, or other specified entity. In England it is said to be located in Parliament. In an absolute monarchy it is located in the king. In the United States it is located in the national government. Some would prefer to say that in the United States it is located in the Constitution or in some amending process. The alternative designation avoids difficulties associated with the American concept of federalism. The Constitution or the amending process, however, are not concrete. There is in them the vagueness and diffusiveness of popular sovereignty. Popular sovereignty may indeed be expressed in these constitutional forms. However it is legal, not popular, sovereignty which is currently being analyzed.

The point under consideration is that in every state, in every political system, some rule-making, decision-making, or policy-making body can be found. There is no question that "authoritative decision making" is central to the political system whatever the process of input, environment, or feedback. Wherever decision-making authority is found there is the determinate legal sovereign. Such a role does not disappear when the names change. That functional role of someone making decisions is the determinant authority.

Indivisible

That legal sovereignty is *indivisible* also means exactly what it says. If it takes both houses of a legislative body to pass a law then the combination of houses is the determinate legal authority. If it takes the agreement of the legislative and executive branches and the acquiescence of the judicial branch to make law then legal sovereignty is located there. There is no question about the legal authority being indivisible in most countries other than the United States. Most countries are like England in governmental form where there is one universally recognized authority.

The legal arrangement in the United States is such that sometimes it takes all three branches for something to be legal. At other times one or two branches is adequate for a binding legal decision. The point about the indivisibility of legal authority is that no two decision makers are equal such that they both can make binding but opposite decisions. At times it may appear that legal authority is divided in the United States. The press speaks of division much more than it actually occurs. Points of division, "constitutional crisis," are rare and have for the most part dissipated over time. There have been lively debates about which branch of government is legally superior. Different answers come according to particular historical settings. It is clear though that no definitive answer is theoretically or practically possible. The branches of the government do not represent warring factions. If they did the result would soon be a divided country. The rivalry between the branches is a popular media lore. There is less substance to it, as will be discussed in a later chapter, than the titillation would suggest.

A graver challenge within the United States to the notion of indivisible authority is the idea of federalism. Federalism, which also will be discussed in a later, separate chapter, means to many that authority is divided between the national government and the states. For the present and to the point of indivisibility it can be noted that the issue was argued at length in the early years of the nation. Most especially sovereignty was argued in the famous Webster-Calhoun debates of the late 1820s and early 1830s. Daniel Webster, supposedly arguing the position of the north and in defense of the nation, presented the so-called federal notion. He argued that sovereignty is divided between the states and the national government but the nation is one. John C. Calhoun, spokesman of the south, argued in more eloquent rhetoric and more consistent logic that sovereignty was "like chastity; it cannot be surrendered in part."[3]

Calhoun was as sound in his theory as he was vivid in his imagery. He was, however, incorrect. He was incorrect in how the theory was applied. The states did not have sovereignty, as Calhoun would have liked. The national government had it. Some readers of historical (hysterical?) inclination may want to dispute the locus of sovereignty. To blunt that quarrel until it can be addressed at length, let us acknowledge that for Calhoun, Webster, or anyone else in any specific situation some final decision-making authority settles disputes. Some *one* making a decision is the point of sovereignty being indivisible. The national government and the states do not make equal but opposed decisions. If that were the case there soon would be no nation. The idea of divided jurisdictions merely hides from the issue. Eventually the main issue must reappear in jurisdictional disputes.

The reason some answers to the question of the locus of sovereignty in the United States are in constitutional terms is to avoid this federalism confusion. It was not avoided here, nor was it settled. If the complexity of government is to be fully appreciated it must be acknowledged. After it is acknowledged it must be held in abeyance while additional points are considered. The attribute that sovereignty would be indivisible can be appreciated in its theoretical form even though its exact practical application may be unclear in some respects in the United States.

Those of us in the United States looking at other countries have no difficulty in finding their sovereignty undivided. Whether in a so-called federal system or in so-called unitary (most) states, we perceive them as undivided. We may observe disputes about authority from time to time but those disputes are over "who" shall possess and exercise authority, not over its equal division. There is no dispute about the location of sovereignty unless there is a rare though real case of secession.

Omnicompetent

Omnicompetence, the third attribute, means finality or completeness. It means there is no restriction on legal sovereignty; some legal body makes final decisions. It could declare murder legal, it could abolish private property, or it could abrogate freedom of speech or religious worship. If some higher body would annul the earlier decisions, that later body would be the legal sovereign.

It is acknowledged that Parliament in England could do all these things and that there is no higher legal body to overrule them. The same is true in all countries once the legal authority is located. In the United States the Supreme Court is frequently cast in the role of the body which makes unpleasant binding decisions. That view of the Court is not exactly accurate. Congress or the President can or could have a role in such matters. To claim recourse to the constitutional amending process may be comforting to some but it should be noted, and usually is not, that then the amending process has precisely those omnicompetent qualities. Refuge in the popular sovereignty dimensions of the Constitution will not disguise the attributes of legal authority. However one takes it, by pointing to a particular person, agency, collection of branches, or to a process, the legal decision-making authority is indivisible, final, and complete.

LIMITATIONS ON LEGAL SOVEREIGNTY

Having said that authority is omnicompetent, there is some need, if it is be understood concretely, to consider what limitations exist on it. This consideration is nothing more than an extension of the examination of the attributes of sovereignty. The purpose of the extension is to fully understand the ascribed character of legal authority. That understanding is preparation for evaluating the nature and end of the state and political authority.

Limitations on sovereignty are traditionally said to be the natural or moral law, human behavior and popular will, and the facts of international life. All three limits are called natural. "Natural" suggests that they arise like signposts in the desert of tyranny, saying "Halt!" to the further advance of despotism. In this way it is assumed that there is a natural or automatic barrier to authority becoming all-powerful, absolute, and unlimited.

Moral Law as a Limit

The natural moral law limitation assumes, for example, that the ethical and moral purposes of the state limit its jurisdiction and authority. Accordingly, those acts of the state which are contrary to morality, which abuse the dignity of human beings, lack the character of legitimacy and are not binding on the individual citizen. That sounds good. Obviously, however, it has had no affect on the dictators of history, Hitler for example. This alleged moral limitation was of no help to the Jews in Nazi Germany who were sent to ovens as victims of a false and immoral doctrine. One could imagine someone standing just outside the door of those human crematoriums whispering in the ear of those who passed, "Psst, you don't have to go in there because it's against the natural moral law." It is not hard to picture who would be first shoved in.

There is no guarantee that the moral law, be it natural or not, will prevent immoral practices. A careful student of natural moral law would recognize that its effect can be destroyed. Aristotle, though he argued in defense of natural moral law, acknowledged[4] that "virtue and vice respectively preserve and destroy first principles." He was saying that the first principles of moral law ought to be preserved but they can be destroyed. If first principles are destroyed by repeated acts which ignore them, then Hitler is possible. That there are many moral citizens under such a tyrant is no guarantee that they will act morally. If the tyrant possesses sufficient power, the tyrant can prevail. This is not to say that morality will always be ignored. It is to recognize that morality has been and can be ignored.

Human Nature as a Limit

The same general observations are true with respect to the alleged limit on legal authority labeled "human behavior and popular will." This second limit contends that no matter how despotic a government becomes it can never totally ignore the customs, beliefs, and practices of a people. It is maintained [5] that the legally omnicompetent British Parliament would no more dare to enact a law abolishing freedom of speech or popular elections than Mussolini would have attempted to legally abolish the practice of Catholicism in Italy.

The contention is that even a tyrant is limited by the psychology of human behavior. In a metaphysical sense that may be true. In a practical sense, in the political world the psychology of human behavior can be effectively manipulated by a dictator. The skillful tyrant would see that it is not necessary to abolish Catholicism in Italy or freedom of speech or popular elections in England. At least the would-be tyrant would not do these things first. These items can be abolished later if it is still important to abolish them.

If the tyrant could have his way in all things important to ruling then it would be unnecessary to abolish the practice of a religion, freedom of speech, or popular elections. The tyrant could let the public have its ''toys,'' so to speak. This appears confirmed in a number of Western democratic nations in the contemporary world, at least according to the critics of those nations. (The reader should pick her or his own examples.) Hitler was popularly elected and popularly supported until the people could no longer control him. The skillful control of the flow of information was key to his establishing absolute rule.

Thus, contrary to the assumption of a natural limit, human behavior and popular will can be undermined. Mass brainwashing is possible. Hitler created a situation which the people then followed. They followed Hitler because they were led to think that what he allowed them to hear was true. We know today that they were misled. At the time the people's ability to challenge the regime was limited institutionally and circumscribed by governmental control of the media. Even the German Catholic bishops, for example, who have been criticized for not challenging Hitler, found that out. As they attempted to challenge practices of the regime, bishops found curates arrested and executed on fraudulently concocted charges.[6]

What is known today is that Hitler was evil and ''should'' have been stopped. That ''should'' is based on the assumption that at any given time tyranny can be restrained just by activating some mechanism. That assumption overlooks the particular circumstances of the regime in question. It overlooks the fractionalized and the necessarily part-time character of those who might be opposed. The belief that, knowing the dangers from this Hitler experience, a futuristic *1984* and *Brave New World* can be avoided is false. A complacency in that belief makes the undesirable possible.

The belief in popular will limiting tyrannical government is supported by the cases where popular reaction has overturned unpopular legislation. The repeal of the Eighteenth (prohibition) Amendment in the United States serves as an example. Next time, such a sweeping policy objective may be accomplished by less direct means. An ''educational'' campaign may be launched extending from nursery school through elementary grades; advertising of the item in question may be banned; and "opposed" commercials may be government sponsored. With such preliminaries there will be no need for a constitutional amendment. A glance at the statistics on the declining per capita use of tobacco by Americans confirm this manipulative capability.

Facts of International Politics as a Limit

The limitation on legal authority that did curtail Hitler was "the facts of international life." By this third limit is meant that the mere existence of other states limits or comes to limit in varying degrees the power of a government within its own boundaries. The effectiveness of this alleged limit may be questioned since many atrocities may occur before notice is taken or intervention is threatened by an external nation. Usually an "international" incident is necessary as an excuse before a sanction can be carried out by external states. Hitler's direct aggression against Poland was the occasion for the Allied countries to finally intervene after a series of indirect aggressions and rumors of internal atrocities evoked only verbal reactions. Again, a skillful tyrant can reduce or even eliminate the factors which provoke intervention.

There is much concern today about the abuse of human rights. "Amnesty International" is a voluntary group of international citizens that looks into alleged human rights violations in various countries. The abuses are found especially in, but not limited to, developing countries. Frequently the only recourse against such abuses is unfavorable publicity. Unfortunately, publicity does not have a great effect on many countries, particularly those that control their media. Some countries become immune from sanctions and scrutiny because they are or become the wards of one or the other of the superpowers. The attempt to invoke sanctions against a "protected" country could result in Soviet/US conflagration. If the ward country is pushed too hard by its protector it can threaten to switch to the other superpower and alter the strategic balance in that particular region. Such are the intricacies and encumbrances on international sanctions for the abuse of internal authority.

The alleged limitation is further circumscribed by the consideration that the long and complicated agreement of mutual "detente" with one's primary adversary can free both parties to do what they please in their own domain. To disrupt detente would be ungentlemanly and would indeed require a more severe provocation than if the agreement did not exist. For these reasons the facts of international life, as with the first two alleged limits, are no internal barrier to the omnicompetent legal authority being all-powerful, absolute, and unlimited.

CONCLUSION AND PERSPECTIVE

The point of the discussion of the limits on legal sovereignty is that they do not limit in any natural or automatic way. They can be overcome by a skillful would-be tyrant. In final analysis the attribute of omnicompetence means just that, omnicompetence. The government, any government, could become all-powerful, absolute, and unlimited. Technology makes this even more possible today. The late Frank Church, when he was chairman of the Senate Select Committee on Intelligence Activities, made a revealing remark which brings this point out well:

> In the need to develop a capacity to know what potential enemies are doing, the United States government has perfected a technological capability that enables us to monitor the messages that go through the air. These messages are between ships at sea, they could be between units, military units in the field; we have a very extensive capability of intercepting messages wherever they may be in the airwaves. That is necessary and important to the United States as we look abroad at enemies or potential enemies. We must know.
>
> At the same time that capability at any time could be turned around on the American people and no American would have any privacy left, such is the capability to monitor everything: telephone conversations, telegrams, it doesn't matter. There would be no place to hide. If this government ever became a tyranny, if a dictator ever took charge in this country, the technological capacity that the intelligence community has given the government could enable it to impose total tyranny, and there would be no way to fight back because the most careful effort to combine together in resistance to the government, no matter how privately it was done, is within the reach of the government to know. Such is the capability of this technology.[7]

What can be concluded from Church's remarks is that tyranny is possible anywhere. Church was not advocating tyranny; he wished to avoid it. He was indicating how technology makes tyranny possible.

A political response to the possibility of tyranny anywhere might be that vigilance is necessary. "Eternal vigilance is the price of liberty," Jefferson and many others are quoted as having said. Vigilance may take the form of curbing the activities of the CIA, the FBI, and the government in general. Vigilance is useful but not enough. It may be misguided. Restrictions on the CIA and the FBI could give unreasonable freedom to the KGB and genuine subversions. Vigilance can lead to vigilantism, which is an equal form of tyranny. A more formidable check on tyranny would be to know the basis for the control of the state (the subject of the next chapter).

Three questions have been left unsettled in this chapter: (1) the question as to whether sovereignty in broad perspective is really absolute, relative, or proper, (2) the question of the content of "proper sovereignty," and (3) the question of the relationship between popular sovereignty and legal sovereignty, how the one "flows into" the other. The first question was not settled in the discussion about the attributes of legal sovereignty or in the examination of the alleged limits on authority. The attributes and lack of limits only point to the *possibility* of absoluteness, not its necessity. Thus the question of the overall character of sovereignty is still open. So is the matter of the content of so-called proper sovereignty. Answers to these many questions will become available with the development of an understanding of the origin of the state. The different views of the origin of the state reveal the character of the state and the basis to control it.

NOTES

1. John Kenneth Galbraith, *The New Industrial State* (Boston: Houghton Mifflin, 1967).

2. Charles E. Lindblom, *Politics and Markets* (New York: Basic Books, 1978).

3. Quoted in Harry V. Jaffa, *Liberty and Equality* (New York: Oxford University Press, 1965), p. 131.

4. Aristotle, *Ethics,* VII, 1151a, 15.

5. These arguments about the limitations, and indeed even the attributes, of legal sovereignty follow the general development in Henry J. Schmandt and Paul G. Steinbicker, *Fundamentals of Government* (Milwaukee: Bruce Publishing Co., 1963). They are, however, turned to make a point different from that of those authors.

6. cf. Guenther Levy, *The Catholic Church and Nazi Germany* (New York: McGraw-Hill, 1964).

7. "Meet the Press," NBC News, Sunday, August 17, 1975.

CHAPTER SIX
THE ORIGIN/CONTROL OF THE STATE

The origin of the state appears to be of historical interest only. That impression is incorrect. Of course there is an historical dimension to the origin of the state, and it preoccupies the attention of many. There is, however, an eventual realization that such knowledge carries little practical information, and with no useful knowledge attained, the examination is abandoned. Such thinking fails to take into account that the origin of the state must be viewed in a double sense.

There is an historical sense of origin and there is a philosophical sense of origin. The latter is much more critical. It spells the basis for control of the state. It will be described at length after a brief look at historical origin.

HISTORICAL ORIGINS

An unusual aspect of the historical origin of the state is that although it comes in three varieties—force, kinship, and social contract—all three can be true. In discussing the nature of the unifying element of the state and in discussing the nature of sovereignty, three theories were confronted, but it was understood that only one could be correct. The same exclusiveness will be the case for the philosophical origin of the state and the purpose of the state. Here, on the historical origin, that is not so.

The force theory maintains that the state, a particular state, originated in the efforts of one great man or group who organized a diverse community into one nation. Charlemagne served this role in France. Simón Bolívar did so in a number of Latin American states. The kinship theory, on the other hand, holds that the state is the product of an evolution from the family and a community of blood relationship. Many nations can claim this evolutionary origin. Obvious examples are the biblical and current state of Israel, as well as many African and Asian nations. The so-called captive nations of eastern Europe and the secessionist movements within many other countries lay claim to such roots. The social contract, which is most prominently exemplified in the United States, holds that the state is the result of representatives of various communities coming together and agreeing to form a larger unit.

Those who study a particular country may dispute which theory of historical origin fits. Some may claim social contract origin for Israel by pointing to the agreements in the 1940s which brought about its current form. Some would maintain that Israel both biblically and historically is a product of force.

Looking to George Washington as an early Simón Bolívar, one could hold that despite the appearance of social contract, the United States is really a force example. In many respects some economic interpretations of the origins of the United States wittingly or unwittingly fit into this mold. France might be viewed as an example of kinship origin rather than force.

Summary views about the historical origin of states give no definitive information. The exact origin of any particular state and a generalization about all states can never be given. What is more important, it does not matter. Historical information is of curiosity value only. As explained earlier, in discussion of history as a discipline, the immediate practical consequences of knowledge about historical events are remote at best. Here for example, no matter what the historical origin of a particular state, no information is provided or justifiably implied in that origin which would bind an individual today to the dictates of the successor governments.

A citizen in any of the states mentioned may be told that the "founding fathers" desired their acceptance of the rules and practices of the successive governments. That justification can be rejected as arbitrary and artificial. It may be true that the founders desired such compliance but there is no binding quality to that desire. Historical justifications in themselves are always arbitrary and artificial. They are subject to the convenience of the immediate interpreter. Such justifications are not acceptable even if—which is impossible—conditions have not changed since the beginning. To bind the individual today, to justify the individual's acceptance of today's rules of this particular government under this particular constitution in this particular state, some explanation must be given which cuts across historical forms.

Some justification must be given which binds the individual of today with the historical conditions, no matter what the form. The individual living today in France or Israel or the United States or any country must be tied in an nonarbitrary way to the state. Unless there is some personal tie, justifications for compliance and allegiance quickly break down. The philosophical theories of the origin of the state provide explanations of personal involvement.

PHILOSOPHICAL-LOGICAL-LEGAL ORIGIN

The philosophical origin of the state may be renamed the philosophical-logical-legal origin of the state. This elongated name better conveys the concept it represents than does the shorter, one-word name. The philosophical origin as opposed to the historical origin is like any philosophical examination of a topic. It attempts to get an X-ray, so to speak, of the entity instead of an external description. In this instance, to know why an individual is bound to a state today as yesterday or a century ago is different from knowing what the ascribed forefathers did.

There are three versions of the philosophical origin of the state. As with the unifying principle of the state and the nature of legal sovereignty/authority, only one version is correct. Whichever is the correct one, it is applicable to all three of the historical forms. The three explanations of the state are called divine, social contract, and natural. These theories claim to answer the question of why the individual should accept what was done by the founders, who did not know today's circumstances. Those who live in the Philadelphia area or who are fortunate enough to visit the beautifully preserved and restored Independence Hall and Park area have visible evidence that the founding fathers did not know them. With the skyscrapers surrounding the low-profile original buildings no one can question that the country today is significantly different from two hundred years ago.

The divine, social contract, and natural theories, respectively, would answer the question of why one is bound to the state in the following manner, "God wills it," "the majority wills it," "your better self wills it." To these three answers one might reply, again respectively, "Ergo I am not free," "I am oppressed," "I will it." The third theory seems favored in these interchanges. As promised earlier, that seeming imbalance will be adjusted in the elaboration on each theory which follows and in the next chapter. The point of these short preview answers is to show that the philosophical approach attempts a type of answer which is different in kind from the historical ones. Each, though, links the individual to the state in a special way.

Divine or Determinative Origin

The divine origin theory, although it uses the terms "divine" or "God," need not be taken in any religious or theological sense. It could also be called the "determinative" origin theory. By divine, as with determinative, what is meant is that some force over which the individual has no control brings about the existence and continuation of the state. This force can be God, or Hegel's *geist*, or a biological force, or the deterministic developmental stages of the Swiss theorist Piaget.

There are serious and there are popularized expressions of this divine origin theory. James I of England or Louis XV of France may claim that God ordained them to be king. President McKinley may claim that God inspired him to retain the Philippines after the Spanish-American war. Jews may claim that they are building Israel because of God's directive, and supporters of Ronald Reagan may claim that he was spared from an assassin's bullet "by the hand of God . . . for a purpose." These claims may be looked on as real or rhetorical. As rhetoric they form a cover for raw power, imperial fact, or a hidden biological pecking order. They may be an elitist self-justification in language pacifying to the ignorant.

Hegel, as mentioned earlier, saw the state as "the march of God in the world." Many today see their brand of liberation or order as God's plan for humankind. The origin of the state and succession within it are viewed in this philosophical theory as a product of spiritual, biological, or environmental forces. In biological terms the state's origin is said to be in a gregarious instinct as in the herd or flock of animals. Various embellishments of the suggestiveness of this biological theory are found in recent writings on biopolitics and sociobiology as well as in popularized writings of Morris and Ardrey mentioned earlier.

The critical point of the divine or determinative theory is that human beings do not control the state. As a consequence humans are not free. By definition the origin of the state is in some force over which the individual has no control. Charlemagne, the founding fathers, the original clan, the historical majority, all are products of the uncontrolled force, whether it be identified as the environment, culture, God, or whatever. The only benefit from this knowledge is a heightened appreciation of the human condition. For practical purposes no change can be effected by it.

Hegel saw his theorizing as "painting gray on gray." Peoples' destinies in this view are set. One studies political signs as one reads the daily astrology reports or the biorhythm charts. It may be consoling to know or understand what is going to occur but the outcome is inevitable. Political science in this view can move beyond false theories of freedom and dignity by seeing that behavior is patterned and predictable. By measuring men's movements sufficiently it will be found that their behavior is as predictable as molecules in a gas. The National Safety Council already does well in predicting the number of traffic deaths on a holiday weekend. Sample opinion polls are statistically reliable for a universal population. Conflict situation responses are predictable. Voting seems hardly necessary because of preelection forecasts.

There are indeed signs that an outside force "informs" human behavior. From "economic man" to econometrics, from "Freudian slips" to biological determinism, from "history repeating itself" to developmental stages, from "fate" to "futuristics," various forms of determinism find favor in scholarly and ordinary discourse. American and generally Western forms of describing the state may have overcome the crude forms of determinism of Hegel, Marx, James I, or McKinley, but the disguised versions just mentioned reveal its presence. We may not regard the President as the father of the nation-family as the Japanese regard the Emperor or as Sadat claimed he was regarded in Egypt. We may all be, however, like ants on a log floating down the river, each thinking we control the direction.

The divine or determinative theory is like the organismic theory of the unifying element of the state: not flattering. It also is not to be dismissed in a casual manner. Many popular contemporary philosophies, those of Camus and Heidegger for example, although not admitting of nineteenth-century determinism, have humans as victims of a "human condition" symbolized in the myth of Sisyphus. They see humanity being thrown in the absurdity of existence contemplating the nudity of the world. Such philosophies and attitudes toward the ruler express the essential element of the divine theory of the origin of the state, that it is not subject to human control.

Social Contract Origin

The philosophical social contract theory holds that the origin of the state is found in some form of voluntary agreement. It is the opposite of the determinative theory. It maintains that in some way, which need not be explicit or overt, humans agree to the existence of the political community. This voluntary agreement is a type of "rational or legal legitimacy," in the words of the German sociologist Max Weber[1], just as determinative origin is a combination of Weber's traditional and charismatic basis of authority. The point of the social contract theory is that humans by their choices control the existence and the direction of the state.

There are, unfortunately for tedium, three different versions of the social contract theory itself. What the three different versions show is that the general theory can fit, as the determinative theory can, a full range of historical situations. This ability must be explicated because there is an inclination to merely associate the philosophical social contract with the historical form, which narrows its applicability.

It must be clear that the philosophical and the historical social contract are different. The historical refers to a particular state with supporting historical conditions. The United States and the activities of the Second Continental Congress are prime examples. The philosophical social contract theory, on the other hand, is meant to explain all states, whether the conditions seem to support it or not. In other words, the philosophical social contract is meant to explain historical events like those of the United States and those of a Charlemagne in France or of states which have evolved from kinship origins.

For explanatory purposes the philosophical social contract can be described as a sequence of events consisting of (a) a state of nature, (b) a contract which is a function of some human control, and (c) the state or the situation which exists following the contract. Described in this way the theory suggests a story line where (a) men originally live in a "state of nature," some original, natural prepolitical condition, and that (b) for some particular reason they enter a contract or agreement, and (c) thereby bring about the existence of the state or whatever it is that the political community is called.

Despite the historical appearance of this story line, the philosophical social contract is not intended to be historical. Unfortunately it is frequently mistaken even by established scholars to be historical. In its philosophical design the social contract intends just the opposite sequence from what the story line suggests. What it intends is (c) to explain the existence of the state (b) by way of a contract (a) so as to avoid what is unacceptable, a state of nature. This understanding of the social contract is supported by examining the different versions of the theory presented by Hobbes, Locke, and Rousseau. Figure 6-1 should be helpful in grasping the story line sequence, the intended sequence, and the key parts of the different versions of the theory.

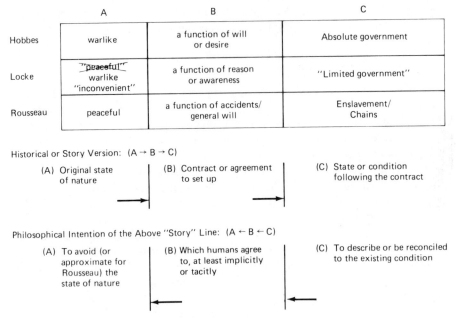

	A	B	C
Hobbes	warlike	a function of will or desire	Absolute government
Locke	~~"peaceful"~~ warlike "inconvenient"	a function of reason or awareness	"Limited government"
Rousseau	peaceful	a function of accidents/ general will	Enslavement/ Chains

Historical or Story Version: (A → B → C)

(A) Original state of nature

(B) Contract or agreement to set up

(C) State or condition following the contract

Philosophical Intention of the Above "Story" Line: (A ← B ← C)

(A) To avoid (or approximate for Rousseau) the state of nature

(B) Which humans agree to, at least implicitly or tacitly

(C) To describe or be reconciled to the existing condition

FIGURE 6-1 Philosophical social contract theory.

Thomas Hobbes

The social contract theories as presented by Hobbes, Locke, and Rousseau are philosophical and not historical, even though their presentations follow the story line closely. Thomas Hobbes, in his *Leviathan*, published in 1651, argued that people originally lived in a warlike "state of nature" where life was solitary, poor, nasty, brutish, and short. In this state of nature the law of the jungle prevailed, meaning that each person had to fend only for himself or herself. As the story goes, desiring to overcome this condition, individuals entered into a contract whereby they established the "Leviathan." They produced the absolute state. Hobbes's Leviathan can in many respects be visualized as somewhat of a Frankenstein monster; it is made from the parts of many persons. The act of creating the state is one in which men

> confer all their power and strength upon one man, or upon one assembly of men, that may reduce all their will, by plurality of voices, unto one will: which is as much as to say, to appoint one man, or assembly of men, to bear their persons, and every one to own and acknowledge himself to be author of whatsoever he that so bears their person shall act, or cause to be acted, in those things which concern the common peace and safety, and therein to submit their will, every one to his will, and their judgments to his judgment. This is more than consent, or concord; it is a real unity of them all, in one and the same person, made by covenant of every man with every man, in such manner as if every man should say to every man, *I authorize and give up my right of governing myself, to this man, or to this assembly of men, on this condition, that thou give up thy right to him, and authorize all his actions in like manner.* [2]

Hobbes goes on to say that this "multitude so united in one person is called a Commonwealth, in Latin, *civitas.*" He calls it the "great *Leviathan,* or to speak more reverently, . . . *mortal god.* . . ." The term leviathan derives from the Hebrew term for a sea monster symbolizing evil, which is ultimately to be defeated by the good. Although Hobbes speaks of our debt to the *mortal god,* "under the *immortal God,*" he twists the original scriptural use of the reference from a monster kept in check by God for man's sake to a monster which dominates men under God. This dominance of men by the monster is reflected in a curious drawing on the title page of the original edition of the *Leviathan* in which a crowned giant, whose body is composed of tiny figures of human beings, overlooks a town. Over the giant is a passage from Job 41:24 saying, "Upon all the earth there is none like him."

Hobbes's meaning is clear; there is a "real unity" in the ruler who dominates all under the approval of the heavens. Hobbes did not mean to say that the state must possess and exercise all power all the time. The state must possess full power so that it can exercise whatever power is necessary to avoid disorder. Hobbes is saying that people desire or will the state in order to avoid anarchy. The state would not need as much exercise of power in 1651 as it might in the 1980s. In either case what is needed is enough power to overcome the state of nature.

The evils of the wars of individuals, of each against each, are such that absolute power is preferable. The ruler who does not possess that power could be replaced by one who does. Without enough power the community would be in danger of falling into the state of nature.

Hobbes's theme can be observed today in the rationale of many martial law regimes and of "law-and-order" candidates for office. These individuals argue that authoritarian rule is needed to overcome and to avoid general disorder and lawlessness. Many easily criticize these modern leviathans. Many others prefer them to the disorders where there is no freedom to walk the street in safety or to tend one's shop or garden in peace. This *preference* for safety is the consent, the agreement, the contract of which the social contract theory speaks. The desire for peace, security, and safety which the regime satisfies is justification for its rules and its power. If the situation is grave enough then absolute exercise of power is justified. That is what Hobbes's theory is saying. It can be seen to strike a responsive contemporary chord.

John Locke

The most widely accepted of the social contract theories is that of John Locke. In his *Two Treatises of Government,* dated 1690, Locke is primarily concerned with "limited government." Locke is usually perceived to view the state of nature differently from Hobbes. For Locke the state of nature ("a" in the sequence) is said to be peaceful, the contract (step "b" in the sequence) is said to be a function of reason, and the state ("c") is expressed as "limited government."

Immediate puzzlement about this version of the story line or the philosophical intention occurs, or should occur. The story does not work. It is not immediately apparent why people would leave a peaceful state of nature to enter a contract and form a government, even a limited one. It is true that Locke insists, against Hobbes, that the state of nature is peaceful:

> And here we have the plain difference between the state of nature and the state of war, which however some men have confounded, are as far distant as a state of peace, goodwill, mutual assistance, and preservation; as a state of enmity, malice, violence and mutual destruction are one from another.[3]

Locke had said in an early part of this work:

> To understand political power aright, and derive it from its original, we must consider, what state all men are naturally in, and that is, a state of perfect freedom to order their actions, and dispose of their possessions and persons, as they think fit, within the bounds of the law of nature, without asking leave, or depending upon the will of any other man.
>
> A state also of equality, wherein all the power and jurisdiction is reciprocal, no one having more than another. . . .[4]

Locke had assured us that "though this be a state of liberty, yet it is not a state of license . . ." since the state of nature "has a law of nature to govern it. . . ." The problem, to repeat, is that if the original condition is indeed peaceful there is no apparent reason to leave it. Locke recognized this peculiarity since he goes on to describe what he calls "inconveniences" in the state of nature.

The inconveniences arise from a consideration of who is going to determine the specifications of the law of nature. Who will judge the law, who will enforce it? To these questions Locke answers that "the execution of the law of nature is . . . put into every man's hands, whereby every one has a right to punish the transgressors of that law to such a degree, as may hinder its violation." The point is unmistakable since he adds, "And if any one in the state of nature may punish another for any evil he has done, every one may do so. . . ."

Clearly this is an inconvenience. Each individual must decide what the law is, when violations occur, and how to enforce it. In other words each individual is legislator, executive, and judge. Locke had expressed this in his opening passage as men doing "as they think fit." Contrary to the reading of many who see Locke's version of the state of nature as peaceful, this condition cited by Locke is just a camouflaged, or Madison Avenue, way of describing the war of each against each.

If everyone does "as he thinks fit," Locke's state of nature is not noticeably different from that described by Hobbes. This changed reading improves an understanding of Locke's social contract theory. If the state of nature is warlike—inconvenient to use Locke's euphemism—then there is in the story line reason to abandon that condition. In the philosophical formulation there is reason to avoid the state of nature. One would reasonably agree to set up limited government to avoid the inconveniences of the state of nature. As it turns out then, the major contrast of Locke with Hobbes is not in the condition of the fictional state of nature. The contrast is in the contract itself and the nature of the state which the contract supports.

The contract is a function of will or desire for Hobbes. For Locke the contract is an expression of man's reason, of his awareness that the state of nature is inconvenient. Government for Hobbes is or can be absolute. For Locke it is always to be "limited." The nature of Locke's "limited government" is of critical importance. It is this individualism and notion of limited government which attracts many to Locke.

The theory of individualism will be described in the next chapter. A conclusion about which theory is preferable should be reserved until at least that time. It should be pointed out now, however, that what Locke intends is that government be precisely limited from doing anything other than overcoming the inconveniences. Locke feels that every individual should be able to do "as he thinks fit," but that the inconveniences interfere with this ability. Government limited to a minimal role makes it more possible for the individual to acquire wealth or do many other things of one's own choosing. Locke's social contract theory therefore easily accommodates laissez faire individualistic views of the state.

This Lockean view can be recognized in contemporary political rhetoric, economic theories, and daily conversations. Its ramifications will be explored later. For the present it is only necessary to see that this version of the social contract theory is saying that this role of government derives from the common agreement that individuals do not want the inconveniences of enforcing the law themselves. They do not want absolute government. They only want to do as they think fit without uncertainty, insecurity, and harm. They do not want to be interfered with as they go about acquiring wealth.

Jean Jacques Rousseau

Rousseau's social contract theory is different from those of both Hobbes and Locke. Although he dislikes government, Rousseau sees a larger role for government than does Locke, even as he condemns its "chains." In many respects Rousseau is the most colorful writer of the three. He dislikes the state and prefers the state of nature which he describes as truly peaceful but unattainable. What is more, there is greater historical realism to his story line. The historical quality should not make any final difference in the acceptance of the theory, but it is also fascinating that his story coincides with biblical depictions of a tranquil Eden.

The opening phrase of Rousseau's *The Social Contract* reads, "Man is born free; and everywhere he is in chains." This means that for him the state of nature is free and peaceful, the state an enslavement. The condition of this enslavement he had made clear in an earlier writing, *Discourse on the Origin of Inequality*, wherein he related that degraded man accepted "the origin of society and law, which bound new fetters on the poor, and gave new powers to the rich; which irretrievably destroyed natural liberty, eternally fixed the law of property and inequality, converted clever usurpation into unalterable rights and, for the advantage of a few ambitious individuals subjected all mankind to perpetual labor, slavery, and wretchedness." The warlike condition described by Hobbes as part of the state of nature is for Rousseau a product of leaving the state of nature. Wretchedness came with the development of private property. Rousseau is critical of both Hobbes's absolute government and Locke's limited government which protects private property.

Rousseau's attitude toward the state of nature as truly peaceful and toward all forms of society as a form of bondage presents a double problem for the social contract theory. The first problem is that the story line does not appear to work. If the state of nature is truly peaceful then there is no explanation either in reason or will to abandon it. The second problem is that the general pattern of philosophical intention does not appear to work either. What exists (''c''), the chains, is undesirable and what is desirable for Rousseau, the peaceful state of nature, (''a'') is generally unattainable. Both problems are resolved by an understanding of Rousseau's transition step (''b''). By a combination of fate and consensus Rousseau fashions an intermediate step which makes both his theory and his story cogent.

In the story line for Rousseau, man left the state of nature because of a series of natural accidents. This expulsion compelled man to invent increasingly elaborate means of survival. The accidents, he says, ''were able to perfect human reason while deteriorating the species.'' What he has in mind is that by being set off from his original condition, man had to invent new devices to aid survival. He invented thinking, then property, and eventually government to protect both the barbarous and the weak. In this connection Rousseau is particularly effective in describing the origin of private property:

> The first person who, having fenced off a plot of ground, took it into his head to say *this is mine* and found people simple enough to believe him, was the true founder of civil society. What crimes, war, murders, what miseries and horrors would the human race have been spared by someone who, uprooting the stakes or filling in the ditch, had shouted to his fellow-men: Beware of listening to this impostor; you are lost if you forget that the fruits belong to all and the earth to no one![5]

The accidents he has in mind are volcanos which caused the fusion of metals and the creation of implements, which in turn produced agricultural tools and weapons. Other physical disruptions produced similar developments. Man learned to adapt to that changed environment. In the process mankind became enslaved to the new development. In other words, man left the state of nature because he had no choice, nature forced it upon him. Here the story line and the philosophical intention conjoin. The ''simple feeling of existence,'' the philosophical goal is desirable. It is unattainable since it is not possible to undo nature. Man must be resigned to his fateful chains.

Although human beings desire the tranquility of the state of nature it is not possible to achieve it. Nature cannot be reconstructed. The human condition is the product of varying adjustments to diverse circumstances. All that man can do is attempt to make the best of a bad situation. This is the role of the general will or consensus for Rousseau. The general will is an attempt to acknowledge man's fate and to approximate the state of nature by being resigned to that fate. Rousseau's writing is a combination of hope and despair, a resignation to chains and a rejection of them. His philosophical position is an environmental determinism and an existential individualism. He would seem at home in twentieth century dour philosophy and literature.

Political fatalism and consensus are expressed in Rousseau's social contract. He describes it as "each man, in giving himself to all, gives himself to nobody; and as there is no associate over which he does not acquire the same right as he yields others over himself, he gains an equivalent for everything he loses, and an increase of force for the preservation of what he has." In this way, he tells us, "each, while uniting himself with all, may still obey himself alone, and remain as free as before." A little later he tells of the need for a "legislator," in effect a dictator, who will instruct the general will. Even here Rousseau's despair is clear, for he admits that to succeed such a legislator "ought to feel himself capable, so to speak, of changing human nature. . . ." This change cannot be brought about because nature in Rousseau's view cannot be changed and because "the legislator occupies . . . an individual and superior function which has nothing in common with human empire. . . ."

It is not hard to see why one commentator spoke of the desperate absurdities of the general will. The general will combines appealing criticism with irreconcilable solutions. It is this combination which may make his fundamental theme so appealing to the advocates of democratic popular control discussed in the first chapter. Criticism of elitism combined with unattainable idealism characterize traditional democracy. The Port Huron Statement's participatory concepts and hidden centrism are vintage Rousseau.

The three versions of the social contract theory are similar in that they impute agreement by the members to the existence of the state. The agreement need not be overt. It need not come about by way of a public referendum. It can be and normally is tacit. Passive consent, resignation, and implied consensus are its trademarks. The "voluntary contractual submission" of the social contract is not written. It can assume written form in some historical expressions, as in the United States. In the law-and-order monarchy or dictatorship, in the consensus "popular democracy," and even in the constitutional republic there is according to the social contract theory an agreement which comes before the regime. It is the fundamental agreement to law and order or to limited government or to the general will.

The theories purport that all mankind desires, finds reasonable, or is resigned to the basic circumstance of the state. The theories are not to be faulted because they lack historical reality. They are not to be faulted because there is no historical or anthropological evidence that such agreements were ever entered into. The theories speak of a philosophical or logical or legal origin of the state, not an historical one. The explanation is "logical," it is not "chronological." The point of the logical origin in a contract is that human control exists. If there is not enough law and order human control can change it, if the "limited government" is not adequate it can be changed, if the general will is unhappy it can undergo change.

The full details and ramifications of the respective social contract theories would require much greater elaboration. The essential character has been identified. The element of control or agreement stands in contrast to the lack of control in the divine or determinative theory. Each of the theories of the origin of the state carry over into respective theories of the purpose of the state.

The linkage of origin and purpose will not be formally developed. The general pattern will be clear. The reader will be able to appreciate a continuity of nature, authority, origin, and purpose. This continuity shows that a determination of the range and limit of government activity is not a matter to be settled by casual preferences. It is a serious interlinkage of many considerations. Before the purpose of the state can be considered, the final theory of the origin of the state must be described.

SOCIO-LOGICAL ORIGIN

The third distinct theory of the origin of the state maintains that the control of the state is neither completely subject to human control nor completely beyond human influence. Frequently this theory is named "natural" on its claim that the state exists by way of human nature and is not an artificial construct. That name, natural, is not being used here since both of the other two theories claim that they are natural, too. Both the determinative theory and the social contract theories read human nature differently, but they nonetheless view themselves as part of nature.

The term "socio-logical" is being used here for the third theory of the origin of the state. The term is being used with a hyphen to distinguish it from the term "sociology." What is meant by socio-logical is that the logic of man's nature understood as a social animal explains the existence of the state. The term sociology, or the unhyphenated sociological does not necessarily imply this logic.

The socio-logical origin theory is Aristotelian. It is Aristotle who claimed that "man is by nature a social and political animal." This view maintains that the state is not purely a product of human control nor is it purely a product of uncontrollable forces. To be "natural" means in this context that "always or for the most part" man would live in society. There can be exceptions to the rule but they are indeed "exceptions." Aristotle had expressed this by observing: "He who is unable to live in society, or who has no need because he is sufficient for himself, must be either a beast or a god."[6]

Aristotle did not go beyond this simple observation and attempt to specify the identifying characteristics of beasts and gods. Because they were so rare, they were self-identifying, and they were not in the realm of the political. The truly nonpolitical and nonsocial person is exceptional. Examples would be limited to the hermit with *no* societal contact. Otherwise pseudo-nonpolitical pretenders live, either figuratively or literally, on the fringe of society in a parasitical dependence on the established order. Such nonpolitical pretense frequently purports godliness on the side of beastliness. The so-called Reverend Jim Jones and his unfortunate People's Temple of Jonestown, Guyana would be a gruesome example.

Most who claim that they are nonpolitical are a far cry from such bizarre events. They are also a far cry from being truly nonpolitical, since they live within and depend upon the existing order. Even those who would desire to change the existing order to one of greater imagined autonomy would be by definition political since they desire some order.

The socio-logical origin theory holds that human beings live in society for two basic reasons. We live in society because of the necessities of life and because of our capabilities. "The state comes into existence," said Aristotle, "originating in the bare needs of life, and continues in existence for the sake of a good life."

On a smaller scale, for example in the family, the same two reasons apply. In the family material necessities of life are provided and, in addition, the ability to share and communicate in an intimate fullness is accomplished. In the family the individual exercises capabilities which are not utilized either in private life or in the larger political community. The intimacy of relationship between the individuals or the entire family is not present in more fleeting social relations. There is a division of labor in the family which provides for the daily material needs. One person is the principal provider, another the principal processor, others are helpers. This division of labor in the family is an economic dimension which, although indeed important, is not the most important ingredient for the socio-logical theory.

The economic dimension of the domestic community is not primary since the family remains a great good even when one no longer depends on it for the necessities of life. College-aged persons can especially appreciate this observation since while frequently in a condition of being self-supporting, they nonetheless love to go home for a holiday or to receive a letter or phone call from a member of their family. That holiday visit or letter are part of "the good life," of living well. The socio-logical origin theory argues that humans would not only live but would live well. Humans live in the community not only because of economic need but because of social need and because of ability. In Aristotle's words,

> Men, even when they do not require one another's help, desire to live together. . . . And we all see that men cling to life even at the cost of enduring great misfortune, seeming to find in life a natural sweetness and happiness.[7]

In every activity, whether piano playing or social living, there is not only its performance, there is its "well" performance. Humankind seeks its own "well" performance in community. Although men and women could live without the community, they could be beastly, they could not live well. Aristotle observed that "man, when perfected, is the best of animals, but when separated from law and justice, he is the worst of all."[8] The family is an attempt at living well through an intimate sharing with another human being. Individuals leave their family of origin and begin to form a new family for purposes not just economic and sexual. They do so for the intimacy of sharing and communicating about life. This is what we observe as individuals pair off in quiet strolls, dine in twosomes, and seek privacy in crowds. All life, its beauty, and its potential are the domain of these two "lovers."

The political community or state, a larger community than the family, is explained by the same economic and social dimensions. As quoted earlier, the state comes into existence for the bare needs of life and it continues in existence for the sake of a good life. Economic sufficiency is a prerequisite of any state. Some obviously fail and their political existence is in jeopardy. This is an especially troubling proposition at a time of international economic superpower competition and threatened insolvency of smaller nations. This real world condition constantly challenges political theory and regularly provides an opportunity for it to show its value.

More important than the economic prerequisite is the social dimension of the state's existence in the socio-logical theory. From the socio-logical perspective, even if the economic needs of the community were somehow provided automatically, the state would continue to exist in fulfillment of the social dimension. This continued existence of the state is contrary to purely economic contract theories which purport that if the economic needs of the community were met then the state could be eliminated. The economic perspective holds that if the state merely provides a traffic cop function and that function were satisfied with electronic traffic signals, then the personnel-operated state could be set aside.

In the socio-logical theory the state is viewed as coming into existence to facilitate the production, distribution, and consumption of material goods, and that it continues in existence for the sake of the good life, for social living. The social factor is like the nonmaterial dimension of sharing and communicating in the family. It is real but nontangible. It is a function or an expression of the ability of a person to extend to the universal community of humankind. More concretely, within the community this ability expresses itself in art, education, religion, athletics, concerts, clubs, and the other means of sharing and communicating.

The sharing and communicating in the civil community are less intimate and of a different character than that between two or a few individuals in the family. Though less intimate, the sharing and communicating in the civil community are no less real or significant. If a person has the ability to communicate to many in a musical concert or in a demonstration of athletic prowess, that concert cannot be performed or the contest played in a chaotic community. Symphony orchestra concerts and international athletic competitions have not been scheduled in Iran or Lebanon in recent years. Since there is a universal need and ability to share and communicate through art, through readings, through religious meetings, through athletic competition, the state exists as expression and fulfillment of that capacity.

By presuming the existence of the individual, the family, and the state, the socio-logical theory reflects a notion of the nature of man which is "multidimensional." By this is meant that it assumes a private or individual dimension, a limited but intimate social dimension, and an extended social dimension whereby communication is universal. That last dimension can be fulfilled only in an orderly community. Through such a community one is able to exercise all one's capacities. It is for this reason that earlier in this chapter, when the respective answers were given to the question of why one should accept the state, the socio-logical answered, "My better self wills it!" Now that "better self" has been introduced. It is the self who would naturally live in the orderly domestic and civil community. It is the self who is able to share and communicate in the family and with all mankind even if the sharing is no more than picnics and good music.

This is the socio-logical view of the origin of the state. Implicit in the view is an acknowledgment that one can choose not to live in the state. One can choose to destroy the state. It is better not to exercise this liberty of contrariety, to rebel against the givenness of things. To reject society is either beastly or godly. Control within the state is doing what is "right," "proper," "responsible," "correct." These control qualities are consonant with human nature. Their implementation is important but it is not automatic. Since, as has been seen, there is disagreement about the content of human nature no set behavior is automatic. To abandon an effort to achieve these qualities because of their difficulty, however, would merely surrender to another theory by default.

CONCLUSION AND PERSPECTIVE

When asked at the beginning of this chapter why one should accept the particular laws of a particular government under a particular constitution in a particular state, three different answers were given. The three answers reflected three different possibilities of control of the state: God wills it therefore I am not free; the majority who specify the contract will it therefore I am oppressed; my better self wills it therefore I will it. This string of alternatives appears to favor, in language if not in argument, the third theory. There is, however, in the third theory a hidden assumption about reality and the nature of human beings which has not yet been fully revealed.

In looking at the purpose of the state each of the theories will be examined one final time and in that examination their full implications will stand out. In that final look the three different theories about the origin or control of the state, the three theories about authority, and the three theories about the nature of the state will be evident as three integrated systems. One theory is still preferred but it does not exist in a way which is utterly convincing to both its predisposed adherents and to its adversaries. If it were so convincing there would be no problem of divergent political views. But there are many divergent views. People take contrary positions because they view political principles differently. It is an awareness of these deeply felt and well-founded principles that one should get out of an introduction to political science. The balance that can be gained from political principles is not just a balance on the scales of logic or worth. It is a balance of reality where all these theories are the contending forces in the daily battles and conflicts of political life.

NOTES

1. Max Weber, *Economy and Society: An Outline of Interpretive Sociology,* Edited by Guenther Roth and Claus Wittich (New York: Bedminster Press, 1968). See esp., Vol. I, Chapter 3 and Vol. III, Chapters 10–15.

2. Thomas Hobbes, *Leviathan* Part II, Chapter 17, paragraph 13.

3. John Locke, *Concerning the True Original Extent and End of Civil Government (Second Treatise on Government),* "Of the State of War," paragraph 19.

4. John Locke, ibid., "Of the State of Nature," paragraph 1.

5. Jean Jacques Rousseau, *On the Origin and Foundation of the Inequality of Mankind,* "The Second Part," paragraph 1. A similar position is argued in his *Social Contract,* Book I, Chapter 9, "Real Property."

6. Aristotle, *Politics,* I, 1253a, 27.

7. Aristotle, ibid., III, 1278b, 21.

8. Aristotle, ibid., I, 1253a, 30-35.

CHAPTER SEVEN
THE PURPOSE
OF THE STATE

Earlier discussion pointed toward three theories of the purpose of the state. Although that anticipation is largely correct, there is some deviation. Collectivism, individualism, and the common good are the primary topics of this chapter. Before we discuss them, a brief consideration will be given to anarchism, which also purports to be a purpose of the state.

Anarchism

Admittedly, the use of the word "purports" in the previous statement is not an objective introduction to anarchism. That subjective introduction was deliberate for several reasons. Anarchism holds that the state should not exist. It regards the state as evil per se. In the anarchist's view the only thing to be done about the state is to eliminate it since there is no justification for one person ruling over another. This view would make it logically and semantically incorrect to include anarchism as a purpose of the state. Despite these reservations a brief description can be given.

There are two varieties of anarchism, evolutionary and revolutionary. Evolutionary anarchism would have no cooperation with the state. It would await the state's eventual decay and collapse as anarchism's noncooperation doctrine spreads from individual to individual. Revolutionary anarchists cannot tolerate any delay in eliminating the evil. They see the evolutionary plan as too slow. More direct and violent efforts to destroy the state are advocated. From such revolutionary attitudes and their occasional implementation all anarchists receive the reputation of bomb throwers.

There are nonviolent and, in fact, quite peaceful anarchists who nonetheless should be recognized as anarchists. Thoreau is one, as are Kropotkin and Buckminster Fuller. Kropotkin in his *Conquest of Bread* (1913) and Fuller in his *Operating Manual for Spaceship Earth* (1969) and other writings would replace government and politicians with engineers and technocrats "who would make things run." It is as if engineering titles would preclude the technocrats from becoming politicians and governing. That view is a surface naivete. One can honestly wonder at times whether even the proponents of this view believe it.

Henry David Thoreau, the American poet and individualist, was more generally instead of technically critical of government. He sought to live on the fringe of society, withdrawing to a cabin on Walden Pond to be free of the world. His poetry is revered by many and his Walden retreat has been preserved as a memorial. An ironic commentary, however, is that it took governmental action to preserve the Pond. It is now subject to a regular parking fee for cars, and swimmers and sunbathers litter the beach. Crowds are such that no one can be "alone" there. In wry sympathy one might say *sic transit gloria mundi*. And so it is for anarchism. That is not a sympathetic presentation. Realistically one has to ask what sympathy could be expected in a consideration of the "purpose" of the state that is practical? Those desiring more attention to anarchism may find comfort later in some of the extreme versions of individualism.

COLLECTIVISM

Collectivism regards the state as an "absolute good." It is the extreme opposite of anarchism since it believes that all worth for the individual is found in and through the state. Hegel's organismic view clearly has this notion of the exaggerated role for the state. The whole which is the state is greater than the sum of its parts and the parts—the individuals—are intended to serve the whole. The view is well expressed by Alfredo Rocco, the philosophical apologist for fascism:

> For Fascism, society has historical and immanent ends of preservation, expansion, improvement, quite distinct from those of the individuals which at a given moment compose it, so distinct in fact that they may be in opposition. Hence the necessity, for which the older doctrines make little allowance, of sacrifice, even up to the total immolation of individuals, in behalf of society. . . . For Fascism society is the end, individuals the means, and its whole life consists in using individuals as instruments for its social end.[1]

There are many different expressions of the collectivist view besides that of fascism. Communism is an obvious example. It is found in other surprising locations as well. In a revealing reaction to criticisms of his book *Beyond Freedom and Dignity,* B. F. Skinner commented:

> I am not doing away with freedom and dignity. I want to go beyond it in a quite progressive sense.
>
> I think that it is clear enough that if people are allowed to have as many children as they want, we are in trouble. If they are allowed to pollute the environment, we are in trouble. I am not interested in imposing restrictions on people. I believe that, somehow or other, we must induce people to take into account things that go beyond their own immediate satisfaction. People do not like to do that, but only the culture which does it is likely to survive. The great question before us is how a culture can induce its members to take its own survival into account. Rome convinced the Romans that it was sweet to die for Rome, and Rome became a great military power. That was fine for Rome but rather rough on the Romans. The Church held up martyrdom as important and that became a great inducement. It was rough on the martyr but great for the Church. Communism made the survival of an economic system the important thing, and the individual then worked harder and he even went to war and lost his life for the system. Now, can we find other ways to get the individual to be aware of the importance of the future of his culture?[2]

Skinner is pointing to the collectivist role of the state and, in his view, the church and communism. At the same time he is seeking "inducements" which will allow for the perpetuation of the culture of today. He finds it necessary to emphasize the culture at the expense of the concepts of freedom and dignity of the autonomous individual. His preference for the culture over freedom and dignity is made clear in his book: "If it [our culture] continues to take freedom or dignity, rather than its own survival, as its principal value, then it is possible that some other culture will make a greater contribution to the future."[3]

The culture becomes in Skinner's usage as collectivist as earlier versions of the state or communism or fascism or the Church. In each case the individual's role is to serve the whole. That whole, the state, which has a permanence greater than the ephemeral existence of the individual, is regarded as paramount. It is needed for the individual's survival in the same way that the herd or flock serves its individual members and the survival of the species.

INDIVIDUALISM

As collectivism would overemphasize the role of the state, individualism would underemphasize it. Individualism sees the role of the state as minimal and as directed to the enhancement of the individual in his or her private capacity. Government is regarded as a "necessary evil." Accordingly, "the government which governs least governs best." These views from Thomas Paine's pamphlet "Common Sense," published at the opening of America's conflict with England in 1776, have developed a somewhat mistaken American identity. They are the views of Paine (pun intended) and individualism. They are not necessarily or correlatively American. Paine's words are colorful and have been adopted by many:

> Society in every state is a blessing, but government, even in its best state, is a necessary evil; in its worst state an intolerable one: For when we suffer, or are exposed to the same miseries *by a government,* which we might expect in a country *without government,* our calamity is heightened by reflecting that we furnish the means by which we suffer. Government, like dress, is the badge of lost innocence.[4]

In Paine's view and in that of those who share it the individual is to be accorded the widest scope of freedom consistent with the freedom and safety of others. Government in the individualist's perspective is to be "limited" to maintaining order, protecting individual freedom and enforcing contracts. These tasks are precisely the inconveniences performed by government for the individual in the theory of John Locke. Other than this limited role, government is to "keep its hands off," *laissez faire,* the affairs of individuals and groups. The best practice is to allow individual competition and natural abilities to control the affairs of mankind.

This doctrine of laissez faire found a harsh expression in the writings of Herbert Spencer (1820–1903). Spencer argued against public assistance or what is called today welfare and social security. His attitude is labeled "social Darwinism" because of its elements of natural selection and survival of the fittest. A curious thing is that Spencer spoke of these elements before Darwin found them in his investigation into the origin of the species.

The viewpoint of Spencerian individualism is that to interfere with the natural laws of society or the physical world will do much harm and little good. Natural selection improves the species. Interference or the constraints of law destroy initiative and stifle incentive. The best policy, according to this view, is that every person be free to pursue individual interests to the highest possible degree. Spencer wrote,

> It seems hard that a labourer incapacitated by sickness from competing with his stronger fellows, should have to bear the resulting privations. It seems hard that widows and orphans should be left to struggle for life or death. Nevertheless, when regarded not separately, but in connection with the interests of universal humanity, these harsh fatalities are seen to be full of the highest beneficence—the same beneficence which brings to early graves the children of diseased parents, and singles out the low-spirited, the intemperate, and debilitated as the victims of an epidemic.[5]

One might express Spencer's attitude as one of " 'everyone for himself,' said the elephant dancing among the chickens."

Most individualism does not come in such a crass form. The usual argument is attractively put in terms of individual ability, government interference, private initiative, doing one's own thing, the individual knows best, or unwarranted intrusion of government. There are shreds of the individualist point of view in both contemporary conservative and liberal political rhetoric. That rhetoric is seasonal.

It seems fair game today to pick on government and to criticize its activities as at other times it was common to constantly propose new programs for expansion of governmental activity. This rhetorical appeal reflects in only a loose way a theoretical attitude toward the state. It can change as quickly as the personal attractiveness of candidates changes. What is necessary for the serious student of politics is some well-founded theoretical principles which can upon reflection stand as measure of the passing appeals.

The large theoretical issues of politics may never be finally settled for many individuals. The principles nonetheless give orientation to many little decisions on budgets, policies, and conflicts. Theoretical positions also give meaning to individuals who seek to know their place and purpose in the vast political universe that affects them daily. Despite the legitimate confusion about the distinctness of the theoretical principles, still they remain separate. Individualism has a trace of anarchism in it if one were to stress the evilness of the state instead of the necessity of the evil. Stressing the necessity shows a trace of collectivism. In this way the theories touch and blend. They are distinct in their emphasis: one on the individual, the other on the whole. The third theory of the purpose of the state, in a special way, emphasizes both.

THE COMMON GOOD

The third theory of the purpose of the state is the common good. It is not readily identifiable in the political conversations of everyday life. Upon first hearing the phrase it is misunderstood as being the same as collectivism. When it is explained to be "the good of the *individual* as a member of the state" it is then mistaken to be a form of individualism. It is neither collectivism nor individualism. It is, in fact, a separate and distinct theoretical position whose distinguishing features are important for practical politics.

What distinguishes the common good from collectivism is its respect for the integrity of the individual. What distinguishes it from individualism is its recognition of the individual as social by nature and the state as a natural instead of an artificial construct. As stated above the common good is the good of the individual as a member of the community, the good which the individual realizes from sharing and communicating. It is a good which is indeed one's own but of which the private benefit is not the absolute measure.

The good of the family, for example, is one's own good but it accrues to the individual by reason of family membership. The good of the family is not the father's good, plus the mother's good, plus each child's good. In other words, it is not the sum of the good of the parts. The good of the family is each and every individual's good but it is a good which each shares by reason of the others' membership.

In the same way the Common Good, which is the state, is the good of the individual, even while it is at the same time the good of each and every individual in the community. That does not mean that their goods are identical. Each good is distinct from but not separate from the good of every member of the state. It comes by way of the sharing and communicating of the community. In one instance it may be the listening to beautiful music and in another it may be the performance of music. In one it may be living a tranquil life without paying attention to politics and in another the lifelong study of politics. For one individual the common good may be in military service and for another it may be collecting antiques or painting houses.

The common good is that fulfillment of the extended social dimension of the individual mentioned in the last chapter under the socio-logical origin of the state. The "multidimensional" individual has a private dimension whereby things are uniquely and incommunicably one's own, a limited but intimate and in-depth social dimension, and an extended social dimension whereby one would communicate with universal mankind. The individual has goods which accrue by reason of each of these dimensions, private goods, the common good of the family, and the common good of the state. Private goods, those that are uniquely and incommunicably one's own, are limited to things such as the food that nourishes, the clothes that warm, and the virtues that perfect one as a private individual. Clothes may have a secondary social effect of appearing attractive to observers but the secondary effect is incidental to the functional one of warmth and protection. The primary private virtue is temperance, whose incommunicableness and uniqueness is principally demonstrated when it has been lacking (as portrayed in cartoons when one complains of a certain type of headache saying, "You don't know the pain I'm suffering!"). Other than these few items there are not many exclusively private goods. Almost everything is the result of communicating and sharing. Education, for example, is a social good, as are books, patience, museums, jazz concerts, transportation, national parks, and most things with which we come in contact.

The common good views the state as providing an environment—material, social, and intellectual—which is most conducive to free, human living. The environment is one which is consonant with human nature. It draws on one's ability, it lets the individual thrive in fulfilling those things of which the person is capable. The common good presumes the individual and the various abilities of different individuals. It presumes the individual developing his or her private, social, and universal dimensions. The common good is not the sum of the good of the parts, as in the family it is not the sum of the singular good of its members. It is at one and the same time the good of the individual member and greater than the sum of singular goods.

Individualism views the state as the sum of singular or private goods. Collectivism views the state as greater than the sum of the parts and something to which the parts must be subservient. The common good is greater than the sum of private goods but it does not subordinate the individual. An attempt to express these relationships in symbolic language is presented in the accompanying chart (Table 7-1). All the relationships are fairly easy to appreciate. They all follow from the verbal descriptions already given. The only formula that presents any difficulty is the last one, the common good. There, despite the distinctions which have been made and the descriptions which have been repeated, the precise nature remains not entirely

TABLE 7–1　*THE PURPOSE OF THE STATE*
　　　　　　IN SYMBOLS

Anarchism

$W = 0$
(The state should not exist.)

Collectivism

$W > P1 + P2 + \ldots + Pn > Pi$
(The whole is greater than the sum of the parts and it is greater than any individual part.)
(Parts are subordinated to the whole.)

Individualism

$W = P1 + P2 + \ldots + Pn$
(The whole is equal to the sum of its parts.)
(Only the parts are real.)

Common Good ·

$W > P1 + P2 + \ldots + Pn \not> Pi$
(The whole is greater than the sum of its parts but it is not geater than the individual parts.)
(Parts are not subordinated to the whole.)

---

clear. As with many other things the differences can be seen more clearly when examples are given.

It is difficult to give examples in which differences are unambiguous. To ask how the different theories of the purpose of the state would respond to an exercise of eminent domain against one's ancestral property for public use is only mildly interesting. The differences blur because the test is not strong enough. While collectivism would rejoice at the contribution they could make, and while individualism would mourn at their forced sacrifice, the common good would mumble something about doing what is right. The end result of all three would not be noticeably different. The property would be taken, some payment would be made, and even the collectivists' approval would not prevent them from accepting it.

Death in the Line of Duty

Other examples or attempts to illustrate the practical difference of the various theories of the purpose of the state would be similarly anticlimactic. All examples would be unsatisfactory except one, which is the ultimate test of the relationship between the individual and the state. Such a test would occur when the state asks the individual to act so that his or her life may be sacrificed in the line of duty. Going to battle to defend one's country in time of war is an example of such an act. There are many similar acts. Routine police work and the job of a firefighter are not as dramatic as wartime events, but death in such circumstances is just as final. There are other occupations where one's life is put in jeopardy for the sake of others. It is this type of situation which presents a more severe test of the purpose of the state. The severity arises from the question of what the individual gains from such sacrifice.

To the situation of death in the line of duty the anarchist, to dispose of their argument quickly, would respond that the proposal is absurd. For the anarchist there ought to be no state or government and therefore a request for sacrifice is impossible. The individual might make a personal choice of sacrifice but this decision is not directed by some outsider or intermediary. In this way anarchism continues to show itself as ignoring and escaping from reality. It is because of this consistently negative view of the state and political reality as evil that little serious attention is given to that theory. The absurdity of war can arouse much sympathy for the anarchist's rejection of individual sacrifice. Despite that absurdity, the unfortunate necessity of war cannot be ignored. If sympathetic feelings formed the standard of judgment, they would have to apply also to the police, the firefighter, and the emergency medical team. Individual sacrifice in these situations is no more or less meaningful. They can hardly be written off as absurd.

Collectivism may regard the death of the individual in the line of duty as unfortunate but as meaningful within the context of the whole. It sees the individual's worth as determined by one's place within the whole. The individual is the means, the state is the end. As Mussolini said in his description of the doctrine of fascism: "Fascism conceives of the State as an absolute, in comparison with which all individuals or groups are relative, only to be conceived of in their relation to the State." Individual service and individual sacrifice both have worth from their contribution to the state, "The fascist conception of the State is all-embracing; outside of it no human or spiritual values can exist, much less have value."[6]

There is no question that for collectivism the individual can be called upon to sacrifice, "even up to . . . total immolation" in the words of Alfredo Rocco, on behalf of the state. From that sacrifice the individual finds value since no value exists beyond the state. A careful distinction has to be made between genuine and humble patriotism. The sacrifice of a Nathan Hale or the service that a John Kennedy asked for differs from the slavish subservience to a "totalitarian" state about which Mussolini bragged. Unlike a Hale or a Kennedy, the collectivist totality sees nothing beyond the state which measures the goodness of the service provided. For that same reason the cultural value of Skinner or scientism fits the category of collectivism. For them by definition there is nothing beyond this principal value. They are as much a philosophy of collectivism as are the more obviously political variants.

Individualism, on the other hand, would react to the call of sacrifice of the individual on behalf of the community with skepticism. Its most visible response might be the one witnessed during the Vietnam era in the United States, where crowds of youth chanted, "Hell no, we won't go!" Unwittingly, the chant had a tinge of collectivism to it in the use of the word "we." "I" would have been the more consistently individualist word. What the chanters meant was that they and not the government should decide what was an acceptable call to duty.

If a majority of "I's" felt that a war should not be held or that an individual should not be called to duty, then the war should be called off. If some individuals felt that they did not want to go to war, then they should not be drafted or sent. Within that same perspective, if some were of a mercenary frame of mind and wanted to take their chances, then they indeed could make up the fighting force. It is all a matter of individual choice.

According to individualism there is nothing to consider beyond the individual. To take up a proposition of something to be served beyond the individual is dangerously collectivist and to be avoided at all costs. This danger leads to an anarchistic dilemma for the individualist. The dilemma arises when the cost of service is the survival of the liberal political community which makes the freedom possible. That logic is either ignored at peril or denied with bravado. "Peril or . . . bravado" is not an evaluation. It is a description of the alternatives that are available in the individualists' perspective. In the denial of peril there is "an act of faith in the abiding good sense of the average human" and a confidence that in the long run the values of individual worth will triumph over the forces that threaten them.

Pericles and Lincoln

The common good maintains what has the appearance of a contradictory position, that death in the line of duty is the good of the individual as well as the good of the community. The good of the community is fairly evident, assuming as is usually done, that the community survives the situation. The benefit appears to accrue chiefly or solely to the community and so the common good seems to be collectivist. The reason the position is not collectivist is that the position does not hold that there is nothing beyond this act of service. Concomitantly it is maintained that there is a benefit to the individual.

Death in the line of duty is an exceptionally individual act. The idea of individual benefit challenges the credulity of the most willing reader. Ancient values such as the preservation of the community of one's family and maintaining order and the rule of law are not insignificant. It is not immediately apparent, however, what accrues to the dead hero. No matter what the preservice conditioning, no person rejoices at their own death as "feeling great." There is no apparent benefit to the individual except insofar as service is considered a good of the individual. There is no other benefit for the individual in this life.

The phrase "in this life" suggests a dimension not previously mentioned. What is suggested is some "afterlife" or some other factor not humanly controlled. The easiest factor to consider is a heaven in which individuals are rewarded according to the quality of their life. This factor is easiest because if it is true then everything follows in symmetrical fashion: as one lives a good or a bad life one will receive proportionate reward in the afterlife, and if one dies courageously one may make up for earlier deficiencies, etc. This is the heaven/hell phenomenon of folklore, religious belief, and traditional thought.

From the time of Pericles, the Athenian general during the Peloponnesian War, to the time of Lincoln and beyond, the war dead have been honored as sustaining the common good. Pericles in his famous funeral oration praised the ones who had died, saying that they sustained their own good while sustaining the good of Athens. The same belief applies to any who die in the line of duty, that their special service merits a greater reward in the afterlife. An important point to note, however, is that this belief does not prove the existence either of personal immortality or an afterlife. Religions believe in heaven, hell, personal rewards, and punishments. It can be shown that Aristotle did not preclude the possibility of an afterlife and that he spoke of the soul as separable from the body. All these religious beliefs and philosophical treatments do not prove their claim as much as merely set them forth. They fit into the context of the discussion by completing the notion of the individual's personal benefit from heroic service.

It should be noted that the afterlife and personal rewards within it are not the only way in which the individual could benefit from death in the line of duty. If instead of personal reward what was involved was less personal but equally universal and real, individual benefit could still be satisfied. If it were maintained that to be "courageous" or "good" or "just" was unqualifiedly better than to be "rash" or "cowardly" or "bad" or "unjust," then one's death in the line of duty could merely be argued to be consistent with that better course of action. In this way then, similar to the religious belief, the individual does not serve some state determined good or some privately determined good but serves an objective and real good. It is better for the individual to die courageously than to live cowardly, to die justly than to live unjustly, etc.

From the common good perspective the individual lives and dies in accord with real universal norms sustained by truth. The individual does not follow private or state determined objectives sustained by selfishness. It is good that the community be afforded fire protection, police protection, military defense. If the individual dies in service to these goods of the community, then the individual has done what is right even if the particular situations requiring protection or defense are questioned or are mistaken. The individual's benefit is not adversely affected by misadventure by political leaders or even, in the case of war, by the defeat of one's country.

Lincoln honored the men of both sides who died at Gettysburg. The men of Athens sustained the common good, as acknowledged by Pericles, even though their side eventually lost the Peloponnesian War. This does not mean that leaders can frivolously decide to send men to battle or street confrontations. It is the individual's life and although it can be shown that there is a real good for the individual in sacrificing for the community, that life is not at the complete disposal of the community. That limit is the difference between the common good and collectivism. The individual is not at the complete disposal of the community, the integrity of the individual is supposed to be preserved. The difference between the common good and individualism is that the service and the benefit are not determined solely by the individual.

Unlike the common good, collectivism and individualism preclude the consideration of afterlife or other universal factors beyond the state on the one hand or the individual on the other hand. Collectivism and individualism measure the state only in purely human terms. The common good's consideration of something beyond this life does not prove the existence of that additional dimension. The foregoing consideration is not proof, it is merely an explanation of what completes the system.

For the common good it is this additional dimension of something beyond this life upon which the independence and integrity of the individual is based. The individual is not dominated by the state or by any collectivist cause because the individual has a higher purpose to serve. That higher purpose is not contrary to the state but it goes quite beyond it. Without something beyond human nature, human beings would make themselves or their creations the thing to be served. Aristotle commented that "Politics would be the highest science if man were the best thing in the universe, but man is not the best thing in the universe."

The common good makes human beings neither masters nor slaves. It is a good which is indeed one's own, but the private benefit is not the absolute measure of this good. The state is not the absolute measure of this good either. The possibility of something better than humans opens a full discourse on the purpose and the role of the state. This discourse will not always preserve the individual from tyranny. At least it does not preclude that freedom by definition.

CONCLUSION AND PERSPECTIVE

Earlier it was promised that this chapter would balance out the three theories with which the state has been examined. The balance was supposed to be some factor or dimension which would take away any advantage that the third system (syngeristic unity, responsible authority, socio-logical origin, and common good purpose) might have enjoyed. It might appear at first glance that the balance has not been established, that the earlier imbalance has been exacerbated. In part that may be true but it is not necessarily true.

The third system, the common good, wants to include more in its universe of discourse than do either individualism or collectivism. What the common good wants to include is not proven to exist. It is perhaps subject to more criticism and doubt today than at any time in human history. If the afterlife does not exist, if objective "truth" or "goodness" or "justice" do not exist, then all that remains are the human alternatives—individualism or collectivism. It is this point of what to include that ultimately separates the three systems.

Whether politics should take as its fundamental point the part (the individual) or the whole (the state, culture, economic system, etc.) or something better than humans in the universe is the distinguishing factor of the different theories of the state. This fundamental point has never been decided in any final way. Various individuals have their private preferences. Those private choices do not determine final truth but they do influence how individuals will evaluate events and direct their actions. In the unproven premises and the relentlessness of their separate disciples the three systems are in existential balance at least.

What has been done in the last four chapters was to lay out the alternative points of view in such a way as to show the respective positions of the different approaches to the state. Since the "correct" approach has not been determined or proven, all that is available are individual personal choices. It might be hoped that each of the readers would make the same choice as the author. It must be acknowledged, however, that everyone decides in the light of many factors including personal background, reason, and comfort. Everyone will, whether wittingly or not, consider what has been said in the light of conditioned preferences and anticipated consequences as well as logical reasoning. Such unconscious and conscious factors of choice cannot be suppressed. To proceed as if only one view will prevail is both mistaken and impractical.

Despite a preference for one or the other approach it should be recognized that there are other individuals who cannot accept its basic propositions. There are groupings of individuals who share the preferences of each of the three basic approaches. Such differences have existed from the beginning of Western thought, if not human thought. It is the start of political wisdom to know and to understand the different approaches. Only with such wisdom can human beings begin to accept the diversity of those with whom they cannot agree.

There are certain harsh aspects of the different approaches. They are so diametrically opposed that violent conflict often occurs. Marxism, capitalism, laissez faire individualism, fascism, socialism, democracy, and anarchism are often mortal enemies. An appreciation of the basis and depth of the differences between the enemies is essential to minimizing hostile conflicts in the future. It is a common human practice to lament the wrongful deeds of some opponent in the past. Those deeds should not be overlooked completely but the important thing is to avoid them in the future by appreciating the depth from which they spring. If the examination and explication of the different views of the aspects of the state has developed an appreciation of the roots of disagreement, then at least a minimal threshold of success has been attained.

NOTES

1. Quoted in Schmandt and Steinbicker, *Fundamentals of Government* (Milwaukee: Bruce Publishing Co., 1963), p. 55.

2. "'I have been misunderstood. . . .' An Interview with B. F. Skinner," *The Center Magazine*, Vol. 5, Number 2 March/April 1972, pp. 63–65. Reprinted with permission from *The Center Magazine*, a publication of the Center for the Study of Democratic Institutions.

3. B. F. Skinner, *Beyond Freedom and Dignity* (New York: Bantam Books, 1971), esp. p. 173.

4. Thomas Paine, "Common Sense," *The Life and Works of Thomas Paine,* Edited by William M. Van der Weyde, Vol. II (New Rochelle, New York: Thomas Paine National Historical Association, 1925).

5. Herbert Spencer, *Social Statics* (1851).

6. *Social and Political Philosophy,* edited by John Somerville and Ronald E. Santori (New York: Anchor Books–Doubleday, 1963), pp. 424–440.

CHAPTER EIGHT
IDEOLOGIES

If one were to organize the four previous chapters and the three principal theories into a grid or matrix, one could get a visual impression of the three organic systems of thought which have been presented. The theories would be to the left side of the grid and the four aspects of the state would be at the top, forming a "three by four" matrix with twelve cells. The theories would be identified by numbers in the order in which they were initially presented and the aspects would be labeled as "nature," "authority," "origin," and "purpose." Theory One would fill the cells of the first row as Organismic, Absolute, Divine, and Collectivism. Theory Two would read across as Mechanistic, Relative, Social Contract, and Individualism. Number Three would read Synergistic, Proper, Socio-logical, and Common Good.

The grid, Figure 8-1, appears very orderly and suggests a neatness which at an initial level is quite acceptable. When Theory One is related to Hitler's Nazism or Mussolini's Fascism or even to Communism, as it easily can be, the simple identifications in the first row appear to work well. Each of those "isms" is understood in one way or another to regard the political unit as larger than and having final say over the individual. At this level each views the state as originating in some historical, physical, or spiritual force. Each regards the state as paramount, at least for the time being, in terms of priorities for the individual.

Theory Two works quite well, too, when understood in terms of laissez faire liberalism. Here the political unit is viewed purely in terms of individual will, sub-

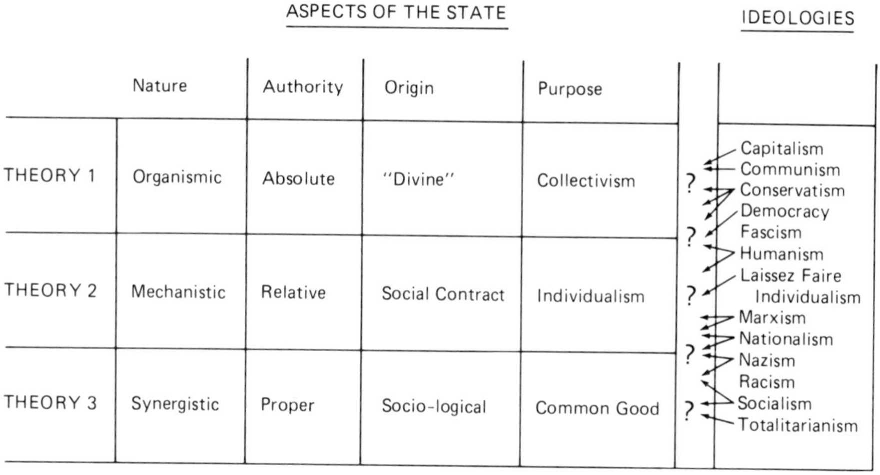

ASPECTS OF THE STATE   IDEOLOGIES

	Nature	Authority	Origin	Purpose		
THEORY 1	Organismic	Absolute	"Divine"	Collectivism	?	Capitalism Communism Conservatism Democracy Fascism
THEORY 2	Mechanistic	Relative	Social Contract	Individualism	?	Humanism Laissez Faire Individualism Marxism Nationalism
THEORY 3	Synergistic	Proper	Socio-logical	Common Good	?	Nazism Racism Socialism Totalitarianism

FIGURE 8-1   Elements of ideology: The grid of theories and aspects of the state.

ject to the disposition of majoritarian change, originating in a contract of the same disposition, and serving first and foremost the private individual. Such a configuration of elements is revered by some and regarded as essentially selfish by others. Its real-life representation is felt by some to have occurred in various governments in the United States, England, and elsewhere during the nineteenth century. There are individuals who regard some or all the twentieth-century presidential administrations in the United States as consciously or unconsciously representing this view. That characterization of particular governments may be misplaced but it should be seen as a way of rejecting the second theory as much as a criticism of specific perceptions.

Unless one is committed in some preset way to Theory One or Two, most people would like to believe that their government, in its best moments at least, and their theory of the right kind of government reflects Theory Three. In other words, most people like to view themselves, and correspondingly their governments, as neither selfish nor unwisely altrustic, as taking a proper and responsible position on issues, whether large or small, as acting in a manner ordained by nature, truth, and goodness, and as serving the common good. It is because of this predilection that there was a consistent inclination in each of the previous four chapters toward the third theory. In the last part of the discussion of the purpose of the state it was pointed out that the tilt in favor of the third theory could be balanced out. That balance was attained by acknowledging the unproved major premise from which it, like the other two theories, proceeded.

The perception of preference for the third theory remains. That perception is no handicap since it is consonant with the human predilection and is something which all theories of the state have had to deal. If one wants to argue in favor of another of the purposes of the state it is necessary first to argue a particular version of the nature of man. So, if individualism or collectivism is the goal, one has to argue that human nature is aggressive, or selfish, or willful, or controlled by history or economic, biological, or spiritual forces. With such an argument one has staked out a cell in the grid. The state's relationship to the individual is organismic or absolute, mechanistic or relative. The origin of the state is either completely uncontrollable or completely controllable.

To this point the grid appears neat and uncomplicated. What is most fascinating is that it is not as tidy as has been described up to this point. The description has been entirely accurate up to a certain level. A complication arises in that the theories work out nicely in the abstract, but when applied or related to concrete political situations and programs the abstract tidiness disappears. For example, it was convenient to refer to communism as fitting Theory One and having collectivism as its purpose. All communist states, as far as we know them, are collectivist, although the reported strong competition among the upper echelons within them somewhat belies that. Our understanding of communist theory, Marxism to be specific, usually reinforces this practical knowledge. However, this common opinion runs into difficulty when we are reminded of the goal of "the withering away of the state" so that the "new man," the Marxian goal, may live unimpeded by any forces foreign and extraneous to himself. This latter goal suggests a radical, almost an anarchistic, individualism. With communism pointing to individuals as an ultimate goal the lines on the matrix begin to cross.

Further line crossing occurs, for example, if one probes laissez faire liberalism. In this instance the goals and the premises appear to be unencumbered individualism. The means, however, are collective insofar as maintenance of the economic system is concerned. Likewise, the very mechanism for the operation of a system of laissez faire liberalism is majority rule, which is itself a collectivist principle. A minority of, say, 49 percent may have little practical or theoretical difficulty in reconciling both individualism and majority rule. For a minority of, say, 10 percent it is a wholly different matter. The antiwar saying that old men, meaning the majority, send young men, the minority, to die is based on this principle.

These anomalies or paradoxes, which unveil the complications of reality, often lead to discouragement about the value of theory. The contrary should be true. This revelation should not cause a pullback from the insights gained by an understanding of the different theories and aspects of the state. It should lead to an appreciation of the practical efforts to explain the basis of politics on a popular level. In fact, appreciation of the difficulties of theory is prerequisite to an understanding of ideology.

DEFINITION

Ideology is an attempt to understand or describe the political world. There is an almost endless variety of books, definitions, and discussions of the term ideology and its various forms. Leon Baradat does a particularly good job in this regard.[1] He describes ideology as "action-oriented, materialistic, popular, and simplistic."

This definition is especially useful because it focuses on the character of ideology, seeking to persuade large groups for specific purposes. The intention of mass appeal easily explains the simplistic dimension. If, as according to the common understanding, the daily newspaper and weekly newsmagazine has to be written on a high school level, so would an ideology. The materialistic dimension is not as immediately apparent but it ultimately has the same root in making popular what Baradat calls "accommodation to social and economic conditions."[2]

LISTS OF IDEOLOGIES

There are so many definitions and discussions of ideology that it is usually not possible to agree on a list of ideologies. Most works describe four or five ideologies. The prominent ones are:

- Democracy
- Fascism
- Marxism
- Nazism

Even this small list causes difficulty, because some lists would not include democracy, others would omit Marxism and instead include communism. Some would insist that the items be forms of socialism, capitalism, or totalitarianism. Others would discuss liberalism versus conservatism. Some would want to include nationalism, racism, humanism, and laissez faire individualism. Accordingly, a more complete list, presented in alphabetic order with a description attached, would look like this:

Capitalism: an economic system based on nongovernment ownership and direction of production and services and regulated by competitive activity among individuals and groups. Capitalism, like communism and socialism, is in one respect principally an economic doctrine, but it, like the others, cannot be completely separated from this social and political context. In cannot be clear whether its successes or failure are purely economic on the one hand or purely political on the other.

Communism: an economic, social, and political system seeking government ownership of production and services directed by a process of scientific administration and universal assent. The process of administration and assent gives it a utopian quality theoretically and an authoritarian practice. Historically, many religious and monastic communities are communistic in principle but they are also voluntary and they operate on a much smaller scale than the political versions.

Conservatism: a point of view that emphasizes tradition and established institutions and thereby appears to give greater attention to social entities than to individuals. Although there is a common association of the Republican Party in the United

States and political parties elsewhere with this idea, it is not an exact relationship, since all parties are generally pragmatic in their practices. In its more exact form, as represented by Edmund Burke, conservatism takes history and tradition as the measure of the true and the good.

Democracy: in its simplest form understood as rule by the people but not as immediately self-explanatory as that phrase might imply (see Chapter 1). While at one point in the last two hundred years democracy was the dominant political and philosophical ideal, its implementation in many disparate settings reveals both its adaptability and its fragility.

Fascism: the system associated with Mussolini in Italy, which emphasized the authoritative direction of the leader and the following of the public in all things. A description such as this has always been easier to give than a precise definition of specific elements. Today no ruler proclaims this doctrine as Mussolini did. Since his time it is a common term of deprecation used by critics of almost any governmental feature or practice with which they disagree.

Humanism: a view which concentrates on human assets to the active exclusion of anything transcendent or spiritual in public affairs. Many different groups, ranging from Marxists to individualists, claim to be humanists. Some of the most strident are actively antireligious secularists like Madalyn Murray O'Hair. There are also relatively calm humanists like the psychologist B. F. Skinner.

Laissez Faire Individualism: an economic, social, and political view which emphasizes unregulated individual competition as the rule for social interaction on the assumption that a natural stratification based on merit will result. It claims to focus on human strengths and abilities instead of frailties. It is associated with capitalism, nineteenth-century liberalism, as well as the final goal of Marxism.

Liberalism: a view which, although emphasizing individual goodness, sees more need for change and improvement in social relations requiring governmental involvement. In a nineteenth century mode it was more associated with laissez faire. In the twentieth century it is viewed as more on the side of state-interventionist socialism.

Marxism: a particularly extreme form of communism, humanism, liberalism and others which calls for the ultimate elimination of the state and all other social institutions, to be accomplished by a transition which will itself wither in favor of radical individualism. It claims a large contemporary following but its success is justifiably debated as being more the result of crude power than the product of the strength of an idea.

Nationalism: a view which stresses loyalty and devotion to the nation-culture group as the greatest vehicle for self-realization and which has witnessed the tripling

Adolf Hitler

Karl Marx

of nation-states in the last forty years. It is not unreasonably regarded as the most powerful simplified, unifying idea of the last two centuries.

Nazism: Hitler's version of fascism, individualism, nationalism, socialism, and racism combined in a particularly virulent form claiming the superiority of some individuals and the natural enslavement of others. The principal way it is distinguished from fascism is the racial dimension whereby a claim is made that one race is superior to others. This claim is in its origin not so much directed against other races (although its effects are) as it is a concentration on innate, genetically, or statistically proclaimed data about one's own race.

Racism: a belief that race is the primary determinant of human abilities and action and that consequently social and political alignments are or ought to be consonant with ethnic stock. It is intrinsically an unprovable and hence irrational proposition, both logically and empirically. It is nonetheless a generalization engaged in by many persons even though they admit its falsity. To argue the natural inferiority of one race is as much racism as proclaiming the natural superiority of another.

Socialism: an economic and political doctrine which advocates governmental ownership and direction of production and services but which would retain existing institutions as the means for regulating them. Marxism would advocate the abolition of these institutions, but until that abolition is accomplished, Marxism is a type of state-socialism. Socialism without Marxism has more of a majoritarian democratic dimension to it.

Totalitarianism: a system in which all individual, economic, social, and political actions are subject to the direction of the authoritarian ruling person or party. Practically it is dependent on twentieth-century technology, especially the advance of communications for both gathering and disseminating information. Theoretically it has much earlier roots in Marx, Hegel, and even Hobbes. Plato's carefully designed Republic has shades of this. In the Republic, everyone was assigned a place as either a farmer, craftsman, soldier, or leader according to whether they were originally composed of iron, brass, silver, or gold. Those original metals were a "clever fiction" for achieving harmony in the community.

The list is long but not necessarily complete. There is also considerable room for disagreement about the descriptions. Depending on the strictness of one's definition of ideology, some would be excluded as "merely" an *ism*. Unfortunately, that reference does not clarify the situation, for ism is in most respects today synonymous with ideology. The distinction between ideology and ism is in the character of ideology as a "systematic" body of concepts or as visionary theorizing as opposed to an ism as a distinctive theory. There is really little difference although large works are written under one or the other rubric. The books about "isms" and the books about "ideologies" are really concerned with the same thing. They are concerned about the above list and its related disputes. The systematic quality attributed to ideology does not reflect any objective character but only refers to the integration of concepts in a plausible theory. It may still be visionary or illusory even though systematic. (The Ptolemaic explanation of sun, moon, and planets rotating around the earth was systematic but illusory.)

ILLUSORY QUALITY OF IDEOLOGY

The illusory quality of ideology harks back to the origin of the word in the late eighteenth and early nineteenth centuries. The French philosopher and psychologist Destutt de Tracy (1754-1836) is said to have first used the word in the mid-1790s. Tracy appears to relate ideology to "the science of ideas" or to "the philosophy of mind." The term has also been attributed to Napoleon, with whose government Tracy was associated, who gave ideology its political connotation. According to the Oxford English Dictionary, various sources such as John Adams, Sir Walter Scott, and the poet Shelley attribute to Napoleon the depreciatory sense of ideology as unpractical or visionary theorizing or speculation. Hence ideology, like ism, the older term, has a disparaging intention in its early usage. As to whether it was Tracy or Napoleon who coined the word, it is but an ephemeral curiosity similar to contemporary commentary about public officials and unseen speech writers.

It is the derogatory sense of ideology that Marx adopted in the mid-nineteenth century. Marx uses ideology to refer to illusory philosophies and doctrines current in Germany at the time of his writing. More specifically, though, he regards any false way of seeing the world as an ideology. Only science can replace ideology, and science is equated with his own method. Furthermore, ideologies, in Marx's view, are not simply the product of errors of thought but instead are rooted in the whole socioeconomic fabric which shapes a person's thinking, acting, work, indeed, whole personality. Religion and the state are in this view ideologies in that they are illusory representations of one's true character suppressed by alienating material conditions. To change the illusions or ideology it is necessary, in Marx's view, to change the material conditions.

The change in the material conditions which Marx speaks of means a complete and total change in all institutions and relationships, from the family to the state and religion. It is for this reason that Marx is rightly regarded as radically revolutionary. For him anything, and that includes practically everything, which stands in the way of a scientific understanding of the world should be unmercifully swept aside. For Marx, science equals Communism, which means a materialist and individualistic, radically new conception of reality. Scientific thinking, thinking which is not illusory, is based on sense-experience. People's actions can be observed, described, and interpreted without illusion. They are empirically observable.

It is ironic that Marx on the one hand adopts the connotation of ideology as false and confused thinking and on the other hand uses science in the sense that Tracy originally did for ideology. Tracy, following Condillac, saw all ideas as derived from sensations. Ideas derived from the senses were in Tracy's intention to be distinguished from "metaphysics," by which he meant traditional or speculative philosophy. Marx had precisely the same intention with respect to science and distinguished it from metaphysics, which he understood in the same sense as Tracy.

It is more than fascinating that the origin of the word ideology and Marx's use of science have the same source. This conjoining of opposites demonstrates that the contemporary confusion about the definition and agreed-upon list of ideologies has a basis in its own roots. Marx would have no sufferance of illusion. On the other hand, as each of the separate ideologies partake of the original primacy of sensations, they are intolerant of anything claiming nonsensational verification or premises other than their own. Which is to say, each ideology is as exclusive and intolerant as the next one. It is for this reason that ideology is said to have an essentially rhetorical character.

RHETORIC AND IDEOLOGY

Rhetoric is the art of using language to persuade. From Greek time down to the present it has been a chief tool of political operatives. Presidents have seen their effectiveness wax and wane in direct proportion to their rhetorical skills. When President Reagan is called a great communicator, what is meant is that he effectively persuades others to accept his policies. President Carter was an effective communicator throughout his first campaign and up to his inauguration. His rhetoric, unlike Reagan's, was not as effective thereafter, either on a long- or short-term basis.

The difference between ordinary political rhetoric and ideology is a matter of scope and duration. Ordinary political rhetoric is mostly piecemeal commentary on current topics with a view toward eliciting popular support. The duration may be no greater than the length of a electoral campaign. This is not a cynical assessment of elections since, as described in the first chapter, it is by this process of scrutinizing and evaluating the credibility of their use of rhetoric that the public is able to judge candidates for office. Ideology on the other hand does have a cynical quality to it, since it purports an integration of all aspects of the sociopolitical realm over an extensive span of time. Each of the ideologies claim that theirs is the best practical guide for political action. Tolerance between ideologies is low since they view their premises and goals as exclusive. One system accepts another only insofar as it sees the other as coming within the confines of its own structure.

Ideology is like a roadmap by which we find our way or review the path we have covered. The map is a simplification of the real road and it leaves out much of the detail. In addition, different maps can be drawn for pilots, truckers, public transportation users, and tourists. Alternative ideologies are like the different maps of the same region. In other words, a different emphasis can be understood to reflect a different original perspective. In this analogy, political rhetoric is like a flashing red light or an amber light. Both lights would mean the same things, stop or use caution, to any traveler. But one can respond to the warning light without a clear set of directions. Understanding the elementary message without any commitment to the details is also true for most political rhetoric. The difference between a map and ideology, however, is that a map's accuracy and validity can be easily tested. An ideology, however, may appear accurate from a few of its elementary signposts, but its general validity must be judged logically and not just empirically.

IS DEMOCRACY AN IDEOLOGY?

At the beginning of this discussion, four ideologies were listed: democracy, fascism, Marxism, and Nazism. These four were listed separately from the longer list which followed. The shorter list represents ideologies that have had recent, clearly identifiable, political leaders who were spokesmen for their distinct ideological position. That is true at least for fascism, Marxism, and Nazism. Democracy has not had a distinctly identifiable spokesperson as much as it has had a long number of champions. There are reasons, hinted at earlier, for not regarding democracy as an ideology at all.

One reason for not counting democracy as an ideology is that almost all the others want to present themselves as a form of democracy. Totalitarianism, Nazism, and Marxism claim in one way or another to truly represent the best sense of the people. The Shah of Iran and his successor Ayatollah Khomeini, for example, claim popular sanction even though they were never subject to an election. A further reason for treating democracy separately, as in Chapter 1, is that it does not claim a solely materialistic or sensationalist base. Some of its modern advocates, from Locke to the present, and some of its critics, like Marx, may impute that limited empirical foundation to democracy, but its classical heritage will not allow it. Aristotle's democracy, for example, may have been "of the people" but this people had a "soul." That soul refers to real, separable spiritual dimensions, something better than humans in the universe, which keeps the political realm from being totalitarian. Marx and other modern commentators on democracy may disagree with this classical heritage. It is precisely the point of this disagreement that returns our attention to the aspects of the state discussed at the beginning of this chapter and in the previous four chapters.

Each of the ideologies takes some of the aspects of the state and either concentrates on and simplifies one view or selects from more than one view and presents a simplified explanation of politics. The particular ideology is intended for popular consumption. It is not an objective examination of the elements of the political community and the relation of those parts. All the ingredients for an ideology are contained within the discussion of the aspects and views of the state. Ideology's purpose, however, is different from a scholar's examination of the political community. Ideology's purpose is to persuade for action. Democracy may be considered an ideology if it is looked at in terms of narrow views of the nature, authority, origin, and purpose of the state. Democracy, however, is not tied to such views. Democracy could just as easily be viewed from Theory One, as from Two or Three. It could have as its purpose collectivism, individualism, or the common good depending on the other aspects and premises. It could have a soul, as classically understood, or it could be measured purely in human terms and thereby be an ideology. In fact, democracy is looked at in all these ways.

It is therefore possible to examine each of the isms or ideologies in terms of the contents of the aspects of the state. Some ideologies may beg for more examination than others as they appear more immediately compelling owing to current political events. The reader is encouraged to undertake this examination by way of using any of the many good books[3] that describe various ideologies at length and by way of integrating the information gained with the grid of aspects and theories presented at the beginning of this chapter. What the reader will end with is not a foreordained set of conclusions, but an array of alternatives from which choices can be made. The author of this text has his own preferences, but all alternatives are presented so that they can be judged on their merits. The same type of choice based on the principles involved should be possible on the difference between ''ideology'' and ''metaphysics.'' That freedom of choice based on merit is the paramount value of an examination of the principles of politics.

NOTES

1. Leon P. Baradat, *Political Ideologies: Their Origins and Impact,* 2nd ed. (Englewood Cliffs, N.J.: Prentice-Hall, Inc., 1984), p. 304.

2. ibid.

3. The reader is encouraged to begin such an undertaking with the suggested works in the selected bibliography at the end of this text.

CHAPTER NINE
SUBSIDIARITY
AND JUSTICE

In moving from the theoretical consideration of the nature of the state to practical considerations of government, a bridge must be provided which shows the juncture of the two. That bridge comes by way of an expansion of the purpose of the state from the one side and an extension of the sum of governmental activities from the other. The structure of the bridge is built from both sides. Furthermore, it will be seen, it has an even deeper understructure which radiates from both regions. One can begin to see the link by examining the concept of the "general welfare."

Discussion of the general welfare often makes it appear as if something more concrete is involved than in the consideration of the purpose of the state. The Constitution of the United States mentions that the government was formed to "promote the general welfare." There is no mention, however, in the Constitution of the common good or other formal purposes of the state. The general welfare phrase appears in the preamble to the Constitution and although the phrase may have wide locution it has no legal standing. The courts have never given the force of law to the provisions of the preamble.

The general welfare is supposed to be an expression of the promotional aspect of the purpose of the state. It is a complement to the protective role of government, also mentioned in the preamble, of defending against external attack and internal disorder. There is a problem, however. Though these protective and promotional roles appear to be concrete, there is as much disagreement about how much or how little should be provided as over the original theoretical positions discussed earlier. A particular problem is the promotional aspect of the state. Here the question is the degree to which the state should promote the material, moral, and intellectual well-being of the people.

Different positions, reflecting the earlier theoretical views of the purpose of the state, are taken on the extent of promoting the general welfare. Anarchism, for example, would hold for no promotive role. Collectivism would desire an extraordinary promotive role for the state. In keeping with its theoretical position, it would eventually see the state assuming total responsibility for individual needs. Individualism would seek a minimal role, consistent with the proposition that the government which governs least governs best. The common good, in the formal sense, would see the general welfare as a difficult balance of individual and social interest.

GOVERNMENT MINI/MAX DECISIONS

All this has been heard before. No progress in understanding is made by repeating the previous discussions of the purpose of the state. However, if the general welfare is considered in the light of the governmental budget, some advance in understanding may be accomplished. The budget is a concrete statement of the sum of governmental activities. It is the single most important policy statement of what the government at any level does. Although governments cannot be measured solely in terms of costs and expenditures, the budget reflects and represents the overall dimensions of governmental activity. All the theoretical views of the purpose of the state, except for anarchism of course, would agree that the purpose of the state is reflected in the budget and the debate over the budget.

Which is not to say that there is a formal discussion of the purpose of the state in the budgeting process. Nonetheless, to advocate the expansion of programs and corresponding costs or to call for the contraction of programs or balanced scrutiny roughly approximate collectivist, individualist, and common good positions. In other words, collectivists would like the government to do more by way of services and controls, individualists would like to see less, and the common good would, as explained before, be calling for "fair" or "just" policies. Whatever their theoretical differences, each of these three theories would agree, and here is the important new point in this examination, that for the present no sharp expansion or contraction can occur. Abrupt changes are eschewed by all.

For all the hue and cry over budget changes that get media attention from time to time, the actual changes rarely amount to anything close to 5 percent of the previous budget. All who approach the budget from any theoretical position are left in a similar practical situation of determining for the present moment the minimum necessary and the maximum possible for the government to do in the next year. Each theoretical position represented in a city council, a state legislature, and a national assembly is, in other words, compelled to make a practical decision along the lines of minimum costs and maximum benefits. Although each protagonist would hold to the original theoretical position and hope eventually to lead the other members and all society to that goal, practical considerations would persuade everyone, except the revolutionary, to make a decision along some such minimum/maximum lines.

The practical minimum/maximum decision is a description of what takes place in any budget process of deciding priorities and price tags.[1] Revenues and expenditure limits are finite for any level of government at any given time. A drastic change in any direction, no matter how desirable, would be disruptive and, very likely, self-defeating. Because of that disruptiveness budget changes are usually incremental, meaning that they come in small steps.

There are other reasons for this incremental change, such as the inertia of institutions, the slowness in getting various structures and parts of the bureaucracy coordinated, and the public's resistance to change. In the present discussion the slowness of budget change is being viewed as merely a function of the practical compromise of the different theoretical position on the role of the government itself. That theoretical disagreement does not appear in a formal way in the actual debates over revenues or expenditures. Nonetheless, the liberal, the conservative, the centrist, the reactionary, and the radical who serve on the governmental bodies each must reconcile their views with practical necessities or become less a part of the actual policy process.

Since this practical compromise with reality occurs at all levels of government, the extent to which the theoretical and the practical are joined in daily governmental activity takes place more frequently than is generally imagined. Even at city and township levels of government people who serve on councils have strongly held views about the theoretical role of government, and these views must be tempered for the moment for practical purposes.[2]

An additional consideration is that each level of government must make its practical budget decisions in light of what the other levels of government are doing. The state of Pennsylvania, for example, must consider what its cities are doing, what the national government is doing, and what other states are doing. In all these deliberations decisions must be made about minimum needs and costs and maximum expenses and benefits. For Pennsylvania to attempt to provide for total social security benefits for its citizens independent of the national program would be as impractical as for it to attempt to provide the police force in each of the cities and towns in the state. The state as the intermediate level of government in the United States can provide neither the welfare promotional role nor the local police protective role. Similar considerations of what is feasible because of practical limitations apply at every level of government. Local governments cannot maintain all the roads or finance all aspects of education. The national level cannot handle the ordinary aspects of refuge disposal.

SUBSIDIARITY

What can be discerned from this pyramid of decisions based on the practical minimum/maximum considerations is that all levels of government, whether they know it or not, operate according to a principle which would see to it that the lowest unit that can perform a function should do so, and if it cannot, some next higher unit should undertake that function. This principle of operation has been identified as the "principle of subsidiarity." The principle of subsidiarity states that "the lowest unit of society which is able to accomplish a particular function adequately, efficiently, and with benefit to the welfare of the whole should be permitted to do so."[3] In examining its background it is unclear whether subsidiarity is a deductive or an empirical rule, whether its origin is in prior theoretical propositions or practical observations of repeated experiences. Whatever the case it is both a useful guide and a helpful description of governmental decision making. E. F. Schumacher, the British economist and essayist, adopts its essential thought in his *Small Is Beautiful*.

Schumacher's principal intention was to speak of large-scale business operations. At one point, however, he refers to "a famous formulation" of the "principle of subsidiarity" and says that though it originally was meant to apply to society as a whole it can apply equally to the different levels within a large organization.

> It is an injustice and at the same time a grave evil and disturbance of right order to assign to a greater and higher association what lesser and subordinate organizations can do. For every social activity ought of its very nature to furnish help to the members of the body social and never destroy and absorb them.[4]

Schumacher interprets this formulation to mean that "the higher level must not absorb the functions of the lower one, on the assumption that, being higher, it will automatically be wiser and fulfill them more efficiently." He adds a few lines later that the principle "implies that the burden of proof lies always on those who want to deprive a lower level of its function, and thereby of its freedom and responsibility in that respect; *they* have to prove that the lower level is incapable of fulfilling this function satisfactorily and that the higher level can actually do much better."

As mentioned a moment ago, Schumacher intended to apply this formulation to large business organizations, pointing out that it is sound organizational, personnel, and economic policy. What is interesting is that the principle is seldom mentioned as such with respect to society, its original intention according to Schumacher, and yet it fits so well in describing that pyramid of practical budget decisions. It is as if to say that government operates according to an organizational principle and does not even know it.

Subsidiarity is both a description of what government does and a guide to remind government of its practical limitations. It is, as has been pointed out, a practical way in which all the theoretical approaches to the purpose of government come to grips with immediate policy and budget issues. No one rejects their theoretical goals but each must make incremental steps toward those goals if progress is to be made. In the Soviet Union, which may desire total government domination of the economy as opposed to the 80 percent, or so, level at which it currently operates, practical or subsidiarity-type decisions have to be made about what control or program is most needed or most important to add next. In England, on the other hand, which may desire less government involvement in the economy from the current 47 percent level of GNP in the public sector, similar subsidiarity decisions must be made about which programs are least needed.

In other words all levels of government decisions to increase or decrease programs, to tax, to regulate, to intervene, to purchase, or to ignore are made in terms of the minimum necessary and the maximum possible, the minimum costs and the maximum benefit. No government, no matter what its will or theoretical position, can make large scale changes without paying the price in disruptions, be they economic, social, psychological, or structural. Despite great revolutionary events the perspective of time shows them to be incremental in final analysis. Revolutions principally change personnel. The actual changes in the total amount of governmental activity is found to be incremental once the revolutionary dust settles. In some instances that is not the case and then all are aware of the disruptiveness which ensues. Cambodia, now called Kampuchea, is a recent example.

The scope of these practical decisions suggests, and is indeed intended to suggest, that the principle of subsidiarity has a wider applicability to government than to just budgets and similar policy matters of size. It applies to the larger question of governmental organization, to revolution, and indeed to the consideration of change as a general concept. The minimum/maximum principle of respecting the lowest unit and allowing for higher level involvement where appropriate has a general usefulness which can be seen in nearly all aspects of government. A glimmer demonstrating that sweeping proposition can be seen in how subsidiarity helps to explain justice, an important but often confusing and neglected concept in political science.

JUSTICE

A casual review of thirty-one different textbooks designed to be an "introduction to political science" reveals that two thirds do not consider the topic of "justice." There is no mention of justice in the index or the table of contents. Four texts had from one to six paragraphs devoted to the discussion of the topic while giving no other mention to it. One text indexed "Justice, Soviet concept of" and gave two brief paragraphs to the special approach to "justice" in the Soviet Union. Five texts gave a good number of pages of attention to justice, equating it with fairness and goodness but admitting the difficult and elusive nature of the concept. This was an admittedly casual survey of textbooks but the proportional numbers would most likely be the same in a more systematic examination. This review lends support to the postbehavioralists' complaint that much of contemporary political science is an apolitical or antipolitical treatment of a methodologically limited topic to the neglect of questions of great concern.

One reason for the void in the consideration of justice may be, as pointed out in Chapter 3, that many of the texts, as a large part of the discipline, tend to be empirical or behavioral and therefore deliberately shy away from philosophical or theoretical, or what they call "normative," considerations, as if there were no theoretical or normative underpinnings to their "more scientific" approach. The problem is, however, that if justice is not considered in an introductory political science text then it is left by default to others. Those others who will set its parameters, like philosophers, sociologists, and religious scholars, lack the empirical knowledge of political scientists for coming to grips with both the compelling necessity and practical complexity of situations which require justice.

Some of the discussion on war and peace in the last two decades has been dominated by disciplines other than political science, giving further substance to the complaint of the postbehavioralist. Men and women of religion, philosophers, sociologists, and many others have legitimate interest in war and peace and justice. They may see the lack of justice in most current arrangements but often they lack a firm grasp of the political realities which allow little immediate change. It is not true, on the other hand, that a grasp of those realities is necessarily informed by a profound sense of justice. The justice the political scientist accepts is often one of default, the inevitability of the situation. That justice is not really justice at all and the avoidance of the study of justice leaves them vulnerable to the criticism of the others.

Two Contemporary Studies

Two contemporary studies in jurisprudence show the type of work possible in combining empirical knowledge and a profound concern with justice. John Rawls' *A Theory of Justice*[5] and Ronald Dworkin's *Taking Rights Seriously*[6] address the question of justice in the contemporary world in a classical manner. They treat current concerns while reflecting on the thought of Plato, Aristotle, Rousseau, Kant, Mill and others. Rawls created the greatest stir and was the subject of seven lengthy reviews in the June, 1975 *American Political Science Review*. The reviews ranged from saying that he made effective use of the classics to saying that he misunderstood all of them. At least the reviews show that some political scientists are prepared to examine justice in detail. Dworkin takes a different tack. He examines Rawls and goes beyond the appearances of contract theory, utilitarianism, and game theory with which Rawls is associated. Dworkin finds a deep theory behind Rawls' original theory based on a concept of rights which are natural. In this way these contemporary discussions of justice get involved in some of the most classical questions in political philosophy. The only question we would raise is, why do not more introductory political science texts reflect this concern?

Classical Discussions of Justice

Justice is a structuring girder in the bridge between the theoretical and practical domains of politics. The girder comes from both sides and requires a knowledge of facts and theory. It must have some structural form to it, otherwise it will not support its surface. It is because of this need for form that most discussions give some attention to the writings of the classical authors. At the beginning of Western political thought, in Plato's *Republic,* at least three views of justice are given. There is the view of Thrasymachus, the Sophist, that " 'just' or 'right' means nothing except what is to the interest of the stronger party."[7] There is the view that justice is a compromise, the lesser evil between inflicting injustice without punishment and suffering injustice without the power of retaliation. Neither of these two views are satisfactory to Plato but they are seen many times in later thinkers.

The view that justice is nothing more than the interest of the strong was adopted by Machiavelli at the beginning of the modern era. In Machiavelli's pragmatic approach to the political world success is the measure of goodness. Under this criterion any means, even unjust ones, may be employed to achieve success. Hobbes's Leviathan took Machiavelli at his word by creating an absolute Prince whose goal may indeed have been order but whose means was power. Lockean laissez faire individualism came along to restore a more individual source of justice but its effect was to make everyone a little Prince. Marx saw this point and in his analysis rejected the "might makes right" of individualistic capitalism. Not too surprisingly, he provided the vehicle for the return of Machiavellian justice in oppressive totalitarian form in the leadership role assigned to the vanguard of the proletariat.

Rousseau, mentioned earlier in connection with the social contract theory, saw justice ideally as a function of the vague general will of consensus. A rationalized general will is what Rawls attempts to work from, but his effort in itself is proof that Rousseau's plan needed more concrete formulation. The utilitarians who followed Rousseau in the eighteenth and nineteenth centuries saw the weakness in his approach and attempted to give substance to justice by their famous formulation of "the greatest good to the greatest number." It may seem strange and improbable but the utilitarian concept of justice twenty-one centuries removed from Plato is similar to the one he rejected. That revival may not have been the utilitarians' intent. John Stuart Mill, for example, sought to protect the individual, but in this instance the stronger party is merely the greatest number.

In place of this rejected view, Plato proposed that justice was "to render what is due." Plato's *Republic* was an elaboration of "what is due." He outlined a scheme of roles and functions within the state and a coordination of individuals who were fit for those tasks. Plato argued that as the individual has certain parts to his or her body which must work in harmony for well-being, so the state has similar parts which must be harmonized. For Plato that harmony of parts is justice. Justice, for him, is the bond which holds a society together, a harmonious union of individuals, each of whom is fitted to an appointed task.

The Republic, in Plato's design, determined what the tasks were and who could best perform them: philosophers ought to be kings or kings ought to be philosophers, brave persons ought to be warriors, persons of domestic skills ought to be artisans or tradesmen. All this performance of respective tasks has an appearance of justice when compared to the sophist's view that tasks and duties are performed according to force and domination. However, there was a tyranny to the assignment of tasks and the rigid structure of the *Republic.* Individuals were not so much free to act as compelled to perform within the outline provided. The latter was one of Aristotle's criticisms of his teacher's concept of justice.

Aristotle, like Plato, saw justice as a harmony within the community, but the harmony had a natural as well as a positive or humanly determined part to it. It is this same distinction between the positive and the natural that constitutes the difference between much of modern writing on justice, including that of Rawls on the one hand and that of Dworkin on the other. Instead of outlining an idealized form of justice as found in Plato's *Republic,* Aristotle looked to various kinds of justice in various relationships. The parts of the community and individual behavior within the community must be taken for what they are for Aristotle. They cannot have an order or relationship imposed upon them from the outside as takes place in Plato. Aristotle seeks to discover what the parts and behavior are and then talks about improved relationships. He does not, as Plato does in his quest for justice, seek a stratified society with a coordinated educational system. Nor does Aristotle seek the abolition and communism of wives and property in the name of greater harmony for the community.

In contradistinction to Thrasymachus' justice of the strong, Plato's is a "rational" justice but it is much too rational. That much too rational plan is what is meant by Plato's ideal forms. The forms are rationally conceived in the mind instead of being the "natural" concepts of Aristotle. Aristotle saw concepts as the product of an interaction of reason and reality. Although Plato's conception is an improvement over force on the one hand or chaos on the other, its structure lacked flexibility. Aristotle's approach provided both structure and flexibility, principle and adaptability. For him there is a natural justice which is unchanging, and that which is evil cannot be made good. Yet Aristotle's justice is not rigid for he admits[8] the profound difference between the world of the "gods," of natural science, and of practical affairs where justice must be applied. What is unchangeable in one way in the first realm is unchangeable in a different way in the other realms. As the modern author Dworkin argues[9], the critical difference is in a deep theory of natural rights.

KINDS OF JUSTICE

One way to approach justice is to describe three kinds of justice: legal, distributive, and commutative. When each of these are examined, it is usually in terms of looking for what is natural or unchanging in them and what is positive or civil. For legal and commutative justice there is little dispute that something is naturally *due* in the relationship. *What* is due, the positive or civil part, may differ from place to place. That an obligation is owed stands uncontested. In this essentially Aristotelian conception the existence of justice itself is unquestioned even though the particulars may be. For distributive justice, however, the concept itself is questioned as well as the particular determinations. For this situation the principle of subsidiarity can make a significant contribution to both aspects. This use of subsidiarity has a double effect. It both contributes to the understanding of justice and it demonstrates the utility as a flexible but structuring principle in political relations. To appreciate subsidiarity's contribution it is first necessary to become familiar with legal justice and commutative justice.

Legal Justice

Legal justice deals with the individual's obligation to the state. An individual may not feel completely satisfied with all aspects of the state. Nonetheless it provides a base from which to seek improvements. Consequently the individual has an obligation to obey the laws that uphold the system. Without a minimum of order, which means individuals obeying the law, it is not possible to bring about change and improvement. This argument may sound self-serving, and indeed it is, but it is at the same time of service to everyone else.

All systems of order are the same. The modern mass communications network from which we all benefit can be disrupted by a handfull of agitators. Arbitrary harassment of a single individual can send fear through an entire community. The order from which the individual benefits requires cooperative observance, otherwise the system breaks down and the consequences are widespread. So what an individual owes the state is more than just getting by, more than not breaking the law. Legal justice says that one must observe the law in the sense of upholding the good of the community. Here is where the natural and civil part of justice come in. Agitators may be exercising their right to free speech but they are disrupting the right of many more. Harassment may not be technically illegal but it is harmful to the individual and the community.

The natural part of legal justice is that one has an obligation to uphold the good of the community, to obey the law which upholds the state. The civil part of legal justice pertains to what the particular law is. In one state or country the particular law may be that of compulsory military service. In another country the law may merely be registration of eighteen-year-olds for a selective service system even though there may be no draft. In a third state the military system may be completely mercenary. In some countries the individual is obliged to tend to certain civic duties like voting or patriotic rituals, while in others these practices are completely voluntary.

These practices in themselves are indifferent. Alone they are neither just nor unjust. It is only when they become a legal statute that they become a matter of legal justice. In the same way other matters such as jury service and the payment of income taxes are part of legal justice. They may seem relatively insignificant on the individual level but when considered as part of the cooperative functioning of the whole system the individual act assumes a larger importance. It is in the context of the whole that the individual has obligations. These obligations are neither arbitrary nor misanthropic. As indicated, the individual benefits from them. The corresponding benefits of the individual will be discussed later.

In the next chapter the source of individual rights will be examined in a more constitutional sense. In the previous chapters on the philosophy of the state there were aspects which had clear implications for the relationship between the individual and the state. Setting all those considerations aside for the time being, there is an interesting question about whether the individual has an obligation to the community beyond the minimum. It is like asking whether one should buy a higher octane lead-free gas for one's car than is necessary to make it run. It is not clear that one must serve on civic bodies or become a worker in political campaigns. These certainly are not legal obligations in the sense of positive law. But there is a larger sense of justice where one may be obliged to contribute in some way to the continued functioning of the community even though the exact actions may be unspecified. Making up passable but nonetheless false excuses for avoiding jury duty is an interesting test of one's sense of legal justice.

The individual may be faithful in paying taxes and obeying the law generally. Some consideration must be given, however, to doing more, because otherwise the community is forced to operate on minimal standards. Consider, analogously, the practices of business. There one can get by with minimum standards for a time but it is the business that goes beyond the minimum, which offers better quality at low cost, which often excels and endures. Communities in which the individual feels inspired to do more for the community than just get by are stronger and have happier individuals. Empirical evidence can be found for this in reflecting on various volunteer programs. The Red Cross's voluntary blood donor program, Little League sports programs, community orchestras, and planting flowers in the public square are only a few of many examples. In these volunteer programs individuals do more that the minimum. They make a contribution to the community and they feel better about themselves because that donation of time and self helped so many others. The individual and the community benefit at the same time.

It is common to look at the legal system in terms of its many rules and obligations and at times to complain about the weight of its excessive statutes. Legal justice accepts that maybe the laws that seem excessive had some original merit and if that no longer applies then those laws can be changed. That outlook is the larger sense of justice. It accepts obligations but does not let them impede individual freedom and growth.

Commutative Justice

Commutative justice is about the relationship between two or more individuals. Commutative justice, like the commutative property in mathematics, is an exchange. Here it is a matter of a fair day's work for a fair day's pay, a fair course for a fair tuition, a fair room for a fair rent. What is fair in work, pay, education, tuition, etc. may be subject to market factors. The point of commutative justice, however, is that once the unit of fairness is agreed upon it cannot be unilaterally changed.

The cashier in a restaurant cannot charge one patron a different price for the same meal than another patron. If I borrow twenty-five dollars from you or if I carelessly damage your textbook worth that amount then in justice, commutative justice, I owe you that amount. The natural part of justice, that an exchange is due, is clear. The positive part is determined by the factors of time and place. It would be contrary to justice if the professor who damaged the student's book pulled rank and intimidated the student out of what was due.

Legal suits which involve property or contracts are often an acknowledgement of the natural part of justice, that something is due. The suit is over the positive part, *what* is due. Commutative justice is a normal part, and a normally clear part, of the political order. Civil suits over property, damages, or divorce are matters of commutative justice. Criminal matters, the other principal form of judicial proceedings, come out of legal justice and involve the actual breaking of the law.

The civil suit is an effort to determine precisely what is due in a particular circumstance. That there are so many suits is not a sign of the lack of justice in the wider community of human relations. One has to consider how many suits were not entered. There is an ongoing agreement on exchange in the community. Most relationships proceed smoothly. When they do not, when a specific determination is necessary, they come to public attention.

Distributive Justice

Distributive justice is an entirely different domain from legal and commutative justice. At first it is not easy to identify or to specify the content of distributive justice. It is frequently called "social justice," which suggests that it has some special social character that the other forms of justice do not. That suggestion is misleading and false. All justice, as can be observed in the previous discussion, is social! Anything that involves two or more individuals is social.

Distributive justice is no more nor less social than the other two. When the redundant phrase "social justice" is applied solely to distributive justice it is singled out and suggests that it alone is social. Such a suggestion is potentially harmful for the following reasons. Owing to the disagreements over the contents of distributive justice some people would like to disregard it and still assume that they are just. Furthermore to fail to regard commutative and legal justice as social puts them in a strictly contractual or positive light. This light ignores the broader natural dimensions which make community life successful. A strictly positive and contractual view of justice reduces all relations to tedious individualistic exchanges.

As to the content of distributive justice, it may be said that it is the other side of the coin of legal justice. In other words, as the individual is obliged to the state, so the state is obliged to the individual. Distributive justice obliges the state with respect to the allocation of the benefits and burdens of society. This allocation should not be wholly from quantitative equality. It should be decided according to the needs, merits, and abilities of the individuals who compose society. In keeping with this mutual obligation of individual and society, each individual has the duty to contribute a just share to the common good, which share is determined in part by the ability of the individual. At the same time each individual has a claim to the advantages of society. The latter claim is measured to some extent by need.

The duty to support society's functioning according to ability is accomplished through a progressive income tax. The distribution of advantages according to need is fulfilled through welfare programs. From these two examples the controversial character of distributive justice should be evident. Contributing according to ability and sharing according to need sounds much like the slogan "from each according to ability, to each according to need." That slogan, because of its association with Marxism and communism, raises many frightening possibilities to large numbers of people. It is easy to see why distributive justice does not get sympathetic attention.

It is true that distributive justice is saying that the individual should contribute to the community to some extent according to ability and that the individual may also receive according to need. This is the natural part of distributive justice: those in need should be helped, those not in need should help. What must be determined is the positive part. The content of what is due must be determined. There are some obvious requirements, at least they become obvious after a little discussion, which is often the way the obvious occurs. Furthermore, upon reflection the requirements reveal a two-way subsidiarity relationship. Through this examination, as indicated earlier, subsidiarity amounts to both a description of how things function and a guide to how they should function.

The obvious requirements of need and support are brought out by considering the situation of a child born to an unwed mother living in poverty. The child at least is clearly in need. A child born into a wealthy family, on the other hand, is clearly not in need of public assistance. The poor child should not be denied help on the grounds that many other children do not require it. It may be said that the taxes to support the poor child come through the state from the wealthy parents of the other child. This redistribution of wealth at the expense of those who had nothing to do with the poor unwed mother is viewed by many to be an offense against justice rather than a practice of it. But, it must be asked, from where is the help for the poor child to come? Is the poor child to suffer for not making a good choice of parents?

The assistance cannot come from other poor people because they are, by definition, not in a position to help. In addition, if the help were to come from those just above the poverty level the results might well enlarge the number of poor. The only reasonable source for financing such services is those who are in a position to pay without being forced into economic hardships. The result is indeed one of giving according to ability and receiving according to need, but this result does not have the character, as might have been the first impression, of *leveling* society.

Leveling would consist of taking the wealth of all and redistributing it on average to the entire population. That leveling or averaging is not involved in the situation described above of the poor child in need of aid. What is involved is some mechanism to see to it that the lowest unit of society, the poor child, can come to a point where it can operate adequately, efficiently, and with benefit to the welfare of the whole. In this way need is functionally determined. It is not purely a matter of relative income comparisons. The ability to pay would have a similar functional content with a progressive income tax system because the revenue would be in inverse relation to need.

The two-sided subsidiarity relationship is, on the one hand, the provision for the lowest unit of society to operate adequately. On the other hand, it is the provision of the tax system which sees to it that those marginally close to poverty are not brought into the lower level by paying what others of higher incomes can more easily afford. So subsidiarity makes it easier to understand distributive justice and the requirements to support it.

In a purely utilitarian sense, which is, strictly speaking, not just, those who are wealthy would want to see the poor come to a point of operating adequately because that point, again by definition, is one at which there is no longer the need to "take from the rich to give to the poor." This utilitarian exchange concept is not just because its intention is selfish. It is a minimalist's position of saying, "Aid the oppressed, not because they are in need but to keep them away from our door."

Here once again in the theoretical question of what is truly just, the different theoretical positions about the purpose of the state and the role of government come to bear. The practical, subsidiarity position that something of a concrete character must be done is present, too. There may be disagreement about what type of help should be given, how much, and in what manner. There may be questions about the particular tax system and whether it is truly progressive or if something else might be more appropriate. Those questions and disagreements about amounts and forms of aid are the positive side of distributive justice. The natural side of distributive justice is that some assistance must be provided to those in need.

CONCLUSION AND PERSPECTIVE

Justice may say that a child born to a poor, unwed mother is entitled to aid. What does justice say about that mother continuing to have more children? Can the government take steps to prevent this from occurring? That further step is a question of justice also. That question is usually taken up in a consideration of rights, and the larger topic of the relationship of the individual to the state will be discussed in ensuing chapters. The point of the above discussion of the poor child in the context of distributive justice was that the principle of subsidiarity can be helpful in understanding the usually troublesome concept of justice.

Subsidiarity can serve as a guide for what governments actually do and at the same time it can serve as a norm for what policies might be considered. The example cited both describes what the government actually does and reminds us of the importance of the policy for all levels of society. Because of this dual role of norm and guide for understanding, subsidiarity has a potentially great role as an organizing concept for many if not most relationships within the state. Schumacher, as pointed out earlier, wanted to use it with respect to large business organizations but he indicated that the principle was intended for society as a whole. What will be seen in the next few chapters is that it is useful in providing a framework for understanding the relationships between the individual and the state, groups and the state, and of states to one another. Later it will be seen that it has a usefulness in understanding constitutionalism, and, perhaps obviously by this point, it has a special utility with respect to the concept of federalism in the United States.

The disagreements over the purpose of the state are not forgotten and they will not fade from sight. Our attention shifts more and more to factual matters but subsidiarity provides a link to the important theoretical points which will appropriately surface from time to time. The structural underpinnings of the bridge between the theoretical and the practical constantly affect both sides.

NOTES

1. This discussion reflects in a broad way the well-thought-out and detailed introductory presentation of budgets, taxes, and priorities found in Thomas R. Dye's *Understanding Public Policy*, 4th ed. (Englewood Cliffs, N.J.: Prentice-Hall, 1981), Chapters 10 and 11.

2. Patience becomes as much a virtue for government officials as it does for the parent or other members of a family. Constant frustration is its alternative.

3. Cf. Henry J. Schmandt and Paul G. Steinbicker, *Fundamentals of Government* (Milwaukee: Bruce Publishing Co., 1963), pp. 114-15.

4. E. F. Schumacher, *Small Is Beautiful: Economics as if People Mattered* (New York: Perennial Library of Harper & Row, 1973), p. 244.

5. John Rawls, *A Theory of Justice* (Cambridge: Harvard University Press, 1971).

6. Ronald Dworkin, *Taking Rights Seriously* (Cambridge: Harvard University Press, 1978).

7. Plato, *The Republic* Book I, section 338.

8. Aristotle, *Ethics*, 1134b, 25.

9. Ronald Dworkin, "Justice and Rights," in *Taking Rights Seriously*, pp. 150–183.

CHAPTER TEN
THE INDIVIDUAL AND THE STATE: A FOCUS ON RIGHTS

In considering the individual's relationship to the state the individual is normally referred to as a "citizen." A citizen is understood to be "one who possesses rights." This is the common framework for discussions ranging from the most minor role of the individual to the most fundamental matters of personal security. Everything is encompassed in terms of the rights of the individual as a citizen. Certainly the focus on rights is legitimate and understandable in the light of modern historical experience of the wholesale abuse of individuals by absolute monarchs and revolutionary mobs.

Historical Perspective

It should be made clear, however, before undertaking that legitimate examination of the individual's relationship to the state in terms of rights, that there is an altogether different way of looking at the relationship. The consideration of the relationship of individual and state in terms of rights is a relatively recent concern. It is important to see a larger context in which the relationship can be viewed.

Considering the relation of individual and state in terms of rights is relatively recent both with respect to the United States and Western history. Although it is true that in the United States the Bill of Rights has been part of the Constitution for nearly two hundred years, active legal recourse to the provisions of that Bill of Rights is hardly fifty years old. If Western history is dated from some point before

Homer and the documentation of "rights" date from the English lawyers of the late Elizabethan period, then here also the concern is relatively recent.

What is meant by "a concern with rights" is a concentrated attention to "what the individual has that the state may not take away." Rights are thought of as "something the individual possesses as against the state." That antagonism between individual and state is not the character of the relationship in Greek or Roman times nor during the medieval era. Even in the early American period, although there was some political haggling over the inclusion of a Bill of Rights in the Constitution, the actual history of "rights" cases does not begin until well into the twentieth century.

The history of rights frequently begins with reference to the Magna Carta of 1215 in England. Careful examination reveals that barons and nobles benefited from this early document. Its general applicability to individuals did not come for many hundreds of years. The efforts of Edmund Coke and other English lawyers in the early seventeenth century mark the beginning of the slow process of making the concept of rights generally applicable to individuals in society at large.

At the time of the drafting of the American Constitution the general concept of rights was current in learned circles. Some experience of the general abridgment of personal liberties had occurred under English rule, yet the practice of individuals needing protection from the state was not widespread in America. American history and American judicial history is divided broadly into three periods: the national period from 1780 to 1865, the business period from 1865 to 1937, and the period of rights from 1937 to the present.[1] It is only in the current era that rights have assumed the prominence with which all history is myopically judged. So dominantly is this contemporary image projected onto the past that many cannot picture any other.

The notion that the individual possesses something which the state cannot take away, the general notion of rights, suggests a negative relationship between the individual and the state. It assumes that there is a natural antagonism between the two. Although there are undeniable historical grounds for this view, the evidence is only partial. More importantly, that assumption of antagonism reflects the individualistic and anarchistic attitudes toward the state. Setting the theory considerations aside, clearly an objective evaluation of the relationship between the individual and the state cannot rest on only those instances when there is abuse anymore than when there is not. The relationship ought to be judged on those periods when there was no oppression as well as when it occurred.

Participation

In classical Greek times and in the philosophy of the state which accompanied them, there was a notion of a cooperation between individual and community. The classical Greek notion of citizen was "one who participates in the life of the community." For Aristotle the citizen was one who "shares" in the offices of the state and in the administration of justice. The citizen, for him, "should know how to govern like a freeman and how to obey like a freeman." The purpose of this sharing was the betterment of both the individual and the community. As he said at length in his *Politics:*

> It is clear then that a state is not a mere society, having a common place, established for the prevention of mutual crime and for the sake of exchange. These are conditions without which a state cannot exist; but all of them together do not constitute a state, which is a community of families and aggregations of families in well-being, for the sake of a perfect and self-sufficing life. Such a community can only be established among those who live in the same place and intermarry. Hence arise in cities family connexions, brotherhoods, common sacrifices, amusements which draw men together. But these are created by friendship, for the will to live together is friendship. The end of the state is the good life, and these are the means toward it. And the state is the union of families and villages in a perfect and self-sufficing life, by which we mean a happy and honourable life.[2]

In Athens, participation was the greatest blessing of a citizen and the greatest deprivation if not possessed. There was no thought of the citizen possessing something which had to be held jealously against the state that wanted to take it away.

In eighteenth- and nineteenth-century America the sharing and cooperative living was rich as it had been in the ancient setting. The rhetoric of constitution making might have spoken of bills of rights. Recent colonial experiences might have convinced some of the need for such bills. The reality was one of individual sharing and growth in a community of friendship. The breadth of the country and its rich natural resources combined with a literal ocean of protection from foreign military and economic adversaries made it possible for the creation of a vast number of communities of like-minded individuals. America was not just an aggregation of individuals forced to live in a common place. People migrated to the United States from Europe because they could grow and prosper in a community which they themselves built. There was enough space so that if friendship did not exist in one place it could be developed in another.

In the American experience, as had been the case in ancient Greece, there was a slavery system which was an ultimate denial of rights. The slavery system in the United States at least served as the principal economic prop of only a portion of the total number of communities. Unfortunately in both the ancient world and in America the question of slavery was not faced as an abstract issue of human rights. When the slavery issue was first faced politically it was not as an issue of human rights but as a political issue of who could be counted in the community. Some abolitionists spoke of the abstract rights of the person but practically those rights were only attended to in the last fifty years.

Slavery was, so to speak, a blind spot for both worlds. It might be said that in that setting participation was at the expense of other individuals. It must be remembered that slaves constituted a small number of the total population. Although those numbers do not excuse the practice, the participation character of citizenship should not to be diminished by this historic fault. Participation played a large role in nineteenth-century American growth. Because of that growth America took on a twentieth-century world role. Eventually the incongruity of legal membership and actual exclusion brought about a change. Emancipation in itself did not accomplish an immediate realization of personal rights. Realization was unfortunately gradual but it was nonetheless steady once it got started.

Although we like to congratulate ourselves for an abstract adherence to rights, it is only with their experience in community situations, and only in a participatory setting that they become something more than words. The people of late nineteenth-century and early twentieth-century America thought of themselves as truly practicing the respects for rights of even the former slave. It was only with the spread of those former slaves and their descendants throughout the country as a result of industrial growth and World War II that participation (really nonparticipation) challenged the verbal assumptions. Western frontiers, the clarion call to participation in the nineteenth century, were replaced with urban and personal frontiers. Homesteading became urban instead of rural. The enjoyment of rights followed this growth rather than preceded it.

Today rights are emphasized and participation is given little attention, the opposite of the earlier period. The inattention may explain why apathy is a greater phenomenon than voting and why legal justice is often viewed in only a minimal sense. Without deciding that point, citizenship should be appreciated in the dual sense of both possessing rights and participation in the community. A lengthy discussion of rights will be taken up in the remainder of this chapter but worth should not be judged in terms of length.

One problem with the participatory aspect of citizenship is that the opportunities for involvement seem often to be limited to either voting or being a candidate. It should be made clear that participation in the life of the community is not limited to such disparate alternatives. It must be understood that the life of the community involves more than the few acts which surround the biannual election ceremony. If people realized that they are participating when they give blood, or help out at the young girls softball league, or serve on a volunteer fire department, or drop money in the Salvation Army canister at holiday time, or perform any other volunteer action, there would be a more positive appreciation of this other aspect of citizenship.

The focus on rights has been such that we have forgotten that the participatory role is still very large. This is true not just in the sense that, like breathing, everyone does it. Studies[3] of various national political cultures show a gradation of participation from low to high. Some countries have greater participation, some have less. The practice of judging participation according to nonvoting levels should be challenged for not counting the other forms of involvement like those just mentioned. Voting and nonvoting may be one factor in a index of participation. Other factors like those mentioned may be more difficult to tabulate. That does not make them any less important.

An interesting study would be a correlation between levels of participation and the actual enjoyment of rights in various countries. Most interesting studies really cannot be done. We will speculate on this one later in the chapter on constitutionalism. As mentioned in the chapter on methodology, the lack of agreement on terms and measuring instruments severely handicaps any such study. One might expect, however, a fairly high correlation between participation levels and the respect for rights. It may be necessary to do no more than to look around for confirmation.

RIGHTS: ARE THEY ABSOLUTE OR RELATIVE?

Do rights come from the state or from some other source? Are they unchanging? Are they relatively durable but not absolute preferences? These questions quickly erode our normally assumed knowledge of rights. If rights come from some external source then individuals are in a dependent position. If they come from some constitutional majority they are not any better off since the majority may change.

In another set of unacceptable alternatives, if rights are relative they lack security and if they are absolute they are unrealistic. To suggest an absolute is to hold that something cannot change anywhere or anytime. If an absolute "right" existed then everyone would know what it is, and if absolute "rights" existed there would be the problem of deciding which is more absolute than the other. If the only alternative to "absolute" is "relative" and relative means subject to time and circumstance, rights do not have a very sturdy footing. These observations show some of the shortcomings of the commonplace ways of understanding rights.

There is an alternative to understanding rights as either absolute or relative. Rights are neither absolute nor relative, they are principles. A "principle" is something which carries with it the importance and respect which the word "absolute" attempts to convey. At the same time principle suggests the need for application and interpretation while not implying the fluidity of being relative. Rights as principles are held most dear, they are fundamental and comprehensive but not dogmatical.

A right taken as an absolute would condemn any abridgment of it, whether in self-defense or by accident. All infractions would fall before the sweeping indictment of violators of the absolute. Understood as a principle to be respected and applied, rights do not have the problem of absolutes, nor do they have the problem of the ephemeralness of being relative.

It is unusual, however, to describe a right as a principle. Most people have not heard rights explained in this way. Nonetheless it is a better and clearer way to understand the relationship of government and state to the individual. There are so many constitutional provisions and there have been so many cases about rights that the common practice of memorizing passages and cases proves increasingly improbable. When the general concept of principle in application to rights is understood in terms of subsidiarity the many different rights and the controversies surrounding them become more manageable. There are hundreds, indeed thousands, of cases involving rights. Some way is needed to understand them that is both efficient and accurate. Subsidiarity provides that understanding.

Subsidiarity, as indicated in the previous chapter, means that the lowest unit of society that can perform a function adequately, efficiently, and to the welfare of the whole should be permitted to do so. Here if the lowest unit is understood as the individual or the activity of the individual then the principle means that the integrity of that particular unit or function should be assumed. As with subsidiarity in general, if the lower unit cannot perform the function and it is a necessary function or if its improper performance is of serious concern to society, then in some way the unit or activity can be interfered with.

The principle of subsidiarity as described earlier can be equated as a principle of "decentralization." This means that if the lowest unit cannot perform a necessary function then there is within the principle a "centralizing" spiral so that the function can be performed with no harm to society. In application to rights, if an individual acts in a manner harmful to society then some level of society can intervene in an orderly way. To appreciate subsidiarity's contribution to understanding rights, a survey of several rights and related problems must be undertaken. The rights examined will be those in the general grouping of life, liberty, and property. Subsidiarity will serve as both a tool for understanding these rights and as a normative reminder of the respect that is expected.

LIFE AND CAPITAL PUNISHMENT

A most basic right is life. All communities have special ceremonies marking the commencement of life and its ending. Likewise all humans have a horror at the artificial termination of life in great calamities or individual accidents. Murder is a crime against life which is subject to severe response in organized or unorganized communities. A significant test of a community's respect for life comes in those circumstances when a murderer is found guilty. Should capital punishment be exercised? Can life be respected in these circumstances?

There is no question that capital punishment can be invoked when there is no other way to secure society from future harm by the convicted murderer. A more crucial question comes when society's security is not in jeopardy and yet the convicted murderer is guilty of heinous actions. It is a question of the severity of the legal response that is central to the controversy about capital punishment. If life were taken as an absolute then there would be no question that capital punishment could not be used. But treating life as an absolute would also challenge all past actions which took life, whether in military or criminal justice procedures.

To condemn capital punishment outright is unreasonable. That would suggest that all past use of it was wrong and would critcize all future use without consideration of circumstances. Such a sweeping position assumes too much. It may also be unreasonable, however, to continue to use this form of punishment at the present time. Given contemporary American conditions it is entirely possible to secure society through adequate prison systems. At a time when prisons were less secure than today, or less secure than most industrial nations are capable of today, capital punishment had to be employed. The principle of respect for life applies differently in those less secure conditions.

Many arguments are raised in the capital punishment debates. One argument is that the murderer did not respect the right of the victim and therefore surrendered the right to life. Other arguments are that the punishment should suit the crime, life in prison is cruel and inhumane and execution is more humane, life imprisonment is too costly (currently $15,000 to $25,000 per year per prisoner), and capital punishment is a deterrent. None of these arguments show much respect for life. One proponent of capital punishment said that it is needed as "a symbol of our concern for life and safety."[4] That is a strange argument indeed. Capital punishment may be a symbol of safety for some but it is hard to imagine how it is a symbol for life. It is as if the guillotine were a symbol of life. To prove that it is wrong to kill by killing is twisted logic. It accepts the premise of the murderer that life need not be always respected if inconvenient to do so. The trading of one life for another is a vengeful brutalization of society contradicting pretensions of respect for life.

Capital punishment's reinforcement of *dis*respect for life was evidenced in a press release for the Independent Truckers Association in opposing the national 55 mile per hour speed limit a few years ago: "If Gary Gilmore [A convicted and executed murderer at the time] can be allowed to kill himself, or be sentenced to death, then the nation's speeding motorists should have the same right."[5] Gilmore, whose brutal murders made headlines, got even more attention when he insisted that the state carry out his death sentence. Subsequently Norman Mailer wrote a book about Gilmore and a movie gave further publicity to this despicable character. Instead of contributing to all this attention two things should have been said to Gilmore: one, "Go back to your cell," and two, "Shut up!" If these things had been done Gilmore would still be sitting there and more could have been written on how horrible it is to sit in prison for the rest of one's life.

An argument used to support capital punishment is that it is a deterrent to crime. Former U.S. Senator James Buckley maintained that capital punishment is "the ultimate deterrent" and that it is "cruel and inhuman to allow a person to linger in prison for long periods of time awaiting death." That same Senator Buckley had argued against legalized abortion as a "new medical ethic" in which "the dignity and sanctity of the person is sacrificed upon the altar of social utility."[6] The argument suggests that it is okay to sacrifice the dignity and sanctity of the person on the altar of social utility if it is a deterrent to crime. There have been many sociological studies about the deterrent effect of capital punishment. The only conclusion that they can agree upon is that the executed murderer is deterred from further crime. That same effect could be achieved by a secure prison.

What Buckley was arguing with respect to abortion was that one person cannot be used just because it is socially useful to do so. That same argument should obtain even when it comes to the murderer whose acts lack dignity and sanctity but whose life, as life, is still to be respected. It truly is a question of whose premises are to prevail. And, it should be noted, if the deterrent argument has any merit, which is not definitively established, then incarceration for life should serve as a greater deterrent. Life imprisonment would be more properly a symbol of life and safety. If it is pointed out that even the prison guards are not safe from some murderers, the answer should be lock that one up and, literally, throw away the key.

A concern with keeping individuals in prison for life is the amount of tax money needed to do this. Expenses for running prisons are begrudged now and would be even more so if needed improvements were made. Warren Burger, before he became Chief Justice, acknowledged the dilemma of the criminal justice system:

> In part the terrible price we are paying in crime is because we have tended—once the drama of the trial is over—to regard all criminals as human rubbish. It would make more sense, from a coldly logical viewpoint, to put all this rubbish into a vast incinerator than simply to store it in warehouses for a period of time, only to have most of the subjects come out of prison and return to their old ways.[7]

Burger has continued somewhat of a crusade for more adequately dealing with prisons and criminal justice practices since he has been on the Court. His is not a proposal to mollify criminals. Nor would he mitigate criminal responsibility by blaming society's environment for the acts of crime. Burger is not proposing a harsh system of incinerators to deal with convicted criminals. A cheaper and more widely used system of capital punishment is not the answer to prison costs. What would be saved or spent by executing all those currently on death row is marginal compared to total prison costs and the amounts needed to rectify inadequacies.

The criminal is to be neither coddled nor abused. What is needed is a tough, adequate, and fair system where overcrowding, homosexual rape, drug abuse, and many other abuses do not occur. To provide such a system more money needs to be spent than is currently done. Most people do not like to think of their hard-earned money, which could be spent on deserving personal projects, going to support the prison system and individuals whose actions could hardly be said to be deserving. It is the case, however, that each year more money is spent separately on liquor, beer, cigarettes, cosmetics, luxury cars, video games, designer swimwear, and other similar nonessentials than on the prison system.

All these items are either personally harmful or transitory. Although they may be a manifestation of individual free choice, when weighed against the value of supporting life it is hoped that the comparison would give most reason to pause. An excise tax or an increase in a sales tax on these nonessential items could support a more adequate prison system and at the same time keep alive all murderers who might have been sentenced to death. The tax would be worth it for at the same time it would maintain support for society's principles. It would also help us cut down on some things that are not particularly healthy for us anyway.

Personal comfort is a desirable thing when taken in moderation. Moderation has to be measured in the context of one's society and its values. If respect for life is truly a value, if it is truly a "right" which concerns all, then society must be consistent in upholding it. Viewing life as a right in light of subsidiarity says that life will be respected, even the life of the convicted murderer, unless there is no other way to secure society from future harm from that murderer. We expect war to be the last resort, we expect the police to resort to force and weapons only when there is no other course of action, and we expect individuals to be nonviolent in personal disagreements. Avoiding capital punishment is consistent with these values.

Wars occur, the police use force, and individuals come to blows, but all these come about, or so we hope, when the action is necessary and there is no other recourse. The series of expectations and events are in keeping with that principle of assuming individual integrity. The individual or individual right is not an absolute, but at the same time society's jurisdiction is not based on majority preference. The principle starts with the individual but when it is demonstrated—demonstration is what a legal system of jury trials and appeals is all about—that the action or person lacks integrity, then intervention may occur. The burden of proof for interference is on society's side.

A few years ago in *Furman* v. *Georgia* (1972), the Supreme Court ruled against capital punishment on the grounds that procedures were arbitrary and capricious, with some individuals receiving the death penalty for crimes for which others received much lighter sentences. A couple of years later, after many states adjusted their sentencing procedures, the Court in a series of cases (chiefly *Gregg* v. *Georgia,* 1976) found the death penalty statutes acceptable and not a violation of the cruel and unusual punishment provisions of the Eighth and Fourteenth Amendments. The Court took note that thirty-five states had enacted death penalty statutes since its 1972 decision, and the Court seemed to defer to popular sentiment supporting capital punishment. The Court said that "a large proportion of American society continues to regard it as an appropriate and necessary criminal sanction."[8]

The Supreme Court is not usually so cravenly political in its decisions. An explanation may be that the Court was caught in the logic of its *Furman* decision. When the states enacted less arbitrary and capricious procedures, the Court either had to accept them or ban capital punishment outright on the grounds of violating cruel and unusual punishment prohibitions. For federalism or decentralization purposes, explained later, it may be best that the Court not be the instrument to ban capital punishment. It would be better for the respective state legislatures to see the wisdom of banning it. Since legislatures and politicians in general are not likely to oppose capital punishment—the individual calling it a symbol of life was a candidate for governor when he, like many others, spoke in favor of it—the Supreme Court will eventually be forced back into the arena.

If conditions in American prisons continue as they have, the Court in coming years will be handing down a large number of widely publicized decisions in this area, including possibly an Eighth Amendment decision outlawing capital punishment. The point about subsidiarity in this topic of "life and capital punishment" is not which level of the legal system makes the decision, but the primary concern of respecting the integrity of life and when the Court will find itself unable to let state legislatures continue to ignore it. The readers will forget that they heard it here first, but in their lifetime capital punishment will be banned once again. Probably, and unfortunately, it will be the Court and not the legislatures which will ban it.

THE RIGHT TO PERSONAL LIBERTY

The previous section, discussing the right of life, showed that life could be understood better as a principle than as either an absolute or as relative. The basic concept was (1) to assume the integrity of the right or individual or activity and (2) to allow that the assumption of integrity can be abridged when it is demonstrated that integrity is lacking in necessary functions. The basic approach, henceforth called the principle approach or the subsidiarity approach, of assuming integrity and allowing interference can be applied to the whole range of rights. In the first area the integrity of life was assumed, but the assumption could be superseded if there were no other way to secure society from future harm.

The principle approach is both descriptive and analytical of the way rights and the whole topic of the relationship of the individual to the state in fact take place. It is also normative in that it starts from a standard of assuming integrity. An outline of the principle approach applied to several specific rights is seen in Table 10-1. Basic to the approach are the two parts, the assumption of integrity and the corollary of what occurs when integrity is lacking. A description of the rights in this way will both clarify the use of the principle and instruct about the actual exercise of rights.

Beyond the application to life itself, the principle approach can be applied to the various physical and mental attributes that human beings possess. This means that no one may deprive an individual of limbs, eyes, brain, reproductive power, or other attributes without just cause. It is hard to imagine what a just cause might be,

TABLE 10–1 PRINCIPLE APPROACH TO RIGHTS

RIGHT	*PRINCIPLE—assume integrity of:*	*COROLLARY—circumstances which limit the right, i.e., the principle applies unless:*
1. Life	1. Murderer's life	1. Inability to protect society from future harm
2. Speech	2. Whatever is said	2. Clear and present danger (Schenck Case) Grave and probable danger (Dennis Case)
3. Press	3. Whatever is printed or produced	3. Libel (after the fact) Obscenity (after the fact)
4. Privacy	4. Personal possessions and surroundings	4. National security is threatened
5. Criminal procedure	5. Innocent person	5. Proven guilty
6. Property ownership	6. Individual ownership	6. Necessary task is not performed adequately

but a medical necessity in which the individual refuses to cooperate and which is harmful to others may be an example. In any such case the decision is not a matter of subjecting the individual to the preferences of the community but is a "demonstrated need" with a "legally established" procedure for determining it.

Some years ago a prominent churchman proposed castration as a penalty for rapists. The proposal was later retracted with an acknowledgment that brutality is not a fit response to brutality. Actual abuses of this principle are reported in the news from time to time, as in the case of the fifteen-year-old girl whose sterilization was sanctioned by a judge at the request of the girl's mother "to prevent unfortunate circumstances to occur" since the girl was "considered to be somewhat retarded." The girl was told that she was having her appendix removed, so that at the age of twenty-one, married and unable to have children, she discovered the facts and brought suit against all parties for $3.25 million. The courts dismissed the suit on the grounds of ambiguous liability but the facts of the case, if accurate, give warning and notice to others of just what to be alert to in order to avoid similar ill-treatment.

Free Speech

Other cases concerning personal liberty are widely available that support and in turn are explained by the principle approach. Freedom of speech is an especially good example. The Courts pay great deference to freedom of speech. However, as established in the Schenck Case[9], if the speech constitutes a clear and present danger it can be suppressed. That particular case questioned laws passed by Congress prohibiting certain types of actions disruptive of the Conscription Act. Schenck, as general secretary of the Socialist Party, had sent out leaflets to men who had been called to military service, urging them to oppose the draft. When he was arrested and tried, Schenck argued that he was protected in his actions by the First Amendment guarantee of freedom of speech and press.

In rendering a decision the Court made clear the protected position of free expression but added that an act must be judged in the circumstances in which it occurs. Justice Holmes pointed out that "when a nation is at war many things that might be said in time of peace are such a hindrance to its effort that their utterance will not be endured so long as men fight and that no Court could regard them as protected by any constitutional right." In other words "the character of every act depends upon the circumstances in which it is done," adding that "the most stringent protection of free speech would not protect a man in falsely shouting fire in a theatre and causing panic."

The Court ruled in this case, and this is the key clause, that if the circumstances "create a clear and present danger" which would bring about "substantive evils that Congress has a right to prevent," then the action of Schenck is not protected. Thus the Court ruled against Schenck in the manner of (1) upholding the protected position of speech and expression and (2) making clear the established legal standards for determining in a factual situation whether the circumstances warrant interference. In other words the lack of integrity of the action or speech must be demonstrated. The burden of proof is on the state, and the Court felt in this instance that it had been met.

There is an immediacy to the circumstances in the Schenck case which would not always obtain in freedom of expression challenges. During World War II, after the period of the 1920s and 1930s with the development of the cell movement of the Communist Party of the United States, the Congress passed the Smith Act (1940), which outlawed the party for teaching and advocating the overthrow and destruction of the United States by force and violence. Eleven leaders of the Communist Party were arrested and convicted under authority of the Smith Act and it is their appeal which is reviewed in the Dennis Case.[10] The eleven argued that since, unlike the Schenck situation, there was no immediacy, their arrest and conviction was unconstitutional.

The Court spoke at length to the merits of First Amendment freedom of expression, saying that the basis of the amendment is "the hypothesis that speech can rebut speech, propaganda will answer propaganda, free debate of ideas will result in the wisest governmental policies." However, the court went on to acknowledge that "the societal value of speech must, on occasion, be subordinated to other values and considerations. . . ." The chief point that the Court took note of here was the distinction between discussion and advocacy. The intention of the Smith Act, it said, was to protect government from change by violence, revolution, and terrorism, not from change by peaceful, lawful, and constitutional means. Going to the heart of the issue of the difference between peaceful change and the advocacy of violence, the court said:

> Whatever theoretical merit there may be to the argument that there is a "right" to rebellion against dictatorial governments is without force where the existing structure of the government provides for peaceful and orderly change. We reject any principle of governmental helplessness in the face of preparation for revolution, which principle carried to its logical conclusion, must lead to anarchy.[11]

And it later observed:

> Overthrow of the Government by force and violence is certainly a substantial enough interest for the Government to limit speech. Indeed, this is the ultimate value of any society, for if society cannot protect its very structure from armed internal attack, it must follow that no subordinate value can be protected.[12]

The "clear and present danger" rule of the Schenck case was altered to what might be called the "grave and probable danger" rule of this case. Quoting from Judge Learned Hand of the appeals court from which the case had come, the Supreme Court stated that "in each case [courts] must ask whether the gravity of the 'evil,' discounted by its improbability, justifies such invasion of free speech as is necessary to avoid the danger."[13] Here was a new but reasonable modification of the circumstance when the assumed integrity of speech can be abridged. The court's lengthy argument in this case indicated that it was concerned about safeguarding

First Amendment freedoms, but it acknowledged at the same time that the very integrity of the constitutional government which guaranteed the freedoms had to be maintained. In the Court's view the government could not be forced to wait until the "putsch" was on the courthouse steps before it could take action to defend itself.

In the Schenck and Dennis cases the court took great pains to spell out the unusual circumstances when the normally assumed integrity of speech could be abridged. That the court was concerned about maintaining the assumption of free expression can be seen six years later when in the Yates case it refined its notion of "advocacy." There it distinguished between advocacy "to do something, now or in the future, rather than merely to believe in something." In *Dennis* there was advocacy and preparations to *do* something while in *Yates* it was "too remote from concrete action to be regarded as the kind of indoctrination preparatory to action which was condemned in Dennis." By making a distinction between action and belief the Court in *Yates* found that the lower court judge had not sufficiently instructed the jury in these matters. The Court reversed some of the convictions and remanded others for retrial.[14]

Later cases reinforced the distinction between action and belief. This area of free speech litigation can be seen as consistent with the principle approach. It should also be noted that by the time of the Yates decision in 1957 the domestic situation had changed to the point where the Communist Party, whatever its doctrine, was a threat to little more than themselves. The danger or perceived danger of just a few years earlier could no longer sway a jury. That change in circumstances is not grounds for arguing that the right is relative. The pains with which the assumption of integrity was always insisted upon documents the basic point of the principle approach. There is always an inclination to argue that something which changes proves its relativity. That inclination fails to grasp the basic character of any principle. Little can be expected from pursuing discussion from such a view since it logically accepts only absolutes or relatives.

Freedom of the Press

Freedom of the press and other forms of expression can also be seen and better understood in the light of the principle approach. The integrity of what is written, printed, produced, staged, performed, etc., is assumed. Legal action can only be taken in the absence of integrity after the performance or distribution of the material. In other words, prior censorship is not practiced. There are indeed libel laws and obscenity laws, but they apply to actions which have already occurred and not to anticipated actions.

An author or a director is not required to obtain approval before the presentation of his or her work but the law does not protect them from penalties if the work is later ruled libelous or obscene. In numerous countries like the Soviet Union and Eastern bloc countries, as well as in certain "martial law" situations this assumption of initial integrity does not prevail. These are exactly the circumstances where it is generally held that true rights do not obtain. The precise legal character of these situations will be examined from a constitutional point of view in a later chapter.

A particularly ironic example of prior censorship was found in Greece in 1967. There the government, while acknowledging the country's historic place as the "cradle" of art and while insisting that it did "not intend to impose any restrictions," nonetheless declared that it would not tolerate anyone "undermining healthy Greek habits and customs and corrupting Greek people, especially Greek youth." (This phrasing is reminiscent of the charges brought against Socrates some twenty-three hundred years earlier of undermining and corrupting the youth of Athens.) The Greek censorship law of May 30, 1967 obliged all theatre directors to submit for approval an application and a copy of their proposed productions. The directors were especially reminded of their responsibility for any alterations made after the approval of the text. Specifically indicating what was expected, the law forbade all theatrical pieces, or musicals and public shows which "1. disturb or could disturb public order; 2. propagate subversive theories; 3. defame our country nationally or touristically; 4. undermine the healthy social traditions of the Greek people and their ancestral habits and customs; 5. touch on Christian religion; 6. attack the person of the King, the members of the Royal Family, and the government; 7. exercise a noxious influence on youth; or 8. exercise a distorting influence on the aesthetic evolution of the people."[15]

Although these criteria stand in ironic contrast to the great Greek literature of the golden age, the previous discussion about Supreme Court decisions and internal disruptions legitimize governmental concern about internal order and self-defense. The provisions of the Greek law, however, should also point out the particularly difficult path of attempting to define and monitor the things outlawed. Some of the terms left undefined and hence subject to the unchecked discretion of the authorities are "disturb," "subversive," "defame," "healthy," "noxious," "distorting influence," and "aesthetic." The ambiguity of the terms will result in arbitrary enforcement, which will leave the government itself the most conspicuous violator of provision number three about defaming the country nationally and touristically.

The Greek censorship law has a common difficulty with all attempts at defining and enforcing restrictions on artistic activity. In the United States there are obscenity laws but the legal definitions are such that enforcement is minimal. The prevailing definition of the obscene is "whether to the average person, applying contemporary community standards, the dominant theme of the material taken as a whole appeals to prurient interests." That definition appears to say a lot but there are huge gaps in it. Left undefined are "community standards," "dominant theme," and "material as a whole." Such gaps lead to many problems when there is an attempt to enforce the law. Legal scholars, literary critics, religious and educational professionals may abhor pornography but find it difficult to agree on the definitions by which they would attempt to fight it.

Most persons may echo Justice Potter Stewart in that they cannot define pornography but they know it when they see it. That sounds like a prime example of the mathematician's "null set," the set which has no elements. The mercurial property of the subject makes it void as real public policy. Everyone knows what is obscene but there are no winnable cases curtailing it. There are increasing complaints about material available on cable television, even though when compared to some magazines and so-called adult entertainment productions, the television material pales. The problem therefore spreads with technological innovation, and the sophistication of dealing with it does not keep pace.

The principle approach insists on two things: one, that the integrity of actions be assumed and two, that there are circumstances when that integrity may be lacking and the assumption can be suspended. With respect to censorship and obscenity we are discussing the lack of integrity in published or produced material but also the inability to do anything about it. There is a certain amount of unwarranted despair in that acknowledgment. Usually it is felt that community standards are lowered because the legal system cannot do anything to limit pornography. The despair may be in the emphasis more than in the fact. A slightly different emphasis may see things as not so bleak.

If there is general acknowledgment that artistic work may be lacking in integrity and that it is subject to moral evaluation, that is certainly a more positive picture than a nihilistic assumption that there are no standards. If a larger context is seen for the establishment of community standards than just the Supreme Court, then the despair is not completely justified. If other courses of action may be taken to promote higher standards, community interests need not be looked at as merely the byproduct of the accretion of rights. Rights are indeed important. They are what this discussion is devoted to, but the discussion of rights sometimes has the effect of narrowing the scope of reality.

Standards do not automatically rise and fall by the dictates of one agency controlling the flood gates. The Court may rule on a legal definition but there are many other actions which influence a community's standards. The number of museums, orchestras, and performing arts groups that are available and the amount of financial support the city gives to them all set the community standards. If the admission price to an art museum is higher than an ''adult'' movie, there is an impact on the community standard. If free summer orchestra and jazz concerts are provided for various communities, then standards are being set. Standards are raised if art programs are promoted in the schools and teachers make references to good literature instead of the most popular television series. The number of parks and recreation programs are a measure of a community's standards. A balance of athletics, arts, education, and civility have much more to do with the denominator of public morality than any Supreme Court decision.

Keeping perspective is important in discussing rights. The area of freedom of expression and the question of obscenity presents problems from a technical outlook. Subsidiarity may lead us to look at the individual and the individual action and it may force us to despair when little can be done where integrity is lacking. Subsidiarity, the principle approach, however, does not impose the Court rulings on all members of the community. The rulings are for the few individuals caught up in the case. All the others members of the community, the vast majority, still have their own integrity. A ruling on movies or magazines or home videos does not mean that everyone must stand in line to buy one. Most court decisions on these issues are a challenge to the educational system and other community organizations for a creative response. That the response has not been creative should not be laid at the door of the Court for blame.

John Stuart Mill

Some argue that First Amendment freedoms are absolute. Justices Black and Douglas in some of their dissents from the majority in Court decisions seemed to argue that the First Amendment provisions, "Congress shall make no law . . .", meant precisely that *no* law shall limit or regulate religion, speech, press, and assembly. It is often maintained that this provision of "no law" is supported by the sound theoretical position of John Stuart Mill who, in his *On Liberty,* seemed to favor absolute freedom of opinion and sentiment. One commentator says that Mill's work is, "together with Milton's *Areopagitica,* the finest and most moving essay on liberty in English, perhaps in any language."[16] Mill said, "If all mankind minus one, were of one opinion, and only one person were of the contrary opinion, mankind would be no more justified in silencing that one person, than he, if he had the power, would be justified in silencing mankind."[17] It is from this statement that Mill gained his great reputation as an arch defender of free speech.

Many texts and authors quote Mill and hold up this view as a standard for society to emulate. There is however a continuation of his thought a little later in *On Liberty* where Mill, more realistically perhaps than some of his "disciples," admits of circumstances which curtail free expression. There Mill states, "Even opinions lose their immunity, when the circumstances in which they are expressed are such as to constitute their expression a positive instigation to some mischievous act."[18]

Combining the two statements shows Mill as consistent with the principle position. He holds the right to free expression most dear, but he acknowledges circumstances when free expression loses its immunity because it lacks integrity. Mill cites an example which is similar to the later Supreme Court cases just mentioned: "An opinion that corndealers are starvers of the poor, or that private property is robbery, ought to be unmolested when simply circulated through the press, but may justly incur punishment when delivered orally to an excited mob assembled before the house of a corndealer."[19] This admission of the role of circumstance is consonant with the "clear and present danger" doctrine. A "grave and probable danger" would only be a slight modification as the Supreme Court found.

Students' Rights

The "principle approach," which now has been identified as (1) assuming integrity and (2) acknowledging circumstances, can be applied to and found in many other areas of the relationship between the individual and the state. The approach can even be used as a guide in matters that are not yet fully developed litigiously. In an area that may be called "students' rights" the Court ruled that "school officials do not possess absolute authority over their students. . . . In our system, students may not be regarded as closed-circuit recipients of only that which the state chooses to communicate."[20]

The Tinker case involved the appeal of students who had been suspended from public school for wearing black armbands as an expression of opposition to the Vietnam War. The Court ruling acknowledged that students are "persons" "possessed of fundamental rights" and held that only when it is demonstrated that the forbidden "activities would materially and substantially disrupt the work and discipline of the school" could the circumstances justify the prohibition. There have been cases in the past where courts have placed the burden of proof on the plaintiff in school discipline cases[21], but the *Tinker* case makes it clear that when fundamental rights are involved the burden belongs to the school board. The 1985 Supreme Court decision on the constitutionality of searching students in school maintains the Tinker principle. The court, while sanctioning the particular search in question, held school officials to a "reasonableness" test. The test, according to the court, is different in the school setting, but it nonetheless intended to protect the "interests of students."[22]

Criminal Procedure

Particular attention should be paid to the cardinal principle of the entire criminal justice system which reflects the principle approach. "Innocent until proven guilty" announces the assumption of the integrity of the accused until it is proven "beyond a reasonable doubt" that the person is guilty. All the specifics of indictment, due process, fair trial, grand jury, petit jury, sentencing, and appeal are expressions of the basic principle. The precise application to these specifics in particular circumstances is what much of the criminal procedure case law is all about.

Individuals may dispute the fairness of their particular case and as a consequence a separate case is made of this procedural claim. The separate claim is what occurred in the famous *Escobedo, Gideon,* and *Miranda* cases. In these cases, which are about the right to counsel and the reading of constitutional rights, it was not, contrary to some popular rhetoric, the criminal who was being protected, it was the innocent. The criminal will, one hopes, be properly apprehended and convicted. It has always been the motto of fair procedure that "Better the guilty go free, than one innocent person be found guilty." The criminal justice system founded on the assumption of innocence serves all. Society does not want the guilty to go free but it wants even less that nonguilty persons be unprotected.

Affirmative Action

In recent years there has developed a policy in American society which seems the direct opposite of the assumed integrity of the individual, unit, or function. The policy area is that of "affirmative action." It involves legal requirements that some owners and administrators of businesses and other large institutions, such as universities, demonstrate that they are not practicing discrimination in hiring and personnel procedures. The premise here is, in effect, that innocence must be proved rather than assumed. If charges of noncompliance are brought against these institutions, the burden of proof is not that of the accuser but of the accused.

How does this affirmative action policy square with subsidiarity? Easily! The policy has been established to protect the assumed integrity of *individuals* who, by reason of being female, black, or some other minority, have been discriminated against in the past. Clear patterns of discrimination, not always consciously practiced but nonetheless true, have been established in businesses and other large institutions, and so the burden of proof is rightfully shifted to the institutions. The policy is not a reversal of the assumed innocence principle. The policy of affirmative action is a furtherance of the principle, since the basic unit of society, the individual, is promoted.

The principle of affirmative action was set forth as a profound truth by President Lyndon Johnson. When he explained the affirmative action principle in a commencement address at Howard University on June 4, 1965, Johnson reminded Americans,

> You do not take a person who for years has been hobbled by chains and liberate him, bring him up to the starting line of a race and say, "You are free to compete with all the others," and still justly believe that you have been completely fair. . . . Thus it is not enough to open the gates to opportunity. All our citizens must have the ability to walk through those gates. . . . This is the next and most profound state of the battle for civil rights . . . the task is to give twenty million Negroes the same choice as every other American to learn, to work, and share in society, to develop their abilities— physical, mental, and spiritual—and to pursue their individual happiness.[23]

Johnson recognized the enormity of the task. What he believed imperative, however, was that individuals who had been discriminated against in the past must be helped so that they might function adequately, efficiently, and with benefit to the welfare of the whole. Affirmative action policy is not easy for many people to accept. At least it stirs our thinking about matters of principle. An additional benefit of the debate about affirmative action is that it is an excellent example of where subsidiarity's assumptions of integrity cannot be applied easily. Such an admission is necessary to make it clear that the principle approach is not simple and automatic. Simple and automatic principles are not principles.

Privacy

Privacy is an area of personal liberty which is new in the sense that there is little statutory or case law setting forth its precise character. It is an area of increased concern and discussion as reflected in congressional hearings, books, articles, and some lawsuits. Some individuals express great concern about data banks, electronic bugs, undesired publicity, and snooping into personal matters. There is no agreed upon position on the issue of privacy, and if society is to await the excretions of case law before having a standard, then the exudations of communications technologies will have all but inundated it in the meantime.

The alternatives to personal privacy are not appealing. Concerns expressed by some suggest a return to exaggerated individualism on the one hand or unavoidable statism on the other. As in most dichotomies the more likely outcome is "neither." In this instance some of the concern may be warranted but it is not as grave as feared. Perhaps the better way to approach privacy and to gain a standard by which one can judge personal concerns is to once again look at it in terms of subsidiarity. One should proceed by way of the assumption of the integrity of one's personal domain and the inviolability of one's records, domicile, and possessions.

The assumption of individual integrity is not going to be an impenetrable shield against determined violators. Privacy should be held most dear. Like other rights it is not absolute, nor should it be. Privacy can be abused to where it is an excuse used to harm others. For this reason privacy can legally be invaded. Through court orders, personal property can be searched, mail can be opened, and telephones can be tapped. That this invasion can today only occur legally through a court order with stated objectives, times, and reasons ought to be a solid indication that things are not so bad. What may be needed is a refinement of understanding based on principles instead of an effort to carve out a new right.

THE RIGHT TO PRIVATE PROPERTY

Life and liberty are but two of the many rights which might be considered in discussing the individual's relationship to the state. Some other rights have been mentioned or touched upon, such as privacy, assembly, and students' rights. There are many other separate or related rights which could be examined such as the right to free movement, the right to religious freedom, the right to employment, and the right to the products of one's labor. Some of these will be taken up later, others must be left to understanding through the general principle as has been outlined.

The only other personal right which will receive separate treatment is that of private property. The only aspects to be discussed here is that of the systems of ownership of property. It is expected that this discussion, like the previous considerations, will show sufficient application of the principle approach that its usefulness can be extended on one's own.

Universal Ownership

There are four basic systems of ownership: individual, corporate, public, and universal. *Universal ownership* is a somewhat vague concept which relates to items like the high seas, the air space above them, and perhaps the resources below them. Universal or communal ownership frequently goes by the phrase "freedom of the seas" or "freedom of the air," etc.

Although custom and treaty acknowledge freedom based on universal ownership, historical reality suggests that it does not work as easily as grand agreement might imagine. It may be argued that no nation may claim sovereignty (exclusive jurisdiction) over a part of the ocean or the air lanes above it. Past experience would suggest, however, that those who have the technical ability to develop a new enterprise and the power to defend that development basically establish the rules for continued use.

Many maintain that the laws of the seas are a product of international law but it is not clear that this international law is not first a product of the practices of those who use the high seas. Landlocked nations did not have a sizeable input into the formulation of sea law. This discussion is obviously jumping ahead to a topic in international relations or, as it will be called here, the relation of states to one another, but the intention at this point is to call attention to the ambiguity and complexity of the basis of so-called universal ownership itself.

The problems related to the inexactness of universal ownership are not limited to the international scene. On a domestic level the difficulty can be appreciated as the high seas creep up to the shore. Here, for example, the question is one of who owns or who should own the seashore or beach? Of the thousands and thousands of beaches in the United States, only a small percentage are open to the general public, even though more than half the population lives within an hour's drive from the water. Most beachfront is privately owned. Where there is some municipal, state, or national park, frequently a fee must be paid to use the sea, which theoretically all people own.

Many of the reasons for private ownership of seafront property and for beach fees for public parks are understandable in their given context. After all, who will pay to pick up the debris that all people leave behind? Nonetheless, it is ironic at least that the alleged universal heritage of human beings is not freely available to them. The immediate usefulness of the concept of universal ownership may therefore be questioned. Immortal verse may tell us that "the moon belongs to everyone" and that "the best things in life are free" but when it comes to booking passage on a lunar flight or preserving the environment and maintaining clean air, reality intrudes forcefully. The concept of universal ownership should not be completely dismissed, however, because it is at least a reminder that there are aspects of ownership not adequately explained by the other three.

Individual, Corporate, and Public Ownership

The other three forms of ownership are best explained in relation to one another. The starting point for discussion is individual ownership, progressing to corporate ownership and then to public ownership. Individual ownership is the beginning point because the individual is the "lowest unit" and because this is the place where the Western and American economic system begins.

It is not the intention to argue here the theoretical foundation or merits of the Western and American economic system. Here the system is accepted as a given. The operations of the system are discussed in the light of the principle of the assumed right of ownership. If it is desired, discussion of comparative economic systems can be found elsewhere. To probe the foundations of competing economic systems may be fascinating but it does not fit into the scope of the current text.

Individual ownership is here taken to be about those things, business things in particular, which the individual can manage and develop entirely on her or his own. Individual ownership is sometimes equated with private ownership but it is not the sole form of private ownership. *Corporate ownership* is also a form of private ownership since it is a combination of two or more private owners. A corporation is formed when two or more individuals decide that a certain function can be better performed in combination.

No one is forced to form a corporation and the system of private property operates on the assumption that if the lower unit can perform adequately, efficiently, and with benefit to the whole, it is permitted to do so. The corollary, though, of nonadequate performance is present here also. The corollary operates in the first instance when individuals join together in a corporation. For the sake of discussion attention is normally focused on the corporation but there are actually other intermediate combinations between the pure form of individual ownership and the corporation. Such intermediate combinations are partnerships and what is known as Subchapter S corporations.

Individual and corporate ownership are called "private" as opposed to "public." *Public ownership* means government ownership or, as it is otherwise called, socialism. To use the word socialism is to immediately bias or prejudice the discussion for some persons who react without reflection either positively or negatively to it. Arguments that have been and still are offered against public ownership are thought by their holders to be irrefutable. Similarly the citing of one or a few cases of successful public ownership is thought by others to establish its universal merit.

Neither unqualified rejection nor acceptance of public ownership is warranted. Simple rules of logic indicate that a universal rule is not established by a few particulars. Furthermore, it should be seen that the very logic of the corollary which moved ownership from individual to corporate would move it from corporate to public. That is, when corporate ownership cannot perform a particular and necessary function adequately, efficiently, and with benefit to the welfare of the whole, then public ownership, as the next form, must see that the function is performed.

As indicated earlier there are intermediate combinations or forms of ownership between individual and corporate. Here there are intermediate steps between corporate and public ownership. The exact nature and kind of intermediate steps does not disturb the logic which leads to the justification of public ownership. There may be cooperative efforts, regulations, subsidies, bail-outs, publicly sanctioned trusts, or public corporations. However many intermediate steps there may be, public ownership is not precluded by some doctrinaire concept of private property.

The logic of the system says that if a function is a necessary function and it is not being performed adequately at a lower level, then some next higher level of activity must become involved so that the function can be performed. The next higher level of activity may be a coordination of units at the same level. It may be a temporary subsidy or trade protection until adjustments and normalizations occur in the market. If the intermediate steps will not work then public ownership may be in order. Which step is appropriate depends on the particular circumstances. What is important is to see that no single solution is mandated and no particular step is prohibited. Each step assumes that the function under discussion is a necessary one for society.

The arguments advanced against public ownership are that it promotes waste, inefficiency, and maladministration by impairment or destruction of the profit motive. It is said to weaken or eliminate competition, lessening incentive and efficiency. It is also said to bring politics into the economic sphere leading to favoritism, mismanagement, and corruption. Lastly, it is argued that political power in the economic sphere will eventually lead to totalitarianism. Each of these objections have some merit to them but taken as a whole they give a distorted picture, they are not always and everywhere true.

For years the Tennessee Valley Authority (T.V.A.), a government operation set up in the 1930s, has been a model of efficiency for public and private corporations alike. T.V.A. has provided effective service to the people of the region it serves with no suggestion of unsoundness or the other maladies said to afflict public ownership. For that matter, except for ownership, there is no difference between the running of the T.V.A. and utility companies and other similar monopolies throughout most of the United States. Competition, such as occurs in the auto industry or the computer industry, does not serve as an incentive for efficiency in the utilities and yet their operation is generally on a par with the private sector.

The profit motive serves no more as an incentive for the worker at IBM, Sun Oil, or TV Guide than it does for the worker at T.V.A. The secretary, the welder, the bundle sorter, and the vast bulk of workers in any corporation are paid fixed wages or salaries. Although some may know that their income is remotely related to profits, it does not serve as a personal incentive. Other incentives, on the other hand, such as bonuses and penalties, are employed equally by businesses as well as by publicly owned corporations.

Recent crises in the American auto industry are said to have introduced a greater amount of worker awareness of individual impact on overall efficiency and competitiveness. This foreign competition induced awareness is, however, an extraordinary situation. The competitive advantage or disadvantage of an industry is less the result of the profit incentive of secretaries or production workers than it is the result of the product design and management controlled inducements, particulary environment conditions. The frequent focusing of discussion on the wage earners shifts attention away from the high-salaried decision makers who have a greater immediate effect on general efficiency. Since these highly paid management individuals can and do easily switch from one company to another, the assumed effect of the profit motive on the efficiency and effectiveness of private business in contrast to government ownership is more theory than practice.

The ripple effect of the profit motive within a corporation has been exaggerated. It should therefore not serve as a major point of contrast between public and private ownership. Corporate and public ownership must be looked at in terms of the function performed, its necessity, and the ability of the different systems of ownership to perform these functions. The argument over corporate and public ownership should not be looked at as fictional results of imaginary differences.

As with the efficiency argument, the contention against public ownership on the grounds of waste, favoritism, mismanagement, and corruption has a partial basis in reality. Such defects are seen in many government operations, especially at state and local levels. However, it should be clear that these deficiencies do not exist in all government operations. Furthermore, and of equal importance, their occurrence is not limited to government alone. The Penn Central will serve for a long time as an example of a private corporation where all the arguments advanced against public ownership apply.

Many other private corporations have or have had problems of waste, inefficiency, maladministration, favoritism, and corruption. For proper perspective, however, it must be remembered that all the examples of deficiencies, whether private or public, are not representative samples. The mismanaged corporation is as much the statistical bad sample as the bungled government operation. The well-run operation or industry is about as newsworthy as the six o'clock news reporting that all commuters got home safely.

Public ownership fits into the systems of ownership in a functional way. If a lower level cannot perform a necessary function adequately, then some next higher unit must see that it is performed. If the next higher level happens to be the government, action is not precluded. Emphasis is still on the lowest unit. Accordingly, if public ownership exists but a condition is reached when the activity might be performed adequately at a lower level, then the government might divest itself of the activity. In other words, what goes up can come down.

The experience of changing the postal service from a cabinet level government agency to a quasi-governmental postal system in the last two decades represents some semblance of a divestiture. The recent attempt to run the postal system on a pay-for-itself basis has resulted in greatly increased postal fees. These increased fees have had the effect, whether intended or not, of reducing the scale of its activity and encouraging competing and alternate delivery systems. Many might argue that the reduction of activity is as it should be, but it must be remembered that it could only come about when the alternate communication systems were available. The postal department for almost two centuries had provided the only long-range societal communications. Through electronic and other media the function can now be satisfied by other means.

Other governmental activities, T.V.A. included, should be looked upon as candidates for divestiture. The question should always be decided on the basis of whether the task can be performed adequately at a lower level. There is no reason that a task assumed by the government should always remain with the government. However, in determining the adequate performance of a task, business and economic factors should not be the exclusive concern. With the postal service, for example, costs and revenue were not the sole concern. For many years the government subsidized the postal service as a means of ensuring reliable and low-cost communications between all the various parts of the country. That knitting of the country together through the pony express and the tradition of "through rain, sleet, and snow'' was a service that could not otherwise be provided at the time. Now that the knitting has been finished, divestiture can be afforded.

When the T.V.A. was created it was not, as some rhetorically argued at the time, a form of creeping socialism. The need to aid the development of a neglected region of the country could not have been accomplished by other means. The Tennessee Valley area was an economically and technically deprived region needing rural electrification and flood control projects. Private efforts could not underwrite those projects. The government creation of T.V.A. brought about an economic development as well as social, political, and cultural enrichment to the region. The region, which had been neglected since the Civil War, took on new life. Here is an unequivocal example of public ownership enhancing individual freedom and initiative rather than diminishing them, as is often alleged.

The essential point in the T.V.A. case was one of whether the functioning of the units of the region could be carried on at a lower level, and since they could not the government stepped in. If the situation changes after fifty years, so can the level of governmental activity. Thus subsidiarity, as applied to the forms of ownership of property, becomes a wholly integrated social, political, and economic principle. It is not doctrinaire but a practical principle based on reasonable judgments of what constitutes adequate, efficient, and sound levels of activity.

CONCLUSION AND PERSPECTIVE

No area of rights can be handled in a doctrinaire or absolutist fashion. The fundamental concerns of life, speech, assembly, and property can neither tolerate absolutes nor afford to be decided on a majoritarian basis. Absolutes in human dealings are attractive but unrealistic. They assume a simpler world than that which experience shows. This does not mean to say there are no absolutes. Absolute values are important. The sacredness of life, the importance of truth, justice, and goodness, are absolute values. If "man were the measure of all things," as some philosophies have taught, where humans alone determine value, rights would have little meaning as they become subject to the final human arbiter. They would become at one and the same time absolute and nothing.

As principles, rights are held most sacred but at the same time their application is not automatic. Rights as a true human concern require study, reflection, debate, patience, and humility. Only by a spirit of respect and tolerance can rights exist which do not produce their own downfall. It is not an easy task. For this reason it is important to understand their elementary principles and not pretend to reduce them to simple rules.

NOTES

1. Robert G.McCloskey, *The American Supreme Court* (Chicago: The University of Chicago Press, 1960).

2. Aristotle, *Politics,* III, 1280b, 30-40.

3. Gabriel Almond and Sidney Verba, *The Civic Culture: Political Attitudes and Democracy In Five Nations* (Princeton, N.J.: Princeton University Press, 1963).

4. These sentiments can be confirmed in editorials, speeches, and letters to the editor columns regularly.

5. As quoted by Robert Sherrill, "Raising Hell on the Highways," *The New York Times Magazine,* November 27, 1977, p. 90.

6. Quoted in the *Philadelphia Evening Bulletin,* January 23, 1974, p. 1.

7. *The New York Times,* May 22, 1969, p. 10.

8. *Gregg* v. *Georgia,* 428 U.S. 153, 179 (1976).

9. *Schenck* v. *United States,* 249 U.S. 47 (1919).

10. *Dennis* v. *United States,* 341 U.S. 494 (1951),

11. ibid., 501.

12. ibid., 509.

13. ibid., 510.

14. *Yates* v. *United States,* 354 U.S. 298 (1957).

15. The enumerated prohibitions are from a closing list in the Circular from the Ministry to the Prime Minister's Office, Athens, May 30, 1967. The entire Circular can be found in *The Drama Review,* Volume 13, Number 4 (T44), Summer 1969.

16. William Ebenstein, *Great Political Thinkers,* 4th ed. (Hinsdale, Ill.: Dryden Press, 1969), p. 542.

17. John Stuart Mill, *On Liberty,* Chapter 2, "Of the Liberty of Thought and Discussion," paragraph 1.

18. ibid., Chapter 3, "Of Individuality, as One of the Elements of Well-being," paragraph 2.

19. ibid.

20. *Tinker* v. *Des Moines,* 393 U.S. 503 (1969).

21. In *Pubsley* v. *Sellmeyer,* 158 Ark, 250 SW 538, 1923 the state court pronounced the commonly accepted rule that it would not annul a rule adopted by a locally elected board unless it is demonstrated that the rule was *not* "reasonably calculated to effect . . . promoting discipline in the school."

22. The case has been referred to as the "Piscataway case" for the name of the school district in New Jersey where the search occurred. Excerpts from the court opinions and commentary are in *The New York Times,* January 16, 1985, p. 7 and January 21, 1985, p. B4.

23. Cited in Thomas R. Dye, *Understanding Public Policy,* 3rd ed. (Englewood Cliffs, N.J.: Prentice-Hall, 1978), p. 63.

CHAPTER ELEVEN
THE STATE
AND GROUPS

In the last chapter the relationship between the individual and the state was discussed in light of the principle of subsidiarity. The principle approach started with the assumption of the right of the individual to life, liberty, and property and then circumstances were described when that assumption of integrity was not warranted. This approach gave an accurate, structured, and systematic way of looking at all rights, not just the few specifically examined.

Systems of ownership of property, the last topic considered, was approached as an extension of the individual. The individual was viewed as "the lowest unit" and other forms of ownership were looked at as appropriate developments when the individual could no longer privately handle a necessary task adequately. In this way business corporations and eventually public ownership of property were viewed as an integrated system flowing from and directed to the welfare of the individual. Some of the state's relationship to "groups" is implicit in that discussion of systems of ownership. Businesses certainly are groups since they are combinations of two or more individuals.

There are many groups other than businesses, however, and some of them, like the family or the church, may even be considered more primary than business. It is necessary, therefore, to more formally address the relation of the state to groups and to develop in some detail the way in which the subsidiarity principle is helpful in understanding the relationship. There are two ways in which the state's relationship to groups can be approached. One way, as has been indicated, is to look at it according to the subsidiarity principle. A second approach is a more descriptive one of classifying and measuring groups to gauge by empirical means the possible effectiveness of groups within the state. This second approach is called "the group model" by political scientists. Brief attention will be given to the group model before continuing with the principle approach.

THE GROUP MODEL

Groups are of various types and sizes and they can be classified in many different ways. Political scientists are first interested in calling attention to the role that groups play in the political process and following that they are interested in attempting to measure and predict the effect of groups in the process. All groups do not have the same characteristics and so what is identified and the precise role within the system differs considerably. Spontaneous or temporary groups arise over particular events or issues. They take the form of a riot or demonstration and normally have only a short-term impact. Such groups do not ordinarily last beyond the event that brought them into existence. During the demonstration the assembled individuals behaved as a group, perhaps even eliciting some governmental response. However, they most likely would never assemble again and so their role as a group would be different from those with greater duration.

There are, of course, other groups with greater permanence than the ephemeral groups just referred to but which also lack an organized character. This second type of group differs from the first type by reason of their duration but they are still not easily identified nor is their strength weighable. This latter type is referred to as nonassociational interest groups. They are based on ethnic, kinship, regional, status, or class identifiers. They have a potential for mobilization but the individuals within them usually go their separate ways, and only extraordinary effort over a long period of time overcomes the prevailing inertia. For example, individuals of Irish descent usually come together and act like an organized group only once a year, except in Ireland itself, but for the rest of the year they do not have the same interests.

If an ethnic or other nonassociational interest group came together on a more permanent basis, elected officers, and began to regularly assert its identity, then the group would begin to take on the characteristics of the more familiar interest groups. The more commonly recognized interest groups which have these characteristics are institutional and associational groups. They are combinations of individuals within the general public or within institutions. They are designed to represent and reflect the interests of the member. Since they can be blocs within institutions or organizations as well as separate entities, they have a more easily identifiable role and so assume a greater importance. They can range in interest from a faction within the Democratic Party to a business-supported conservative think tank. In either case they receive the attention of political scientists.

When political scientists consider interest groups they do not simply attend to those with obvious political roles. The group model takes into consideration all groups. Attention is not limited to those with headquarters in Washington or in state capitals or those who play a role in elections. All permanently organized groups, even those with no ostensible political role, fit into the group model. It is the interplay of the groups as such that the model is all about.

The group model, or group theory as it is sometimes called, maintains that all meaningful political activity is to be understood in terms of groups. Sometimes the activity is one of struggle, other times it is one of quiet carrying out of a dominant interest. Some political scientists who work within the model view policy makers as constantly responding to group pressures. They see struggle between groups as the normal mode of political reality. Politicians are seen as forming coalitions of groups in order to mount successful election campaigns. Public policy is described as the temporal equilibrium reached in the group struggle. Others do not view the group interaction as being so forceful. They do not see politics as only a matter of "struggle." The common aspect of the group model is the interplay of groups in the ongoing process of public life.

Not all political scientists subscribe to the group model. When discussing the political system it was pointed out that some political scientists see the systems model as the best way to describe and understand the political world. In the chapter on methodology many other models for capturing the secrets of the political world were mentioned. Among the variety of models there is an institutional model which gives emphasis to the dominant force of established institutions in the making of public policy. There is the elite model, seen in the earlier discussions of democracy, which sees a few select individuals in society as controlling its direction and character. There is an incremental or evolutionary model, which sees political life explained by slow and almost inevitable steps determined by past practice. Some other models are game theory, power, role, communications, rational, and individual-psychological. Sometimes these models are seen in combination, as are the game and rational, whereas at other times the particular political scientist proponent holds them to be unquestionably separate.

Each model claims that its technique is a better way to capture political reality than the other models. It is not unusual then that political scientists disagree on the dimensions and the significance of the group model. An attractive feature of political science is that it acknowledges the complexity of the political world and offers a variety of ways to attempt to understand it. All who are students of politics must learn the various models because in so doing we learn of politics itself.

A special feature of the group approach is its identification and measurement of groups in terms of their possession of certain characteristics. This feature catches much attention and has the appearance at least of offering some practical utility. The characteristics are those of leadership, size, cohesion, status, wealth, doctrine, and organization. The possession of these primary characteristics together with the absence of certain adverse factors, such as overlap and latent groups, combined with a positive affect of the multiplier of time, should mark a group for success. The

American Red Cross and the American Cancer Society are prime examples. Both possess all the primary characteristics in a positive way. They are not adversely affected by overlapping appeal to each other or other health groups. Nor are they threatened by new groups which would weaken the older group's popular appeal.

Positive possession of the group characteristics means that the group has effective or dynamic leadership, good size, cohesive membership, well-developed organizational structure, a sound doctrine, is well received by the public, and has a solvent treasury supported by a self-sustaining membership. Although many organizations and interest groups possess these characteristics, some possess them to a greater degree than others. Some may be lacking in leadership or size, others may be weak on cohesion or wealth. Positive possession of all the characteristics means, among other things, greater access to the public and to public officials and a correspondingly greater chance of success when requests are made.

New groups, like an antinuclear organization, whatever the merits of their particular doctrine, will have reduced chances of success unless their relative newness is offset by overwhelming numbers. A group seeking handgun control may surpass the National Rifle Association in doctrine. The Second Amendment, contrary to the NRA's contention, ties the right to keep and bear arms to the existence of a "well-regulated militia" which is accomplished through the National Guard. The NRA's membership size, national leadership, local chapters, communication networks, and experience over time make them, however, almost untouchable in group competition. All efforts at gun control have met stiff resistance from the NRA, and legislators approach with caution any proposal which might incur NRA opposition. The brief application of the group characteristics to assess the likely success of the NRA and competing groups shows that the model has some realistic basis. Following this example the model could be applied to groups such as the Dairy Farmers Association, the AFL-CIO, or computer users groups. Depending on the possession of the characteristics, the ability of the group to influence public affairs can be gauged.

It would indeed be worthwhile if the procedure of weighing and measuring group strengths were able to gauge the amount of effort needed to ensure legislative success of a desired policy. Likewise it would be useful, in hindsight at least, to know for sure whether one group instead of another is most responsible for a particular policy. But this goal itself singles out the principal weakness of the model. The weakness is that in obvious cases, where the numbers (on the positive possession of the characteristics) load up clearly on one side, the applications are easy. In the nonobvious cases, where measurability is problematic, the model is no more useful than any other competing theory. There are too many factors in closely fought policy issues for strengths and weaknesses to be reduced to numbers alone. If one group found the formula for success from the study of the model, others would quickly discover the same formula and no one would be any better off than before. One must conclude that the model has descriptive merits in letting us know more of the size and strength of competing interests. The model, however, cannot go much beyond that, and it is especially limited on prescriptive tasks.

The group model with its descriptive rendering of the political world is a prominent feature of twentieth-century political science. It is not entirely new, however. Plato and Aristotle each spoke of the competition among various groups within Athenian society. Long before the group model was a major feature in political science, American historians were speaking of the struggle between the Tidewater, the Piedmont, and the frontier interests in early American society. Similar descriptions of competition and rivalry can be found in all developed and developing countries, even though formally organized interest groups exist in fewer than thirty-five of the nations of the world.

The group model has some descriptive merits and some analytical weaknesses. It can help evaluate the strength of various interests but it cannot access responsibility or predict outcomes. The group model cannot draw a practical distinction between formally organized groups and formal interests nor can it show when one becomes the other. Even the classification scheme, though conceptually neat, must ultimately collapse when put to harsh practical tests. For these reasons some political scientists choose not to pursue the model. The model may fail but before judging everything in that final light the richness of the descriptive insights should not be completely overlooked.

SUBSIDIARITY AND GROUPS

We now shift attention to the subsidiarity relationship of groups to the state. This approach does not involve the elaborate descriptions of the group model. The subsidiarity approach takes the units as givens and explains how they can be affected by the state. To be considered are the family, voluntary associations, the church, and other states. As to why these particular groups are singled out for attention, they are representative groups that have some special problems associated with them, so that an examination of them will lead to a fuller understanding of both the principle and the groups themselves.

THE FAMILY

The consideration of the family, as with the previous topics, basically assumes the integrity of the unit or the activity associated with the unit and acknowledges that there are circumstances when, because of the lack of integrity, intervention is necessary. In the corollary situation, once again, the lack of integrity which justifies interference must be demonstrated. The family as a primary association which most persons form may be considered under three topics of possible interest to the state: formation, size, and development.

We understand that the individual may marry whomever he or she prefers without prohibition or directive from the state. This understanding is the basic assumption about the "formation" of the family. This freedom of choice for the individual was not always the case. Students of today may be surprised to learn that in earlier centuries planned or arranged marriages were the regular practice. This practice still exists in some countries. The state's role in this situation is one of sanctioning societal and religious practice. In those circumstances there is little interference in what families or kinship groups had already decided. There are some rules against certain types of marriages but these mostly reflect societal or religious agreements.

Today, however, individual choice has become the prevailing practice. The state only regulates in those areas where it is demonstrated that the assumption of integrity of individual choice is lacking. What the state does today is set minimum age limits, prohibit marriage between persons within certain degrees of blood relationship, require blood tests and refuse to issue licenses to those with certain contagious diseases, ban the marriage of mental defectives, and prohibit plural marriages. These regulations are designed to protect innocent parties. The innocent party may be one of the partners or the children who would result from such a union. The requirement of obtaining a marriage license is not a matter of the individuals' obtaining permission to exercise their choice but is a means of enforcing the other legitimate concerns. The actual role of the state in this area is still passive. What the state's role might be in an environment of increased cohabitation is worthy of speculation, although current income tax regulations and laws on landlord-tenant relationships do not describe a completely neutral role.

On the matter of family size, the state's role is not small. It may appear that the individual family units may choose to be whatever size they please. That is not entirely true. In many places today family size immediately raises the issue of overpopulation. Some countries speak of limiting, or actually do limit in some way, the number of children. Many view country and world overpopulation as a problem of gigantic proportions. That problem is counterposed, in the view of others, by the personal rights and integrity of individuals and families, which rights and integrity would be violated by the country that interferes with family size. Added to the personal and family side of the issue is often a religious dimension. These factors combine to make an especially intense issue.

Limiting population and family size has only been regarded as a problem in recent years. Not long ago underpopulation was the concern. States in the past encouraged population growth through homestead acts, tax exemptions, and family allotments. When the state encouraged population growth it was not neutral and there was general support for its policy. If the state could encourage growth in the past, those who object to discouraging growth must be fully aware of the subtleties of the issue. In practical procedures yesterday's tax encouragement can be turned into today's discouragement. The question today becomes, therefore, what is the "limit" if any to the state's role on family size?

Can the state require an individual family to obtain permission, take out a license, in order to have children or to have more than a fixed number of children? This is but one of many proposals that have been raised for limiting population growth. This is not just a theoretical issue since reports of it as a practice have emanated from China in recent years. From India there have been reports of required sterilization or instances of sterilization in exchange for a free transistor radio worth a couple of dollars.

There are other less severe proposals for population management in various countries. All the proposals amount to some involvement by the government. Among other measures are the postponement of the legal age of marriage, thus reducing the childbearing years, while maintaining current proscriptions against illegitimate birth. The increasing problem of teenage pregnancy in premature parents reveals how unrealistic such a simply legal measure would be. Other proposals are for lower taxes for single persons than for married ones, the end of the tax exemption for children, government funding of birth control supplies and abortions, and even the establishment of a ''child tax.'' Another proposal is that women should be given equality in educational and employment opportunities so that they could develop alternative interests to the family.

Many of the proposals are in effect to some degree. Most have no more chance of success than the one on raising the legal age for marriage. The one about giving women an alternate interest to the family presumes that it is only women's interest in children which has been the cause of large families. Women receive more equal treatment today in many areas. To say that fairer treatment is deliberately planned for population control purposes confuses many issues. The tax situations which discourage large families already exist in varying degrees but most have not come about deliberately. Decades of inflation and bracket creep in income tax practices have converted the old exemption incentive into a disincentive. Proposals for more direct incentives or discouragements is precisely the issue that has to be faced.

Subsidiarity has been helpful thus far in giving a fairly clear idea of how to view a problem. It creates an understanding of what receives preferential treatment and it shows on what grounds intervention may occur. As to population and family size, a simple answer is not possible. The principle approach does not give answers. It gives a structured outline to priorities. Subsidiarity says that the lowest unit, in this instance the individual family, should be assumed to have integrity and if integrity is lacking that lack must be demonstrated and the need for intervention for the public good must also be demonstrated. The difficulty is that the population issue is viewed by many as well beyond the stage of theoretical debate. So great is the population in some countries, and the projected world population for just a few decades from now is so large, that many people are giving attention to some of the more drastic proposals mentioned earlier.

Some concrete figures should be given to appreciate the context of the problem. World population, which took about nineteen hundred years since the time of Christ to quadruple, has quadrupled again in the last one hundred years. Projections are that it will quadruple again in the next seventy-five years. Subsidiarity would first urge respect for the integrity of the individual family unit and, if that integrity is lacking, find some moderate measure which would induce responsible family growth. There is a problem with inducements, however. They do not work with some and they work too well with others. At some point inducements give way, as in India, to more direct measures and more difficult problems of coercion come up.

Simple answers like the absolute rights of individual families or the preference of the majority within a state begin to appear attractive. They are attractive until it is realized that they do not solve problems as much as they hide them and create others. Subsidiarity, on the other hand, although not providing a direct answer, would urge that principles be involved in the painstaking process of attempting to see that the problem does not get worse. "Principle" answers are not dramatic. They require making distinctions, delving into other's firmly held views, being patient, and minimizing tension. Such actions are hardly perceptible. They are sounder, however, and have a greater chance for eventual success than the more dramatic, simple answers.

As there are more governmental activities regarding the size of the family than about its formation, so there is an even greater amount of activity in the area of family development, that is, if development is taken principally to be education. Development is more than education, however, and so the statement of the larger role of the government is only partially correct. There are many aspects of family growth which are not directly and formally related to education, but education does have a very large role and its activities have been relegated for the most part to the state. Since the time of the one-room schoolhouse in the seventeenth century, education has been a very large concern of the state.

It is still recognized that "the child is not the mere creature of the state."[1] Nonetheless the adequate performance of the task of education is now assumed to be the responsibility of the state, and the parents must demonstrate that they can perform the task if they seek to be exceptions to the mandatory attendance laws. There have been instances in several states where, under special circumstances, parents have not had to comply with state requirements. This has occurred with the Amish or in instances where gifted parents instruct their own gifted children. The normal assumption today in favor of the state instead of the family seems a reversal of the integrity accorded the lowest unit. Actually the assumption in favor of the state looks toward protecting the integrity of the individual child and that "person's" opportunity for an adequate education.

The state's role in the family should not give the impression that it is engulfing all the areas of responsibility previously reserved to the family. There are many and more subtle aspects of family development from which government is far removed. It may be convenient to focus on education as primary but that ignores the truly subtle and complex dynamics of family development. Mark Twain said, "Education ain't what it used to be, and never was!" That statement could just as easily be applied to family. The family is a basic and familiar social entity. Most individuals directly experience two families. The subtleties of the family as an institution surround us without our being directly aware of them. For someone to say that the family is in decline because of some one or two perceived factors is unwarranted. With the family, like many other familiar social entities, there is a tendency to simplify the past and correspondingly to misunderstand the present. This simplification misrepresents both past and present. The state's role in education is large but there is still an exceedingly large area of responsibility for the family where the assumed integrity operates without state contact.

VOLUNTARY ASSOCIATIONS

Voluntary associations are the various types of entities discussed in relation to the group model. They are generally understood to be any combination of two or more individuals. According to this definition even the family could be considered a voluntary association, although it is usually singled out, as was done here, as a separate primary association. In this same respect the church could be regarded as simply a voluntary association but, as will be discussed below, it also receives separate attention because of special considerations associated with it.

When speaking of voluntary associations, usually considered are groups related to business, labor, professions, political organizations, social and fraternal interests, athletics, theater, etc. People voluntarily form these associations, hence their title. Such groups play an important role in reflecting and expressing the freedom within the community. They undertake tasks which, if they are important enough, the government would have to perform.

Once again the basic relationship of these groups to the state is one of assuming the integrity of the group, but recognizing that there may be circumstances where state action is required if it is demonstrated that the integrity is lacking. To put the basic relationship into words slightly different from those used before, it can be said that there is a twofold relationship of the groups to the state, one positive and the other negative. On the one hand, the state should encourage and foster the existence of voluntary associations in recognition of the principle of their assumed integrity and their benefit to society. On the negative side, it can be said that the state should refrain from interfering with groups or that there should be the least interference possible. This twofold relationship acknowledges that the state may intervene when the lower unit does not perform its function adequately, efficiently, and with benefit to the welfare of the whole but there should be as little intervention as possible.

Many voluntary groups perform functions which are helpful to the community but which the state would not undertake if the organization failed. Such organizations are engaged in activities which are important but which are not imperative for the community. Little League baseball and soccer for the youngsters in the community might be very positive activities but the local government would not necessarily step in if fathers and mothers no longer contributed their time. The Red Cross, on the other hand, is so important that if it failed as a continuing voluntary organization the government would have to intervene immediately.

Normally any group is assumed to have integrity. No one has to obtain anyone's permission to form a group whether the individuals be motorcyclists, singers, knitters, or collectors. However, if the organization consisted of "Weathermen" or "Minutemen" there might be clear grounds for government intervention. Interfere with weathermen or minutemen? Yes, when the weathermen referred to are "the Weathermen Underground," a radically liberal, bomb-building group responsible for many acts of violence. The "Minutemen," similarly, are a radically conservative group preparing a storehouse of ammunitions to allegedly defend the country when the government will not. In both instances the groups are a threat to the safety of the community, even though they both claim to be concerned with the "true" interests of the country. It would be entirely unsafe if they lived in the house next to yours with a basement or attic full of contraband munitions. Governmental intervention for the safety of the community would indeed be in order.

As made clear previously, any government action would require employment of the established legal process. The rules of evidence obtain. The burden of proof is on the state instead of the group. Innocent until proven guilty applies as much to groups as to individuals. It is understandable that the state might act in a negative manner toward groups which threaten the security, safety, or health of the community but the requirements of procedure still favor the group. That preference is not unreasonable since there are many more groups that proceed according to integrity than there are groups that lack it.

THE CHURCH AND THE STATE

The positive and negative aspects of the state's relationship to voluntary associations also applies to the church. In treating the church as no different from other voluntary associations, the state would encourage and foster its existence and would refrain in the same way from interfering. The question then arises about why the church should be discussed separately from the other voluntary associations. In many respects the church is no different, for example, from a country club. Some individuals go religiously to the country club every Sunday to play golf while others go to church.

Churches themselves and believers maintain that the church is different from other voluntary associations and that this difference imposes a unique relationship with the state. That different relationship must be examined because of both its historic and continuing political dimensions. What must be considered are the claimed differences and the ramifications of those differences. The differences can be described and the implications of the differences explained. Proof of the claim will not be explored. Such proof will have to be investigated with the church. The task of examining the relationship in terms of subsidiarity is difficult enough. It should be undertaken because religion plays a large role in society and a delineation of the place of the church would clarify the range and limit of both institutions. What we will do is consider the relationship (1) as if there were no difference and (2) as if there were.

The first part of the consideration is relatively easy and has already been sketched. If the church is no different from other voluntary associations, then the basic relationship of assuming integrity and the corollary of intervention apply. The state would encourage and foster the church the same as any other voluntary association. Secondly, there would be the least interference possible. In these terms the state's barring the practice of polygamy, or barring the use of poisonous snakes in religious ceremonies, or forcing compulsory inoculation upon those who refuse on religious grounds, or inducting into military service those who have conscientious objections would all be viewed in purely secular grounds. Each of these state actions, which would involve interfering in practices regarded as being religiously prescribed, would be, in the words of the Supreme Court in a polygamy case[2], "actions regarded by general consent as properly the subjects of punitive legislation."

The justification by the court of the government's actions against polygamy could be regarded as general grounds for state action involving fringe religious practices. Without a truly separate religious dimension there is no problem with the state interfering with the use of poisonous snakes by private clubs or the refusal of inoculation by an individual family or the practice of plural marriage by any private person or simple refusal to comply with the military draft. All these can be interfered with on the purely secular grounds of being regarded as properly the subject of punitive legislation. But there is a problem with this generalization.

In the polygamy cases, where the court set forth the rationale for government action in religious cases, the settlement was purely secular and not religious. The cases falsely serve as examples of the way in which the state may interfere in religious practices. This normally cited legal precedent for interference in unusual religious practices is not a valid First Amendment religious freedom case. The lesson that can be learned from the polygamy cases about the treatment of voluntary and religious groups is not particularly apt. Some points can be learned from the cases, however.

The court appears to have made the *Davis* v. *Beason* case a clash between the legitimate criminal laws of the state and the practice of religion when it said, "However free the exercise of religion may be, it must be subordinated to the criminal laws of the country. . . ." The court had acknowledged that "with man's relations to his Maker and the obligations he may think they may impose, and the manner in which an expression shall be made by him of his beliefs on those subjects, no interference can be permitted. . . ." The court immediately added that this was so "provided always the laws of society, designed to secure its peace and prosperity, and the morals of its people, are not interfered with." Clearly the court had set the case in the framework of a dispute over a religious practice and the First Amendment.

Despite these words the case was not decided on a First Amendment basis. The case was decided on the constitutional grounds of Idaho's territorial status. Idaho, like Utah in similar cases, was a territory at the time and as such subject to the absolute jurisdiction of Congress. In several other than religious freedom cases the principle of Congress's jurisdiction over territories has been tested and all the cases were decided on the side of Congress. The only provision of the Constitution which applies to territories is the one giving Congress jurisdiction. Congress can change the territories' tax system, their court system, set conditions for admission as states, and deny the application of the Bill of Rights. Congress had proscribed the practice of polygamy in Idaho and Utah and this was the technical grounds for the Court's decision.

By the time the Idaho and Utah territories were admitted as states, the religion involved had changed its doctrine on polygamy. If the doctrine had not changed the legal situation would be entirely different. With statehood the First Amendment would be applicable and a true constitutional religious freedom conflict would have arisen. The confrontation on First Amendment grounds never occurred in the courts. It occurred in reports about the case but not in true legal standing. Unfortunately the territorial basis of the decisions was never fully acknowledged. The assumed First Amendment justification for the government action has been used in other cases, which compounds the misunderstanding of an important issue.

Most people would probably have little concern for government actions limiting polygamy, the use of poisonous snakes, and other bizarre or unusual religious practices. "General consent" would most likely regard these practices as "properly the subjects of punitive legislation," as matters to which "the law of society, designed to secure its peace and prosperity" should apply. However, most people would be much less complacent if by general consent it was decided that religious practices of majority religions were prohibited. There would be an uproar if some jurisdiction decided that for the sake of health, drinking from a common cup or many hands breaking bread from a common loaf should be prohibited. And there would be little equanimity if legislation prohibiting the glorification and display of violence were applied to the crucifix. "Genuine" religious issues would be under attack and the reaction would be broad-based. One does not have to agree with their beliefs to see that those who use poisonous snakes, refuse inoculations, etc., would like the same serious attention given to their religious practices.

The discussion of interference and court cases may create the impression that the relationship between church and state is chiefly negative. There are many positive things which the state does. It "encourages and fosters" the existence of religious groups. Encouragement is given to religious organizations by their tax exempt status, by the public sanction given to religious holidays and days of worship, by the chaplaincy service in the military, by the prayer services which are part of official ceremonies, by the respect generally accorded religions and religious officials. The positive aspects of the relationship are of benefit not just to the organizations but to the state and to individuals. The state is therefore not indifferent toward religion. It may be remarked with some justification, however, that many of these encouragements extended toward religion are also available to charitable organizations who do not have any religious affiliation.

The essentially religious aspect of the church as a voluntary association that distinguishes it from the nonreligious group is difficult to specify. The church regards itself not only as different from other voluntary associations, it regards itself as bigger, better, and greater than the state. The state is viewed as originating in human nature and natural law. By contrast the church is seen as instituted by a direct act of creation, as originating in divine law, as receiving its authority directly from God. The claimed differences are significant. They have a political significance in themselves because of what appears to be a challenge to the authority of the state. They also have a political significance in that many people who are also citizens believe them and can be mobilized as an interest group. Whether true or not the belief in superiority therefore becomes a political concern.

With the church presented as superior to other voluntary associations and to the state itself, a whole new set of questions arise. Under the claim of superiority, is there a need for encouragement and fostering from the state? Does the state, as a lower unit, have any right at all to intervene in the affairs of the church, as a higher unit? (Remember that the actual superiority of the church to the state has not been proven here. The question of superiority is merely taken up to examine its logical and practical consequences.) It may be, in answer to such questions, that there should be precisely ''no'' interference and ''no'' encouraging and fostering. This would be consonant with what some, for different purposes, read as the requirement of the First Amendment. There are, however, some problematic consequences to such an absolutist position.

If there were to be no encouragement and fostering then the church would in effect be discriminated against, because it would receive less regard than other nonreligious voluntary associations. If, in the second instance, there were to be no interference whatsoever, then the evidently fraudulent and harmful pretender at religion could literally get away with murder under protection of a claimed religious origin. There may be little harm, as long as children are excluded, from the religious practices of Christian Science or even from the use of poisonous snakes in religious ceremonies. The latter may indeed take their inspiration from *Mark 16*, ''In my name they will cast out demons, they will pick up serpents, and if they drink any deadly thing it will not hurt them.'' The occasional death of an individual being struck in the temple, pun intended, by a poisonous snake may be explained by ''divine will.'' The same tolerance may not be extended to instances when strychnine is used as a communal drink. Tim Leary, the hippie guru of the 1960s, reportedly attempted to claim at one point that the use of the drug LSD in his commune was a religious service in a newly found religion called the League of Spiritual Development. (Leary apparently fashioned the name to fit the drug.) He did not succeed with this effort. Others, unfortunately, have been successful in religious fraud to the harm of many. Such was the case with so-called Reverend Jim Jones and his People's Temple.

Fraud in religion is difficult to detect because the distinction between sincere belief and harmful intent is not easily discerned. Respect for sincere and genuine religious belief requires the state to tolerate more than it would for a nonreligious group. There is a limit to such tolerance but it is the method and criteria for setting these limits that test both church and state. The problem is that if religion truly comes from God, then who is the state to tell God what the definition of religion should be? By specifying what church and religious practice is acceptable, the state in effect puts words in God's mouth. On the other hand, if Tim Leary or Jim Jones can get away with fraud in the name of religion, then the whole internal protective role of the state for its members is undermined.

There have been small town efforts to have every homeowner in the community claim to be a minister and his or her home a church. This is done to avoid local and other taxes. So the state is forced to get into the business of defining legitimate religions. Both the established churches and the state would like to avoid such conflicts but they will most likely never be completely absent. All that can be reasonably hoped for in this area of church and state relations is that there be a deference and respect paid to claims of religion greater than that paid to nonreligious voluntary associations. That deference and respect, however, cannot go to the point of absolute noninterference because of the harm that can occur. Where and how to draw the line is truly a test of fairness, tolerance, and concern.

THE CHURCH OVER THE STATE

What follows in the next few pages is an extended treatment of church-state as an issue in politics. It is presented as a case study. It is offered as a model by which many (and what appears to be an increasing number) specific issues of a church-state nature can be understood. The broad range of particular issues will become evident as the discussion continues. What also will become clear is that this is not a parochial issue. It is one that involves all of politics, at all levels, and in almost all states mentioned at the end of this section. For a start, and to establish the model, the relationship will be discussed primarily in terms of one church.

There are three possible ways to look at the relationship between the church and the state: (1) to view the church as no different from other voluntary associations, (2) to view the church and state as separated by a wall, and (3) to view the church as higher than the state. These three approaches are depicted in Figure 11-1. The first possible relationship was examined in the previous section, where the point was not to prove the church's superiority but to examine the relationship given the understanding of the church as different or as no different from other groups. It now becomes necessary to extend the examination to the point of the logical and practical consequences of the church as the higher unit. In the process of this examination the proposition that there is or should be properly a wall separating church and state and that consequently there should be no practical contact between the two will also be considered.

To be considered here is the church's relation to the state if the church is higher on the ladder of subsidiarity than the state. That proposition entered the previous section but there the concern was about instances when the church might act in a manner that lacked integrity, such as using strychnine in a communion rite. Where normally the principle of subsidiarity would work such that the lower does not interfere in the higher, in the instances cited it has to be assumed that the purported higher unit is a fraud and does not deserve respect. What has to be considered at this point is the situation when the actions of the state lack integrity in the eyes of the church. If the state engages in activities which in its judgment are necessary for the welfare of the community, yet which lack integrity from the church's view, may the church intervene in such state affairs?

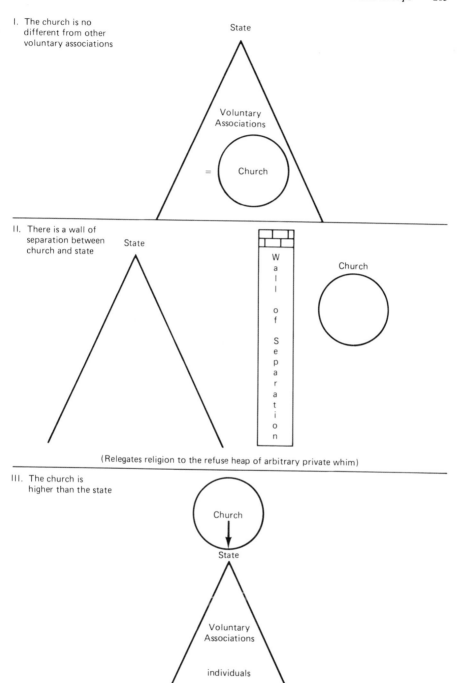

FIGURE 11-1 Three views of church-state relations.

This question may at first appear to be of historical interest only. In medieval and early modern times the church was involved in state affairs to the point of deposing heretical monarchs, settling territorial and property lines, and interdicting various state policies. With the level of state activity today church involvement in state affairs is not of the magnitude of that earlier period. Still there are occasions when the mixing of religion in politics appears particularly intense. As those occasions increase in frequency both in the United States and abroad, additional attention to the issue is warranted. Abortion, textbook censorship, prayer and bible reading, separate schools, the morality of economic systems, the Vietnam war, and nuclear deterrence are examples of contemporary issues which have been the objects of lively church-state debates. Some regard the debates as not so much academic disputes as instances of church interference in state affairs. It is precisely that issue of interference, undue interference, that must be clarified both for the state and for the church.

Over the centuries there has always been some overlap in the claimed jurisdiction of church and state. The question of the proper relationship is that if the church regards some action by the state as improper, can it intervene in such a way as to bring about a reversal of that action or law? The intervention issue is not a matter of the church acting merely as an interest group. The issue is one of sectarian belief or practice being imposed on all. Recent events in Iran and the Middle East in general, Poland, Northern Ireland, northern India, Latin America, and the specific issues in the United States point out the relevance of the issue for political science.

One way to come to terms with the question of the legitimacy of church intervention in state affairs is to consider briefly the theoretical positions on church-state relations in the history of Catholic thought. The Catholic Church is used as a model not to "pick on" or "promote" that church. It is done for convenience: the documentary record is available, it is relatively straightforward, there is continuing involvement. Other religions, the Jewish religion for example, have such a record but are more complicated because of historical circumstances. For some religions involvement is not always as institutionally distinct and therefore the example would lack clarity. Used as a model, the long experience of this one church can help identify various theoretical principles involved and show insight to current and future conflicts.

Theories on Church-State Relations

Discussion on the issue of church-state relations in Catholic thought dates back to the writing of Augustine in the early fifth century and Pope Gelasius in the late fifth century. Since that time many churchmen and others have written on the topic. Their various positions can be summarized in the form of three theories usually called the direct theory, the disjunctive theory, and the indirect or unitary theory. Figure 11-2 depicts these theories. These positions will be briefly described to give a historical perspective. That perspective will show that the positions may have historical roots. It will also show that contemporary experiences are not as new as we frequently imagine.

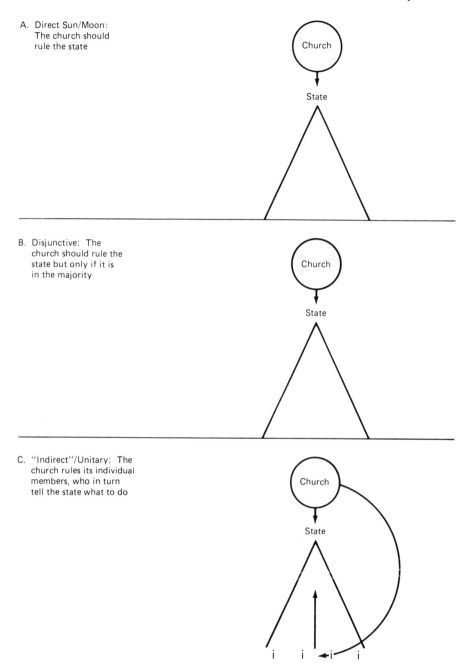

A. Direct Sun/Moon: The church should rule the state

Church

State

B. Disjunctive: The church should rule the state but only if it is in the majority

Church

State

C. "Indirect"/Unitary: The church rules its individual members, who in turn tell the state what to do

Church

State

i i i i

FIGURE 11-2 Three traditional views of church-state relations if the church is higher.

Direct Position

The direct position holds that the church may directly or unilaterally intervene in the affairs of the state because the state is a mere creature of the church. As expressed by Pope Boniface VIII in 1303 in the church document entitled *Unam Sanctam,* the relationship of the church to the state is like the relation of the sun to the moon. As the moon receives only the reflective light of the sun, so the state receives only the authority which the church chooses to give it. Many found it an appealing argument, even though before Boniface the position had been rejected by Thomas Aquinas. In discussing the position Aquinas had pointed out that the state preceded the church in temporal existence, therefore the state could hardly have only the reflective power of the church.

Some suggest that the direct theory of church-state relations became obsolete, for practical purposes anyway, when the thirteenth-century situation of one dominant religion in society no longer prevailed. The direct theory should not be so quickly dismissed, however. The argument of practical obsolescence begs the theoretical question for one thing, and for another, the position is not practically obsolete. The Catholic Church may no longer be in the dominant historical position as it was during part of the Middle Ages, but the theoretical sun/moon theory is shared by small groups of fundamentalists in almost all religions. A particularly prominent example is the Iranian Islamic Republic where religion is the directing force of the state. The Iranian experience is not an isolated incident. Many others in the Middle East, and indeed in all parts of the world, have similar stirrings. We may not like the direct position and it may not represent the Catholic Church but it does give an insight into real political matters.

Disjunctive Position

The argument that the direct position is "obsolete" logically gives way to the disjunctive theory. The disjunctive position holds that the Catholic Church ought to be the established church if it is the predominant religion in society. That position appears opportunistic. It holds that the church is opposed to "establishment," which means officially sanctioning one particular church, unless the Catholic Church is in the majority. This proposition is speciously religious. It appears religious but it is really political. It is political because it is based on numbers. Most actual instances of church establishment have just such a circumstantial base. Whether in France, Italy, England, Scandinavia, Iran, or Israel a religion is not "established" unless it is supported by numbers. The recent activities of the "Moral Majority" are but a variation on the disjunctive theme.

This point about the disjunctive position being based on numbers is important in contemporary experience. Although there are many states that still have "established" or official religions, they are experienced mostly in a ceremonial sense. The critical concern is the "establishment" of the practices and prohibitions of that majority religion on all the state. It is that establishment of beliefs and practices that arouses nonmembers against the "Moral Majority," the "Moslems," the "Catholics," or whatever group appears to be advocating a distinctive position. The disjunctive theory does address this question in terms of numbers. It speaks of a majority and it implies a minority. The political realities of majorities and minorities makes almost everyone uncomfortable in talking about religion, and therefore a more comfortable "indirect" position is sought.

Unitary or Indirect Position

The unitary or indirect position maintains that the two spheres of church and state are and ought to remain distinct. It claims that only when spiritual matters become involved has the church the right and duty to denounce the law that endangers souls. In these instances the position holds the church touches the temporal order but should do so only indirectly through the individual members who as citizens use the available political means. This is said to be a pluralistic position particularly well adapted to the realities of American society. By this is meant that since there are many different religions in the United States, the church demands no dominant position and only acts through its members instead of through the institution's leaders.

The indirect position is attractive but it contains hidden problems. On the one hand it hides from the fact of hierarchical direction of church affairs. On the other hand it turns doctrinal decisions over to the laity, something which the Catholic Church at least does not accept. Either the church members are presented all sides of an issue such as abortion and told to make up their own minds as citizens, or they are told the position of the church as determined by its leaders and are urged or expected to support and carry out this position. Neither alternative is indirect. Both are direct, either with the citizen determining doctrine or the citizen carrying out doctrine. The indirect/unitary theory is prominent because on first impression it satisfies both religious and societal needs. Upon closer examination it is not consistent with either.

All three theories, direct, disjunctive, and indirect, are wanting in the reality of religion and politics. Politics may be temporarily satisfied with this unitary or pluralistic position. This has been the case in the United States for many years. When religion starts operating according to the terms of this position, however, then those on the other side become concerned and they have no theoretical position to cite. If the Moral Majority operates through citizen majorities, they utilize both the unitary position and they become disjunctive. If antiabortion religious groups and others operate in the same way, there is a similar problem. The theoretical alternatives to the question of church intervention in state affairs all run into difficulty because they appear to lack full respect for the integrity of the state, or of other churches, or of individuals either within their own church or other churches. Subsidiarity provides a way out of this dilemma.

Subsidiarity Position

To the question of intervention of the higher unit in the affairs of the lower unit subsidiarity would answer, "Yes!" That may sound like the direct sun/moon position but it is not. Implicit in any application of the principle is the expectation that it will respect the integrity of the lower units of society. Subsidiarity would have the higher unit take over a task only if it is demonstrated that it is both a necessary function and that there is no other way to preserve society from harm. For church-state relations, the lower units involved, whose integrity must be respected, are not only the state but all units of society, including other churches and all individuals.

Throughout this discussion of the issue of church-state relations, reference has been made repeatedly to "the church" and particular reference has been made to "the Catholic Church" as if to equate the two. This dual reference has been deliberate to draw attention to the fact that there are many churches. Each church regards itself, and properly so, as "the church." Catholics, Baptists, Jews, Lutherans, Methodists, Muslims, Mormons, etc., regard their own as the one true church. Individual members of each religion regard it as something special, determined not so much by them as by God. For one church to intervene in the affairs of the state by imposing its views on public policy is to tamper with the integrity not only of the state but also of the other churches and the individual members of the other churches.

Subsidiarity, therefore, gives a fourth and more precise answer to the relations of church and state. The Catholic Church, whatever the impression received from other theories, appears to subscribe to this position, at least as seen in the statements made about religious freedom in the synod of the mid-1960s called Vatican II. In one of that synod's documents on *Religious Freedom* it explained religious freedom to mean "that all men are to be immune from coercion on the part of individuals or of social groups and of any human power, in such wise that in matters of religion no one is to be forced to act in a manner contrary to his own beliefs." The explanation went on to say, "nor is anyone to be restrained from acting in accordance with his beliefs, whether privately or publicly, whether alone or in association with others, within due limits."[3] Those words are clear and specific: no one is to be forced to act in a manner contrary to his or her own belief nor are they to be restrained from acting in accordance with their beliefs. The respect for the integrity of individual belief seems unequivocal. The phrase "within due limits" appears not so much a limitation on integrity as a recognition, as discussed earlier, of those situations of the Jonestown type where integrity is completely lacking.

This position on religious freedom taken by the Catholic Church in Vatican II is consistent with subsidiarity and is entirely acceptable in itself. It may appear not wholly consistent with church history and stories about the treatment of individuals like Galileo and victims of the Inquisition. Historical inconsistencies of that nature, however, appear to be acknowledged and explained a little later in the same document where the synod spoke of religious freedom having its "foundation in the dignity of the person" and that "the requirements of this dignity have come to be more adequately known to human reason through centuries of experience."[4] Whatever the synod had in mind about the historical record, it does respect the contemporary freedom and integrity of other churches and of individuals who are members of those churches.

The statements acknowledging the religious freedom of individuals and churches also seems to encompass the freedom of some individuals to have no religion. The statements speak of ''all men'' being free from coercion and of ''no one'' being forced to act in a manner contrary to his or her own beliefs. Some individual's belief may indeed be ''no belief'' and though they may be, from the view of the church, in error it is not to be coerced. This principle of religious freedom should not be taken, however, as an indifference toward belief. Such an indifference would be both contradictory to religion itself and to the principle of subsidiarity under which the issue is being examined. Religion says that belief is important but also that it is a gift. The notion of ''gift'' explains both the variety and absence of belief. The idea of the importance of religion says that it is not indifferent to the concerns of the world but also that religion should not act so that it harms itself. Thus it can neither accept a wall of separation nor impose its beliefs on others who freely do not believe.

The wall of separation suggests that religion and politics or church and state have nothing to do with one another. The notion of a wall of separation has been cited in Supreme Court cases but it does not appear in the Constitution itself. Its precise constitutional character is not our current concern. The theoretical idea that the spheres of church and state ought to be separate is the concern of our discussion. Many would like to understand the separation of church and state as a matter of the church staying out of state affairs and the state staying out of church affairs, that the one should not get involved in the jurisdiction of the other. If that is all that is meant nearly everyone would agree to it. The point however is a matter of what happens when the two spheres overlap.

Institutional overlap occurs when church and state claim jurisdiction over a common area of social activity. Concrete examples are the abortion issues, or the conduct of war, or educational issues. A wall of separation would have the two spheres separated such that religion would be, as expressed in the surprising commentary of Marx on the First Amendment to the United States Constitution, ''relegated to the refuse heap of arbitrary private whim.'' Marx in this comment was not defending religion. Marx saw the First Amendment as protecting religion and supporting laissez faire individualism. He opposed laissez faire private whim for its antisocial character. If there were to be a wall separating religion and politics, it would in effect endorse the individualism.

The church-state question must be conceived in a way which neither endorses individualism, church dominance, nor state dominance. The difficulty with the church-state issue as discussed so far is that it seems impossible to see a role for religion or the church without reverting to some of the past practices which unduly interfered with the integrity of others. That need not be the case. A solution consistent with subsidiarity is possible. The solution would piece together all the ingredients of subsidiarity and would respect religion and churches, the state, and individuals.

In another of the documents from the Catholic Vatican II synod, *The Church in the Modern World,* the Church stated that, ''It is always and everywhere legitimate for her [the Church] to preach the faith with true freedom, to teach her social doctrine, and to discharge her duty among men without hindrance. She also has the right to pass moral judgments, even on matters touching the political order, whenever basic personal rights or the salvation of souls make such judgments necessary.''[5] Which is to say, the church, any church, can teach, preach, and pass moral judgments on abortion, on the conduct of war, or on any social issue, but in doing so it would not, consistent with the document on religious freedom, impose its belief on others who are not of that same faith. This relationship is depicted in Figure 11-3.

Teaching, preaching, and passing moral judgment appear passive. Efforts on a constitutional amendment to overturn the Supreme Court's abortion decision, protest marches on train tracks scheduled to transport nuclear materials, sanctuary movements in behalf of Central American aliens, and pastoral letters on nuclear strategy are not as passive. The observer should notice, however, that no belief or practice is imposed by the church on anyone. The demonstrators and speakers are

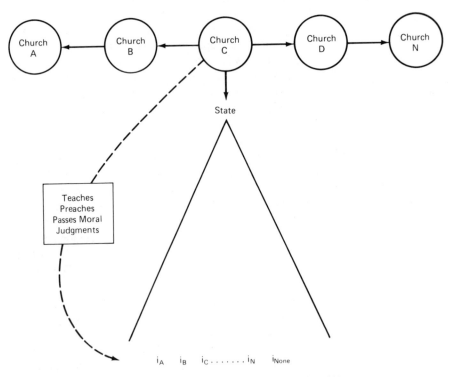

Church C respects Church A, B, D, . . . N and individuals A, B, C, D, . . . N and None

Church C teaches, preaches, and passes moral judgment and attempts to reach individuals in this way. It does not by law impose its beliefs on other churches or other individuals. Church C has much to do.

FIGURE 11-3   A fourth view (subsidiarity) of church-state relations.

acting according to their beliefs. What they advocate will not be accepted as policy unless it is agreed to in the normal policy-making manner. Unless other groups, including other religions, indeed a constitutional majority, become persuaded to support the policy it will not become law. If it does become law it is no different, except perhaps in origin, from any other public policy. All policy, whether wise or unwise, has the support and opposition of an amalgam of the community. If there are officials of the Catholic Church who have taken a leadership role on the issue of the abortion amendment or the war pastoral, there are others who, although not disagreeing on the doctrine, see the policy issue differently. If the policy advocated were ever enacted it would be as public policy and not church policy.

The Jesuit Father Drinan once observed that public policy ought to minimize the number of deaths, should teach the sanctity of life, should provide for proper counselling and physical care, and should avoid the imposition of the requirements of a belief on those who do not share that belief. The Supreme Court's decision allowing abortion seems consistent with Drinan's reasoning. Without legalization, abortions would take place anyway but more deaths would be involved and the counselling and physical care would not be available. Without legalization the life of mother and child are in jeopardy. With equal sincerity one could argue, as President Reagan and others do, that the legalization imposes a belief on the unborn to whom the services of counselling and care are not available. Clearly this is an area where the issues are as intense as they are profound and in need of careful reflection.

The job of the churches as well as of the state does not end with an official pronouncement or policy decision. War, poverty, abortion, oppression, all bring severe mental and physical anguish. Religion and churches have a continuing role to heal the wounds of society, to aid those who anguish over troubling issues. Religion's task, by definition, is much larger than momentary acts or particular legislation. It deals with that part of human beings that cannot be defined in the law and that cannot be limited by time. It calls all persons to a life and a practice of which they prove themselves from time to time incapable. Its inspiration and content is said to come from a source beyond the human domain.

Proof of religion's claim has not been offered in the foregoing discussion. Presented was a consideration of the respective roles of church and state given the claim of religion and the denial of that claim. The issue is by no means settled, but subsidiarity provides a way in which the topic can be viewed in an orderly and understandable manner. If the topic were ignored because it is unfamiliar and complex, that would relegate religion to the refuse heap of arbitrary private whim. To ignore a topic establishes a principle, the principle of a private domain neither touching nor touched by politics. That principle in itself has profound political implications. The burden of this section has been to bring to the surface principles that affect political life so that they are recognized for what they are and are not hidden from view. It is by those principles, by the model presented, that many other topics and issues can be understood in the future.

It may be well to list some of the other issues in church and state relations so that the larger range of the topic can be appreciated. Citing a few other issues should also stress the importance of having subsidiarity as a way to understand them. Other issues in the area of church interest are the general issue of population control, prayer in public schools, the role of the "Moral Majority," aid to non-public schools, censorship, unionization, social justice, Islamic politics, religious freedom in Communist countries, the religious dimensions of the problems in Northern Ireland, Lebanon, and the Middle East in general, the role of religion in Latin America, Haiti and many other countries. Even this list is partial and may reflect a limited perspective. What is important is not the completeness of the list. What is important is the way to approach the issues. Subsidiarity starts with a perspective which accepts the relationship and is willing to work out differences with patience. Such an approach reflects a maturity in the ongoing attempt to understand the reality of political life.

THE STATE'S RELATION TO OTHER STATES

One final relationship has to be considered, that of the state to other states. It involves such topics as international relations, international law, the sources of law, international organizations, regional organizations, international commerce, international economics, war, the settlement of disputes, and diplomacy, to name just a few. Each of these topics could and do in fact constitute the subject of entire courses if not complete programs, depending on the level of study and the university. It will not be possible here to go into these topics beyond what their titles might imply. What will be done, and the reason this broad relationship is included in this chapter, is to suggest that the relation of the states to one another can be understood most effectively and efficiently in the framework of subsidiarity that has informed the previous discussions.

The basic concern in the relation of states to one another is what happens when they do not get along adequately, efficiently, and with benefit to the welfare of the whole community of nations. The most familiar manifestation of their not getting along is some form of invasion. Invasion is usually thought of only in military terms, but the twentieth century has shown new forms of it. Invasion can be economic and cultural, where in a seemingly benign way the invaded country loses control of its resources and heritage. Investments from abroad and enrichments from new cultures are normally welcomed. They can come in such amounts, however, that the results are no longer beneficial. A few examples can illustrate the nonmilitary forms of invasion.

The Japanese accepted the American military occupation after World War II as well as could be expected. It was the effect of American cultural practices on Japanese life which disturbed them. The United States normally has a friendly relationship with its neighbors to the north, but Canada does at times express a concern for its separate identity. As a result of this concern there is a deliberate effort in Canada to maintain the difference between the two countries by way of deliberately different magazines, newspapers, television, and even rules for football. A concern for the threat of OPEC petro-dollar invasion was felt by many in the United States a few years ago. That concern can serve as a reminder of what many countries have felt for many decades about the United States. Investments both within and outside the United States are not unwelcome. It is the extent of the investments that contributes to a concern that outsiders will have a larger say in one's domestic affairs and that sovereignty could be lost. That concern is about a form of invasion. Economic, cultural, as well as military invasion are similar in that one nation does not respect the integrity of another when unilaterally entering into the other's affairs.

The greatest continuing concern in the relation of states to one another is the threat of war. Closely related to this is the concern for economic deprivation, which frequently leads to war. When conditions of war and economic deprivation exist, the relations between states are, by definition, not adequate, efficient, and beneficial to the welfare of the whole. The essential subsidiarity question in this situation is whether some higher level of government is necessary to establish order. When the lowest unit, which happens to be the highest available unit, cannot perform its function adequately, does subsidiarity require movement one step higher to some form of world government? Subsidiarity up to this point has carried from the lowest unit of society through various steps along the way up to the state at the top of the ladder. The question remains whether there is an appropriate next step beyond the state.

World Government

The proposal of having world government intervene when states do not settle their disputes peacefully is centuries old. Dante, the poet famous for *The Divine Comedy,* advocated a single world government in a work entitled *De Monarchia.* He argued that the human potential for growth can best be carried out only when human beings enjoy the quiet and tranquility of universal peace. Such peace cannot exist when states are in conflict with one another; it can only be brought about, he argued, under a single world government with universal law. Many others have argued the same point invoking Aristotle, Cicero, Augustine, Aquinas, various Popes, and other authorities to establish their case. The general contention is that the present international system of independent states without a common authority is tantamount to anarchy and should be replaced by a world government of some sort.

A sketch of the relation of states to one another is presented in Figure 11-4. It depicts various states of differing sizes. Each has a ladder of subsidiarity within it. The assumed relationship between the states is one of equality. There are a couple of states not on the line of equality. Equality is not a matter of size but of worth, integrity. Most of the states currently are members of the United Nations, where their equality and independence is assumed. The question arises as to whether subsidiarity leads to world government when the relationship between states breaks down in war or some other form of invasion. To ensure the tranquility necessary for growth, that Dante spoke of, is some step beyond current arrangements needed to accord all states equal respect?

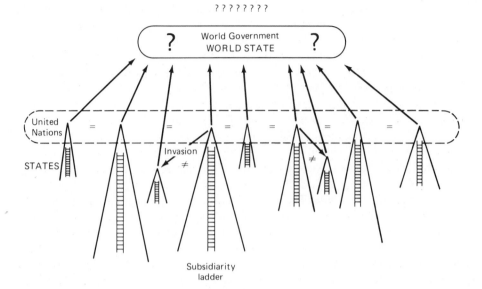

FIGURE 11-4   Subsidiarity and state-to-state relations.

A contemporary group seeking to bring about a common world authority are the World Federalists. They seek to achieve a governed world by changing the present United Nations organization from its confederate form to something they call "world federalism." In the later chapter on federalism there will be a discussion of the concept itself and the contention by some serious thinkers that federalism is merely a fiction used rhetorically for political purposes. Here, in discussing the world order, it is not necessary to examine the theoretical questions of federalism; it is enough to consider what the World Federalists seek and to evaluate this in the light of subsidiarity.

A constant theme running through the literature of the World Federalist Association is that they seek a strengthened United Nations which will be given "power to . . . prohibit any nation from using force or threats of force"; that the strengthened United Nations have power to "govern" the seabed, that it have "taxing power"; that the expanded United Nations judiciary have "final authority"; and that there be universal membership without the right of secession. The World Federalists want the UN Charter changed to handle those areas and any other problems not adequately dealt with by the individual state relations.

The proposals by the World Federalists and the theme enunciated by Dante seem wholly consistent with the principle of subsidiarity; if the lower unit cannot perform a necessary function then some next higher unit should see that it is performed or assume the function itself. World government would handle only those problems of war, disarmament, nuclear weaponry, the seabed, trade, or human rights which cannot be adequately solved at the present national level. It is therefore expected that the world government would be established on a "federated" basis with the constituent members and lesser groups retaining their original autonomy over matters properly within their respective spheres. In this way, as in the theory of "federalism" as applied within particular countries, on the world level diversity is retained in unity, pluralism is maintained in common purpose, harmony is achieved in contrariety (as occurs musically in the case of the bow and the lyre).

Diversity in unity, pluralism in common purpose, harmony in contrariety are poetic phrases. They are inserted deliberately to point out the rhetorical mode to which the discussion frequently turns. The problems, complexities, and painful situations of international conflict lead to a desire for dramatic solutions. Dramatic solutions are simple and appealing, but they are inadequate. The situation where states do not perform their function adequately does not automatically lead to a decision in favor of establishing world government.

In all the previous discussions of subsidiarity the emphasis was that a unit should perform its function. In discussing individual rights, private property, groups, and religion, the assumption of integrity primarily focused on the unit coming to perform its function. If a function could not be performed, other units should come with assistance or even assume the task of a weak unit if necessary. The point was always that a unit should perform its function, the units should give according to ability, and if they could not function they should receive aid according to need. Subsidiarity, so to speak, focused downward to lower units performing their functions rather than upward to some higher unit taking over. This downward focus was insisted upon until there were no other way for a necessary function to be performed.

The tasks of lower levels of government or society were not to be automatically assumed by the next higher unit until efforts had been made to see if there were other ways to make it possible for the lower one to perform its function. This was especially emphasized in, but not limited to, the consideration of corporate and public ownership of property. Furthermore, in all the previous discussions there was always a next higher unit already in existence when the time came that it was needed. These points become critical in considering the proposal for world government. In assuming the validity of the step to world government, it is forgotten that world government does not now exist and that it would have to be created in some way. An additional problem is that the process of awaiting the creation of this higher government becomes an excuse for the existing states to neglect their obligation to function adequately in international terms.

The current structure of the United Nations is as a confederacy. A confederacy is a loose union of independent states legally free to reject proposed rules and free to withdraw at will. The freedom and independence of states can be abused as is sadly witnessed in invasions and other irresponsible activities. Corrective actions against such abuses would be desirable. It is possible, however, that the creation of a world governmental body could result in harm greater than that which it would seek to prevent. The world government would have to be "created." The precise means of the "origin" of that state could present practical as well as theoretical problems.

On the theoretical side, the issue of the origin of the state has not been finally settled at the domestic level. It is not clear, as discussed in the earlier chapter on this precise topic, whether the state originates in a social contract, is the product of some socio-logical origin, or that the "divine theory" is the proper explanation. When states are formed, leaders do not sit around and debate the theoretical justifications for the origin of political authority. When world government is discussed, those theoretical matters are debated. Practical justifications are important but in this instance the theoretical differences are going to play a much larger role. Because the consequences are so great and because of the intense theoretical divisions between states, the justification for a world mechanism will have a profound effect on everyone's future. The issue of world government becomes more significant than originally thought.

Aside from the theoretical disagreements and philosophical divisions which cloud the discussion of world government, the issue is further complicated by practical considerations. Nationalism, the emphasis on one's own nation to the exclusion and sometimes the harm of other states, is a practical and not just a theoretical problem in international affairs. Irresponsible and violent displays of nationalism have been exhibited many times. Much has been written about nationalism. Before World War II it was on the wane. It has not disappeared, however. Since 1945 more than one hundred nations have been created and many more yearn for recognition. Their membership in the swollen United Nations brings a breakdown in the discussion and exchange for which the organization was created. It is not unusual now for sessions of the General Assembly of the United Nations to witness unprecedented numbers of member nations lamenting the practical ineffectiveness of the world organization. If the United Nations was created to remedy the evils of nationalism it itself is becoming the victim.

Unsatisfied nationalism spreads in Europe, Africa, the Caribbean, and the South Asian crescent. And nationalism is just one of the practical problems and caveats to world order. Among other problems are those seemingly minor details of the structure of the world governmental body. Technical questions of gigantic proportions are whether the world body should be bicameral or unicameral, what type of equitable financing should be arranged, and who its administrators should be. The United Nations has problems enough of this nature and it is not even a government. Currently the United States pays a disproportionate amount of the UN costs. This greater payment may be as distributive justice requires. However, in the face of increasingly hostile stances within the UN toward the United States, it seems impractical to expect continued American support let alone increased support for a larger membership.

The so-called minor details of structure and organization for the world body become potentially more divisive than the more general ideal itself. Disagreement on theoretical issues may inhibit and delay action, but disagreement on practical matters such as financing or the implementation of resolutions can lead to strife. The quiet tensions of the United Nations as currently constituted could give way in a strengthened organization to armed conflict. Under a ''united'' world such conflicts would be called civil war instead of world war. The differences might be semantic; the consequences would be seismographic.

To oppose world government does not mean to give in to present injustices or to surrender to the forces of laissez faire in international relations. In the contemporary world many states do not perform their function properly and many others are unable to function adequately. It is important in terms of their own needs and in the terms of the principle of subsidiarity that the states function adequately, efficiently, and with benefit to the welfare of the whole. If world government is not an appropriate step to ensuring that adequate performance occurs, then other means must be sought.

Practical Alternatives

The other means available may be less dramatic than the twin alternatives of laissez faire or world government. Although journalistic coverage of the political world has conditioned students of politics to look for and expect the dramatic, the hard work of progress seldom comes in that form. A few proposals for improving the possibility for all states to function more adequately may at first seem modest. Brief examination of the modest proposals reveals the intricate complexity from which improvement must be wrought. The furtherance of free trade, the development and expansion of arrangements for international banking, and the regulation of multinational corporations are three proposals for improving the relations between states without resorting to world government.

These proposals are not particularly new. They require great amounts of time, patience, and tenacity. They have the advantage, however, over the more dramatic alternatives of accepting and building from the best aspects of the present international system. These proposals accept the current world framework. They would seek to accentuate aspects that can build relations and improve conditions; they do not focus on only what is wrong. The key to the proposals is that they seek to advance the integrity of existing individual states on a worldwide basis.

Respecting integrity is the cornerstone to the whole subsidiarity concept. In international conflict, whether military, economic, or cultural, the parties involved do not treat each other as equals. The ''invading'' party in a military conflict seeks to subordinate the other party; it does not ''respect the integrity'' of the other nation. In economic affairs, trade barriers call attention to the lack of equal exchange. Tariffs and quotas are a defense against or the beginnings of unfair treatment. Strings-attached, bilateral foreign aid links international charity and coercion. Strings treat the states which need aid as pawns to be manipulated by the lender. Multinational corporations whose origins are in one country are said to treat the countries in which they do business in a subservient manner because there is always a third country to welcome them if the second does not cooperate. All these practices are instances of breakdowns in the presumed integrity of states.

Free Trade

Free trade, international banking, and regulation of multinationals are counterpoint to the above practices. The remedies seek to take the existing framework of states and enhance the respect for all the states involved. Free trade, like the other measures, starts with the assumption that the parties engaged are equal at least in statehood. Free trade—fair trade might be a better description—would seek to foster equality by eliminating artificial barriers. This would avoid the subordination which comes with external decisions of foreign states regulating a nation's commerce. There is a fear that free trade supports harmful unregulated competition injurious to all parties. That concern has to be judged in light of its alternatives of massive manipulations and no greater chance of success and fairness.

Today's environment of international commerce is not so much a matter of formal trade barriers by tariffs as it is a matter of indirect barriers and national subsidy to promote selected economic sectors. Whatever the form, barriers erected to the free and fair flow of commerce become the cause of international inequity. The chances of realizing an international free trade environment are not imminent. Unrelenting efforts to bring about an improvement are at least a concrete step to better the relations among nations and the health of those nations. It is to lessen the inequities that the international GATT (General Agreements on Tariffs and Trade) organization and other trade conferences are dedicated. These efforts are the hard realities of international politics. They can make positive contributions to the relations among nations without awaiting the dramatic formation of a world legislature.

International Banking

In similar fashion expanded international banking arrangements would improve the relation among states. Some international banks already exist, such as the World Bank (properly called the International Bank for Reconstruction and Development) and the Asian Development Bank. The International Monetary Fund and affiliates of the World Bank, such as the International Development Association and the International Finance Corporation, also serve in the same capacity of seeking to aid needy nations through loans and various forms of development assistance. All such programs need added resources but there is a reluctance caused both by economic strain and philosophical outlook that holds developed nations from being entirely forthcoming with investment funds.

The traditional mode of economic assistance on the international level was a system of bilateral loans and grants from wealthy nations to those other nations which the wealthy ones choose to help. Along with the personalized selection process of who assisted whom there was always a factor, as in all personalized lending arrangements, that economic aid bought political loyalty. Thus implicit, and frequently explicit, with economic aid came strings which prescribed certain political expectations. Even where the strings were not intended in the beginning they were added in time. Where pure beneficence existed there came to be a perception of a dependence that was originally unrecognized, and resentment and hostilities developed.

It is frequently argued in defense of the practice of tying strings to aid, that if others want a wealthy nation's assistance then they ought to be grateful. Political support to the helping country and the system which made the aid possible is not too much to ask. Resources are limited for even the wealthy and it is only reasonable for them to choose to aid those who would not abuse the benefactor. It is not as if the wealthy need to "buy" friends. It is a matter of giving aid to those who would be friendly. This position is argued in both domestic and international politics despite the fact that in personal lending practices it has long since been realized, in the words of the adage, that "If you want to keep a friend, don't lend money to him." The adage is based on the experience that suspicions and resentments crop up even among the best of associates.

On the personal level what most reasonable individuals do is invest their resources in full service banks, savings and loan associations, credit unions, or the like. Others then borrow from these same institutions, paying a reasonable interest for the use of the investor's funds. The practice of private lending is fraught with danger. It is on this analogy that the international banking idea is proposed. International banks would depersonalize the contacts between nations and let aid be accomplished through businesslike banking channels as it is in local banking practices.

International lending would see that the loans were secure, made for legitimate purposes, and have sound investment purposes. Concern for repayments, extending credits, refinancing, credit limits, and all other arrangements would be handled on a business basis so that the political or personal dimensions would not get in the way of development. This is not to say that political and personal considerations are not important in international dealings, yet they sometimes interfere with other sound political principles and impede progress. When temporary political concerns get in the way of respecting the integrity of other states, then short-term interests adversely affect long-term goals to the injury of all parties.

The integrity and equality of all states are principles which even the advocates of an improved world order espouse. Efforts in their behalf should have general support rather than be looked upon as something harmful to the well-being of free nations. What is harmful to free nations is a process of subordination of states, whether it comes about through military forms of domination or through strings attached to bilateral aid.

Regulating Multinational Corporations

The rapacity of multinational corporations is another factor which brings about the subordination of nations to an external force. Although abuses are universally condemned, precise measures for mitigating the harm and restricting the practices which bring them about are noticeable only by their absence. The "invaded" country or countries are in no position to fend off the corporations, which are often economically more powerful and organizationally more effective. The countries benefit economically through the investments and the resulting jobs. However, they are also harmed through the inability to regulate working conditions or products and through some correlative corruption which often accompanies large business contacts.

The countries which spawned the multinationals are themselves not in a very good position to regulate these companies. The country of origin fears that the businesses could slip away to another country (like auto plants have moved to Mexico and textile plants to the Far East), and then there would be an even lessened ability to influence offensive practices. In addition there is a resulting gratuitous loss of capital and jobs. Since many nations share this problem but face it from different perspectives, the likely solution will come from the economically and politically powerful nations joining together at some point and agreeing to some restrictions which will benefit large and small nations alike. Such an approach to regulation will not come about easily and it will not be universally accepted. Nonetheless, delayed solutions which satisfy the interests of the powerful countries as well as the wealthy corporations are more likely and will respect the integrity of existing institutions. Successful unilateral action or international legislation are both unlikely. The terrible disaster at the Union Carbide plant in Bhopal, India may have a beneficial effect if it quickens concern for dealing with corporate and political accountability.

There are already several international organizations which regulate or facilitate commercial contacts between nations. Although the regulation of multinationals is much more complex than the commercial activities currently encompassed by these bodies, they do offer a precedent and design for more extensive efforts. The International Postal Union, the International Civil Aviation Organization, the World Intellectual Property Organization, the International Telecommunication Union, the World Meteorological Organization, and the International Labor Organization are a few of the organizations established in the last forty to seventy-five years to promote or facilitate a particular aspect of the interaction among nations and their peoples.

It cannot be claimed that these existing international organizations preclude any breakdown in the areas in which they operate. Their practices and procedures, however, are so superior to what would occur if the organizations did not exist that their value is manifest. Necessity was the mother of the invention of these earlier organizations. It might be speculated that similar developments may produce the regulation of the multinationals. The early organizations functioned without interfering in the legal rights and autonomy of the participating states. Their functioning enabled all the states to conduct their own affairs more smoothly. Such results are as would be expected with the application of subsidiarity. They give hope that in time arrangements will be found which will apply effectively to business.

DISCUSSION

It might be argued that improved free trade practices, enhanced international banking, and coming to grips with regulating multinationals is nothing more than what world government would want to do. There is a difference however. The legal means by which the changes are brought about are crucial. Retaining state autonomy may mean that some may still be free to act irresponsibly. Yet that behavior would not be precluded even in a world government. With autonomy all would continue to exercise that pluralism of choice requiring cooperation which makes politics at every level both challenging and beneficial. With world government massive planning and coordination would be necessary and these abilities are not even proven on the domestic level.

It is true at this level of international politics, as Aristotle had said regarding domestic politics, that the recognition of the differences in humans is of the essence of politics. Accepting differences is the chief factor which distinguishes a political science of forced unity, as in Plato, from one of freedom. The goals of world government are a subtle and seductive distraction, like Plato's *Republic,* from doing effectively the hard work necessary on a practical level. More realistic goals will better serve the future peace of the world than idealistic dreams upon which there is great disagreement.

The modest proposals of free trade, international banks, and the regulation of multinationals clearly do not constitute a surrender to the continuation of laissez faire on the world scene. They are instead means to practice distributive justice in the relation among nations. They would make it possible for the lowliest nation-state to come to function adequately, efficiently, and with benefit to the welfare of the community of humankind.

It may be asked why one nation which is prosperous should have to help another which is poor? This question has occurred in other contexts earlier, usually in the form, ''Why should those who have earned their keep through their own industry help those who have not?'' There is a great inclination to answer that question in utilitarian terms, that if the wealthy do not aid the poor there will be economic disruptions to the extent that the wealthy will pay in the long run. This utilitarian sense of justice sees the deprived as eventually revolting or causing some disorder which the wealthy will have to pay to rectify. Ghetto conflagrations, prison riots, and domestic revolutions are offered as evidence of the utilitarian thesis. Such logic does call for some efforts in behalf of the deprived but their satisfaction requires nothing more than the minimum. Utilitarian answers are alleviative instead of curative or preventative.

The difference between a minimalistic response and one out of a fuller sense of justice is illustrated in a story about an earthquake in Guatemala in 1976. When an American relief team began setting up camp on its own at a local village after deplaning and driving to the damage site, residents came running to ask what they were doing. The Americans explained that they were there to aid the quake victims. The surprised Americans were told by the villagers that the quake area was actually a number of miles further up the road, that the conditions in the village were the way people normally lived.

Aid in the time of dramatic events is what the minimalist utilitarian logic comes to. The condition of the village would never have been noticed except for the special event of the earthquake. Distributive justice would require preventative and corrective measures on the situation of the ''normal,'' but until disaster strikes neglected, villages. They should be assisted because they are ''in need,'' as the first part of the disaster relief team had concluded. In justice the prosperous should help the poor because they are in need and for no other reason.

Justice on the international or domestic level does not mean the leveling of all societies, all men, and all nations. It means at a minimum that all persons should be able to operate in a manner which is adequate, efficient, and beneficial to the welfare of humankind. The common good within states is the common good among states. Subsidiarity in the relation of states to one another is intended to bring about that common good.

NOTES

1. *Pierce* v. *The Society of Sisters*, 268 U.S. 510; also *Tinker* v. *Des Moines* previously cited.

2. *Davis* v. *Beason*, 133 U.S. 333, (1890).

3. *Documents of Vatican II*, "Declaration on Religious Freedom," Chapter I, Section 2.

4. ibid., Chapter II, Section 9.

5. *Documents of Vatican II*, "Pastoral Constitution on the Church in the Modern World," Chapter IV, Section 76, paragraph 7.

CHAPTER TWELVE
CONSTITUTIONALISM

The idea of constitutional government is deeply imbued in Americans. The indignant cry, "It's unconstitutional!" or the proud assertion, "It's constitutional!" are echoed and reechoed throughout American history and politics. Despite the ease with which constitutionalism is referred to, it is not well understood. Confident individuals may explain it as "rule according to law and not men." That confidence would fade when reminded that "men make the law" or that "not all rule according to law is good since the law itself might be bad law." As with the concept of democracy with which this text began, the idea of constitutionalism can well use explication. Appreciation of both constitutionalism's unchanging fundamental character and its dynamic qualities can be gained by reviewing its classical roots, its modern dimensions, a classification scheme for constitutional government, its growth characteristics, and its definite but elusive "spirit."

THE ROOTS OF CLASSICAL CONSTITUTIONALISM

The word "constitution" means different things to different people. Most fundamentally there is an ancient or classical meaning and a modern meaning. Each is a special type of constitutional "root." To the average American the term "constitutional" refers to a written document which sets forth the structure of the government and specifies the power of those who serve in its offices. The emphasis in this American view is on limits and the idea that government should be conducted in accordance with fixed rules as opposed to expediency or whim. To the Britisher, on the other hand, constitutionalism denotes not a single document or few closely related documents but the whole body of laws and customs which go to make up the character of the government.

In this broad or more classical sense of the roots of constitutionalism the basic reference point is not a particular written legal document to which lesser legislation must conform. It is instead the whole life and scheme of living of a community. Aristotle had referred to the constitution in this sense as "the way of life of a people." In this way one refers to the constitution of the community as one would refer to the constitution of a human being. Aristotle thought of the state as its constitution, just as a human being is its "disposition." The broad, Aristotelian, or classical view of constitutionalism was basically that of a moral force which guided government but which lacked specific legal or political techniques for ensuring compliance.

The broad positive roots of constitutionalism were seen in a different light when modern times produced a break with the previous unified conception of moral and political life and witnessed the quicker and more immediate impact of governmental actions on private individuals. In this new milieu more specific means of checking unacceptable governmental practices were needed.

THE ROOTS OF MODERN CONSTITUTIONALISM

The development of legal and institutional means of restraining arbitrary rule is what characterizes modern constitutionalism. This development is commonly identified with that American view of written limits set forth in a document carefully laid down in advance. Embodied in this view is the idea that to guide government, a fundamental charter is needed which spells out the broad outline of powers and the rules of procedure. This amounts to establishing "a fundamental law that defines the organs of government, prescribes how they shall function, and outlines the basic relationships between government and the private citizen."[1]

Basic to most commonly accepted descriptions of modern constitutionalism is the element of a "written" fundamental document. Because of this element it is mistaken to say, as is commonly done, that modern constitutionalism had its beginning with the English "Glorious" Revolution and parliamentary supremacy principle of 1688. More accurately, if less commonly, the genesis of the tradition of a written constitution can be traced to the Mayflower Compact of 1620, the Fundamental Orders of Connecticut of 1637, and the many other charters, compacts, and agreements which coexisted with the beginning of most American "colonies." The practice of working with and beginning with a written document was so ingrained that when the Americans in the 1770s found themselves talking about independence from England, the first thing they did was draft a "Declaration of Independence" and *at the same time* sanction the drafting of a common constitution, the *Articles of Confederation*.

When it was quickly discovered that the Articles were not well drafted, they were altered within ten years in the Constitution of 1787, which is the present Constitution. The American practice soon became the model of constitutionalism and was copied in the efforts at written documents in France in their revolutionary era. The practice spread in the succeeding decades in other European countries and more especially in their newly independent colonies. Today this practice of written "constitutional" restraints exists in most all major states in the world except England and, surprisingly, Israel. Consequently, the elementary contemporary contrast between modern constitutionalism and classical constitutionalism is between the American and the English respectively.

The contrast between the modern and the classical notions of constitutional government can be expressed in terms other than just referring to their nominal countries of origin. The contrast is also, respectively, between written and unwritten, narrow and broad, legal and moral, emphasis on restraints and on the way of life, limits and reason, and negative and positive. The contrast between negative and positive based on the emphasis on restraints is expressed by one author who wrote,

> Some thinkers are so preoccupied with the abuses of power that their interpretation of constitutionalism is a series of negatives. Their rule of law degenerates into a bundle of prohibitions. A government must be prevented from doing this, that, and the other. To devise checks, controls, restraints, and limitations becomes the essence of constitutionalism and the prime guarantee of human freedom. . . . The state should be envisaged as a canal through which political power may flow, releasing its energy for the benefit of mankind, rather than as a dam to hold it back. . . . While tyrannical governments destroy freedom, other governments may enlarge it. Many of the functions that the modern state undertakes are designed to make opportunities more nearly equal for everybody and to protect weaker individuals from the rapacity of the strong.[2]

This author correctly implies that the essential conception of constitutionalism reflects one's overall view of government and the purpose of government. One's view can be narrow or broad, emphasizing limits or opportunities. It is this contrast that distinguishes modern and classical constitutionalism.

CLASSIFICATION OF CONSTITUTIONS

The set of parallel but opposing qualities makes it possible to set up a classification scheme of governments from which much can eventually be learned. The scheme is of four parts distinguishing between legally limited and legally unlimited government and actually limited and actually unlimited governments. A legally limited regime is one in which rules of conduct are carefully laid down in advance. An actually limited government is one where the regime conducts itself according to expected standards of behavior whether it is written down or not. Conversely, a government is legally unlimited where there are no written guides, and a government is actually unlimited when it conforms to no standards of conduct. Laid out in a two-by-two matrix the scheme would look like this:

LEGALLY

	Limited	Unlimited
Limited		
ACTUALLY		
Unlimited		

According to this scheme the United States, which has a written constitution and which is regarded as living in conformity to it, is classified as legally limited and actually limited. The Soviet Union on the other hand, which has a written constitution very much like that of the United States, is said to be legally limited but actually unlimited since it is regarded as not living in conformity with constitutionalism and its own constitution. England, since it has no written constitution, would be classified as legally unlimited, but since it is guided by and acts in accordance with constitutional expectations, customs, and traditions, it would be listed as actually limited. Legally unlimited and actually unlimited is a category which fulfills the four-part scheme. Actual examples of the fourth category may be hard to enumerate since many of the nominees, like Uganda under Idi Amin or Cambodia under Pol Pot or Libya under Colonel Qadhafi, while practicing unlimited rule, had some written constitution, even though it may have been counterfeit. To complete this category the reader is asked to name their favorite despotic government or simply leave it as regime "X." Written out the scheme would look like this:

Legally limited and Actually limited : USA
Legally unlimited and Actually limited : England
Legally limited and Actually unlimited : USSR
Legally unlimited and Actually unlimited : "X"

The analytical merits of the classification scheme appear slim since it reveals little more than that the category of legally limited versus the category of legally unlimited refers to the presence or absence of a written constitution. The only contrast reflected between the United States and England is the possession of a written constitution. That same possession is likewise the only similarity between the United States and the Soviet Union. The more important contrast of being actually limited or actually unlimited is unspecific. It is the pursuit of this point that can lead to a more fruitful understanding of the whole concept of constitutionalism.

THE SPIRIT OF CONSTITUTIONALISM I

England and the United States are understood to be actually limited and are generally classified as "constitutional" regimes. The United States and the Soviet Union, although both have written constitutions, stand in sharp contrast in the area where it really counts, in actual compliance with constitutional rule. What is usually implied in this contrast is that the United States adheres to the intention of its constitution and the Soviet Union does not. More specifically the difference is explained in terms of the Soviet Union enacting policy, whether it be constitutional changes or ordinary legislation, by the legal bodies perfunctorily approving what was already decided by the leadership of the Communist Party.

In the United States it is understood that all policy is enacted by following the prescriptions of the Constitution and using the legal bodies of the government as intended. In this way the United States is said to act in a manner consistent with "the spirit of constitutionalism." The Soviet Union is thought not to act consistent with that spirit. Extralegal means of policy making or the overriding of the legal machinery by political dictates are regarded as not used in the United States but are viewed as a common practice in the Soviet Union. This commonly agreed upon "spirit of constitutionalism," here labeled "Spirit I," undergoes a severe test, however, when examined in the light of the process of constitutional growth, particularly when applied to the United States. A review of the process of growth suggests that the normally ascribed differences between the two countries are not entirely accurate. The constitutional contrasts appear to break down.

CONSTITUTIONAL GROWTH

Constitutions grow in two ways, one formal, the other informal. Formal growth or change is the process provided in the constitution itself for amending the original document. In the United States, Article V of the Constitution provides that two thirds of both houses of the Congress shall propose or two thirds of the states shall petition Congress to call a convention for proposing amendments, and then three fourths of the state legislatures or special conventions within the states shall ratify the proposed amendments.

Even though England has an unwritten constitution, there is a formal amending process according to which, by generally accepted convention, no fundamental change will be made without an express mandate from the electorate. Proposals for major changes such as the nationalization or denationalization of industry or the possible elimination of the House of Lords follow an agreed upon procedure. Such proposals would be considered by one membership of Parliament but would not be enacted until another membership was chosen at an intervening election.

Variations on these amending themes can be found in all countries and constitutions. According to its formal process, the United States Constitution has been amended seventeen times with twenty-six amendments. In contrast, the California

State constitution has been amended 438 times in a little more than one hundred years. The formal amending process can be employed sparingly or extensively, depending on varying circumstances in different jurisdictions.

The informal constitutional growth process involves means other than the formal by which change is effected. There are four categories of informal change: judicial interpretation, congressional or legislative enactments, presidential or executive initiatives, and custom, convention, or usage. An examination of each of the informal growth processes will show that the methods other than judicial are each equally interpretative even though that interpretative character is not usually acknowledged in the designations.

Judicial Review

Judicial interpretation refers to the process whereby the courts in the course of their normal business expand, limit, or otherwise alter the previous understanding of part of the constitution. In any legal system the exact meaning and application of a law is often not explicitly or perfectly detailed in the statute itself. The refinement or detail of the application of the law is worked out in what is known as case law. Case law is law as the product of decisions in particular controversies or disputes. Judges normally attempt to apply the laws and precedents of earlier decisions to the particular case before them. Where the ruling of the court deviates from what the legislature originally had in mind, new correcting legislation can be enacted. When the law that the court applies in a particular case is the basic law of the constitution, then the court in its decision is interpreting the constitution. If the court expands or limits the content of specific provisions of the constitution as understood up until that point, it has amended the constitution in a way other than through the formal amending process.

In the United States judicial interpretation is especially noted in judicial review where the court, particularly the Supreme Court, can declare actions of the Congress or the President unconstitutional. The basis of the court's interpretative power is its ability to say that the legislation in question is not consistent with a provision of the Constitution. The provision to which the court refers happens to be the court's own interpretation of what is important and what it means. Since the Supreme Court's pronouncements provide the norm for all lower courts it, rather than the legislature, has "made the law" for the society. It is normally understood that the only way to reverse such a decision of the Court is to take extraordinary measures, such as passing a formal constitutional amendment. That understanding is not entirely accurate since it is possible for the Congress to alter the Court's jurisdiction or to alter the Court's membership. Since these congressional measures are marked by disuse, the perception of preeminence becomes the reality.

It is instructive to note how the courts in the United States acquired the power of judicial review. They did so not by some particular provision of the constitution which explicitly gave them the authority but by a decision in a case, *Marbury* v. *Madison,* 1803. In other words they acquired the power of definitive legal interpretation of the Constitution by a case in which they interpreted the Constitution. The case was a classic in political and legal skill. The court ruled on something it was not asked to do and avoided what had been asked because it was unenforceable. The rule that it established, that it could declare an act of Congress unconstitutional, was used sparingly and so in time it became an accepted practice raised to the level of a doctrine. Even though its second use in the *Dred Scott* case was unsuccessful, its use in the following decades was skillful enough that it became a well-established element of the American constitutional system.

The practice of judicial review is not limited to the United States. It is also found in West Germany, Italy, Japan, and many other countries, and its historical origins have some roots in English practices even before Edward Coke at the opening of the seventeenth century.[3] Judicial review is a soundly logical practice given certain basic assumptions such as the equality of the various branches of the government and the sacredness of the language of the original constitution. On the other hand it is fundamentally unsound from the perspective of parliamentary supremacy. Court primacy is unacceptable from the view that the body elected by the people has the ultimate determination of what is law.

Whether judicial review is to be preferred or not depends on premises about the forms of government which precede the examination of the question of judicial review itself. Judicial review does not exist in its final lawmaking character in parliamentary systems, and therefore its existence in some systems is only partial. A more careful look at the premises of the forms of government will come later when the parliamentary and presidential (separation of powers) systems are examined. In anticipation it is not incorrect to look at judicial review as being for the most part uniquely American.

Congressional Enactments

Despite the attention that judicial interpretation gets, the other methods of informal growth are equally interpretative and equally important. Legislative change involves enactments which significantly expand, limit, or otherwise alter the arrangements specified in the original Constitution. Examples of such changes can be found in the creation of the independent regulatory commissions which add a structure to the government not mentioned in the Constitution. There are many such commissions, starting with the Interstate Commerce Commission in 1887 and extending to the now familiar Securities and Exchange Commission, Federal Reserve Board, National Labor Relations Board, Federal Communications Commission, Civil Aeronautics Board, to name only a few of about fifty. Each such commission was created by Congress to be independent of Congress, the President, and the courts and to exercise independent legislative, judicial, and executive powers in their area of concern.

Since the time of their original creation, each of these agencies has become so powerful that they have come to be referred to collectively as the "fourth branch of the government." The appellation is not inappropriate, as special studies of governmental organization have advocated that they be placed under presidential direction more consistent with the constitutional outline of the three branches. The intention in creating these separate agencies was to remove them and their area of jurisdiction from the ebb and flow of partisan politics. That essential point sustains their continued independence. In creating this new structure, Congress expanded the Constitution without a formal constitutional amendment. It is small consolation to constitutional purists that this legislative expansion received the approbation of the courts and of the President as one interpretation reinforces another.

Often cited as an example of judicial interpretation and lawmaking is the 1824 case of *Gibbons* v. *Ogden*. In that case the Supreme Court is said to have given the authoritative interpretation of the meaning of the commerce clause of the Constitution which also sustained the national government's jurisdiction over that of the states. In this instance of judicial review, which is broader than merely extending to acts of the Congress or the President, the Court overturned a navigation act of the state in favor of a navigation licensing act established earlier by Congress. In a case which usually focuses on the interpretative role of the Court, the original interpretation was that of Congress which in 1793 had decided to enact the licensing law. The *Gibbons* case is important because it made clear the jurisdiction of the national government in the vital area of commerce. It is legally the constitutional basis for the later actions establishing the regulatory commissions. Our immediate interest in it is as an illustration of one interpretation, that of the Court, reinforcing another, that of Congress.

Presidential Interpretation

Examples of presidential interpretations are in executive agreements ranging from the Louisiana Purchase in 1803, to the controversial lend-lease initiative in 1940, to diplomatic and war powers of the contemporary era. Each exercise of presidential initiative is entirely reasonable in the context of its particular exigencies. Jefferson could not wait for formal congressional and constitutional debate before purchasing the Louisiana territory because the opportunity would have slipped by once notice was given of the prospect. Presidents today, in carrying out foreign policy, have to have a flexibility beyond the treaty and other limited provisions of the Constitution. Crises in the foreign policy area are not arranged to occur during the working hours of the day when Congress is in session. To subject the President to the niceties of Congressional approval on every exercise of authority could be contrary to the interests of the Constitution.

Both Lincoln and Franklin Roosevelt went beyond accepted constitutional practice during wartime. They defended their action on the argument that they acted to preserve the Constitution itself. Roosevelt in particular was not known for justifying his actions in other than very broad terms of "war power" or "the statutes." He did not cite chapter and verse. Recent congressional efforts in the "War Powers Act" to restrict the authority of the President will come up later in the context of comparative forms of government, as will the philosophical question about the final character of judicial review. In the case of a surprise attack in the middle of the night during a congressional recess, the ability of the President to act seems mandated rather than precluded by the Constitution. What should be clear is that this debate on war powers involves competing interpretations of the Constitution. The issue is not yet settled. The Court has not even become a serious part of this particular issue. It is significant, however, that no one is talking about a formal amendment as a resolution of the issue.

It is convenient and perhaps necessary for Congress through hearings to question various exercises of presidential war power. Those hearings usually occur after the fact since any attempt to conduct military operations "by committee" would be potentially disastrous for both the committee and the military. George Washington had made clear during the Revolutionary War that as far as he was concerned, Congress could not run the military aspect of the war. That has been the position of all Presidents. For the most part tampering has not been great, though there have been cases of it. In most litigious challenges the courts have upheld the executive showing once again that interpretation reinforces interpretation.

Many additional examples are available on each of the informal means of constitutional growth. Those examples can be saved for an American Government text. The point of interest in this introduction to political science text is the concept of informal change in the formal constitution. American examples are used because they are most familiar to the readers of this text and also because of their prominence in the general literature of the field. The same familiarity and prominence is generally true in the area of informal change referred to as "custom, usage, and convention," although this is not exclusively the case. This last category gets closer to the whole notion of an unwritten constitutional "way of life," and so its illustrations are easier to picture as applying to other than American settings.

Custom and Usage: Political Parties

The chief example of the custom and usage form of constitutional expansion is the American political party system. It is an important example because it points to a definite part of the American political system which in many respects defies constitutional formulation. The party system is universally recognized as part of the political system but it cannot be put into constitutional language.

The American party system has several components: two major parties, passive tolerance of minor and third parties, and the possibility that over time smaller parties will grow to replace one or both major parties. The system evolved from a one party arrangement at the time of Washington through the flux of parties in the nineteenth century to a relatively stable arrangement of the Democratic Party and the Republican Party in the twentieth century. These two current parties appear to be permanently fixed in the system. Occasionally the media anguish over the future of one party or the other as election fortunes change.

Technically only candidates run for office and all candidates are treated equally. Party groupings came to be recognized in the passage of state election laws. This recognition gave greater prominence to party candidates, which contributes to the permanence of the party. More recently some limited national party rules have been supported in the courts, which contributes further to strengthening the existing parties. The full implications of the recent rulings are not yet known and probably cannot be fully evaluated for years. The system has evolved over time and will continue to do so no matter what sporadic legal effort might suggest.

The political party system is important because it is only through the major parties that the otherwise unworkable presidential election system functions effectively. Furthermore it is through the parties that the constitutionally separated branches of government become fluid and less rigidly dysfunctional. The parties have been aptly called the lubricant which makes the wheels of government run smoothly. Despite the usefulness of the system and the seeming permanence of the present parties, they lack constitutional standing. Many of the laws that are thought to regulate parties are actually regulations of elections.

Attempts to regulate the parties themselves, particularly in the area of election and campaign finance, have faltered on the rocks of, of all things, constitutional fairness. It is true that much of this regulation fails due to a lack of will. Inadequate enforcement procedures of financial regulation of campaigns in the past has doomed well-intended reforms. The test of fairness is a large stumbling block. Fairness is a three-part dilemma: (1) to establish in law the present two major parties would be unfair to the minor and third parties and deprive them of the historic role of potentially replacing the major parties; (2) to give equal treatment to the minor and third parties along with the major parties would be harmful to the major party component of the system and the contributions it has made to the political system; (3) to do nothing would be to leave the system to the voraciousness of unregulated competition for votes, money, and mass media attention. Additional legal regulations beyond the experimental campaign reform and campaign finance laws of the last decade can be expected. Nonetheless, the serious questions of fairness and constitutional formulation which will continue prove the point of the important role for informal constitutional growth.

Discussion of Informal
Constitutional Change

Informal changes in the Constitution have played a large role in altering the original Constitution of the United States. Some individuals are inclined for reasons of constitutional strictness to oppose this process of change. They would prefer that all growth be authorized through use of the formal amending process. Those who object to informal change are particularly upset at the idea that the informal changes have played a larger role in altering the original Constitution than have formal amendments. Even so, there is an objection to the practice of informal change in itself. The comparison issue will be examined in a moment. First, the issue of informal or "other than formal" change should be addressed directly.

A good way to approach the justification of informal change is with a question about a specific circumstance: Should the President in a time of emergency be permitted as "Commander-in-Chief of the armed forces" to direct the Air Force to evacuate Americans from a crisis spot in some distant location? The obvious answer is "Yes!" Unfortunately, the answer is incorrect. The President is not Commander-in-Chief of the Air Force, nor of the armed forces. He is Commander-in-Chief of "the Army and Navy." The Constitution was never formally amended to include the Air Force or the other armed forces. To this annoying constitutional caveat might be added a question about the legal status of the FBI as, in effect, a national police force. The FBI was created by interpretation and not by any explicit provision of the Constitution.

Both the question about the President as Commander-in-Chief and about the FBI might be dismissed as nit-picking about matters that are justly implied in the Constitution. The reply of something being "justly implied" in the Constitution can remind us of the strict constructionist position of former President and later Chief Justice William Howard Taft. Taft wrote:

> The true view of the executive function is, as I conceive it, that the President can exercise no power which cannot be reasonably and fairly traced to some specific grant of power or justly implied or included within such express grant as necessary and proper to its exercise. Such specific grant must be either in the Constitution or in an act of Congress passed in pursuance thereof. There is no undefined residuum of power which he can exercise because it seems to him to be in the public interest.[4]

Taft's rhetoric conveys the sense of limited constitutional powers. His words convey something else. The words "reasonably," "fairly," "justly," "necessary and proper," and "in pursuance thereof" constitute loophole after loophole which could legitimize all the informal changes already mentioned. Taft's statement might have been effective rhetoric for whatever purposes he had at the time. Technically all that his statement does is point out that informal constitutional growth must be judged and decided upon through the limits of reason and not by some automatically operative legal yardstick.

The critical role for reason providing the limit to constitutional interpretation is further supported by the consideration that it is chiefly through interpretative reasoning that even formal amendments have come to have their primary importance. An examination of the twenty-six amendments to the Constitution reveals that they fall into just a few categories; those that clarified some chiefly mechanical detail in the original document, those which were foregone conclusions before they were passed, and those which did not assume the importance now given to them until they became subject to the interpretative process. By way of a lengthy parenthetical illustration, a review of the amendments is in order. The review will show their role as responding to interpretation instead of setting in place unequivocal constitutional dictates.

The first ten amendments were enacted among much clamor following the ratification of the Constitution. Some individuals insisted that a bill of rights was imperative. Others said that it was not necessary. In retrospect it seems that the latter position was borne out, because there was no major protective application of the Bill of Rights until the twentieth-century First Amendment cases. It was interpretation by the Court which delayed the application of the Bill of Rights in the first place, and it was later interpretation which gave a large role to them in the twentieth century. The Twelfth, Twentieth, Twenty-second, and Twenty-fifth Amendments were designed to clarify or rectify detail provisions in the Constitution about the election, term, and succession of the President and, to a lesser degree, of the Congress. The limit on the number of terms for a President is probably very significant. The direction of the significance however is not completely clear. For example, the two-term limit for Presidents may be consistent with the democratic principle of rule in turns, but it may harm another principle like the effectiveness of policy leadership.

To continue, the Eleventh Amendment which proclaimed the states' immunity from suits was easily circumvented by the Supreme Court when it later allowed the states to be brought into court on appeal of actions initiated by them and when the Court did not exempt the officers of the states from suit. The Thirteenth Amendment was important, but it was enacted almost three years after the presidential Emancipation Proclamation had already abolished slavery in reality. The Fourteenth Amendment is of great significance but it came to be so only gradually. The Court initially, in the Slaughterhouse and Civil Rights cases of the 1870s, reduced the Fourteenth Amendment to the equal of battlefield monuments of the era. The "life, liberty, and property" guarantees of the Fourteenth Amendment were gradually applied by the Court in reverse fashion—first to business, then to individual liberty, and then only recently to the former slave population for whom it was originally intended. The Fifteenth Amendment, prohibiting racial discrimination in voting, is like the Fourteenth in that it was not implemented according to its literal intention until recently.

The Sixteenth and Seventeenth Amendments were foregone conclusions when they were formally proposed for ratification. They were much debated and discussed twenty years prior to their enactments, which made their later passage easy. An income tax had been enacted by Congress before the passage of the Sixteenth Amendment; twenty-nine out of forty-eight states had already taken steps in the direction of popular election of senators before the Seventeenth Amendment. The Eighteenth Amendment, Prohibition, was repealed by the Twenty-first. The Nineteenth Amendment, women's suffrage, was like the Twenty-sixth, the eighteen-year-old vote, and the Fifteenth, in defining the electorate. All three, however, did not have the concrete results of expanding the actual number of voters as much as had been expected prior to their adoption. These results show that constitutional theory frequently runs ahead of actual practice. In that light, the expected higher participation may yet occur.

The Twenty-third and Twenty-fourth Amendments, on the enfranchisement of the District of Columbia and the prohibition of a poll tax, respectively, were part of a larger symbolic enfranchisement of ensuring participatory rights for all citizens. Nonetheless, the overall voting rate has continued to decline instead of improve. It is ironic that the more amendments that are passed concerning voting the lower the voting rate becomes. The proposed Twenty-seventh Amendment (at least before the defeat of its ratification) on the equal rights of women had its main legal provisions already covered in the Fourteenth Amendment's guarantee of equal protection of all "persons" and in other national and state statutes.

The proposed passage of the Equal Rights Amendment was, like most formal amendments, to be primarily symbolic. The effect of the defeat of a symbol is equally hard to evaluate. Symbols are not unimportant but their effect is slow and uncertain. That uncertainty is precisely the point of interpretative reasoning affecting the formal amendments. The role of interpretation to achieve constitutional significance is clear from reviewing the formal amendments. In this way they are not different from the process of informal change itself. Only purely technical matters like the time and date of session of Congress or the inauguration of the President are free from interpretation.

THE SPIRIT OF CONSTITUTIONALISM II

The discussion of the difference between formal and informal constitutional growth came about as a result of the effort to draw a contrast between the United States and the Soviet Union in terms of constitutional practice. The contrast had been made originally in terms of the spirit of constitutionalism, labeled "Spirit I." According to Spirit I it was understood that change in public policy and in the constitution itself followed the prescriptions of the Constitution in the United States but were brought about through extra-legal means and chiefly the role of the Communist Party in the Soviet Union. The discussion of the informal methods of constitutional growth in the United States shows that extra-legal means and even the political parties play a large role in the American political system. The American practice does not therefore stand that far removed from what Soviet practice is imagined to be. In fact, and here is a momentarily disturbing statement, if one looks at the Soviet constitution and practice one finds that the Soviets follow the letter of their constitution better than the United States does theirs.

Following the letter of the constitution is observed so closely in the Soviet Union that they will change the entire document, as they did in 1924, 1936, and most recently in 1977, so that it conforms to their practical objectives. Furthermore, in the Soviet constitution there are many specific items not found in the American Constitution. Some of these items legitimize Soviet practices, which we criticize, and others place the Soviets one up from the United States in constitutional competition. In particular, Article 6 of their constitution clearly establishes the Communist Party as "the leading and guiding force of Soviet society and the nucleus of its political system, of all state organizations and public organizations...." In contrast we recall that the political party system defies constitutional formulation in the United States. In addition the socialist economic system is established in Article 10 of the Soviet Constitution of 1977. Furthermore, there is no debate about the inclusion of an Equal Rights Amendment in their constitution, it is already there in Article 35.

A scrutiny of other provisions of the Soviet constitution will reveal the mention of many rights like those of speech, press, assembly, conscience, education, housing, health care, privacy, and inviolability of the home. The last five are not specifically mentioned in the United States Constitution. Other fascinating provisions of the Soviet constitution concern the elimination of physical labor and the obligations of children. Article 21 reads, ''The state concerns itself with improving working conditions, safety and labor protection and the scientific organization of work, and with reducing and ultimately eliminating all arduous physical labor through comprehensive mechanization and automation of production processes in all branches of the economy.'' That sounds like the Soviet version of establishing the Occupational Safety and Health Administration (OSHA), a ''controversial'' regulatory agency in the United States, and a reversal of the curse of the expulsion from Eden at the same time. Article 66, on the other hand, sustains a traditional parent-child relationship when it obliges citizens ''to concern themselves with the upbringing of children, to train them for socially useful work, and to raise them as worthy members of socialist society.'' It further states the ''children are obliged to care for their parents and help them.'' That provision might be recited to the American child, who upon receiving the seventh grade introduction to the Thirteenth Amendment, quotes the passages prohibiting ''involuntary servitude'' to parents when told to take out the trash or wash the dishes.

Despite the list of seemingly positive provisions, the Soviet constitution itself, like its Article 38 about granting ''the right of asylum to foreigners persecuted for defending the interests of the working people and the cause of peace,'' has a particularly hollow ring to it. Seldom if ever is there news of genuinely heroic escapes *into* the Soviet Union, of going from West to East over the Iron Curtain. It is this reality that returns the discussion to the basic constitutional contrast between the United States and the Soviet Union. The Soviet constitution may speak of many rights both within and beyond the scope of the American Constitution. Each of the Soviet provisions is, however, qualified with statements like ''as provided by law,'' ''by the development of,'' ''by providing conditions,'' ''in the manner prescribed by law.'' In other words, each of the alleged rights can be legally but cynically inoperative because the necessary development has not yet taken place, if the conditions are not yet right or the law does not prescribe that manner of implementation. The constitution is realistically accurate. The fault for incompleteness is not with the constitution, it is with outside forces not yet controlled, which prevent the full realization of Soviet socialist promise.

The Soviet rights to freedom of speech and press are truly proclaimed by some to be free. This claim is made in the sense that there is only one truth and that truth is already possessed by the government. One is free to profess the truth proclaimed by the government but not to oppose it since that would be to profess falsehood. It is on the same grounds that only one political party is legalized and only one slate of candidates nominated at elections. To have two parties or candidates would suggest that the one did not possess the truth, which cannot be so in a ''scientific communism.'' Those who oppose the government would, in the Soviet view, be professing error which could be harmful to the interest of the people. Since the government is the people in the Soviet formulation, opposition is a form of self-injury and is therefore unacceptable.

The contrast between Soviet words and the reality of freedom reveals a fundamental point about the concept of constitutionalism. One can be literal but not constitutional, or one can be constitutional while not literal. If the Constitution of the United States were to be amended according to its legal means so as to abolish all except one political party, that action might be perfectly legal but it would hardly be "constitutional." To formally amend the constitution so as to abolish freedom of speech or religion might maintain the literal form of legally limited government, but constitutional government would no longer exist. This point about literal constitutionalism demonstrates how closely constitutionalism is linked to the discussions in the earlier chapters on the nature and end of the state and the origin and justification of political authority.

The basic philosophy that one has on the purpose of the state and the nature of authority determines in large part what comprises constitutional government. This philosophy is a more critical test of constitutionalism than the usual proposal that "spirit" means conformity of practice to the intentions of the framers. The spirit of constitutionalism has a deeper meaning than literal conformity, in the same way limited government is something more real than merely following a written document. In these distinctions there emerges a "Spirit II" of constitutionalism which relates to the philosophical outlook as opposed to "Spirit I" which referred to the literal sense of constitutionalism. It is on the test of Spirit II that the United States is "actually limited" and the Soviet Union is "actually unlimited." The classification scheme discussed at the beginning of this chapter finds a more fruitful dimension under Spirit II.

Despite its informal constitutional change, which may stand in poor stead by way of Spirit I, the United States according to Spirit II has a soundly constitutional government. It exercises authority within a framework of moral force, it conducts itself in a manner consistent with respect for the individual, and it is guided by principles higher than the determinations of the government itself. The Soviet Union may be literally constitutional, nonetheless it is "actually unlimited" because of its one-party system, its rigid governmental system, and its totalitarian (meaning total or one-truth) perspective. It is an affront to the spirit of constitutionalism in anything but an organismic-collectivist sense of the nature and end of the state.

CONSTITUTIONALISM, POLITICAL STRUCTURE, AND POLITICAL CULTURE

The discussion of constitutionalism is basically a consideration of the conduct of government and how the appropriateness of that conduct is determined and judged. Up to now the discussion has been in traditional terms of conformity to documents and principles. The nature and end of the state are the final determinants of the appropriateness of governmental activity. In this way even the Soviet activities could be deemed appropriate if it was decided, as they have, that the organismic-collectivist system was the correct one. This is why the earlier discussion of the nature of the state was developed.

There is another way of looking at the conduct of government with an eye toward constitutional differences. It can be viewed according to some political system concepts used earlier in this text. This approach can give a deeper understanding to the difficult task of judging regimes. It can also show that although the approaches to political science differ significantly, they are not completely antithetical.

The political system model, it is to be remembered, is that abstracted description of the political world which spoke about inputs, outputs, conversion processes, environments, and functions instead of states, powers, authority, and persons. Identifiable institutions or political structures and political cultures or environments were important to the system approach. A question that the system approach may entertain is that of the relationship between political culture and political structure. It was explained earlier that structures differ by degree, called differentiation, and that cultures differ by degree, called secularization in a developmental sense. A comparison of the relationship of structures and cultures can be descriptively satisfying. It also has underlying elements of a constitutional nature which give further insights to the character of governments.

Political Structure

"Political structure" is not a difficult concept in the context of the political system. It is "a pattern of related roles or established relationships among people."[5] Structure is traditionally identified with formal organizations such as the courts, the executive, and the legislature. Here the concept is broadened to include informal as well as formal relationships. The informal relationships consist of party organizations, patterns of voting, or the pattern of power distributions in international politics. All are patterns of related roles or established relationships. The traditional approach has little trouble accepting the broadened concept. Political structures can still be usefully related by way of analogy to physical structure such as an Eskimo house or a skyscraper.

We can think in terms of a simple governmental structure, like that of a small town, as similar to the simple structure of an igloo. We can think of a more complex governmental structure as similar to a skyscraper with all its accompanying support systems. In this manner we speak of degrees of differentiation in physical structures and political entities. Some political structures, or indeed entire systems, are very simple and undifferentiated and others are very complex and differentiated. The acknowledgement of this differentiation should suggest that political structures and political systems can be compared according to degrees of differentiation just as buildings or other physical, measurable, objects can be. At least political systems can be compared in that manner if it is assumed that there exists a "structure micrometer" or measuring instrument which can precisely register the exact differences discovered between systems. This is a huge assumption. The existence or nonexistence of a precise micrometer of governmental structures, however, will not disturb the imagined comparison. Even if detailed measurements cannot be made they can be imagined and put to effective uses.

Political Culture

Political culture can be approached in the same manner as political structures. Culture is understood to be the pattern of attitudes and orientations of a distinct community of people. Political culture is composed of attitudes and orientations toward politics. It is a subjective realm which underlies and gives meaning to the political system.[6] The concept of culture is somewhat less concrete than that of structure. Nonetheless, as Almond points out, it involves a set of phenomena which can to some extent be identified and to some degree measured.

Political cultures are broadly classified into three groups: parochial, subject, and participant. The classification is based on a community's awareness of and participation in political events. In a broad sense it can be said that all the aspects of the life of a particular community comprises its culture. The life surrounding the igloo is simple compared to the life surrounding a complex skyscraper community. Extending the earlier analogy, the political culture of the igloo community is parochial in that there is little or no awareness of or participation in separately acknowledged political activity. In the complex skyscraper community there is both awareness and participation. In a subject culture, which has an authoritarian political system, there is awareness but no participation. The movement from parochial culture to subject culture to participant culture is what is known as secularization. The classification of cultures does not imply the relative worth of levels of development. It does not imply that participant is "better than" parochial, it merely states that they are "different by degree." However, in all honesty those claims of nonnormativeness may be suspect due to human aspirations at least.

Relating Political Structure and Political Culture

If (again, a very big if) there existed a "culture micrometer," then all the political cultures could be lined up according to their precise degree of difference, from the simplest to the most complex. This political culture scale, together with the political structure scale which exists in our imagination, can be used as the basis for a larger comparison. It can reasonably be expected that the political culture of the igloo community is compatible with the political structure of the igloo community. Technically, the the igloo community is said to be an intermittent political system, in that they have an undifferentiated structure and a primitive political culture. Nonetheless their structure and culture are said to be in continuity. Continuity means that structure and culture are in step with one another, compatible, or more technically that they have an isomorphic relationship. If there were a disparity between structure and culture, that would be referred to as discontinuity.

If perfect continuity existed between all structures and cultures, there would exist a perfect world. Comparing the two imagined micrometer-determined scales made up of all 159 present members of the United Nations (thus excluding the igloo and skyscraper communities) the country found at position number 47 on the imaginary structure scale would be found at exactly position number 47 on the imaginary culture scale, and so on through the two scales. If the world were not perfect, if there were discrepencies or discontinuity between the structure and culture of a particular country, then the scales would reveal how serious that country's problems are. If a country were five steps out of place or thirty-five steps out of place, one could judge mild or grave discontinuity.

Examining the two scales, even though the effort is purely imaginative, should give another basis for comparing the United States and the Soviet Union. One might expect to find that the Soviet Union, like the United States, has a highly differentiated structure, but unlike the United States their culture is not as highly secularized. In a generalized sense the exact degree to which lag or lead of either structure or culture exists can be speculated upon with respect to the amount of authoritarian rule that is necessary. In a highly authoritarian state, however, the degree of discrepancy between structure and culture is more than marginal. What is suggested here is a contrast between the United States and the Soviet Union by way of an imagined empirical measurement. This contrast has underlying elements of a constitutional nature.

Figure 12-1 depicts the relation of structure and culture. The United States is pictured as having continuity of structure and culture, and the Soviet Union is viewed as discontinuous. This depiction might be regarded as expressing a traditional malignment and misrepresentation of the Soviet Union. From a strict theoretical-Marxist position, however, the Soviet government would have no trouble in being portrayed as a vanguard leading to an eventually advanced classless culture, indeed an eventually classless world. From this position there is no quarrel with a discontinuity between a vanguard structure and a still not entirely liberated culture. From this same perspective a Marxist would have no trouble in admitting the continuity of structure and culture in the United States. From a Marxist perspective "false consciousness" runs rampant in American and other alienated cultures. In these alienated systems neither the structure nor the culture is consciously aware of their continuity in capitalist evil which is why a vanguard structure has to take a leadership role.

The continuity traced between the imaginary scales of structure and cultures suggests that the regime or constitution is in accord with the "way of life of the

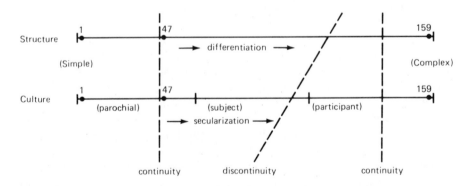

FIGURE 12-1 Political structure and political culture (imaginary) scales.

people." This is, we can recall, the essential element of constitutional rule for Aristotle. When political structure and political culture are compatible, a constitutional accord exists. Aristotle acknowledged that it was possible for an evil regime to be in accord with an evil people. In that situation, too, there would be continuity between structure and culture. The question of the goodness and badness of a system had to be handled in a separate consideration. Discontinuity, however, would make that separate consideration irrelevant so at least the continuity was a starting point for constitutionalism.

A provocative aspect about the Soviet and American comparison is that the Soviets cannot, according to their theory, admit of continuity between structure and culture until their dominance is "worldwide." If continuity occurred earlier the Soviets would be under the obligation to begin the "withering away" of their structure. If this happened when there are competitors still around who might take advantage of the dismantling of the apparatus of the USSR, the achieved continuity would be undone. From the Soviet perspective, basic Western covetousness is the source of all concern. These two positions once again emphasize the importance of theoretical principles which precede practical constitutional judgments.

Infrastructure

Another aspect in the consideration of the political system, and indeed a close reflection of the continuity and discontinuity of structure and culture, is the character of the infrastructure. The political infrastructure is the internal part of the structure. An igloo, to revert to the earlier analogy, has few internal parts. A skyscraper has many units on many floors as well as air-conditioning ducts, electrical wirings, plumbing, elevator shafts, and much, much more. The infrastructure of a political system consists of political parties, election apparatus, interest groups, the media of mass communication, public opinion networks. All these infrastructure parts process and feed information into the system.

In comparing democratic and totalitarian political systems in terms of the freedom of the infrastructure Almond describes the democratic infrastructure as relatively autonomous while the totalitarian one is subordinated to the government.[7] In the democratic countries, it should be noted, the infrastructure is "relatively" autonomous since absolute autonomy would be tantamount to anarchy. There is, however, a clear contrast between democratic relative autonomy and close, hierarchic articulation of infrastructure and government in the totalitarian system. In the latter situation the media, interest groups, and individuals would not act or speak except in a manner consonant with the ruling group. The official position on all public matters is the only one expressed unless one wants to take a chance with being branded or brought to trial as an enemy of the people or a maligner of the state.

Relative autonomy is found in the United States and subordination is found in the Soviet Union. This relative autonomy versus subordination is equivalent to saying that subsidiarity is practiced in the one setting and not in the other. Hence examining the degrees of relative autonomy or subordination in comparative political systems contains another constitutional measuring device. The device is constitutional on the grounds that the spirit of constitutionalism "II" includes the principle of subsidiarity as well as the other considerations of the nature and end of the state and the origin and justification of political authority.

CONCLUSIONS ABOUT CONSTITUTIONALISM

Constitutionalism has basically been concerned about the conduct of government, how it is judged, and how that judgment is arrived at. As a concrete exemplification of the conduct of government, attention has been drawn to the contrast between the United States and the Soviet Union. Three different approaches have been used to contrast these regimes: (1) a comparison in terms of the fundamental "spirit" of constitutionalism based on overall political philosophy; (2) the comparing of continuity of structure and culture; and (3) the comparing of relative infrastructure autonomy.

The first item, at least in the sense of what has been called "Spirit II," relates to legal and actual limits on governments and their relationship to fundamentals of political philosophy. The second point, which is about continuity and discontinuity, was shown to be a way of imagining in a graphic manner the classical notion of constitutionalism as reflective of the way of life of a people. The third basic comparison, that of infrastructure autonomy, tells of the subsidiarity relationship between the government and the units of society. As the media, political parties, or interest groups would be relatively autonomous, subsidiarity would prevail, and as they would be subordinated, the principle of assumed integrity would be ignored. These three basic contrasts are instructive both in comparing the United States and the Soviet Union and, more importantly, in understanding constitutionalism.

Evaluation of the United States
Constitutional System

To the above considerations, one additional point should be made. It was suggested at the beginning of the chapter that constitutionalism in the United States was basically "modern" in the sense of stressing negative limits on government. What was implicit throughout the later discussion, particularly on informal growth in constitutions and on political culture, is that the United States Constitution is no longer simply a single document. Today the United States Constitution includes the whole life and scheme of living of its people. In other words, over time the United States Constitution became classical and is not just modern. It is today, like the English constitution, not just a single document, instead it is the whole body of laws and customs which go to make up the character of the government.

Any attempt to copy the successes of the United States by copying the legal structure outlined in the Constitution is doomed to failure unless the contrasts between classical and modern constitutions are kept in mind. One country adopting the legal structures of another country must be attentive to the accompanying environments. In the United States the peculiarities of the American culture have been blended over time into the larger American Constitution. The similarities and differences between the American culture and the adopting culture must be examined carefully before any changes are recommended. To pay attention to only the strictly legal and structural aspects of constitutional government is to miss a substantial part of constitutionalism. The brief case study which follows reveals one prominent example of such a failure, and it occurred with substantial American prompting.

A CASE STUDY—THE PHILIPPINES

Unfortunately, in the nineteenth and twentieth centuries many countries copied the American legal form. This is something we were proud of at the time and to some extent still are. The Philippines as well as many Latin American nations followed the American model closely when drafting their own constitutions. The specific reasons for the legal and structural practices which were copied varied from country to country. For the Philippines the adopting of American legal forms had historical roots in addition to the normal explanation of having a relatively small set of alternatives to choose from in the first place.

The Philippines was occupied by the United States after the Spanish-American War, which was chiefly a conflict over Cuba. That conflict is not a particularly proud part of United States history because of the greed apparent in some American motives and because of the role of the press at the time in stirring up some unfounded troubles. The Philippines were a long way from Cuba but the upshot of the war saw Cuba independent from Spain but under American military control for three years and the Philippines, along with Guam and Puerto Rico, coming under complete control of the United States. In light of the world power rivalry at the time, chiefly between many European nations, the American seizure of the Philippines may indeed have spared them from that larger domain of conflict.

There was a native Philippine resistance to the American takeover, which sought to establish the independence of the country. The independence effort did not succeed at the time but it did contribute to a quicker than usual promise by a colonial power, in this case the Americans, to eventually grant independence to the colony. The actual promise of eventual independence came in 1916 and the concrete steps of constitution making preceding full independence came in 1935-1936. Independence was scheduled for July 4, 1946. Although a world war with devastating effect in the Philippines intervened, independence was carried out as planned to the delight of both nations.

The Philippine constitution was designed in a somewhat hesitant manner in the period from 1934 to 1940. The process of constitution making lagged for several reasons, including local rivalries and American policy concerns. The interest in this case study is to draw attention to the role which the model of the United States Constitution played in the design of the final product. In the period from occupation to constitution making (1898–1934) the United States poured money and teachers and an educational system into the Philippines. The education dimension proved far more important than any other monies expended. In that short span of three and a half decades, the education effort produced a nation whose lingua franca was English instead of either Spanish from an earlier heritage or any indigenous language of the nation.

Philippine identification with the American instruments of government came with the thorough immersion in American educational ways. Philippine children grew up reading ''See the apple'' and reciting the Pledge of Allegiance even though their country did not grow apples and the Stars and Stripes was not the native flag. Because of this educational immersion there was a somewhat ''natural'' affinity for American constitutional ways since they had been indirectly inculcated as they are in most educational situations. This is a concrete example of the so-called socialization process described at the end of Chapter 2. Here, through informal learning as well as through deliberate efforts, Filipinos came to accept American ways. In addition to learning about American products and American habits and customs, the positive values of the American political system were stressed and Philippine leaders came genuinely to embrace them.

It should come as no surprise to learn that the records of the debates related to the drafting of the Philippine constitution reveal arguments as if from American textbooks over the relative merits of various governmental structures. The drafters of the constitution were all Filipinos. There were no formal ties to any American advisors. One can well imagine, however, the careful attention to American practice as the resulting document became almost a photocopy of the American Constitution. The record of the debates at the Philippine constitutional convention clearly indicates that the copying was not from paper but from what had been inculcated in their spirit in the process of socialization. The photocopy characterization is true except for avoiding what were perceived even then as ''mistakes'' in the American design.

The main features of the Philippine constitution were a separation of powers among three branches, including an independent judiciary, and a bicameral legislature. There was also a bill of rights and, as in all constitutions, a preamble and provisions for amendments. The new ingredients in the Philippine constitution were all items which had been omitted from the American Constitution. Over many decades many of these omissions in the American Constitution had been added to it or had come to be regarded as important parts of the constitutional posterity. These missing ingredients included the definition of citizen, specifications on suffrage, establishment of a general auditing office and a civil service procedure, and provisions for the protection of natural resources. All these items had become part of the larger American constitutional system but only the first two had come to be formal amendments to the Constitution.

One structural change of particular note in the new Philippine constitution was the procedure for electing the President. American academicians and others had come to regard their indirect system of election through the electoral college as anachronistic and would not advise its use in any other system, let alone their own.

Heeding this conventional wisdom of the time, the Filipinos opted for the direct popular election of the president.

Another change in the Philippine constitution from that found in the original American Constitution but which had also undergone mutation was the system of electing Senators. One hesitation point in the design of the new governmental structure was over whether the Philippines should have a unicameral or a bicameral legislature. Eventually the bicameral form was chosen with a Senate and a House of Representatives (using the identical names as in the American legislature). The arguments in favor of bicameralism were familiar to Americans: "Two heads are better than one," "To avoid hasty and ill-considered legislation," "It would be less susceptible to bribery," "It would attract more mature, experienced, and able office holders." The criticisms of bicameralism, like the arguments in favor, were echoed in textbooks at the time: "Deadlock, delay, duplication, and diffusion of responsibility."

In settling on the two-house legislature there was little difficulty in determining the representational base for the lower house. It was to be, as in the United States, on equal population districts. The Senate was not as easy. Senators were to be popularly elected, as had recently come to pass in America, but the representational base was problematic. Established territorial districts comparable to American states were not readily available in the Philippines. Islands could not be used as a representational base because they varied tremendously in size and there were too many, more than 7000, of them. Provinces and language or dialect areas likewise could not be used since they also varied in size and they were not fully developed in political identity. The stratagem chosen was to have all Senators elected from the nation at large with one third elected every two years for a six-year term. Clearly this final design closely followed the American model with only the representational base being different.

Fully implemented in 1946, the Philippine structure worked according to design for twenty-five years except for one problem—no president was ever reelected to office. The chief executive was continually challenged by other national leaders, particularly senators. The rivalry between President and Senators encouraged a rivalry between the executive branch and the legislative branch resulting in policy stalemate and confusion. A complete picture of the Philippines and its government cannot be taken from this brief case description. The reader should not get the impression that everything went poorly. There were, however, definite governmental problems and accompanying social and political frustration.

An attempt to overcome the defects in the Philippine constitution was undertaken in a constitutional convention of 1971–1972. The convention had been mandated earlier but the particular circumstances of its occurrence may have brought as many problems as it sought to eradicate. The convention was held during the second administration of President Ferdinand Marcos. Marcos was the first president to be reelected, which occurred in an election said by some to be more irregular than usual. At the same time there was a growing restlessness in the country about economic hardships, corruption, and subversion. The convention moved in the direction of proposing a shift to a parliamentary form of government, meaning one house electing a prime minister, and as the convention was coming to a close other events seemed to move the president to declare martial law and to rule by edict. The convention finished up its work in the months following the declaration of martial law, and the parliamentary proposal which came forth from the convention was then looked upon as a vehicle for Marcos to continue in office for an unlimited number of years. The exact motivation for the switch in governmental forms and its link to the incumbent executive are not clear even a decade later.

Marcos has continued in office. It is not certain whether his continuance is in accordance with the plan of those who initiated the parliamentary proposal or whether, as some evidence suggests, it is contrary to that plan. In any case it is clear from a purely structural consideration that the proposal to convert the established Philippine constitution from a system with three branches and a bicameral legislature to a parliamentary unicameral legislature would receive tremendous opposition, whatever its objective merits. A further consideration in analyzing the changes is that a period of authoritarian rule could temporarily provide a forced calm in which the dramatic structural changes might be introduced. Senators in particular might be expected to oppose the new parliamentary form since their special legislative and societal position would be abolished. It is possibly noteworthy that prominent among those arrested during the early days of the martial law era were some former senators and other legislators. Logically, however, it is reasonable to expect that political leaders would take "the lead" whether in opposition or support, so no definite conclusions can be drawn from the role of the former senators.

It is difficult to sort out the constitutional and structural aspects of the changes and their partisan and personal dimensions. As a case of structural constitutional change it can be seen that the parliamentary move would eliminate both the personal rivalry of the president with each of the senators and the rivalry of the president with the Congress. By the change also, the problems of representational base and multiple representation were settled once and for all since the offices of president, vice-president, and thirty-six senators would no longer exist. If martial law was in any way coordinated with the needed transition period from the earlier constitutional form it could be viewed, in that respect at least, as salutary. The institution of the senate and the whole governmental form modeled after the American form was well ingrained not just after twenty-five years of independence but after seventy years of immersion in American ways. Change to a new form, even if highly desirable, would be difficult under the best of conditions.

Old forms do not undergo change easily, even if they are entirely unworkable. France experienced this difficulty at the end of the 1950s in its transition from the extremely weak Fourth Republic to the more unified and, at least as initially perceived, more authoritarian Fifth Republic under General Charles de Gaulle. Martial law in the Philippines has continued well beyond the point of what might normally be regarded as a reasonable transition period. Furthermore, the original parliamentary recommendation in the Philippines has been modified in the direction of the French mixed form, which will be discussed in a later chapter, so it is still impossible to judge the structural changes in themselves. The original and continuing reasons for the imposition of martial law may be wholly independent of the constitutional changes. The legal form of martial law was lifted in January, 1982 but many of its powers continued in other forms. The continued turmoil in the country makes it difficult to expect to judge the structural changes for some time to come.

It is not known by objective observers whether the eventual successor to Marcos will see to the continuation of the reforms adopted, in exceptional circumstances to be sure, since 1972 or whether a successor will attempt to revert to the old, American-style, constitution. Based on the demonstrated need for a system more compatible to the local situation, a personal hunch is that the reforms will be retained. The observance of disorders in many countries throughout the world does not give a high degree of confidence to that prediction. One glimmer of hope might be that if the analogy of the Philippine situation to the constitutional changes in France has any merit, there has been no move to undo the Fifth Republic despite the equally bitter opposition to it when first proposed.

The constitutional source of the Philippine troubles was not just the structural defect resulting from the design of the presidential and senatorial elections, but the underlying fact that the design was not well attuned to the indigenous circumstances. In the inclination to follow the successful American structural model, rivalry unwittingly became overplayed instead of minimized. When this constitutional design problem is combined with the usual social and economic problems of a developing country the difficulties are almost insurmountable.

There is no established objective criteria for measuring the effectiveness of regimes so it is not possible, nor will it be possible in the future, to judge the merits of an incumbent government. There is no question that change in volatile situations will bring about resistance and turmoil from those adversely affected. However there is no denying that the old order would bring about its own form of turmoil. It is the nature of political issues that the situation will not stand still to allow time for historical judgment. As mentioned earlier, before the new parliamentary form was even fully implemented so that its operation could be compared to the former presidential system a new change was adopted, in 1981, which introduced the French-style strong presidential office.

It is difficult to say whether the latest change will be better suited than the previous attempts to the needs of Philippine political life. The changes undoubtedly reflect the judgment of the current ruler, President Marcos, and his advisors. The source of a constitution is not the test of its effectiveness. Time and experience will instead be its measure. Still, as Aristotle saw, the chief lawgiver may be the principal benefactor of a people but only if that law reflects the internal natural liberty of the people. The alterations in the Philippines, and they are not alone in this, need neither be a sign of weakness nor devices for perpetuating personal rule. The attempt at change may indeed be a sign of strength in attempting to adapt structure and culture. Whether such strength can succeed before the impatience of time and "events" take over is becoming increasingly precarious.

CONCLUSION

The Philippines' experience is an example of visualizing constitutional crisis in terms of the discontinuity between political structure and political culture. The aspects of political culture were reflected in the indigenous situation, which was not amenable to the American constitutional structure. The Americans who sincerely advised or encouraged the Filipinos to draft an original constitution similar to that of the United States seem to have done so with insufficient or no attention to subtle changes in their own constitution. The American constitution had become ''more than a single document'' or few closely related documents. Through formal and mostly informal growth it had become an adaptation of structure and culture. The parliamentary reforms introduced into the Philippines in the 1972 constitution could be justified as an attempt to adapt their structure more to their particular culture.

The Philippine situation, as representative of most countries, demonstrates once again that constitution making, structure making, is not an easy thing. Constitutions cannot be made in the abstract, although many think of them in this way and classroom analyses encourage such views. That those countries that have continuity between structure and culture do not themselves have a perfect textbook grasp of what their success is made of, that they do not know what formula goes into making ''continuity'' of structure and culture, is demonstrated by their inability to export constitutional stability to the many other countries desiring it.

Constitutional government remains an inexact art. It is not much of a science at all as a momentary mental review of the nations of the world will show. Various attempts at scientific proposals for ''nation building'' have been put forward. Those programs often turn out to be merely new versions of the old art of tyranny now pushed with the aid of a plethora of allegedly scholarly consultants. The precise nature of constitutional government remains elusive even for those who have had the good fortune of enjoying it.

NOTES

1. J. A. Corry, *Elements of Democratic Government* (New York: Oxford University Press, 1951), p. 35.

2. Leslie Lipson, *The Great Issues of Politics,* 3rd ed. (Englewood Cliffs, N.J.: Prentice-Hall, 1965), pp. 238-239.

3. On the latter reference see the classic study by Edward S. Corwin, *The ''Higher Law'' Background of American Constitutional Law* (Ithaca: Cornell University Press, 1955).

4. William Howard Taft, *Our Chief Magistrate and His Powers* (New York: Columbia University Press, 1916), pp. 139-140.

5. Jack C. Plano et al., *The Dictionary of Political Analysis,* 2nd ed. (Santa Barbara: ABC-CLIO, 1982), pp. 153-154.

6. Gabriel Almond and G. Bingham Powell, *Comparative Politics* (Boston: Little, Brown, 1966), p. 50.

7. ibid., p. 47.

CHAPTER THIRTEEN
FORMS OF GOVERNMENT: GEOGRAPHIC DISTRIBUTION OF POWER

One great question of government or of any large organization is how to combine effectiveness and efficiency. In separate ways this question applies to small entities as well as large, since they also can be inefficient and ineffective. The manner in which governments are organized with respect to the dispersion or concentration of power is categorized as unitary, federal, and confederate. These categories of the real or imagined ways in which authority is distributed between national and local levels of government are usually referred to as the forms of government.

There is another set of categories referred to earlier as forms of government, namely, parliamentary form and presidential or separation of powers form. What should be understood is that ''forms of government'' refers to two different considerations. One consideration is the geographic distribution of power or authority between the national and local levels of government. The other consideration is the functional distribution of power or authority. The geographical forms and the functional forms can theoretically be mixed in any combination of ways. They must be described separately to understand them clearly. The geographic forms will be discussed in this chapter, the functional forms in the next.

PRELIMINARY DEFINITIONS OF FORMS

Some distribution of governmental duties is found in all countries. The distribution is not always known by the already mentioned categories. The categories are names assigned by observers, political scientists, to reflect the concentration or the dispersal in a particular state. It should be understood, however, that all states have some centralization as well as some localization. The degree of national versus local jurisdiction and the locus of who decides on the distribution is the essence of the geographic forms. A description of the forms will show their real and imagined characteristics. The examination will also extend the earlier discussion of sovereignty by way of a concrete consideration of exercises of political authority.

Confederacy

A *confederacy* is a loose union of states where each state retains its sovereignty, freedom, and independence, and is free to withdraw at will. For present purposes the best examples that can be given are the United Nations, the old League of Nations, and various alliances such as the British Commonwealth, the North Atlantic Treaty Organization (NATO), the Organization of African Unity (OAU), and the European Common Market. The point of these organizations is that the members freely associate with one another and can just as freely choose to break that association. France left the military command of NATO in the 1960s, and various countries have been in and out of the OAU and the British Commonwealth.

The Constitution of the Confederate States of America of 1861 is so similar to the United States Constitution from which the southern states were claiming secession that it cannot serve as a viable example of a confederacy. The government of the ''Articles of Confederation'' of the United States has special considerations which complicate its use as an example of a confederacy. They will be discussed later. The point that should be remembered about a confederacy is that each member unit retains autonomous decision-making authority. If a member decides to withdraw from the organization, it can do so; if it remains it does so on its own terms.

Unitary Form

A *unitary* state is one in which final decision-making authority is vested in the central government. It is the central or national government which decides the distribution of powers for the country. It decides what powers will be distributed and how much power will be dispersed. England and France are both examples of unitary systems, even though they differ widely on centralization and local autonomy. In England local units have a greater share of political power than in France. In France the central government sees fit to retain more control. It is not the case, however, that in France all power is centralized; it is just that in comparison to England there is less local autonomy. In both countries any decision about distribution is made by the central government, whether the decision means less local rule or more.

It is the central government's power to decide the distribution that makes both France and England unitary systems. In the last few years the new socialist government in France, which many expected to further centralize power, took steps to abolish the prefectural system and its "image" of extreme centralization. The outcome of such moves does not normally become clear for many years. Whatever the final results, the essential point is that the changes came about by direction of the central government.

Within the United States each of the respective states has the relationship to its local governments that the central government in the unitary form has to its local jurisdictions. For example, within the state of Pennsylvania, as in England, the local cities and towns are granted or not granted decision-making authority by the central government. According to the state constitution, the state legislature can grant to local cities, counties, or towns "home rule" charters whereby the local units receive a greater amount of autonomy. Discussions of a similar nature have occurred in England about granting home rule to Wales and Scotland. Whatever the "degree" of autonomy granted in such plans of devolution, unless complete autonomy is granted the local unit still remains subject to the final jurisdiction of the central government. Complete autonomy is something utterly unthinkable in American states and only true in England with respect to former colonies.

Home rule requires central government approval and it can be taken away in whole or in part without local approval. Usually home rule is taken away in piecemeal fashion by the passage of new state legislation with no exceptions mentioned for "home rule" entities. Home rule in large part is a rhetorical device as well as a genuine administrative device. As a tool it satisfies temporary concerns while long term solutions are worked out by the process of time and experience.

A confederacy is a loose union of unitary states. Each state which retains its "sovereignty, freedom, and independence" is unitary in relation to the larger confederacy. Each unit independently decides whether it will go along with the other states on any matter whatsoever. Stressing this fundamental aspect of confederacy points out that so far as unitary and confederate go there is only one form of government, the unitary. Confederacy pretends to be a government but in essence it is not, since it does not have separate decision-making authority except by consent of each member. To call a confederacy a form of government is for the most part a rhetorical concession made to temporary unions which are on their way to either falling apart or creating a real unified rule. The United Nations and other international associations are therefore, as mentioned earlier, the better examples of this "form of government," because it is known in advance that the separate states do not concede to them independent "governing" authority.

Federal Form

The United States, Canada, the Soviet Union, and several other countries are said to be examples of the *federal* form of government where authority is said to be divided between a central national government and local units. In the federal form it is expected that any distribution of governmental power is done by the basic constitution, and it is understood that the distribution cannot be altered by the unilateral action of the central government. In federal systems the distribution of powers to local units of government may be broad as in the United States or Canada, or it may be in effect minuscule as in the Soviet Union.

The Soviet Union is a difficult state to classify. Its constitution identifies it as "a unitary, federal and multinational state, formed *on the basis of the principle of socialist federalism and* as a result of the free self-determination of nations and the voluntary union of equal Soviet Socialist Republics." What the Soviet constitution is saying is that the Soviet Union is unitary, federal, and confederate. The confederacy part is based upon the membership of the nominally autonomous republics, two of whom have membership in the United Nations as independent states. In reality the Communist Party so dominates all the republics, because of the "solidarity of the workers of all nations," according to their rhetoric, that it is usually and accurately thought of as one unitary state. It is because of the combination of unitary and confederate factors that the Soviet Union is loosely referred to as federal. In any practical consideration, however, it should be classified as unitary.

The Problem with Federalism

The problem with the federal form is not just a result of the discrepancy between theory and practice in the Soviet Union. The problem is intrinsic to the concept of federalism itself. The earlier discussion of the "indivisibility" of legal authority in Chapter 5 points to the theoretical problem for federalism. That particular attribute meant that authority, or sovereignty, could not be divided. Just as one cannot be "half pregnant," authority cannot be divided in half. The federal form, federalism, suggests that the authority of the state is divided. It suggests that the national government has some authority over some matters and that the local governments have authority over other matters. The distribution is supposedly made by the constitution, which is what identifies the federal form.

The major question of federalism is that of *who* decides on the distribution and redistribution. If the authority to decide is vested legally or practically in one particular level of government, then that ought to be examined carefully to see if it does not identify the form as different from that imagined. This point will have to be examined further, but before that a small classification scheme and an appraisal should be done to make clear the primary aspects of the forms.

CLASSIFICATION AND APPRAISAL

Using the theoretical forms of unitary and federal it is possible and normal to classify governments in the following manner:

1. Legally federal and actually federal—the United States
2. Legally federal and actually unitary—the Soviet Union

3. Legally unitary and actually federal—England
4. Legally unitary and actually unitary—France

The United States is listed as legally and actually federal because the division of powers is said to be constitutionally guaranteed and because relative decentralization does exist. The Soviet Union, on the other hand, despite its proclaimed federal form, is classified as actually unitary because of its highly centralized reality. England is said to be legally unitary and actually federal because of its centralized authority but also because of the presence of a fair amount of local self-rule. France, at least as compared to England, is legally and actually unitary because it is centralized in theory and practice. Whether the practice in France will really change as the new socialist government promises will only be clear in time and in any case there is no discussion of changing the legal form.

Certain advantages, in theory at least, are said to hold for the competing forms. The unitary form is said to provide unity, simplicity, uniformity, efficiency, and flexibility. By this is meant that there is very little discrepancy in practice between various parts of the particular nation under examination. Governmental and legal procedures in one part of the country are the same in another part. Government procedures in such a unitary state are therefore said to be simplified, producing greater efficiency. Furthermore, since under such a form change can occur all at once without awaiting local approval, there is enhanced opportunity for flexibility.

The unitary form is admitted to have certain liabilities. The liabilities turn out to be the advantages of the federal form. The liabilities of the unitary form are the absence of local autonomy and local incentive for handling responsibilities, the inadaptability to a large state with a heterogeneous culture, the lack of experimentation for innovation in government policy or practice, the lack of opportunity for greater levels of citizen participation in government, and the tendency toward the development of a centralized bureaucracy contrary to the claim of simplicity and efficiency. The corresponding advantages of the federal form are then said to be the presence of local autonomy and local incentive for handling responsibilities, the adaptability to a large state with heterogeneous culture, the presence of experimentation for innovation in government policy or practices, the opportunity for greater levels of citizen participation in government, and the lack of a centralized bureaucracy thus giving simplicity and efficiency in governmental operations.

These disadvantages and advantages work out nicely in any *theoretical* consideration. In a practical consideration they do not hold up. One political scientist calls attention to the discrepancy between the theory and practice of federalism. In citing matched pairs of unitary and federal regimes, he points out the misunderstanding that usually occurs. It is useful to quote his observations at length:

> Consider Australia and New Zealand, both of which sprang from the same political culture, mostly mid-nineteenth century, lower class England. Australia is very much a federalism and its federalism is the subject of a steady stream of books and articles. New Zealand, on the other hand, tried federalism in the 1850s and 1860s and then consciously rejected it. But it does not seem that the presence or absence of federalism

makes much difference, for the quality of life is quite similar in the two nations. Certainly, the things that are under local control in one political system, like schools, police, etc., are under local control in the other. If a citizen of Wellington moves to Sydney, about the only difference in his political life is an unfamiliar level of government. And if a citizen of Sydney moves to Wellington, it is doubtful that he misses the elections for the legislature of New South Wales.

[T]he unitary state of Ghana probably allows more tribal autonomy than does the federal state of Nigeria.

Comparing Chile and Argentina . . . rather than supporting localism and diversity, federalism in Argentina seems as a practical matter to encourage dictatorship and centralization.

Despite the Yugoslav assertion of federalism . . . when one compares Yugoslavia and Poland one is really comparing two unitary governments, one of which simply has a facade of federalism. Nevertheless, most students of life in eastern Europe would agree, . . . that local autonomy and cultural freedom are closer to realization under the government without the pretense of federalism than under the one with it. [1]

The actual situation in the countries composing the matched pairs may have changed since the time those remarks were written. Any change would not alter the essential point of the lack of practical differences in countries claiming opposite forms. The similarity in practice of regimes thought to be of different legal forms can be expanded from the above set of matched pairs. The list is limited though since the total number of regimes said to be federal is only about twenty-eight out of the one hundred and sixty or so nations. Federalism appears somewhat loosely correlated with large geographic size. The notable exceptions of China, Sudan, Algeria, and Zaire, all large but not federal, prove that correlation specious. A momentary, or longer, reflection on the world scene of many different regimes, with various bureaucracies, different levels of citizen participation, and greater and less complexity and efficiency, reveals no pattern of preferred form. Some political scientists or experts like to announce that one form is definitely better than another but no such proposition can be reliably established. The conclusion from the appraisal of the different forms can only be that conclusions cannot be arrived at.

RESERVE POWERS

The classification of the forms looks neat and accurate. The appraisal shows that no practical distinction can be made and that the federal form in particular is quite ambiguous. The problem in federalism arises from the discrepancy between the legal expectations and the practical operations. A constitution may spell out what an initial distribution of powers may be, but what is important is how the powers come to be exercised and how adjustments are made in the functioning regime. Since no constitution can possibly spell out how all future contingencies are to be handled, it is necessary to have some provisions or procedures for redistribution of power. How redistribution is handled has a profound bearing on the exact nature of the form.

In a unitary state decisions about redistribution are legally and actually the responsibility of the central government. Local units in a unitary system may take some initiative in introducing new practices or policies, but if the central government wishes to prohibit the moves or to assume them for itself there is no question about their authority to do so. In the federal system, on the other hand, there are elaborate and diverse provisions on how to handle redistribution. The essential nature of federalism suggests that redistribution is supposed to be reflected in the constitution. Supposedly a constitutional amendment would specify more powers for the central government and less for the local governments, or the other way around. Since amendments are not always possible or practical, some other provisions are made in the original constitution for allocating the ''reserve powers.''

Reserve powers or residuals are powers that are not mentioned in the original constitution. They are ''leftovers'' which accrue to one level or government or another according to the provisions of the constitution. Which level actually receives these reserve powers or benefits from this form of redistribution is not the final determinant of the form. As mentioned before, a unitary form can allow for local autonomy, as occurs in England and the American states. The actual form of government is determined by *who* decides whether a questioned power is national or local. Some person or agency must decide such issues since the constitution cannot speak for itself.

United States

In the United States the reserved powers and, according to general understanding, the basic statement of federalism is found in the Tenth Amendment. It states:

> The powers not delegated to the United States by the Constitution, nor prohibited by it to the states, are reserved to the States respectively, or to the people.

By reason of this statement the Tenth Amendment is commonly called the ''federal amendment'' or the ''federal principle.'' The amendment is taken to mean that powers not mentioned in the original Constitution belong to the states. Despite this impression of intended local growth, the actual growth over nearly two hundred years has been national. New powers have accrued to the national government, and even powers thought originally to belong to the states have through a steady stream of court cases been assigned to national jurisdiction.

Canada

The United States may be the chief example of the federal system but it is not the only one. Other countries, like those mentioned earlier in the set of matched pairs, have growth patterns which are the opposite of that expected by the legal form. Distance makes it difficult to study many of those other countries but one country, Canada, is near and provides a surprising growth pattern in comparison to the United States. The growth in Canada is also in contrast to what appears to have been legally intended.

The Canadian constitution, known as the British North American Act, provided that the national parliament, after certain specified powers were granted to the provinces, would have the authority "to make laws for the peace, order, and good government of Canada in relation to matters not coming within the classes of subjects by the Act assigned exclusively to the provinces." According to this provision the residuals were supposed to belong to the national or Dominion government and not the local government or provinces. In many respects the growth was actually local. Even with that local growth there was a restlessness in some provinces with what they saw as national domination. This kindled separatist feelings in Quebec and in some western provinces, who sought even more local growth. All this has occurred despite the constitution placing reserve powers at the national level.

There has been a recent rewriting of the Canadian constitution. Both the dominion (national) government and the provinces sought to consolidate their position in the new act and both claimed that they succeeded, although not completely. Because of this change and because of the absence of any imminent separatist crisis, the new constitution's character has not been fully tested. Quebec did challenge the new charter but lost in the Canadian Supreme Court. Although some of the provisions of the new constitution do grant exclusive jurisdiction over some responsibilities to the provinces, the real test of the ostensibly federal ingredient can only come when there is a dispute. If the provinces and the dominion government disagree on an area of exclusive jurisdiction, that dispute, like Quebec's challenge to the constitution itself, will be settled in the courts. As we will see in a moment, that manner of settlement answers the question of legal form.

Federalism: Centripetal or Centrifugal?

The discrepancy seen in the operation of federalism in the United States and the general discrepancy seen between legal expectation and actual practice is intrinsic to federalism as a concept. In any federal form there must be either a centrifugal or a centripetal movement. Authoritative decision about residuals and redistribution must be made by either a national or a local agent. The constitution, the document of the original would-be distribution, cannot itself make the decision. In the United States, and as just mentioned in Canada too, final decisions about reassignment of powers has always been by one of the branches of the national government, chiefly the Supreme Court.

In the United States the Court is not the sole arbiter of national-state relations although it usually receives the greater amount of attention. Often the landmark decisions of the Court are really an upholding of an earlier action by the Congress or the President. In the *Gibbons* v. *Ogden* case (1824), when the Court is said to have established the national commerce jurisdiction by its interpretation of the Constitution, the Court decision actually ruled in favor of earlier action by the Congress. In

McCulloch v. *Maryland* (1819), concerning an attempted state tax of a national entity, the Court ruled in favor of presidential and congressional actions. The same was true when the Court helped the Congress and the President get around the Senate's treaty power in order to legislate on wildlife policy, which is usually reserved to the states *(Missouri* v. *Holland,* 1920). Even in the instances when the Court rules "in favor of" the states, the centripetal force still prevails since it is a national agent, subject to other national branches, which makes the decision.

Federalism in Theory and Practice

The theoretical legal definition of federalism states that the distribution is made by a constitution which cannot be altered by the unilateral action of the central government. In the United States the Constitution has been, can be, and is changed most significantly by the unilateral interpretative actions of the national government. When judicial, congressional, or presidential actions alter the Constitution it is done without the formal amending process coming into play at all. The process of informal constitutional growth has played the dominant role in defining and redefining the jurisdiction of the national government and the states. The interpretations which result in national growth are not usurpations by a voracious government. The growth that occurs is usually a necessary response to a particular set of circumstances.

National growth is most often the response to a demand for uniformity needed to overcome the confusion and dysfunction of disparate state rules. National highway legislation financed construction *and* provided for uniform materials, widths, shoulders, etc. National business regulations, particularly the too much maligned Occupational Safety and Health Administration, support uniform standards and prevent certain businesses from hiding behind state law to take advantage of workers and consumers. There is a geopolitical logic to the growth of national powers in the United States. The land area of the United States combined with its population and resource distribution necessitates national rules and national rule makers. National rules are necessary if there is going to be interdependence rather than disorder.

Interdependence produces both problems and solutions. A labor strike or disaster or agricultural problem in one part of the country quickly affects most all parts of the country. When such situations occur there is no concern that the Northeast should not be helping the Southwest. There is fair recognition that the sections of the country have interchangeable roles of producers, consumers, developers, marketers, borrowers, lenders, friends, and neighbors. All the parts of the country profit together so they help out and suffer together. In Canada, to refer again to their counterdynamic practice, the combination of area, population, and resources is different from the United States. With a population one tenth that of the United States in the same size territory, there is much less interdependence, and therefore more localizing developments occur. The instrument to oversee this national dynamic in the United States is bound to be either the Congress, President, or the Courts, or a combination. Even under the new Canadian constitution, though there have been signs of concessions to the provinces, there is a necessity for a national overseer and so it also is not an exception to this centripetal force.

Unfederalism

In the United States, the chief "federal" example, the inevitable national growth has its foundation, most surprisingly, in the "federal amendment" itself. The Tenth Amendment is thought to proclaim local growth. It speaks of powers that are "delegated" to the national government and powers that are "reserved" to the states. The delegated powers are expanded through the implied powers doctrine of the "necessary and proper" and other clauses of the Constitution. This doctrine holds that certain additional powers are implied in the powers specifically delegated to the branches of the national government, although it should be noted that the Constitution itself does not use the word "specific." There is no longer any important dispute over the concept of implied powers.

What makes the "federal amendment" the source of the national growth is that there is nothing in the Constitution which is specifically "reserved" to the states. There is no substantive power of government that the Constitution mentions as belonging to any government unit other than the national branches. Originally, for example, the specification of voting qualifications belonged to the states. Out of necessity this power to define voters was over time mostly taken away from the states. In any case this power was a procedural and not a substantive responsibility. It might be thought that the switch from state to national jurisdiction in the matter of voter specification had to be accomplished by formal constitutional amendment, which therefore proves the true federal character of the system. That argument is reasonable except for the consideration that the history of the various voting amendments shows that they were only effectively implemented with the interpretative efforts of the national government.

There is, it must be admitted, a single provision of the Constitution which grants a specific substantive jurisdiction to the states. That provision is the Twenty-first Amendment and the power granted there for the states to establish local prohibition if they so desire. This is the only provision in the Constitution which is an exception to the Tenth Amendment not specifying anything to the states. Few people, especially young people, want to expand upon this substantive state power of prohibition. The recent action by the President and Congress to force the states to raise the drinking age to twenty-one in all states because of the problems associated with drunk driving seems, however, to take even some of this specific state power over drinking laws away. The twenty-one-year-old drinking law, like the automobile air-bag law, are recent examples of reasonable national action when the states cannot, even though they might like to, regulate.

The recognized "police powers" of the states, the authority to promote and safeguard the health, morals, safety, and welfare of the people, is itself not based on a specific substantive provision of the Constitution. The police powers are based on the interpretation of the reserve clause itself. Since what can be interpreted into the reserve clause can also be interpreted out and since nothing is specifically reserved to the states except for the anomaly of prohibition, the "federal amendment" turns out to be not so much federal as *"un*federal." In other words, because of the reasonableness of implied powers and the lack of substance to the reserve powers, the Tenth Amendment turns out to be the undoing of federalism. The United States is therefore *un*federal or unitary rather than federal.

SUPPORT FOR *UN*FEDERALISM

The main casualty of unfederalism is the doctrine of states' rights. States' rights maintained that the states had a core of sovereign power which could never be taken away. Unfederalism would contend that the states never had that core of authority. Justification for unfederalism comes from the many considerations of necessity, interdependence, and the desire for uniformity already mentioned. "Support," however, is a matter of citing past or present factors which contribute to the general condition of unfederalism without formally intending to do so. There are many such supports.

The Articles of Confederation

One perhaps unexpected support for unfederalism would be the Articles of Confederation. This document, which was the first Constitution of the United States, is said to have established the "confederacy" which preceded the "federal" Constitution of 1787. In the process of showing that the "federal" Constitution is not so federal, it becomes important to see that the Articles of Confederation were not so confederate. This venture may seem preposterous when it is acknowledged that Article I of that first Constitution states, in its original spelling, "The Stile of this confederacy shall be 'The United States of America.'" That should make the situation fairly unequivocal; the Articles of Confederation established a "confederacy."

The Second Article should conclusively establish that the intended form of government was a confederacy. As it is normally quoted, the Second Article states, "Each state retains its sovereignty, freedom and independence." The essence of a confederacy, as indicated earlier, is that the member units retain their sovereignty, freedom, and independence. There is a problem, however. The usual quote from the Second Article leaves some material out and this quoting out of context makes a big difference. To quote that article completely, it states,

> Each state retains its sovereignty, freedom and independence, and every Power, Jurisdiction and right, which is not by this confederation expressly delegated to the United States in Congress assembled.

Upon first reading that article may not seem to make much of a difference. Attention should be directed, however, to the distinction within it between delegated and reserved or "retained" powers. Though the article speaks of "expressly" delegated powers, that word does not take away the division. A look at the expressly delegated powers shows that they are the same powers stated in the same manner as in the Constitution of 1787 which replaced it. A close reading of the Articles and the Constitution shows a great similarity of powers of the national government, restrictions on the states, and obligations of the states to one another, such as full faith and credit, privileges and immunities, and rendition. In these respects then, the Articles are similar to the later Constitution.

The Articles of Confederation did not, however, provide for a well-designed government. Its mechanism for interpretation, its decision process, and its means of implementing policy were clumsy at best. The reasons for the Articles' faulty procedures may be that a genuine spirit of confederacy motivated their framers, or it may be the result of optimistic assumptions based on existing unity. After all, the Americans had just successfully waged war against England. The euphoric unity of wartime was broken, as often occurs, by the rivalry of peace.[2] Whatever the explanation for the defects in the Articles, it is clear that the political leaders at the time saw a need for change almost immediately. In a series of meetings at Alexandria, Annapolis, and then Philadelphia, the leaders brought about the drafting of the present Constitution, which replaced the Articles within six years of its ratification.

The argument that the Articles are not convincingly confederate relies on more than the reserve clause within the Second Article and the similarities with the later Constitution. A striking contrast to a truly confederate intention are the many passages which speak of the confederation as a "perpetual union." The union is referred to six times as "perpetual." Furthermore, it is stated twice that the Articles shall be "inviolably observed," which is then followed by the phrase that "the union shall be perpetual." These statements hardly suggest a primary focus on the sovereignty, freedom, and independence of the states. The sovereignty business is mentioned only once in the entire document. The right to withdraw at will is not mentioned even once.

The "more perfect union," of which the later Constitution's preamble speaks, may indeed reflect a perfecting of a union which already existed. No final determination has to be made here about the precise character of the Articles of Confederation. The point of interest in this discussion was to show that there is a basis even in the earlier document for the contention that true union was the intention in the design of the Constitution of 1787 despite its convincing rhetoric of "federalism."

"New" Federalism

A more contemporary but no less surprising source which supports the suggestion that the United States is unitary, or at least *un*federal, is the "new federalism" proposal of former President Nixon back in 1969. President Reagan has also given much attention to new federalism. The two views on new federalism do not differ essentially but the statement by President Nixon has a more developed character. That developed character makes it more appropriate for study and since it is farther removed from immediate political debate it has less of a partisan flavor to its examination. In an evening address to the nation Mr. Nixon discussed public welfare and other reforms and announced a plan of revenue sharing which was the keystone to the plan of new federalism. The point was, as he said, that for a long time "power and responsibility have flowed toward Washington—and Washington has taken for its own the best sources of revenue." Accordingly, the new federalism proposed

> . . . to reverse this tide, and to turn back to the states a greater measure of responsibility—not as a way of avoiding problems but as a better way of solving problems.

Along with this responsibility, he continued:

> . . . should go a share of federal revenues. I shall propose to the Congress next week that a set portion of the revenues from federal income taxes be remitted directly to the state—with a minimum of federal restriction on how those dollars are to be used and with a requirement that a percentage of them be channeled through for the use of local governments.[3]

There was much fanfare for the idea of new federalism's returning responsibility to the state and sharing the largess of national revenues with the states. There are, however, several noteworthy aspects to the proposal which might lessen the federalism euphoria:

1. the President was making the proposal,
2. the proposal was going to Congress,
3. the "federal" restrictions were not so minimal,
4. the channeling of funds was the first state restriction.

Mr. Nixon used the term "federal" effectively. From an objective perspective it should be noticeable, however, that here was one national agent, the President, making the proposal to another national agent, the Congress. That one long sentence in which the proposal was announced contained the first national rule about how the program was to be operated. New federalism, like the old one, was *un*federal from the night it was announced.

A not so small footnote to the new federalism and revenue sharing proposal is that although it was enacted as the president requested, it did not last long. Like many proposals and programs before and since, revenue sharing ran aground on the shoals of state and local rivalry for guaranteed amounts and administration of the funds. Another problem was that the national government, understandably, did not want to completely turn funds over to other levels of government without some say in how and under what condition those funds were to be spent. As with many large expenditure programs there was also an amount of graft and corruption. What is striking is that these problems of corruption did not arise so much at the national level as at the local level. It was precisely to monitor such dysfunctions and to keep an eye on its task that Congress in particular wanted to maintain a say in the rules and administration of the various programs. President Reagan with some flare and even President Carter to some small extent sought to begin other programs to readjust national and state responsibilities, but there have been no breakthrough developments.

Statistics on Unfederalism

Another source of support for unfederalism can be found in the statistics which reflect the growth that has occurred over the years in the national government's domain. Simple budget figures point out the massive shift from local to national power. In 1902 local governments spent 59 percent of all governmental budgets in the United States, the states spent 6 percent, and the national government had 35 percent of the expenditures. By the 1970s the local figures hovered around 24 percent, the state figure had increased to around 16 percent, and the national percentage had increased to about 60 percent or higher for a number of years. Even these figures are misleading because about one third of state revenues are currently derived from national sources which would translate into a higher national percentage of total expenditures and a lower state and local percentage. The figures merely show that the national government has grown vis-à-vis the states and local governments.

Some contend that this growth is primarily a result of the better national revenue source as a result of the Income Tax (Sixteenth) Amendment. Aside from the questionable *post hoc, ergo propter hoc* reasoning, the contention does not even look into the real situations which compelled national action in order to provide necessary uniform practices. The grant-in-aid programs which provided national monies for the building of highways, airport terminals and runways, hospitals, educational facilities, and many other undertakings are the result of the need for certain minimum national standards. These programs are not the result of a reasoning which says, "we've got the money, let's find a way to spend it."

There are many other national programs which are not the result of revenues but which instead suggest the response to the need for minimum uniform standards. These are programs in labor practices, banking procedures, food and drug handling, and building and safety standards. The national standards in all these areas make certain that unscrupulous individuals do not hide behind state laws to take advantage of consumers or the public. There is also a convenience in national requirements which seems to outweigh the inconvenience of the remote bureaucracy administering them. The convenience is the certainty, when conducting business or traveling in different parts of the country, of knowing that standards and practices will be the same. On an individual level, one can imagine what it would be like to undertake an automobile trip from Florida to Oregon and find in each state along the way different rules and road specifications. It would be like traveling through fifteen Canadas and Englands where ''They drive on the 'wrong' side of the road.''

Statutory Supports for Unfederalism

Additional evidence of the actual growth of the national government can be seen in an area entirely different from statistics about relative expenditures. Chief Justice Warren Burger has pointed out in an address to state court judges that aside from the traditional upward movement of litigation, Congress has also contributed to the expansion of national courts' duties. He lamented that in recent years, Congress has enacted forty-eight statutes which expand the jurisdiction of the national courts at the expense of the state courts. The Chief Justice's concern was for the ''piecemeal shifts of jurisdiction away from state courts and into Federal courts.''[4] He opposed these shifts and asked the state judges to thoughtfully and effectively inform Congress that the state courts could do a better job. His comments document that shifts have occurred in favor of national growth, and the comments also indicate that Mr. Burger takes a view divergent from others in the legal system.

Congress has not reversed the statutes Burger questioned, which suggests that they were enacted precisely to overcome the disparateness of different state rulings. The Court itself, with Burger and two others in dissent, a couple of years later continued the expansion of national courts' responsibilities by enlarging the justification for citizens to sue their states (*Maine* v. *Thiboutot,* 1980). A year later Burger was again lamenting the ''double-digit inflation'' of national court caseloads, which he explained were the result of ''sloppy draftsmanship'' of statutes.[5]

The Chief Justice's complaint about minor cases clogging the court docket may be well taken when he cites examples of the man who brought suit on the grounds that his constitutional rights were violated when he was not permitted to drive his Sherman tank on the streets of Cincinnati. Everyone might wish that other procedures could resolve such disputes without involving the national courts. It must be considered, however, that these minor matters may well be the price which must be paid to maintain a system that handles more substantial cases. Caseload efficiency may be very desirable but it can create more social costs than it saves.

The Rhetoric of Federalism

Several times in the preceding comments federalism has been referred to as rhetorical. In many respects that is *all* federalism is, a rhetorical term used for political purposes. At the beginning of this chapter a political scientist was cited who drew attention to matched pairs of unitary and federal systems and found that there was not a discernible difference in the effective functioning of the two forms. That political scientist, William H. Riker, had put his thoughts as a question, ''Does federalism exist and does it matter?'' He gave a scholarly qualified ''No!'' to that question. This chapter would make the ''No'' a little more emphatic.

Riker calls federalism a ''fiction.'' He was commenting that scholars accept federalism as real while ordinary citizens treat federalism as a fiction. Ordinary citizens do not ''concern themselves often or seriously about federalism.'' He argued that

> Scholars, on the other hand, have treated it as a real thing, probably because they have been overly impressed and indeed misled by the valuable and important function this fiction fulfills in persuading regional politicians to accept the formation of a central government. The main theme of this review [of other scholars] is, however, that, no matter how useful the fiction of federalism is in creating new government, one should not overlook the fact that it is a fiction.[6]

More forthright words are seldom written by political scientists.

Federalism Undone

In this chapter federalism has been undone as a form of government. An examination of the usual forms in their concrete setting shows that basically one has a government which can effect decisions or one does not. There is no in-between. The original three forms of unitary, federal, and confederate are reduced to one, the unitary. The confederate was seen earlier to be a loose union of unitary states. The federal has been shown to be unfederal. The earlier classification breaks down as based on a legal fiction. However, the practical distinction of being actually federal or actually unitary remains important for it refers to the degree of centralization or relative decentralization that obtains in the particular country.

The term federalism still has some referent value. It should be understood, however, not to have the legal content previously assumed. A consoling revival of some utility for the friendly old term of federalism will be developed further in a moment. First it might be said that having exposed the fiction of federalism and the reality of unfederalism, it may be useful to remind the reader of the brief discussion of federalism in the earlier context of ''world federalism.'' The reader might want to reflect on the consequences of the fiction in that earlier context and then to reexamine the proposals. One should reflect on what the World Federalists hope to achieve and the seriousness or indirection of the methods of those advocating it.

FEDERAL CONSOLATION AND THE FUTURE

The fiction of federalism and the reality of unfederalism may be upsetting to many who have been ingrained with the importance of federalism. Pointing out the fictional character of a perception does not change the reality but only, if even that, the perception. B. F. Skinner makes the consoling and wise observation, perhaps to calm those who get so upset at some of the things he writes, that ''a theory does not change what it is a theory about.'' It is not necessarily true that a theory does not change what it is a theory about, but it is sufficiently true to merit some consideration. What Skinner's statement amounts to is that one should not get terribly upset when one first comes across something which deviates from previous assumptions.

What has been done in this chapter is to show that federalism is not necessarily what it is usually described to be. Such new knowledge which challenges set assumptions can and should be a healthy thing. Not everyone will be convinced immediately or ever in some cases. Nevertheless it is useful to be aware of the challenge to the concept of federalism. Because a major element in the conventional stock of political science and American government was scuttled in the comments on unfederalism it may be wise to expand on the changed perception a little further.

The revealing of the fiction of federalism does not change the Tenth Amendment itself, it only changes the perception or understanding of that amendment. The unfederal understanding eliminates the basis for the old doctrine of states' rights according to which the states were thought to have, but never practiced, some degree of autonomy. In place of the old reading of the Tenth Amendment, the new one would understand it in terms of the principle of subsidiarity. To say that ''all powers not delegated . . . are reserved'' is merely to hold that a function or power ought to be assumed as best performed at a lower level before it is taken over by the national government. If the states can perform a function rather than the national government, they ought to do so, if the people can perform a function rather than the states, they likewise ought to do so. This subsidiarity reading of the Tenth Amendment is a perfectly reasonable proposition. It is far superior to the old states' rights view which held that there was an unspecified area of governmental jurisdiction which was absolutely off-limits to the national government.

In the past some individuals proclaimed this doctrine of states' rights, but it was not practiced except in a temporary obstreperous delaying fashion. Consequently, the only significant change in the new doctrine of unfederalism is to admit the possibility and legal authority of national jurisdiction and to deny the legal doctrine of states' rights. If ''federalism'' itself is understood as *no more* than a statement of subsidiarity, then there would not even be a problem with the term.

States Continue to Exist

It is important, if the national government has the right, as in any unitary system, to decide what powers shall be exercised nationally and what shall be expected locally, that there be some mechanism whereby the national and local interests can be effectively debated before decisions are made. In the United States that mechanism is provided in the whole structure of the government ranging from the two houses of Congress, to the separation of powers, to the electoral system, to the guaranteed existence of the states and their guarantee of a republican form of government. According to the latter guarantees, (1) the states may not be divided up nor added to another state without the state's consent, (2) the national government must come to their defense, (3) the states may not be denied their equal representation in the Senate, and (4) their representational form of government shall be assured.

This representational or republican form of government merely means that internally the states can continue to elect their governors and other state officials. A fascinating aspect of this assurance of a republican form of government is that the Constitution thereby guarantees the existence of the states and the continued election of governors even though there is no guarantee, according to unfederalism, that the states and governors will have anything to do. The better part of wisdom would suggest, therefore, that since the existence of the states is fixed they ought to be utilized and given something to do. That is what subsidiarity in this context and the "new federalism" are about.

Political Party Structure

The whole governmental structure and the guarantee of states' existence, and the republican form of government have another mechanism whereby the national and local interests can be aired effectively. That additional mechanism is the political party system and the electoral process which accompanies it. American political parties, despite the appearance of being national in character, are in reality loose coalitions of state parties. The national parties are confederacies of state parties. The state parties are confederacies of local units of the party. This inverted pyramid of party organizational authority is a result of voter turnout as the ultimate electoral authority. If the voters or a local party organization decide not to support a county, district, state, or national candidate there is little that the higher party unit can do to demand a reversal of this decision. The higher level can try to circumvent the local organization, but always at a higher cost and lower effectiveness.

At the national level the parties come together only once every four years to nominate candidates for the presidency and vice presidency. At those national conventions the parties often openly demonstrate their confederate character by failing to unite behind the nominee, except perhaps nominally. When the state units or lower units of the party fail to unite behind the "party" nominee extraordinary effort must be mounted to overcome the handicap. Furthermore, the recalcitrant lower units of the party cannot normally be disciplined because that would only drive a larger wedge, adversely affecting future elections. The same lack of unity and lack of disciplined voting enforcement applies to the organization of the parties within the Congress and state legislatures. Party loyalty is not legally binding within these bodies and frequently legislators are found voting according to local wishes instead of according to the wishes of the party leadership.

Uniformity and Reality

The confederate character of the party system when combined with the unitary (unfederal) legal system in the United States results in a federalism in the overall political system. This system federalism is not a legal one. It is a product of the dynamic interaction of the unitary and confederate parts of the political system. This interactively realized federalism may not be a satisfactory substitute or consolation for the familiar fiction of federalism. It does, however, identify more accurately a major means of local input on the decision process concerning national and local interests. That identification should help in insuring that decisions are as biased for local preference as is reasonable. That bias is perfectly consistent with subsidiarity's assumption of the competence and integrity of the lowest unit until it is reasonably demonstrated to be lacking. That competitive political parties appealing to local voters contribute to the dynamic of a "federalism" in society is partially demonstrated by what happens in one-party systems where centralization of responsibility throughout the political system often stifles real growth at any level.

The need for uniformity which can be handled only through national action was evident a few years ago in a report on some items which would hardly seem to be the subject of national concern. Birth certificates, death certificates, and drivers' licenses seem the quintessence of local jurisdiction. Yet a Justice Department study in 1976 pointed out the need for uniform standards and procedures in these and other identification card areas. The need for uniformity flows from a growing criminal use of false identification in illegal immigration, check, credit card, and other business frauds, welfare fraud, and drug abuse through false identification. The study estimated that such criminal use was costing at least $20 billion a year, with welfare and related fraud being the least costly although the one most likely to receive attention. This false identification problem requires national legislation because state action would be piecemeal, producing gaps and loopholes which would perpetuate the situation. (Spokesperson for the Justice Department at the time was Assistant Attorney General Richard L. Thornburgh. In 1978 Mr. Thornburgh went on to a different governmental position, Governor of Pennsylvania.)

Only minimum standards established by Congress can bring uniformity of practice. Such uniformity is looked upon as being the first step in establishing a national identity card. Some see such a card as a type of internal passport and a threat to civil liberties. It is viewed as an ominous mark of the national government in the pocket of every individual in the United States. Those with a sense of history will remember that the social security card and even the dollar bill were regarded in the same way. The challenge to the "national" currency was settled long ago. The social security card as a common identity number is in one respect the source of the need for a more sophisticated card. The social security number is used in banking to insure that unscrupulous persons do not cheat on taxes, and it is used as faculty and student identification numbers at universities. Because of its wide use it has the same problems of counterfeiting and fraud as currency. These problems prompt the call for a better designed card.

The point of national standards or a national card is to bring uniformity of practice, so that individuals who today sneak around the existing state practices will not be able to abuse the system in the future. When the United States finally has the new standards it will be the result of necessity and not usurpation. Hopefully it will be explained in that manner instead of having a great national debate based on emotion. The recent national legislation on the legal drinking age bears out the willingness to act when necessity and reasonableness conjoin despite a tradition of state responsibility.

NOTES

1. William H. Riker, "Six Books in Search of a Subject or Does Federalism Exist and Does It Matter?" *Comparative Politics* (October, 1969), pp. 135-146; reprinted in Ernest D. Giglio and John J. Schrems, *Future Politics* (Berkeley, Calif.: McCutchan Publishing Corportation, 1971), pp. 93-102.

2. This assumption of unity is a conclusion which I draw from Robert E. Brown's critique of the conventional conspiracy thesis of United States origins. See his *Charles Beard and the Constitution* (Princeton: Princeton University Press, 1956) as well as his *Middle Class Democracy in Massachusetts* (Ithaca: Cornell University Press, 1955).

3. Text of President Nixon's address to the nation on public welfare and other reforms, August 8, 1969.

4. *The New York Times,* March 20, 1978.

5. *The New York Times,* June 2, 1981.

6. Riker, "Six Books," p. 146.

CHAPTER FOURTEEN
FORMS OF GOVERNMENT: FUNCTIONAL DISTRIBUTION OF POWER

In addition to the geographic distribution of power, the subject of the previous chapter, there is also a functional distribution category. Functional distribution is a consideration of how government is organized at a particular level rather than what organizational relationship exists between the levels. It is assumed that all governments have certain common functional activities, namely, making law, enforcing law, and judging violations of the law. Plato and Aristotle spoke of these separate activities in ancient times. Polybius, the author of the earliest history of Rome, wrote of a separation of powers and a system of checks and balances which he said made Rome great. Locke and Montesquieu in modern times gave special attention to them also.

Functional distribution is the consideration of how government is organized to handle the three activities of making, enforcing, and judging law. Separation of powers is one of two general ways the distribution is handled. Fusion of powers is the second way of organizing the distribution. There is a third way, called "mixed," which will be described, but primary attention will be focused on separation and fusion.

SEPARATION OF POWERS

Separation of powers refers to the practice where separate branches of government perform the separate functions. The title usually ascribed to that system is "presidential.'' It is called presidential because of its separately elected, fixed-term president or executive with real, not just ceremonial, powers. Having a separate president necessarily implies that there is also a separately elected, fixed-term legislature which has activities and responsibilities independent of the president. In addition to the legislative and executive branches, the system has an independent judiciary.

The best example of the presidential system is that of the United States, where, according to what might be called a ''nursery rhyme,'' it is understood that ''Congress makes the law, the President enforces the law, and the Courts judge the law.'' The rhyme is based on the constitutional prescription which vests legislative power in the Congress, executive power in the President, and judicial power in the Courts as found in the opening passages of Articles I, II, and III, respectively, of the Constitution. There is a certain sharing and overlapping of powers, also prescribed in the Constitution, which produces the checks and balances that prevent undue concentration of power. The functional value of avoiding concentration is, as Aristotle, Polybius, and Cicero saw in ancient times, that law and policy come to reflect the wishes of the diversity of the community and not just the preferences of a few.

According to the Constitution, the President is to become involved in the making of law by signing or vetoing legislation. He is also entitled to propose legislation to the Congress. The legislative body becomes involved in executive responsibilities by way of the requirement that they approve appointments of executive officers and that they ratify—the Senate at least—treaties. The courts are part of the checks and balances function by reason of their membership being subject to presidential appointment and Senate confirmation, even though once the appointment is completed, the Justices normally serve for life. Their exercise of judicial review of acts of the legislature and the executive completes their part of the balance.

The constitutional prescriptions for separation of powers are all adhered to as are the provisions for checks and balances. Congress legislates, the President enforces, and the Court judges. It appears as if the system works in the manner intended. There are some impediments to the perfect fulfillment of the design, however. The annoyance comes in several forms: with respect to the Court when it exercises judicial review, with respect to the President when he determines war more than the Congress, and with respect to the Congress when it makes foreign policy. These examples raise some question about the precise relationship between the branches and the exact distribution and separation of powers. That question will be addressed later after first introducing the fusion system.

FUSION OF POWER

The fusion of powers form is usually entitled the Cabinet or the *Parliamentary* system. By fusion is meant that the legislative, executive, and judicial powers are fused into one body, understood to be the cabinet or the parliament as a whole. England is the primary example of this form, but Canada, Japan, West Germany, and many others could just as easily serve. A parliamentary body is usually composed of two houses, an upper house with mostly ceremonial roles, and a lower house or "commons" where the fusion of powers is found in more specific form. The members of the commons are elected from separate districts and these members in turn elect a prime minister who exercises executive power. In the parliamentary form there is no independent supreme court which can veto acts of the prime minister or the commons. There is a separately functioning court system but it lacks the judicial review function. This lack only reinforces the fusion of powers in the parliamentary body. There are some anomalies to this generalization about judicial review. Canada, for example, as mentioned in the previous chapter, lets its Supreme Court decide disputes between the provinces and the dominion government. The word "let" maintains the fusion identity, however.

In the parliamentary system the prime minister has the power to call election at will. There are some limitations on this power but it does constitute a major contrast to the regularly fixed date of elections in the presidential form. The ability of prime ministers to schedule the date of elections gives them the advantage of selecting the most opportune time to take on their opponents. This power, combined with a discipline they exercise within their own party, gives the prime minister a leadership edge which presidents lack. This edge does not always work to the advantage of the government, however. Other factors make some parliamentary governments strong and others weak.

Strong and Weak Parliamentary Systems

In England, Canada, Japan, West Germany, and other "strong" parliamentary systems, the fusion of powers is really found in the prime minister and in the cabinet, which is appointed by the prime minister. The locus of power in the cabinet explains the alternate title, "cabinet," given to this form. In contrast to the strong parliamentary system, there is a "weak" counterpart, as in Italy, Portugal, and Spain. The contrasting terms, weak and strong, do not refer to the degree of fusion or even whether fusion occurs. It refers to the *location* of the fusion. In the strong system the prime minister or the cabinet are the ones who really exercise the power. In the weak system the locus of the fusion is more accurately found in the parliament or assembly. This parliamentary locus often means that power is sluggish or dormant. In the strong cabinet system, there is usually a two-party system so that one party has a true majority at any particular time. Third parties and coalitions do exist in the strong systems, but their existence does not disturb the major parties who continue to dominate the political scene.

In the weak systems it is precisely the existence of many parties that undermines any potential strength of the government. In Italy for example it is not unusual to have three- or four-party coalitions who form a parliamentary majority to select a prime minister and cabinet. This situation is inherently unstable. At any time one party within the coalition can withdraw its support, causing the government to lose its majority, and the process of selecting a prime minister within the parliament has to begin again. These changes in prime ministers frequently result in new elections. The results of new elections usually differ little from the previous distribution of members in the assembly, since the voters have no clearer focus of issues or candidates than earlier.

The wide variety of choices available to the voters in a multiparty system is said to be more representative. However, the lack of concentration of responsibility which comes from such a practice makes it less likely that the public can translate its preferences into specific policy orientations. This makes the system in the final analysis less representative. In a two-party system where there is a choice between somewhat contrasting policies or personalities, the voter preferences will ultimately be registered in the composition of the government. This makes the two-party form more representative in that respect. When the parliamentary system is compared with the presidential system for respective advantages and disadvantages, it is only fair and reasonable to use the strong form as the point of reference. A sketch of the presidential and parliamentary systems and the strong and weak versions of the latter are provided in Figure 14-1.

PRESIDENTIAL VERSUS PARLIAMENTARY SYSTEMS

The parliamentary system is said to have the advantages of unity, efficiency, and flexibility. At least these are purported advantages in comparison with the presidential system, which lacks them. The presidential system is noted for deadlock, delay, and buckpassing. In the parliamentary system there is by definition a unity between prime minister, cabinet, and commons. In this unity the prime minister and the cabinet set policy, which is ratified by the commons, since it is dominated by the prime minister's party. If the parliamentary body did not support the policy of the prime minister, there are two likely outcomes. One, the prime minister would resign and be replaced by a new leader of the majority. Two, the parliament would be dissolved and new nationwide elections would be held. The result of either of these two outcomes would be the restoration of the unity between the leadership and the commons.

In the presidential system, by contrast, the president at any given time may be of one political party and the legislature of the other party; the two houses may even be of opposite parties. The courts would be independent of the other two branches, but the judges would be a mixture of individuals from both parties. In this system the policy objectives of the three branches can differ widely and the situation cannot be changed until possibly the next election. When the president and the congress are of two different parties, neither will voluntarily resign and seek to be replaced by someone from the other party to achieve unity within the government. Historical experience shows, however, that having the legislative and executive branches controlled by the same party is no guarantee of unity. Lyndon Johnson found this out in the last two years of his term.

From unity in the parliamentary form follows efficiency, flexibility, and ef-

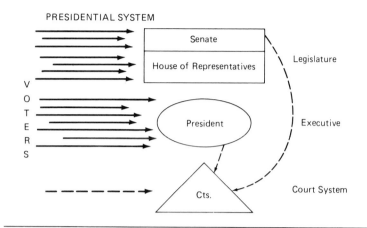

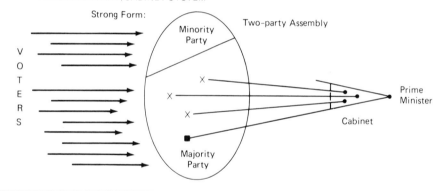

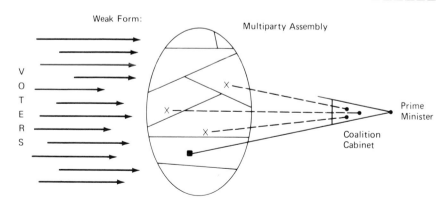

FIGURE 14-1   Presidential and parliamentary systems.

fectiveness. Unity means that there is no delay in awaiting the approval of another branch. Once a policy is decided upon, it becomes policy. If the prime minister and cabinet are convinced of the merits and importance of a policy, it can be enacted without concern that some legislative chairperson can obstruct. The policy can be implemented when it is needed in the judgment of the executive. Therefore the only limitation on the efficiency and effectiveness of policy is the timing and judgment of the prime minister.

In the parliamentary system responsibility is clear and elections are contested on the basis of the performance or the potential performance of the candidates for prime minister. There is no confusion in this system of the candidate for the executive holding the legislature or the courts responsible for policy or the failure of policy. There is no exploiting of partisan differences for electoral advantage in one branch or the other. Individual members of the parliamentary body assume less importance than the party and its leadership. Consequently, the public is not distracted by colorful but impractical proposals by all sorts of candidates who could never be held responsible even if elected. The same "irresponsible" posturing from the presidential system is in evidence in the multiparty parliamentary system also. When and if elected, the party or candidate who makes unreasonable promises can always blame everyone else for the inability to get the policy enacted. In the two-party parliamentary system, attention is focused sharply and clearly which stands in contrast to the diffusion in the presidential system.

It must be pointed out, however, that although there are grounds for the advantages just cited for the parliamentary system, they do not lead to an unqualified endorsement of the form. The advantages and disadvantages just discussed of the two systems may be classified as "theoretical." Theory is not to be taken lightly but theories differ in quality, especially weak empirical theory which is neither universal nor necessary. The problem with the theoretical advantages of the parliamentary over the presidential system is that, although the observations about the different partisan and structural configurations may be mostly accurate, the actual performance of the two systems is not noticeably different.

The governments of England, Japan, Canada, and West Germany are not clearly superior to the government of the United States in managing their economies, in handling foreign affairs, in establishing tranquil domestic policy, and in undertaking all those other things that government does. One country may handle one area of responsibility better that another country for a period of time. It may appear, indeed many may be ready to conclude, that a temporary better policy is a result of better governmental organization. Then the performance record may shift and there is no correlation between organization and policy. West Germany's and Japan's "management" of the economy were for a while set out as examples of the superiority of their systems and policies. A few years later that boast could no longer stand up.

Despite all the efforts of generations of politicians and scholarly experts who claim to have discovered the formula for solving problems, the political world remains serenely independent. Political, social, economic, cultural, religious, and other variables no more conform to expert plans than the weather. That does not mean to say that organized and scientific efforts are useless. That suggestion would be completely unreasonable. The science of politics may never be any more exact than the science of meteorology, but few of us would fly in the face of a hurricane warning any more than we would vote for a committed anarchist. Exact cause and effect relationships have not been established in the world of politics, and there is no scientific basis for saying that one organization scheme is superior to another. That is no sound reason to abandon government as such or a particular governmental design.

The reason theoretical advantage is usually assigned to the cabinet system, even though it does not show up in an obvious practical way, is that the presidential system is viewed according to exaggerated notions of "separate but equal" branches. Great attention is usually given to the separateness of the branches, to their rivalry over power and prominence, and to the threatened erosion of their constitutionally intended equality. Much is written about "the era of Congress," or about the "imperial Presidency," or the "usurpation" of power by the courts. Scholars, newspapers, newsmagazines, radio and television stories, candidates, and officeholders all speak of the separate but equal branches and how one branch is intruding on or falling victim to another.

These accounts of the rivalry between the branches overlook several things. For one, the phrase "separate but equal" does not appear in the Constitution. Separate but equal is a principle derived from the provisions of the Constitution. An equally acceptable derivation would be to say that the branches are "merged and co-dependent" because the checks and balances bring them together as much as they separate them. A further point is to take a step backwards from the tussling of the political world and observe that the United States does in fact have a government. The United States does have a foreign policy, it does have an economic policy, it does have various domestic policies. The policy that the United States government has is not the policy of the President or the policy of the Congress, though it is most often described that way in news reports. It is the policy of the United States. However the policy was arrived at, through the initiative of the President or the insistence of the legislature, the policy "in effect" is that of the United States.

An American looking at the policy of England, or France, or West Germany does not ask about the policy of the Bundestag, or the Chancellor, or the Prime Minister, or the National Assembly, or the President, or the Commons, or the Queen. The interest is in the policy of France, or England, or Germany, or whatever country. That is the way that policy is received by those whom it affects. The recipients of foreign aid or Air Force bombs view the United States as responsible, not the Congress or the President. In the same way, the American coal miner, the malnourished child, the criminal, or the farmer is the recipient of policy even though there is an inclination to point to or credit one branch or another with dominant influence in the making of that policy. Because of this simple but often overlooked truth, the reality of governmental policy is missed and attention is focused on the theater of partisan competition.

Partisan competitors within the Congress and between the branches of the government often draw attention because of a dual and mutually self-serving relationship with the media of mass communications. The partisans love to exploit the media's desire for colorful stories of competition which excite the interest of the public. The media love to cast the partisans in a competitive role for the same purpose. There is never any inquiry about whether this is the best and most accurate way to report the news because that inquiry would be too time-consuming and too theoretical to interest anyone but a few scholars. The focus of the news within the United States is on what one branch of government does to another branch. The news is presented as if it were a never-ending civics lecture about what Congress, the President, or the Court did *to* each other. It is not a very attractive news story to say, "Government works!" It is a case of always hearing about the trees and never the forest. The effect, however, is always one of the forest despite the "twigs."

The recipients of governmental action are affected by the policy no matter who the media says sponsored it. The misdirected attention on sponsorship, in the attempt to be informative and interesting, makes news about the American political system both widely listened to and irrelevant. What is crucial is that there is a government and it works, and it works as good as anyone else's. What is normally said about government would hardly lead one to that conclusion. Rivalry between the separate but equal branches is the normal message about American government. That the government functions at least no worse than any other country is the common experience which is seldom recognized.

A SHIFT WITHIN THE PRESIDENTIAL SYSTEM

Because of the attention to form and rivalry instead of the substance of merged and co-dependent partners, a change in the role of the branches is viewed with alarm. A shift in the powers of the courts or a shift in the management of the war powers or in foreign policy management or changed responsibility for direction of the economy are looked upon as threats to the constitutional structure. If the classic separation of powers is referred to as a nursery rhyme or if it is said more bluntly that a quite different division of labor exists, then the system is thought to be eroding, if not on the verge of collapse.

Indeed, a shift in the original division of labor has occurred. This shift is important to understand if the comparison between the parliamentary and presidential systems is to be properly carried out. The shift does not endanger the presidential system but instead strengthens its structure in the comparative situation. Gabriel Almond has written that "a generation of students of the courts, Congress, and the executive have established a division of labor quite different from th[e] classic separation of powers–checks and balances doctrine."[1] The new division of labor sees the courts as lawmaker because of the judicial review function, the executive as lawmaker in the sense of principal source of the rules, and the Congress as the ratifier of the rules and spokesperson for interests and not much of a lawmaker at all.

The shift in policy responsibilities from those in the Constitution does not leave Congress powerless. Congress is, or can be at least, more powerful. The size and composition of the Congress makes it better suited for some tasks than others. The design of the division of labor between three branches intends that each be effective and efficient and not duplicate one another. Furthermore, good design intends that effort not be wasted in endless disputes over jurisdiction. On the congressional side, this design is fulfilled by the organizational scheme, whereby the hundreds of members of both houses are divided into many committees and subcommittees. Each committee and subcommittee is specialized in its tasks, but then the entire house and then the other house must approve the recommendations of these respective committees.

To have policy initiated in the Congress would be a slow and frustrating process since there is no one individual within the structure who can compel the hundreds of others to follow through on a proposal. Each member within their respective chambers, as each chamber itself, is equal. No one has legal standing over another. The same structure, however, which cannot be used effectively for policy initiatives can be used effectively in another manner. The more effective use is to respond or react to the policy proposal made from outside the structure. To review the initiatives from the executive, to give administrative oversight to the bureaucracy's implementation of policies already agreed upon, is an effective use of the congressional structure. Acting in this way the Congress serves as the legitimizer of the initiatives taken by the President. With Congress exercising this review or oversight function, the presidential system maintains both the necessary policy leadership and the responsiveness which all systems require.

The review function attributed to Congress is not just a theoretical construct to salvage the separations of powers–checks and balances doctrine. Recent prominent examples of Congress exercising its review function were in the Watergate investigations, the hearings on the Southeast Asian and Vietnam policies in the mid-to-late 1960s, and the reviews of the Great Society programs in the late 1960s and early 1970s. Most Congressional hearings are of a review nature since what they do is look at presidential proposals, budget or otherwise, and judge them on past performance. Congress is in a better position to judge what has occurred than what might occur, since they are on the receiving end of reports from their constituents about what has or has not worked properly. Suggestions about what new measures are needed become as diverse as the number of correspondents, which makes the Congress much less effective in policy initiatives.

Once a program is passed under presidential initiative and implemented under presidential direction, the Congress is in a position to review it. Congress can respond to constituent input that a program is not working as intended, that the program is wasteful, or that it is creating more problems than it sought to solve. Congress would respond to such input with inquiries to appropriate administrative agencies. They would hold hearings and seek official testimony for the record if the inquiries do not give satisfactory results. Occasionally Congress would suggest improvements. If the problems are not abated then Congress might decide to hold further hearings, withhold funds, require changes, or drop the program.

The role of the President as the source of rules is not particularly new. It can be seen in the policy initiatives of William McKinley, Theodore Roosevelt, and Woodrow Wilson, if not earlier by Lincoln. In a formal way the Congress urged the initiative on the President in the Budget and Accounting Act of 1921, where they said that the President should be responsible for organizing and managing the budget which was previously primarily their responsibility. Congress had struggled with compiling the budget, with all its policy implications, for many years and they said in the 1921 act that henceforth the responsibility and the accompanying opportunities were to be the President's. Recent changes, as in the Budget Reform Act of 1974, have not altered the basic relationship between President and Congress set in 1921. The 1974 act only served to better prepare the Congress for responding to the full implications of the executive budget.

The President's role as chief policy initiator in foreign affairs started even before the nineteenth century, so there should be little surprise that twentieth-century Presidents request a "declaration" of war only after the country is already in a state of war. By one count[2] the United States has been engaged in more than 100 overseas military actions since 1789, and Congress has declared war only five times. More recently, in the Korean and Vietnamese conflicts, there has not been a formal declaration of war. In many respects it was most appropriate that formal declarations of war not occur, since that would have only succeeded in escalating the conflict. It is best to keep all conflicts as limited as possible. Congress still has a role in appropriating the funds to finance foreign and defense policy and in questioning those policies, but its role is one of response rather than initiative.

In addition to foreign policy and defense initiatives and to general policy initiatives, the President is looked upon as chief director of the economy because of the general economic tone set by the presidential budget responsibilities and other economic policies. It is well that the President be the principal source of policy because, as discussed in Chapter 3, policy or legislative initiative is a matter of "predicting the future." This is so in the sense that all new policy can change or affect only the future. No policy can change the past or the present. Predicting future policy requirements is a task better left to one person than to many. One person, the President, can be responsible for coordinating and giving priorities to all sorts of studies, analyses, forecasts, trends, and speculations. If such a task were given to two legislative bodies composed of 435 and 100 members, respectively, the necessity to reach unity through majority agreements would be extremely handicapped.

Presidents may not always be successful in having coherent programs of integrated priorities explained adequately to the public and to the Congress. Presidents begin at least with unity, which is more than can be said of Congress. It is this initial unity which the Congress seemed to recognize in mandating the executive preparation of the budget and in allowing the President the policy initiative in more and more areas in over a century of development. The Congress itself could only approach this necessary unity if it organized itself more strictly along parliamentary lines, something which would be especially difficult to do with two independent legislative houses.

The whole congressional process leaves the initiative to the executive branch but it does not leave the legislative branch empty-handed. Today there is no such thing as a congressional policy initiative being imposed on the President. Various members of the Congress might propose health programs, tax programs, weapons programs, farm programs, or banking programs. If they do not receive the approbation of the President they are not going to get anywhere.

This change in the basic function of Congress, although different from the traditional impression, does not mean that Congress is functionless or that the review function is merely the leftover. The change means, as said earlier, that there is a different division of labor, a different function than what the nursery rhyme suggests. It might be said that Congress, in now performing a review function, "sees to it that the law is faithfully executed." Most would recognize this as a clause from the second, or presidential, article of the Constitution. The clause does come from the presidential section of the Constitution and it does truly describe Congress's basic role today. In this way the reversal of the original division of labor is completed.

In one sense laws are still made by Congress, the President still enforces them, and the courts still judge. At another level the President makes the law as chief initiator of policy while the Courts are lawmaker because of their final veto power and Congress is a law enforcer as it attempts to ensure that the policy is carried out as intended. No constitutional amendment was passed to bring about this new division of labor. It has come about through almost two centuries of evolution.

For years textbooks in political science and history have reported on the evolution of the powers of the presidency. It has been shown that the presidency has grown gradually through the use of the constitutionally specified powers of addressing messages to the Congress, the power of the veto, the appointment power, and through use of all the other details of the Constitution. There also have been reports on the changed responsibilities of the Congress and the courts. For the most part the changes within the branches have been viewed separately and not as a whole government. The separate focus thus gives the impression of usurpation and rivalry, whereas a composite picture over time would suggest more cooperative adjustment to new circumstances.

When seen not separately but in terms of functional efficiency, the changed division of labor can be appreciated as a continuation and strengthening of the original constitutional design. What is clear is that there is still a division of labor between legally separate and independent branches. The branches might not perform what they used to do and the public may not perceive the functions in the neat summarized form of a nursery rhyme, but the system still works. No one branch has an undue concentration of power. Law and policy still reflect the wishes of the diversity of the community.

FUSION OR SEPARATION

England does not have the situation just described in the United States. With the fusion of legislative, executive, and judicial powers there is no question about who is lawmaker, who should initiate policy, or who can or cannot veto legislation. The

Prime Minister and the party hierarchy are responsible for policy leadership. There is no question about the role of the Commons or any other body. If the public is dissatisfied with the way "things" are going, the party in power is replaced at the next election. There is one thing, however, which the parliamentary system lacks. The parliamentary system lacks an institutional base for a review function.

There is no distribution of legislative, executive, and judicial roles into separate institutions in the parliamentary system. The basic institution of the parliament has only one electoral contact point with the public. More contact would give legitimacy, or legal standing, to one part of the government independently checking on another. Because this is lacking there is no formal means for reviewing the acts of the government except through general elections. Haphazard questioning by the minority party and occasional nagging by the House of Lords is not an adequate substitute for formal review. The House of Lords is, for the most part, impotent, elections are a broad form of public commentary, and minority party questioning has the weakness of being dismissed as simply partisan.

There is in general no discernible way for England or the parliamentary system to formally institutionalize the review function. This gives an edge to the presidential system in the institutional comparison. In England a scandal may bring about a resignation and eventually a report. A challenged foreign policy may bring about much political carping. In neither case will there be a formal and systematic review by a legally independent body free of partisan determination of the resolutions. Even legally independent reviews can be suspected of having partisan motivations, but nonindependent reviews, from the minority party or the majority party, can never be free of such suspicions. An independent review board on a particular issue may undertake and accomplish a completely objective study, which will preclude a partisan dimension. The lack of a partisan sting will almost ensure that the report will only have a long-delayed effectiveness, if that.

In contrast it is political considerations which can keep the legally independent review from becoming partisan in the United States. An investigation by one branch of any other branch could backfire politically if it were not conducted in an objective and unbiased manner. The Watergate hearings had that burden and succeeded because of the painstaking efforts to be politically neutral while emphasizing legality. From the break-in to the ultimate Nixon resignation, almost twenty-six months elapsed. Much of those twenty-six months were spent in assuring that all the individuals involved were accorded due process of law, whether before the courts or in the congressional hearings. In England, if a Watergate-type scandal were to occur, there would be an almost immediate resignation of the chief persons involved. Eventually there would be a white paper or even a blue book[3] report by a blue-ribbon panel giving the details of who did what to whom for what purpose. The resignation would come so quickly, however, and the report so much later that there is no assurance either that the report would be widely read or that due process would be served in the first instance.

There is a recent exception to the generalization that there is no way for the parliamentary system to exercise an effective independent review function. In response to the Israeli role in the massacre in Lebanon in September of 1982, political pressure forced the parliamentary government in Israel to agree to the setting up of an independent commission to investigate the incident and to agree to abide by the findings of the review. Those conditions were fulfilled and resignations did follow the completion of the inquiry, which came less than five months after the massacre. Rather than a breakthrough that could serve as an example for other parliamentary systems the Israeli experience with the independent commission appears to be an exception flowing from the tremendous political pressures related to Israel's special domestic and international situation. Similar circumstances would not prevail in other parliamentary systems where an independent review might seem appropriate and therefore the likelihood of the government agreeing to such terms is highly unlikely. The presidential system, therefore, formally retains the advantage over the parliamentary system of having an institutionalized base for the review function. It provides an institutional answer to the classical question, *Quis custodiet ipsos custodes?* (Who guards the guardians?)

There is another advantage aside from that of the institutionalized review function in the presidential system. In the presidential system the public has more of an opportunity to actively express its views on the public's business than it does in the parliamentary system. In the United States separate elections are held for members of both houses of the Congress and for the presidency itself. Unquestionably it is difficult to interpret the results of the many elections conducted at staggered time periods of two years, four years, and six years. The staggered elections may explain why policy directions and preferences are so mixed. The diversity that the mixed results give, however, are in step with the pluralism of the country. The system reflects more accurately the variety of the public without hindering the requirements of policy leadership. The diversity remains even when the three branches are dominated by the same political party, because the timing of elections and appointments ensures that different expressions of public sentiment are registered every two years.

Which Is Better?

Despite the earlier cited advantages of unity, efficiency, and flexibility of the British system, there are offsetting advantages of the review and more frequent elections of the American system. There is no noticeable advantage in the achievements of policy leadership in either country. The final conclusion, then, that one would have to reach about which is the better form would be country-specific and only marginally form-specific. In other words, the best form is the one which best suits the needs and experience of the particular country. That conclusion may be a defensible rule for forms in general, as the earlier discussion of political structure and political culture suggests. It may be possible to make valid generalizations about governmental forms, but only to the extent of considering their applicability within a particular country, not cross-nationally.

The applicability, or more likely the inapplicability, of the presidential form within England or the parliamentary form within the United States can be discussed as generalized forms, but the universal advantage of one form over the other is a topic of little practical value. There may indeed be a limited number of generalized forms—two or three—but even at that the country-specific qualities make hazardous any attempt at final conclusions. The case of France and the newly evolved "mixed form" clearly illustrates this point.

THE MIXED FORM

The mixed form is said to combine elements of the parliamentary and the presidential forms. The qualifying words "is said to" are used because, although all the appearances confirm the elements of the other two forms, the mixed form is sufficiently new that conclusions about its final outcome may still be premature. The principal example of the mixed form is the French government under the Fifth Republic, the constitutional reform instituted by Charles de Gaulle in 1958. In this form there is a separately elected, fixed-term, strong president and there is at the same time a separately elected parliamentary body which elects a prime minister or premier. The president nominates and, in effect, appoints the prime minister and the cabinet and so there is a great concentration of power in the executive.

Even though selected at elections a month apart, the president and the majority of the National Assembly have always been of the same political party and so the structural tension seemingly built into the system has never been tested. A test may come when separate Assembly elections are scheduled, but even if they result in party contrast, the challenge to the system would not occur until after the presidential election two years later. Even then the results would not be conclusive, since presidential elections would bring forth new Assembly elections. The French presidency has a seven-year term, longer than any other democratic Western nation, and powers unequaled in other presidential forms. What the results would be in a conflict with a determined Assembly are unknown.

The Fifth Republic's mixed form with its strong presidency clearly seems to have eradicated the fundamental weakness of the previous Fourth Republic and its parliamentary, multiparty system. The earlier form was a primary example, as Italy is today, of the weak parliamentary form with its frequent change of coalition governments. A chief contribution of the strong presidency has been the polarization of issues and candidates, so that France is now for the most part a two-party system. As in all two-party systems, even the United States, there are third and minor party efforts which could theoretically revive the multiparty turbulence. That revival does not appear imminent. Even the five-year gap between the presidential election and the next required Assembly election appears to contribute to the two-party polarization rather than to the revival of multiparty factions.

The mixed form with its strong long-term presidency and multimember parliamentary Assembly may have an appeal which the other two original forms lack.

With the strong executive and the legitimizing character of the Assembly, the French form, if successful, may serve as a model for developing countries who are in need of both qualities. Already the Philippines in 1981, in a constitutional reform, adopted the French model. The exact character of the Philippine adaptation is not yet clear; although elections occurred in May of 1984 full implementation will necessarily be slow. The situation in a developing country is hard to evaluate in any case.

The strong leadership and popular assembly that the mixed model allows seems particularly appealing in the situation of developing countries with a democratic tradition or democratic aspirations. The situation in these countries, like that in France itself, is sufficiently unclear on the durability and workability of the form that it would be hard to say whether the model has practical merit. A conclusive judgment on the success of the mixed form will require a great deal more experience to see whether this special combination of democratic and leadership elements functions according to promise. It may turn out, as was suspected in de Gaulle's time, that the mixed form is merely an elaborate device for working the will of a single personality. A fair amount of evidence is available in France in that regard; whether it is cumulative with respect to developing countries remains to be seen.

NOTES

1. Gabriel Almond and G. Bingham Powell, Jr., *Comparative Politics* (Boston: Little, Brown, 1966), p. 129.

2. Thomas R. Dye, Lee S. Greene, and George S. Parthemos, *Governing the American Democracy* (New York: St. Martin's Press, 1980), p. 449.

3. In England a "white paper" or a "blue book" is a general reference to a special investigative report filed by a committee appointed to look into public questions to discover and reveal public wrongdoings.

CHAPTER FIFTEEN
POLITICAL CHANGE

POLITICAL SCIENCE AND CHANGE

Change is intrinsic to politics. The study of the political world differs from the study of the physical world in the nature of the types of change possible. In the physical world, trees lose their leaves, volcanos erupt, atoms split, rivers overflow. Changes in the physical world follow exact patterns, which enables scientists to explore and explain them. Patterns in the physical world are so constant that scientists are even able to produce change, like the splitting of the atom, which makes further change and understanding possible. Change in the political world is entirely different.

Accomplishments in the physical sciences may make outer space weapons systems possible. There are no equally available insights which make the use of new weapons predictable. That there is a discoverable fixed pattern to human behavior is an assumption that some political scientists make. The aggregate of human beings do have fairly constant birth rates, accident rates, and voting habits, but even these are subject to unpredictable variations. How one particular citizen will behave may be predictable but insignificant, how one ruler will behave is unpredictable and significant. That is the most salient point about political "science."

We call political science a science to distinguish it from haphazard, unsystematic, random, and purely emotional explanations of political activity. Common sense is a quality which hopefully all persons enjoy. Even this quality has to be informed with alternatives, underlying motivators, long-range goals, short-term irritants, and personal predilections which influence political events. It is the attempt to consider all these factors which distinguishes the scientific effort at politics from common sense. If common sense is careful, however, it is not basically different from what goes by the name of political science.

These remarks about political science may disenchant many who want to see more successful control of the political world. It is desirable to avoid wars, to stabilize the economy, to eradicate poverty, to eliminate crime, and to establish justice. If human beings can succeed in all the marvelous technical advances with which the twentieth century is familiar, can we not expect the same success in the social and political world? The answer to that question is found in all the previous chapters. Depending on the principles which one finds most appropriate, the possibility and desirability of controlling change will vary.

THREE VIEWS OF CHANGE

The three basic approaches to change are contained in the chapters on the state (Chapters 4 through 7). Change is either completely beyond human control, completely subject to human control, or partially subject to human control. The proposition that change is beyond human control maintains that human behavior is determined by some physical or mystical force. As a result of this determined behavior, all that humans beings can do is discover the underlying forces and attune their behavior to them. At least half of the ideologies described earlier take that position. Human behavior is determined economically, biologically, racially, spiritually, sexually, psychologically, astrologically, or in some other set way. It is from this premise that the rigid scientific approach to politics begins.

The idea that political change is completely subject to human control is not greatly different from its verbal opposite. If behavior is merely a function of personal and collective choice, then the consequences can be as much a totalitarianism as under the determinative aegis. If by definition there is nothing that ought not and cannot be subject to human control, then the principle by which the control is exercised is potentially as determinative, though more flattering, than the other positions. Looked at in this way, democracy is sometimes viewed as an ideology.

Democracy is not an ideology if it holds to the proposition that it is but a form under a constitutional standard of unchanging principles. If there are certain fixed values not subject to human manipulation, though subject to understanding and debate, then democracy presents itself as the continuing approximator of what is best instead of the determinant of what is good. As an approximator of what is best, allowance has to be made for being wrong, which allowance is precisely the place of rights, constitutional procedures, and minority privileges in truly nonideological, democratic systems. This nonideological view of democracy accepts change as being only partially subject to human control.

The raw data about political change give conflicting impressions about what really describes the political world. As constitutional change is observed, the impressions of partial, complete, and uncontrolled change are all confirmed. Public referenda on constitutional amendments, seemingly spontaneous revolutions, coups d'etat, guerrilla warfare, and sociologically determined structural alterations are all forms of constitutional change. Some of those forms suggest the stable growth of partial change, some suggest complete radical change, others suggest uncontrolled change.

CHANGE: APPEARANCE AND REALITY

Revolutions

The appearance of complete change and of uncontrolled change are deceptive. Revolutions frequently are viewed as reflecting complete change and uncontrolled change. Neither is correct, although there are grounds for both impressions. The Russian revolution appeared to be a sharply radical break with the past and to be under the direction of one leadership group. In actuality the leadership group took advantage of forces of change already in motion and succeeded only by restoring an authoritarian structure under a new name. The new leadership went on to direct other changes but only with much struggle over a long period of time. Purges, great loss of life, shifts in general policy, and contradictory alliances marked the first fifty years of the Russian revolution.

Many commentators and readers have a romantic notion of revolutions as representing sweeping changes, but they are all alike. Whether revolution occurs in the United States, China, Cuba, France, Nicaragua, or Russia, it will have the appearance of great change and the reality of slow growth. The substratum of society and its institutional arrangements only change incrementally, as discussed earlier in relation to both subsidiarity and the relationship between political structure and political culture. A more than incremental change puts strains on the system which will slow it down eventually despite an initial appearance of major change. The "cultural revolution" of the 1960s in China, or in the United States if it can be looked upon in that way, are examples of that truth. The late 1970s and early 1980s in both countries saw a shift back in the direction of the original prerevolution position.

The French revolution had its "restoration," which can be regarded as beginning not with the abdication of Napoleon but with his arrival. There is even a basis for arguing that the French restoration started before Napoleon. The revolution of the "Commonwealth" under Cromwell in England had its own restoration, and the American revolution is interpreted by radical historians in the same way. This phenomenon of restoration has led to the generalization that "revolutions restore the tyranny which they replace." That certainly is true in most recent times in the Islamic Revolutionary Republic of Iran.

Third World Change

In the so-called "third world" nations of Africa, Asia, Latin America and the Middle East, this restrained rate of change is also true. The countries may give the appearance of a sharp break with their past. A look below the surface shows the traditional folkways, superstitions, festivals, primitive health and hygiene practices, rural centered life, and centuries old belief systems. To make these remarks is not to imply that developed or "advanced" countries are better than those which are developing or "primitive." Better or worse, good or bad, do not apply in this context, as was the case in comparing political structures and political cultures. The only point is to recognize the level of development for what it is. Neon signs, traffic congestion, and urban crowding in a capital city give an impression of great change that deeper examination belies.

Electoral Change

Even in "revolutionary" electoral changes, the appearance of change occurs while the old order is maintained. In noteworthy changes to socialist governments in France and Spain in the early 1980s, substantial changes were expected and yet the results were more apparent than real. The first year of the new regimes gave the impression of great shifts in public policies. When the initial fanfare is over, the governments moved back in the direction of traditional practices and incremental change. Likewise in the United States it was the conservative, anticommunist, Richard Nixon who opened relations with China and entered into detente with the Soviet Union. The predictability of revolutionary change following observable patterns of past behavior is notoriously unreliable. That is why the making of a science of political change is undesirable.

DEMOCRACY, CHANGE, AND SCRUTINY

It is ironic that change is least likely in what are known as revolutionary regimes and more likely in stable democracies. This occurs because democracies with their stability can tolerate change. Within the confines of their pluralistic systems change is manageable and nondisruptive. Revolutionary and authoritarian regimes, whether in Eastern Europe, Africa, Asia, Latin America, or the Middle East, are always on the brink. They see any unsanctioned change as threatening their position and hence as unacceptable. What is unfortunate is that democracies constitute only about three dozen, if that many, of 159 or more nations of the world.

When the United Nations was founded in 1945, two thirds of its fifty-one members were democracies. Today the number of members has more than tripled, while the actual number of democracies is about the same as in 1945. In this way the United Nations has changed as an institution, gradually changed, and yet the opportunity for change within the member states has been curtailed. It was mentioned a moment ago that it is undesirable to make a science of political change because the patterns are so unreliable. It is likewise unreliable to speak of exact "degrees of freedom" of tolerating change within countries. One group, Freedom House of New York, has attempted to rank countries in a "Comparative Survey of Freedom."[1] Their survey in 1981 suggests that fifty-one countries are free, fifty-three are partly free, and fifty-eight countries are not free. The measurement and judgment of the criteria of freedom are as likely to be questioned as are the evaluations of Amnesty International, which makes surveys of oppression. What is nonetheless striking is that these entirely different groups agree on the importance of freedom within countries. It is those degrees of freedom which tolerate or repress change.

Internal Subversion

The greatest challenge to freedom and change in any country is internal, instead of external. Attacked from the outside, the enemy is identifiable. Appropriate responses can be mounted, rebuttals prepared. Challenge from the inside is about using freedom to undermine it. That was the concern in the Schenck, Dennis, Yates, and other freedom of expression cases mentioned in the discussion of individual rights in Chapter 10. It is that same threat to undermine freedom, only on a larger scale and with more imminent dangers, which occurs in the liberation movements in many countries today. With opposition groups taking advantage of what freedoms currently exist, a partly free regime is overthrown and replaced with one which soon becomes or is recognized as "not free." The "liberationists" may have promised freedom but when they arrive in office they find that circumstances cannot permit the freedoms they insisted on. As in Cuba, with no elections in twenty-five years, and Poland, with a fleeting experience of a free trade union, freedom and openness to unsanctioned change never come.

The United States and other stable democracies can, so far, manage to tolerate such internal challenges. Even the clever ploy of "psychic guerrilla warfare" ostensibly proposed as a challenge to the New Left in the late 1960s in the United States[2] can be absorbed by stable regimes. The New Left, campus disruptions, and protests of the late 1960s and early 1970s in the United States, France, West Germany, and elsewhere have gone the way of other anomic and noninstitutional interest groups, as discussed in relation to group dynamics in Chapter 11. The multiplier of time eroded the initial popularity of these media-highlighted glamor groups of disruption. With the passing of time their membership either faded from sight or became part of diverse established institutions. The change which they paraded proved ephemeral.

Scrutiny

In unstable countries, before time can erode a movement's strength, they have overthrown a regime or the military does it for fear of weakness. Neither action produces real change. Only the name of the regime might change and occasionally the affiliation with a major power may be altered. This is not to deny that change has occurred, for example, in Cuba in twenty-five years. Change has indeed occurred. Many social services, health, and education are reportedly much improved today over pre-Castro practices. But these improvements alone cannot be counted as a gain for the country. That admission would have to factor in "costs" as well as "benefits." The data on those criteria will never be available. That is a lesson which has been learned from the Hitler experience. The data is in on his atrocities and the conclusions of history have been drawn. No latter-day Hitler will allow the books to be opened for public scrutiny. Refugees may surely be counted. The dead and stifled cannot be numbered.

Stable regimes are scrutinized all the time. They change as a result of the scrutiny. The Watergate experience in the United States is an example of scrutiny which produced stable change. Scandals, embarrassments, failed policies, unfulfilled promises, and credibility gaps here and elsewhere have defeated incumbents and changed governments. Lessons are learned from such experiences, policies change, and new scrutinies occur. Stable regimes accept their fallibility and as a result are open to change as a strength. Authoritarian and unstable regimes accept neither fallibility nor change and become obsessed with their own weakness.

SLOWNESS OF CHANGE

Although change has an acceptable place in stable systems it does not come easily or quickly. The discussion of formal constitutional growth in Chapter 12 pointed that out. The proposed Equal Rights Amendment (ERA) is a particularly good illustration. A majority of Americans have supported the idea of such an amendment for many years. The majorities have not been enough, however, to satisfy the formal requirements of constitutional change. That impediment does not obstruct all efforts to establish the policy in other ways. Many regard the basic point of equal treatment to be already expressed in the equal protection provisions for all "persons" in the Fourteenth Amendment. Also, the absence of a specific amendment in the national Constitution need not preclude separate state constitutional provisions or other national or state and local laws and policies, which in effect accomplish the same objective. Change is therefore frequently a matter of many opportunities instead of a single option which passes or fails.

In open and stable systems change is dynamic and multifaceted. This is why constitutional growth in those systems are both formal and informal and yet can remain true to the spirit (II) of constitutionalism. In unstable and authoritarian regimes change is static and as controlled as possible. The United States Constitution has several provisions on presidential selection, inauguration, limit on terms, succession, and disability, yet the basic selection process is managed by the political parties, which are not even mentioned in the Constitution. In the Soviet Union, on the other hand, which has had a number of presidential changes in recent years, there is not a single provision of their constitution on the actual presidential selection process, although their one political party which does the selecting is established by the constitution. It is as if control would be threatened by a formally established selection process. Thus the subtleties of growth processes work differently according to the circumstances. The suggestion made by some that the American and Soviet systems are becoming more alike, called the "convergence theory," cannot be based on any constitutional detail.

Change Without Success

There have been numerous proposals for changing the United States Constitution which have not even gotten to the formal stage that the Equal Rights Amendment has. The failed proposals, as well as the serious suggestions, are as much an expression of change as those which succeed. Unsuccessful efforts confirm that the system is dynamic and the attempt produces better understanding. In contrast to static systems, those open to peaceful change have less need for repressive measures. There may be frustration for many individuals who have worked for years on a proposal which is never accepted, but the frustration cannot compare to those who are precluded from even making a proposal.

For many years some individuals have seriously proposed amending the Constitution to eliminate the electoral college in the presidential election process and replacing it with direct popular election. Occasionally that proposal gets to the stage of being introduced in Congress, but it has never reached the point of being approved by even one of the two houses. There are many convincing arguments against the electoral college and many in favor of popular election. The arguments may be persuasive but they are not compelling. Furthermore, there are many uncertainties about the ramifications of any change. The uncertainties relate to the effect of the change on the character of presidential campaigns, the President's relationship with Congress, the insulation of the President from the dynamics of group competition, whether the length of the term of the President should be altered at the same time, and whether the President should be limited to one term in office.

Change After Crisis

Because of these questions about the ramifications of the change, the proposal is not likely to get any further in the future than it has so far unless there is a crisis in the electoral process. This prospect in itself tells much about the process of change. We like to think of it as planned and rational, especially in stable democratic systems. On that score stable systems are not different from unstable and authoritarian ones. Necessary change is usually a response to a crisis instead of the product of calm foresight. The difference is that in the stable systems the changes were anticipated and discussed openly in the society many years before the crisis. The earlier discussion prepares society for the changes. It is similar to my talking about a new roof several years prior to the midwinter leak and then calmly responding to the crisis even though it is in the middle of Christmas.

New Constitution / New Understanding

Some scholars concerned with the American system of government have gone to the point of proposing a whole new constitution. The Center for the Study of Democratic Institutions in Santa Barbara, California made such a proposal in 1970. They would reduce the number of states from fifty to twenty or less, change the presidency, Congress, the Bill of Rights, everything. Their proposal was not subversive and it did not cause much excitement. It did provide an opportunity to appraise and appreciate the existing practices. Those who proposed the whole new constitution were serious about the changes. They did not intend a mere civics lesson for their efforts. They were not, however, upset at its failure. They were not regarded as criminals for making the proposal and hounded into exile. They made a proposal and it failed. As a byproduct, those who gave the proposals some attention learned more about the present Constitution. Such efforts and successes as well as failures are the nature of change in stable democratic societies.

The discussion of change focuses on a "shift" in existing practices. Equal attention should be given to the "existing practices." Frequently a change is celebrated or advocated when the past or existing procedures are not fully understood. That is so even for revolutions. It is easy to tear down; it is much more difficult to build. It is because of this difficulty that revolutions find themselves becoming tyrannical shortly after their success, as mentioned earlier. The lack of full understanding of past or existing procedures is not limited to the large issues for society. There are longstanding institutional arrangements which are not fully understood. A consideration of these gaps in our knowledge points out what can be done about change and how this discussion of change is related to the earlier discussion of "principles of politics." The earlier discussion of the parliamentary and presidential forms of government, for example, brings out the gap in our knowledge about institutional arrangements and change. An understanding of principles can help us around this concern.

The presidential and parliamentary forms were applied to the national level of governments in the countries then under discussion. The same discussion of forms can also be usefully employed to analyze intermediate and local forms of government. That extension of analysis is not usually done. In the United States, for example, the state level of government utilizes only the presidential form as seen in their separately elected governor, legislature, and independent court system. At the local level in the United States the presidential and parliamentary forms are seen respectively in the mayor-council and the council-manager (as well as the school board-superintendent) systems. In Canada the parliamentary form predominates at the intermediate, or provincial, level with no more justification for it than the opposite form at the state level in the United States. In many countries outside of the United States, the strong mayor, similar to the French presidency, predominates as the local form. Why the pattern of intermediate and local forms exists has no clear explanation except imitation. Why there is so little variety and change where there is no compulsion to have a prescribed form is unexamined and unexplained. Institutional traditions have as solid a grip on local government forms as folkways in more primitive cultures.

WHERE PRINCIPLES FIT

Principles are involved in the forms, both practical principles of fusion and separation and theoretical principles of the necessity of rule. Common forces are at work at all levels of government in all countries. Choices are made about the best means to achieve effective rule. Change or the lack of change can be considered as the response to principles to sustain a particular course of action. Support or resistance to change is not separate from the principles for which change is advocated. Change can be neither accepted nor rejected on its own account. Change for the sake of change is no more justified than unreasoned resistance. The reasoned consideration of change is the place for principles in political science. Dealing with principles gives an accurate and workable understanding of the functioning of government and the changes which are constantly occurring.

In the introduction of this text it was pointed out that there is a parallel contrast between the scientific and popular or "poetic" explanations of the physical and political worlds. The argument was that scientific explanations are more accurate and valuable that poetic ones. The astronaut may poetically speak of the sunrise even though scientifically it is known that the earth rotates. On this score, however, the scientific and poetic explanations do not interfere with each other. In the political world the "scientific" and poetic were posited to be in conflict and that the contrast did make a difference. It is now possible to point out that the consequences of the contrast in the political realm are both more important and less important than originally suggested.

That democracy is, contrary to the poetic understanding, not "popular control" is not so much a scientific explanation as an elaboration of what popular control means and what alternate views on democracy are. "Federalism is a fiction" is not so much a scientific wonder as an explication of the fundamental subsidiarity character of federalism, which everyone has an original intuitive grasp of anyway. That the separation of powers doctrine does not work exactly as imagined does not greatly disturb anyone since the system still works and voters do not debate such technical issues in an election in any case. The most important consequence of examining these conflicting views is that a better understanding of politics is gained in the process. This improved understanding is illustrative of the potential for personal growth that was an important ingredient in the popular selection view of democracy. The simple beginning positions are not so much rejected as improved upon and deepened.

What is found while examining democracy, federalism, separation of powers, rights, and group interaction is that there are certain basic principles of politics which effect all aspects of political life. The nature and end of the state, the origin and justification of political authority, the nature and place of justice, and the concept of subsidiarity and constitutionalism all have a profound effect on particular political activities. It is on these principles that change and variation in political activities can be evaluated. It is imperative to remember, however, that all the principles come with alternatives. Popular control (1) is seen as a myth (2) and as replaceable with popular selection (3). Collectivism (A) is opposed to Individualism (B), which is opposed by the Common Good (C). There are principles but there are also choices about principles.

That there are good and bad, acceptable and unacceptable, principles is not to be denied. What is good or unacceptable is what study, reflection, reading, and inquiry are all about. It is still the case that there are no ready-made answers in the back of the political science textbook. Choice is still the order of political inquiry. We pursue a knowledge of the facts so that our understanding of the application of principles is accurate. The facts alone however will get us nowhere or they will be organized by default according to an unarticulated principle.

CONCLUSION: GOVERNMENT WORKS

There should be no great disappointment if one completes the study of an introduction to political science course without a definitive knowledge of a number of aspects of the political world. After many years of study that definitive knowledge would still be elusive since the political and social world is like so much unencumbered quicksilver—shiny and alluring but difficult to grasp. It seems appropriate to recall the observation by Einstein cited earlier that "politics is infinitely more complex than physics and relativity." It may well be that Einstein was using the word "infinitely" with a well-informed sense of its implications.

With Einstein's confession as a consolation one should be happy to come away from an introduction to political science with a knowledge of some principles which offer a coherent explanation of the political world. The principles may be in the form of not entirely resolved competing theories, but if the world is looked at in those terms there is a much greater chance of understanding what is going on than if it is approached from a single, though exhaustive, perspective. The experiences of the Western and the non-Western world seem to support the broader approach.

What can be concluded from this principle approach to politics is that government does make sense, even though there is much disagreement on which approach is correct. Different individuals and different groups of people have widely divergent views on the nature and end of the state and the origin and justification of political authority. That those views can be grouped into three general perspectives should help immensely in coming to an understanding and appreciation of the political world. Knowing the principles which separate people will not automatically or quickly lead to reconciliation. The principles are too divergent and deeply held to be reconciled. This knowledge may, however, lead to respect for the differences. From respect may come tolerance. It is tolerance which is the beginning of civility, the first virtue of politics. With the realization of civility, political prudence, the virtue by which all principles are implemented, has a chance to be effective.

NOTES

1. As reported in the *Information Please Almanac 1982,* 36th ed. (New York: Simon and Schuster, 1981), pp. 123-126.

2. See G. William Domhoff, "How to Commit Revolution," found in Ernest D. Giglio and John J. Schrems, *Future Politics* (Berkeley: McCutchan Publishing Corporation, 1971), pp. 81-90.

SELECTED
BIBLIOGRAPHY

As a selected bibliography the following list is meant to get the reader started. It is not exhaustive. Any one reading branches off into many others. The professor or the student using this text may use the list to supplement the respective chapter. Sometimes, but not always, readings mentioned in the chapter or footnotes are repeated in the bibliography for emphasis. The list includes some movies, novels, biographies, and other writings. These "unusual" works, which will be annotated, are included because of the insight they give and because political scientists learn not just from one another but from the world of reality with which we must always keep in touch. The bibliography follows in a chapter-by-chapter order. Chapters 4, 5, 6, and 7 are grouped into one list because of the interrelated nature of the topics on the state.

Chapter 1

ASHER, HERBERT, *Presidential Elections: Voters, Candidates, and Campaigns since 1952* (Revised edition). Homewood, Ill.: The Dorsey Press, 1980.

BACHRACH, PETER, *The Theory of Democratic Elitism: A Critique*. Boston: Little, Brown, and Company, 1967.

BINKLEY, WILFRED E., *American Political Parties: Their Natural History* (3rd ed.). New York: Alfred A. Knopf, 1959.

BURDICK, EUGENE, *The 480*. New York: A Dell Book, 1964. A novel from the early 1960s about a computer-assisted presidential campaign.

CAMPBELL, ANGUS, PHILIP E. CONVERSE, WARREN E. MILLER, AND DONALD E. STOKES, *The American Voter*. New York: John Wiley and Sons, Inc., 1960. A classic study of voting and voters.

DAHL, ROBERT A., *Dilemmas of Pluralist Democracy: Autonomy versus Control*. New Haven: Yale University Press, 1982.

PLAMENATZ, JOHN, *Democracy and Illusion: An Examination of Certain Aspects of Modern Democratic Theory*. New York: Longman, 1973.

POWELL, G. BINGHAM, JR., *Contemporary Democracies: Participation, Stability, and Violence*. Cambridge: Harvard University Press, 1982.

RIKER, WILLIAM H., *Democracy in the United States* (2nd ed.). New York: The Macmillan Company, 1965.

ROSE, RICHARD, *What Is Governing?* Englewood Cliffs, N.J.: Prentice-Hall, Inc., 1978.

SPITZ, ELAINE, *Majority Rule*. Chatham, New Jersey: Chatham House Publishers, Inc., 1984.

TOCQUEVILLE, ALEXIS DE. *Democracy in America*. The classic early 19th-century study, still relevant today.

Chapter 2

ALMOND, GABRIEL, "Slaying the Functional Dragon: A Reply to Stanley Rothman," *The Political Science Reviewer,* Vol III (Fall 1973), 259-268.

DAWSON, RICHARD E., AND KENNETH PREVITT, *Political Socialization*. Boston: Little, Brown and Company, 1969.

DEUTSCH, KARL, *The Nerves of Government: Models of Political Communications and Control*. New York: The Free Press, 1966.

EASTON, DAVID, *A Framework for Political Analysis*. Englewood Cliffs, N.J.: Prentice-Hall, Inc., 1965.

EASTON, DAVID, "Systems Analysis and Its Classical Critics," *The Political Science Reviewer,* Vol III (Fall 1973), 269-301.

MILLER, EUGENE F., "David Easton's Political Theory," *The Political Science Reviewer,* Vol I (Fall 1971), 184-235.

ROTHMAN, STANLEY, "Functionalism and Its Critics: An Analysis of the Writings of Gabriel Almond," *The Political Science Reviewer,* Vol. I (Fall 1971), 236-276.

Chapter 3

BRAMS, STEVEN, *Game Theory and Politics*. New York: The Free Press, 1975.

CONWAY, M. MARGARET, AND FRANK B. FIEGERT, *Political Analysis: An Introduction* (2nd ed.). Boston: Allyn and Bacon Inc., 1976.

CRICK, BERNARD, *In Defense of Politics*. London: Weidenfeld and Nicolson, 1962.

FINIFTER, ADA W., *Political Science: The State of the Discipline*. The American Political Science Association, 1983. Nineteen essays commenting on the approaches to understanding and analysis in many of the subfields in political science.

GARSON, G. DAVID, *Handbook of Political Science Methods* (2nd ed.). Boston: Holbrook Press, Inc., 1976.

HACKER, ANDREW, *The Study of Politics: The Western Tradition and American Origins* (2nd ed.). New York: McGraw-Hill, 1973.

JOUVENAL, BERTRAND DE, "Political Science and Prevision," *The American Political Science Review,* 59, no. 1 (March 1965), 29-38.

LINDBLOM, CHARLES E., AND DAVID K. COHEN, *Usable Knowledge: Social Science and Social Problem Solving.* New Haven: Yale University Press, 1979.

RICCI, DAVID M., *The Tragedy of Political Science: Politics, Scholarship, and Democracy.* New Haven: Yale University Press, 1984.

RIKER, WILLIAM, *The Theory of Political Coalitions.* New Haven: Yale Univeristy Press, 1962. This example of mathematical political science may be too much for many readers but Chapter 10, ''Reflections on Empires: An Epilogue on the United States in World Affairs,'' suggests its power in the light of subsequent developments.

SOMIT, ALBERT, AND JOSEPH TANENHAUS, *The Development of the American Science of Politics: From Burgess to Behavioralism.* New York: Irvington Publishers, Inc., 1982.

Chapters 4, 5, 6, 7

ALLAND, ALEXANDER, *The Human Imperative.* New York: Columbia University Press, 1972. Counters the work of Ardrey, Morris, and others.

AQUINAS, THOMAS, *The Political Ideas of St. Thomas Aquinas: Representative Selections,* ed. with an Introduction by Dino Bigongiari. New York: Hafner Publishing Co., 1969.

ARDREY, ROBERT, *The Social Contract.* New York: Atheneum, 1970. Human social organization compared to patterns of animal behavior.

ARISTOTLE, *Ethics.*

——, *Politics.*

BLUHM, WILLIAM, *Theories of Political Systems: Classics of Political Thought and Modern Political Analysis* (3rd ed.). Englewood Cliffs, N.J.: Prentice-Hall, Inc., 1978.

FULLER, R. BUCKMINSTER, *Utopia or Oblivion: The Prospects for Humanity.* New York: Bantam Books, Inc., 1969. Like all of Fuller's writings a sweeping view of the universe with equally sweeping views of the role of government.

GERMINO, DANTE, *Beyond Ideology: The Revival of Political Theory.* New York: Harper & Row Publishers, l967.

HOBBES, THOMAS, *Leviathan.* 17th-Century classic.

HUXLEY, ALDOUS, *Brave New World.* A futuristic novel.

KROPOTKIN, PETER, *The Conquest of Bread.* A classic anarchist view of how things could run better without the state.

LEVIN, IRA, *This Perfect Day.* Futuristic novel of life run by a totalitarian computer regime.

LOCKE, JOHN, *Two Treatises of Government.* The ''limited government'' answer to Hobbes.

MCCOY, CHARLES N. R., *The Structure of Political Thought: A Study in the History of Political Ideas.* New York: McGraw-Hill, 1963. A study of the meaning of classical and modern thought.

MORRIS, DESMOND, *The Human Zoo.* New York: A Dell Book, 1969. Biological explanations for human behavior.

————, *The Naked Ape.* New York: A Dell Book, 1967. A book on man as animal.

NELSON, BRIAN R., *Western Political Thought: From Socrates to the Age of Ideology.* Englewood Cliffs, N.J.: Prentice-Hall, Inc., 1982.

ORWELL, GEORGE, *1984.* A novel.

PLATO, *The Republic.*

PLUTARCH, *Lycurgus.* Classic biography of an early Greek leader which predates but parallels Plato's *Republic.* (Found in *Great Books of the Western World,* Vol. 14, pp. 32-48.)

"ROLLERBALL." 1975 movie which shows a futuristic world where corporations have replaced the state as the final authority.

ROUSSEAU, JEAN JACQUES, *The Social Contract.*

SCHALL, JAMES V. *The Politics of Heaven and Hell.* Lanham, Md.: University Press of America, 1984.

SOPHOCLES, *Antigone.* Ancient Greek classic on authority and human conscience.

TINDER, GLENN, *Political Thinking* (3rd ed.). Boston: Little, Brown, and Co., 1979.

Chapter 8

ARENDT, HANNA, *The Origins of Totalitarianism.* New York: Harcourt Brace and World, 1968.

BARADAT, LEON, *Political Ideologies: Their Origins and Impact.* Englewood Cliffs, N.J.: Prentice-Hall, Inc., 1984.

CARPENTER, FINLEY, *The Skinner Primer: Behind Freedom and Dignity.* New York: The Free Press, 1974. An analysis and critique of B.F. Skinner's work.

DEUTSCH, KARL, *Nationalism and Its Alternatives.* New York: Alfred A. Knopf, 1969.

EBENSTEIN, WILLIAM H., AND EDWIN FOGELMAN, *Today's Isms* (8th ed.). Englewood Cliffs, N.J.: Prentice-Hall, Inc., 1980.

FROMM, ERICH, *Marx's Concept of Man.* New York: Frederick Ungar Publishing Co., 1969.

HALLOWELL, JOHN J., *Main Currents in Modern Political Thought.* New York: Holt, Rinehart & Winston, 1950.

KOHN, HANS, *The Idea of Nationalism, A Study in its Origins and Background.* New York: The Macmillan Company, 1960.

MACRIDIS, ROY C., *Contemporary Political Ideologies: Movements and Regimes* (2nd ed.). Boston: Little, Brown and Company, 1983.

SUCHTING, W.A., *Marx: An Introduction.* New York: New York University Press, 1983.

TUCKER, ROBERT C., ED., *The Marx-Engels Reader* (2nd ed.). New York: W. W. Norton & Company, Inc., 1978.

Chapter 9

DWORKIN, RONALD, "JUSTICE AND RIGHTS," In *Taking Rights Seriously.* Cambridge, Mass.: Harvard University Press, 1978.

FRIEDRICH, CARL J., AND JOHN W. CHAPMAN, editors, *JUSTICE.* NOMOS VI. New York: Atherton Press, 1963.

RAWLS, JOHN, *A Theory of Justice.* Cambridge, Mass.: Harvard University Press, 1971.

SCHUMACHER, E.F., *A Guide for the Perplexed.* New York: Perennial Library, 1977.

————, *Small Is Beautiful.* New York: Perennial Library, 1973.

Chapter 10

CLOR, HARRY M. *Obscenity and Public Morality.* Chicago: University of Chicago Press, 1969.

FRIEDMAN, MILTON, *Capitalism and Freedom.* Chicago: University of Chicago Press, 1962. The Nobel Prize economist's view of the proper role of competitive capitalism.

GOODMAN, PAUL, "The Black Flag of Anarchism," *The New York Times Magazine,* July 14, 1968.

HAND, B. LEARNED, *The Bill of Rights*. Cambridge, Mass.: Harvard University Press, 1958.

McCLOSKEY, ROBERT G., *The American Supreme Court*. Chicago: University of Chicago Press, 1960.

MILL, JOHN STUART, *On Liberty*. 19th-Century classic.

ROCHE, JOHN P., *Courts and Rights*. New York: Random House, 1961.

Chapter 11

Free Trade Union News: AFL-CIO. Monthly newsletter on international affairs published by the Department of International Affairs of the AFL-CIO, Washington, D.C.

Harvard Nuclear Study Group: Albert Carnesale, Paul Doty, Stanley Hoffman, Samuel P. Huntington, Joseph S. Nye, Jr., Scott D. Sagan, *Living With Nuclear Weapons*. New York: Bantam Books, 1983.

KERR, ANTHONY J. C., *The Common Market and How It Works*. New York: Pergamon Press, Inc., 1983.

ROMMEN, HEINRICH H., *The State in Catholic Thought*. St. Louis, Mo.: Herder Books, 1945.

RUSSETT, BRUCE, *Trends In World Politics*. New York: The Macmillan Company, 1965.

TRUMAN, DAVID, *The Governmental Process: Political Interests and Public Opinion* (2nd ed.). New York: Alfred A. Knopf, 1971.

VISSCHER, CHARLES DE, *Theory and Reality in Public International Law*. Princeton, N.J.: Princeton University Press, 1957.

Chapter 12

BROGAN, D. W., AND DOUGLAS V. VERNEY, *Political Patterns in Today's World* (2nd ed.). New York: Harcourt, Brace & World, Inc., 1968.

CORWIN, EDWARD S., *The Higher Law Background of American Constitutional Law*. Ithaca, New York: Great Seal Books, A Division of Cornell University Press, 1955.

DEUTSCH, KARL, *Comparative Politics: Politics of Industrialized and Developing Nations*. Boston: Houghton Mifflin Company, 1981.

KADARKAY, ARPAD, *Human Rights in American and Russian Political Thought*. Washington, D.C.: University Press of America, Inc., 1982.

PENNOCK, J. ROLAND, AND JOHN W. CHAPMAN, *Constitutionalism*. NOMOS XX. New York: New York University Press, 1979.

ROCHE, JOHN P. *Shadow and Substance: Essays on the Theory and Structure of Politics*. New York: The Macmillan Co., 1964.

SOLZHENITSYN, ALEKSANDR I., *The First Circle*. New York: Bantam Books, 1968. The Nobel Prize author's "novel" on contemporary Russia.

STEVENSON, WILLIAM, *A Man Called Intrepid*. New York: A Ballantine Book, 1976. A biography which reads like a spy novel dealing with the British intelligence service and the founding of the American CIA in the late 1930's and early 1940's.

Chapter 13

BEITZINGER, A. J., *A History of American Political Thought*. New York: Dodd, Mead, and Company, 1972.

BLAIR, PHILIP M., *Federalism and Judicial Review in West Germany*. Oxford: Clarendon Press, 1981.

DOLBEARE, KENNETH M., *Directions in American Political Thought*. New York: John Wiley and Sons, Inc., 1969. Classical writings in American political thought plus challenging essays by Dolbeare.

JOHNSON, NEVEL, *State and Government in the Federal Republic of Germany*. New York: Pergamon Press, 1983.

LEVY, LEONARD W., ED., *Essays on Making the Constitution*. New York: Oxford University Press, 1969.

McDONALD, FORREST, *We The People*. Chicago: University of Chicago Press, 1958. History of American constitutional origins.

MORGAN, EDMUND S., *The Birth of the Republic*. Chicago: University of Chicago Press, 1956. History of American constitutional origins.

RIKER, WILLIAM H., *Federalism: Origin, Operation, Significance*. Boston: Little, Brown and Company, 1964.

ROCHE, JOHN P., "The Founding Fathers: A Reform Caucus in Action," *American Political Science Review*, 56 (March 1962), 799-816.

TRUDEAU, PIERRE ELLIOTT, *Federalism and the French Canadians*. Toronto: Macmillan of Canada, 1968.

Chapter 14

ANDREWS, WILLIAM G., *Presidential Government in Gaullist France*. Albany: State University of New York Press, 1982.

BEER, SAMUEL H., *Britian Against Itself*. W. W. Norton & Co., 1982.

BUTT, RONALD, *The Power of Parliament*. New York: Walker, 1967.

CRICK, BERNARD, *The Reform of Parliament* (2nd ed.). London: Weidenfeld & Nicolson, 1968.

DAVIS, JAMES W., JR., *The National Executive Branch*. New York: The Free Press, 1970.

HOXIE, R. GORDON, *Command Decisions and the Presidency*. New York: Reader's Digest Press, 1977.

KAVANAGH, DENNIS, AND RICHARD ROSE, EDS., *New Trends in British Politics*. London: Sage Publications, 1977.

KESSLER, FRANK, *The Dilemmas of Presidential Leadership: Of Caretakers and Kings*. Englewood Cliffs, N.J.: Prentice-Hall, Inc., 1982.

LIVINGSTON, WILLIAM E., "Britain and America: The Institutionalization of Accountability," *The Journal of Politics*, 38 (Nov. 1976), 879-94.

VOGLER, DAVID J., *The Politics of Congress* (2nd ed.). Boston: Allyn and Bacon, Inc., 1977.

WILSON, FRANK L., *French Political Parties Under the Fifth Republic*. New York: Praeger, 1982.

ZUMWALT, ELMO, *On Watch: A Memoir*. New York: Quadrangle/The New York Times Book Co., 1976. An autobiography of the chief of the navy for four years in the early 1970s which gives insight into matters of state and how they are conducted.

Chapter 15

"DANTON." A 1983 movie, in French with subtitles, which gives a marvelous view of the French Revolution and revolutions in general.

DOLBEARE, KENNETH M., ED., *Power and Change in the United States: Empirical Findings and Their Implications*. New York: John Wiley & Sons, Inc., 1969. Essays and analysis of change by a variety of authors.

DRUCKER, PETER, *The End of Economic Man: The Origins of Totalitarianism*. New York: Harper Colophon Books, 1969. Originally published in 1939, this daring book tells much about political change.

HOROWITZ, IRVING LOUIS, *Three Worlds of Development* (2nd ed.). New York: Oxford University Press, 1972.

HORWITZ, ROBERT H., *The Moral Foundations of the American Republic*. Charlottesville, Va.: University of Virginia Press, 1977. A collection of essays which reflect on the origins of the American community and give us a perspective with which to evaluate change.

LIPSET, SEYMOUR MARTIN, *Revolution and Counterrevolution: Change and Persistence in Social Structures*. New York: Basic Books, Inc., 1968.

RIKER, WILLIAM H., *Liberalism Against Populism: A Confrontation Between the Theory of Democracy and the Theory of Social Choice*. San Francisco: W. H. Freeman & Co., 1982.

INDEX